Tidewater by Steamboat

Steamer _Lancaster_ clears the wharf at Irvington, Carter's Creek, Virginia, about 1900. From the collection of David E. Willing. Courtesy of the Mariners' Museum

Tidewater by Steamboat
A Saga of the Chesapeake

The Weems Line on the Patuxent, Potomac, and Rappahannock

David C. Holly

The Johns Hopkins University Press
Baltimore and London
Published in Association with
The Calvert Marine Museum

Johns Hopkins Paperbacks edition, 2000
9 8 7 6 5 4 3 2 1

The Johns Hopkins University Press
2715 North Charles Street
Baltimore, Maryland 21218-4363
www.press.jhu.edu

The paper used in this book meets the minimum requirements of American
National Standards for Information Sciences—Permanence of Paper for Printed
Library Materials, ANSI Z39.48-1984.

Library of Congress Cataloging-in-Publication Data
Holly, David C.
  Tidewater by steamboat : a saga of the Chesapeake : the Weems line on the
Patuxent, Potomac, and Rappahannock / David C. Holly.
      p.   cm.
  Includes bibliographical references and index.
  ISBN 0-8018-4168-2 (alk. paper)
  1. Steamboat lines—Chesapeake Bay (Md. and Va.)—History. 2. Steamboats—
Chesapeake Bay—History. 3. Weems Steamboat Company—History.
I. Title.
HE630.C4H65´ 1991
387´.009163´47—dc20   90-27826

ISBN 0-8018-6530-1 (pbk.)

To my wife, Carolyn, whose love and steadfastness
through the years have carried me through

Contents

Illustrations

Acknowledgments

At the outset, I have to admit that the scope and structure of this book did not follow any preconceived plan. Instead, the material itself took the lead, and any specific notions about the history of the Weems line and its steamboats disappeared in a wealth of information which placed the Weems line at the center of the unfolding panorama of the steamboat era on the Chesapeake. A number of individuals helped shape the direction and form of this study. At the beginning, the invitation to undertake a book on the Weems line was extended by Ralph Eshelman, director of the Calvert Marine Museum, whose interest and dedication to regional maritime history impelled the project into existence. Robert H. Burgess, curator emeritus of the Mariners' Museum, noting the involvement of the Weems line in the Potomac and Rappahannock regions and in a route at various times to Norfolk, offered the view that the book could not escape a background coverage of steamboats out of Washington and Norfolk, as well as out of Baltimore. The concept led to enrichment of the text with the pageant of the steamboat era throughout the Chesapeake, with the Weems line as the vehicle for the telling of the narrative. Advice from others brought about extensive portrayal of the regional economic, social, and cultural background, which gave life and meaning to the steamboat era.

With gratitude and pleasure, I wish to acknowledge my indebtedness to a host of patient librarians and archivists who endured my endless inquiries and went far beyond the call of duty in unearthing material for this book. The list is lengthy: at the Maryland Hall of Records, archivists Jane McWilliams, Richard Blondo, and administrator Christopher N. Allan, for their invaluable assistance and expertise; at the Maryland State Law Library, director Michael Miller, for opening avenues of research, and librarian Shirley Rittenhouse, for her perseverance in locating elusive legal and journalistic materials; at the Maryland Historical Society, maritime curator Mary Ellen Hayward, volunteer Lewis Beck, and archivist Karen Stuart, for their valued assistance; at the Maryland National Capital Park and Planning Commission, manager of the history division John M. Walton, Jr., for researching his files and discovering original materials concerning the Patuxent and Potomac regions, and director of conservation Richard J. Dolesh, for gathering together a quantity of information from his own files and sources and presenting it for incorporation in the text; at the Calvert Marine Museum, board chairman and librarian Paul Berry, for research assistance and advice, librarian Robert Hurry and curator Paula Johnson, for their help at crucial times; at the Chesapeake Bay Maritime Museum, curator Richard J. Dodds, for his interest and generous use of library resources; at the U.S. District Court in Baltimore, clerk Ron Wiley, for researching court records and obtaining assistance from the Philadelphia Federal Archives; at the mayor's office in Baltimore, curator Jeanne March Davis, for locating the portrait and information on Mayor George Stiles; at the Mary Ball Washington Museum and Library in Lancaster, Virginia, and the Northern Neck of Virginia Historical Society, Montross, Virginia, librarian Ann Lewis Burrows, for helpful leads to sources of important information; at the Historical Society of Pennsylvania, librarian Joel T. Loeb, for extraordinary efforts in locating information on the origins of *Eagle* and shipyards on the Delaware; at the Virginia Historical Society, librarians Frances Pollard and William Obrochta, for courteous and knowledgeable assistance in leads to valuable Virginia sources; at the National Archives, archivist John Vandereedt, for a monumental effort to extract enrollment and other documentation on steamboats of the Weems line; at the Maryland Room of the Enoch Pratt Free Library, librarian William Sleeman and others, who helped uncover a wealth of information from various sources; at the Library of Congress, numerous expert staffers, who produced old newspaper files in original or on microfilm and historical maps of major importance; at the Hagley Library, researcher Marjorie McNinch; at Fort McHenry National Park, ranger and archivist Scott Sheads, who researched information concerning the War of 1812 and the Civil War; at the Steamship Historical Society Collection of the University of Baltimore, librarian Laura Brown, who cheerfully waded through files of photographs and other materials to help with the project; and, importantly, at the Mariners' Museum, librarians Benjamin H. Trask and Kathryn B. Braig and archivists Roger T. Crew, Jr., and Charlotte Valentine, for enduring days of delving into the invaluable resources and collections of the institution.

Several aficionados of Chesapeake steamboating offered technical advice at various times. H. Graham Wood and Harry Jones, using their own extensive files, cross-checked data in the manuscript and offered suggestions, a lengthy and arduous engagement of their time and energy. Charles Efford contributed his recollections of steamboat engineering. Harry E. Slye, former master of steamboats on the Potomac, including some vessels that had originally operated under the Weems line, added his firsthand knowledge.

I extend a special note of appreciation to a great number of residents along the Potomac and Rappahannock, who contributed to this book: A. Thomas Embry, Jr., for his knowledge of upper Rappahannock landings; Charles T. A. Larson, for his recollections of steamboat days; Alice Taylor, for the background information and candid portrayal of her grandfather, Charles R. Lewis; G. Edwin Thomas, for the newspaper files and county records concerning the trial of Charles R. Lewis; Carolyn H. Jett, for her introduction to G. Edwin Thomas and access to his information; Steven Thomas of the Northumberland County clerk's office, who furnished the reference data on the trial; Linwood Bowis, master of *Captain Thomas*, for the time and effort he spent in locating the sites of upper Rappahannock landings on a cruise to Fredericksburg; Fielding Dickinson, Jr., for calling upon his own knowledge and research to furnish the historical background of Rappahannock landings on the run to Fredericksburg, for opening Saunders Wharf, which he had restored as it was in steamboat days; and Diana Dickinson, his wife, who supplied her own research on the history of the wharf and Wheatlands, the estate that it served.

Concerning the Patuxent River and its landings as well as Fair Haven on the Bay, the list of contributors is equally important: John W. McGrain, who brought his knowledge of industrial history to bear on Hills Landing and the Patuxent bridge; Roland and Helen Sasscer Sliker, for supplying the valuable drawing of Hills Landing and some of the history of Green Landing; Marie Wallace and Kevin and Barbara Malloy, for their efforts to develop the history of Fair Haven; Judge Perry Bowen, Jr., for his recollections of Patuxent landings; Clyde Watson, for his anecdotes of steamboat days at Magruders Ferry Landing; and Kenneth F. Brooks, Jr., for his knowledge of people and places related to steamboat days on the Patuxent.

Some individuals have contributed directly and importantly to the research for this study. One such individual, whose mark on this book is indelible and highly significant, is William J. Bray, Jr., who not only delved into his own voluminous and painstakingly acquired files on Rappahannock steamboat history to furnish important material but also sounded the alert on the need for further and lengthy research to uncover information hitherto unknown and immensely valuable.

Most certainly, this book could not have appeared in its detailed form, particularly with respect to the Weems family and its trials and tribulations in the development of the steamboat line, without the enormous contribution of the descendants of George and Mason L. Weems, progenitors of the Weems line. In the hands of the Forbes family were the manuscript records and correspondence vital to the span of coverage and essential to a comprehensive history of the Weems line in the steamboat era on the Chesapeake. To David Weems Forbes, who opened the door to the research materials, to his mother, Elizabeth Pendleton Forbes, to Richard M. Forbes, and to Alice Forbes Bowie, I owe a profound debt of gratitude for their openhanded generosity. Especially to Alice Forbes Bowie is this sense of indebtedness most keenly felt. She brought to the study her own understanding of the historical significance of the manuscript collection, and she contributed beyond measure to its compilation and assimilation for research.

I am greatly indebted to Robert J. Brugger, editor and distinguished Maryland historian, for his personal interest in the manuscript and worthy advice. And I am most grateful to Marjorie Nelson for her expertise and kindly understanding in copyediting so complicated a manuscript.

There are many others I should thank, who, through personal or telephone contact, provided bits and pieces of information or who, through acts of kindness, helped further the project.

In an effort of this sort, errors may inadvertently appear, and for them I offer my apologies. To everyone who tolerated a researcher, I extend my thanks and good wishes.

Prologue

The grand white fleet of steamboats vanished from the Chesapeake Bay. Very little remained to remind succeeding generations of a colorful era important in the nation's history.

For a century and a half (1813–1963),[1] some 300 vessels steamed out of Baltimore, as many as 140 out of Washington, and up to 150 out of Norfolk. Although these numbers may include a few boats listed as steam-driven barges, tugs, and other craft scarcely worthy of classification as steamboats (in the conventional and aesthetic meaning of the term), the total of at least 500 reflects the size and importance of the industry. At its height, from around the turn of the century until the First World War, some 50 steamboats at one time operated out of Baltimore alone, and perhaps half the number steamed out of Norfolk and Washington. Tidewater could never have developed as it did without them. In turn, the economic centers, especially Baltimore and Norfolk, could never have prospered without the development of the Tidewater region that supported them. Steamboats connected planters and merchants to the markets, industrial might, overseas outlets, and cultural and social attractions of Baltimore. Norfolk, near the mouth of the Bay, drew its strength from its trade with northern ports (earlier the West Indies) but held fast to its ties to tidewater Virginia.

Steamboats plied the length of the Chesapeake, running 195 miles from the Susquehanna in the north to the mouth between Cape Henry and Cape Charles, and threaded their way through the rivers and creeks that made up its nearly 2,000 miles of navigable waterways. From its majestic waters flowed the great tidal rivers of the Western Shore. The Patuxent extended for a distance of 40 or more miles to the head of navigation; the James, Potomac, and Rappahannock reached inland for a distance of nearly 100 miles to the fall lines at the Piedmont, beyond which steamers could not pass. Between them were other estuaries—the York, Piankatank, Great Wicomico—blending their waters with the Chesapeake. To the north, on the Western Shore, lay the South, West, Rhode, Severn, and Magothy Rivers, navigable for some 10 miles, more or less, inland, and the Patapsco, where stood the economic magnet, Baltimore. Across the flatlands of the Eastern Shore flowed a vast canallike network of rivers and creeks—the byways of Pocomoke Sound; the Nanticoke, Wicomico, Little Choptank, the Great Choptank, Miles, Tred Avon, Chester, Corsica, Sassafras, and Elk Rivers, running 10 to 40 miles through the marshes and heavy soil of the long peninsula. At no point on the Eastern Shore was a planter more than a carriage ride from a waterway.

Chesapeake steamers served several functions. Aside from double-ended ferry boats, which shuttled faithfully across the Bay at various locations but which, with a few exceptions, earned the scorn of true steamboats aesthetes, there were five classes of Chesapeake steamboat. First, the open-decked excursion boats carried their voluminous human cargo to joyous pleasure at the amusement parks. *Louise,* buxom beauty of the Tolchester line, and *Dreamland,* fast-floating beer-and-dance hall (its theme song was "Meet Me Tonight in Dreamland"), running excursions to Chesapeake Beach and moonlight cruises, were classic examples. Second, some day steamers combined excursions with utilitarian service to river landings. The beloved *Emma Giles* of the Tolchester line not only ran as relief boat to Tolchester Beach but also served the Little Choptank, South, West, Rhode, and other rivers for freight and regular passengers, making each trip a sort of daytime vacation as well. *Mobjack* for Mobjack Bay served a similar function out of Norfolk. Third, handsome steamers ran a fast shuttle service at various points. *Cambridge* out of Baltimore ran to Claiborne for rail connections to the Eastern Shore and ocean resorts; *Elisha Lee* crossed the mouth of the Bay from Norfolk to Cape Charles, bearing freight and passengers to connect with rail service up the Delmarva Peninsula to Philadelphia and New York. Fourth, the queens of the bay, the fleet of large, fast luxurious packets, ran between Baltimore and Norfolk, and Washington and Norfolk; for years, the service included the York River. *Alabama, State of Maryland, President Warfield,* and others of the Old Bay Line, *Yorktown* and *City of Norfolk,* among others of the Chesapeake line, ran overnight service from Baltimore to Norfolk; and *Northland* and *Southland* were examples of first-class steamers operating between Washington and Norfolk. Most of the Norfolk packets were large, 250 to 300 feet of steel, white-walled splendor.

A separate class—indeed the largest class—of steamboats on the Chesapeake comprised the medium-sized (150- to 200-foot) overnight packets, whose purpose was to serve the multitude of landings on 1,000 miles or more of rivers and creeks throughout the Tidewater region of Maryland and Virginia (in some instances, as on the Nanticoke River, they reached into Delaware). At the peak of the steamboat era, there were more than 300 of these landings, scattered—often in isolated areas—from the Bay to the upper reaches of navigation. Some of these landings, as in the case of the service performed by the Tolchester Steamboat Company, were reached by day-excursion boats. But the overwhelming majority were served by the grand white fleet—the handsome, purposeful, seaworthy, sturdy, and elegantly equipped vessels that ran out of Baltimore, Norfolk, and Washington. Baltimore, as the commercial hub of the Bay, overwhelmingly dominated the trade.

The steamboats of the Chesapeake were a sturdy lot. Unlike those on the Mississippi, which were built with expendability in mind and rarely lasted more than 4 or 5 years, Chesapeake steamboats were constructed to endure for 50 years, and many steamed much longer. Their engines were built for a life span of a quarter-century. Many were pulled from sunken, burned, or abandoned vessels and continued functioning; some ran for as long as 60 to 80 years. Chesapeake steamboats were designed to meet the rougher seas of the lower Bay—with more enclosure of freight and cabin space and with a more decided sheer than their western-river counterparts. Although similar boats traveled the Hudson and Delaware Rivers, Long Island Sound, the waters of New England, and many lakes, there developed on the Chesapeake a type of steamboat that wore its own hallmark. The Chesapeake itself designed it.

The steamboat era was inescapably romantic. It smacked of plantations, gracious living, and a leisurely pace unmeasured by time. It smelled of the salt air of the sea, oyster shells mountains high, masses of seaweed rotting on a sandy shore, the fragrance of pine and loam and honeysuckle from the passing forest, the stench of a fish factory pressing menhaden for oil and "chum" for fertilizer, the aroma of roasting coffee and old wooden wharves and smoke and the harbor of Baltimore at sailing time. It told of sun-drenched days on the Bay, hampers filled with ham and fried chicken and the makings of a picnic on the beach, of fresh breeze and endless vistas of sea and sky, wooden roller coasters, miniature railroads, and carousels belting out unending organ-grinder tunes, little wavelets splashing on a sandy beach. It spoke of velvet nights under star-studded skies when the waves whispered beneath the guards, and the lookoutsman at the bow called out a plaintive "all's well." It recalled the steamboats themselves, trim and graceful, their white sides glistening, paddleboxes glowing with gold leaf, tall stacks belching smoke, walking beams teetering—breasting the chop of the open Bay or slipping quietly through its creeks and byways.

But steamboat life on the Chesapeake was not a continuous reverie. Its history was beset by disasters and trouble. Steamboats caught fire and destroyed themselves, passengers, cargo, and owners' investments. Collisions, groundings, and sinkings occurred more frequently than steamboat lines were willing to acknowledge. Hurricanes and gales swept the Bay, devastating shipping and demolishing landings. Ice jammed the channels of the Bay and formed packs in the rivers, effectively blocking passage for weeks on end. The steamers themselves were often scenes of ruffianlike brutality and rough behavior. Brawling among passengers was not unusual. Deckhands got to gambling and fighting; and bludgeoning by contenders or officers trying to quell the fighting was not uncommon. Professional gamblers rode the steamers for their own purposes, and plantations were often filched from their owners on a flick of the cards.

Rate wars, depressions, vicious competition, overweening monopoly—the flexing of individual and corporate muscle—characterized much of steamboat management. People who built the steamboat lines, manned the boats, and saw them through years of adversity dealt with difficult and often soul-shattering problems that tested their mettle and stubbornness. In the end, they all succumbed to competition over which they had no control—that of the automobile and the truck and the highway improvements that they brought with them. The steamboat lost its role in the economic life of tidewater Maryland and Virginia. The Great Depression was the final blow.

The steamboat era can be cataloged by a list of the boats, their owners, and the routes they served. Its story can be told by a narrative of individual steamboats, symbolic of the times, and of the men and women who gave them meaning and the entire era substance. Such a boat was *Emma Giles*, beloved by generations of excursion-bound Baltimoreans and residents along the shores of Dorchester and Anne Arundel Counties, where she plied for nearly a half-century. But the annals of steamboating on the Chesapeake can be recounted in a more significant and compelling way—through the narrative of the one steamboat line that lived its life from the beginning of the era to its very climax. The name of one steamboat line on the Chesapeake became virtually synonymous with the steamboat era.

The name *Weems*, and the Weems line, symbolized nearly the entire epoch of the steamboat on the Chesapeake. It began life in 1819 in the visionary and impractical purchase by George Weems of an experimental boat called *Surprise*. It suffered through enormous hardships—explosions, burnings, undercutting opposition, rate wars, near bankruptcy, the depredations of the Civil War, collisions, successive depressions, and the death of its progenitors under tragic circumstances. Yet the courage and Scottish stubbornness of its founder, the persistence and hardheadedness of his son, and the calm vision of the latter's successor carried the line from incipient collapse to triumph at the turn of the century in the "golden age" of the steamboat era. In 1905, it sold out to a subsidiary of the Pennsylvania Railroad at the height of its power. Its 10 steamboats—the most magnificent of the overnight river packets on the Chesapeake—symbolized the heyday of that class of steamboats on the Bay.

Many of these steamboats continued to run to the great rivers of the Western Shore of the Chesapeake long after their sale to subsidiaries of the Pennsylvania Railroad. One of them, *Anne Arundel*, made a sad trip in September 1937 from Baltimore to Fredericksburg, the last run made by an overnight river packet on the Chesapeake.[2] Under another name, she continued to sail after that as an excursion boat. In effect, the steamboats that carried the name of Weems spanned the history of the steamboat era on the Bay for almost 120 years.

The story of the Weems line is the story of a dynasty of sturdy men—the story of their courage in adversity, their mistakes in judgment, their persistence in the face of failure, their loyalty to family, their humanness in the depths of tragedy, and their exultation in days of triumph. It is a tale of encounter with less principled men. It is a story of disappointment, humility, humor, anguish, deception, tempestuous clashes, and monopolistic power. It speaks of gentility, honor, and a sense of fair play.

The story crosses the threads of the nation's history. In the Tidewater country of the Patuxent, Potomac, and Rappahannock, where the Weems steamers sailed, the course of the republic was shaped. During the Civil War, the Weems steamers were forced to participate, in unexpected, sometimes exciting, and often rather humorous ways. The social and political history of Baltimore offered a colorful backdrop to the steamboat era and the Weems family.

The story presents the contribution made by the steamboat to the economic life of the Tidewater region. In the case of the Weems line, the valleys of the Patuxent, Potomac, and Rappahannock owed their development over the span of decades in large measure to the service of the steamers. In the absence of railroads and passable highways for travel, these steamboats offered the only lifeline to the outside world.

The Weems line dramatized the entire steamboat era, its rise and fall, its pageantry and its pain.

Tidewater by Steamboat

CHAPTER 1

The Quest for Steamboats: Trial and Error

The summer of 1818 drew down to a sultry end. Over Baltimore, the humid pall that had beset the city for most of the season cleared by the day to ease the tempers of its inhabitants. Residents who had lived with the stench of sewage in the streets and in the harbor and the ever-present thickening smoke from forge and shipyard around the basin and Fells Point took heart when September gusts off the Bay freshened the air.

In mid-1818 Baltimore bustled with sudden and contorted growth. Its population, numbering some 13,000 inhabitants in 1790, had doubled by the turn of the century, had doubled again by 1810, and by 1818 stood nearly at 60,000.[1] It held a burgeoning conglomeration of tradesmen profiting on overseas commerce and the region's enormous export of tobacco, entrepreneurs bent on a quick yield from the rapid spread of industry in the city, workmen from coppersmiths to machinists to carpenters and skilled laborers who flocked to the congested city in increasing numbers for employment, shipbuilders whose yards were filled with forests of masts of vessels under construction, men of the sea and the Bay whose sailing vessels crowded the wharves and anchorages, and several thousand slaves who furnished much of the manual labor and who served the gentry in their Georgian or Federal-style townhouses gracing the tree-lined streets. Around the harbor, industry had overtaken the narrow streets, where so much of the population had settled in rows of unpretentious dwellings; houses and smelters and warehouses and shipyards melded in unpalatable confusion. Bawdy taverns entertained workmen and sailors, in spite of the exhortations of churches and temperance societies.

Baltimore at the end of the summer of 1818 took its stance on the upper Chesapeake. It saw itself for the first time as a center for industrial growth, as a link between the expanding interior of the country and overseas markets, and as a focal point for the trade of tidewater Maryland and Virginia. Its disheveled appearance and unsavory smells and sounds only reflected the suddenness of its disorderly bulging.

Two men with the given name of George were particularly restless at the end of that summer. One was a 26-year-old shipmaster, George Weems. The other was no less than the Honorable George Stiles, mayor of Baltimore, age 58. In spite of the difference in their age and status, the reason for their restlessness was the same. It concerned a boat. Not an ordinary boat. Instead, a novelty. A steamboat. And a most unusual steamboat at that.

George Stiles was a man of many facets. He had earned his wealth from a fleet of clipper-schooners trading in the Far East. On the return trip, these vessels often brought to Baltimore exotic cargoes, such as quantities of grass linen sheets, which, spread beneath cotton or flax sheets, proved their coolness against the heavy summer humidity. He commanded his own ship during the period of near hostilities with France. His ships roamed the seven seas and earned money for him. Although he kept a dwelling in Old Town Baltimore, on Queen Street near Granby, he spent most of his time on the fringe of the city at his estate, Harlem.[2]

George Stiles was revered by the people of Baltimore as one of its defenders when a British squadron advanced on Fort McHenry in September 1814. Earlier, on May 21, 1812, he was one of a body of Baltimoreans who assembled at the Fountain Inn to voice their indignation at the British for the impressment of American sailors on the high seas, and he joined 50 representatives of Baltimore in signing a resolution urging the president to declare war. In May 1813, he put together the Corps of Seamen with himself as captain and assisted in the mounting of batteries in defense of Fort McHenry. He contributed to the design of a steam battery which, after fundraising by the citizens of Baltimore for its production, was discontinued for lack of federal funds. The city itself constructed barges and galleys to be manned by the Corps of Seamen under Captain Stiles. In the defense of the city in September 1814, this unit manned five 18-pound field guns at the juncture of Philadelphia Road and the road to Sparrows Point.[3] As the ultimate gesture, Stiles placed his own ships in the line of blockade to prevent movement of the British

George Stiles, defender at Fort McHenry, mayor of Baltimore, machinery manufacturer, and builder of *Surprise,* which was powered by the experimental rotary engine. Courtesy of Mayor Kurt Schmoke and the curator of City Hall, Baltimore

squadron toward Fells Point.[4] Several of these ships were deliberately sunk to impede the British advance.

Fear that Vice-Admiral Cochrane and his squadron, reinforced by other British units from Halifax or Bermuda, might return for a second assault on Baltimore prompted the city's Committee of Vigilance and Safety to order all "free people of color . . . to attend daily . . . at the different works erecting about the city for the purpose of laboring therein, and for which they shall receive an allowance of fifty cents per day together with a soldier's ration" and to "earnestly invite . . . our fellow-citizens who are exempt from military duty . . . to labor on the fortifications either in person or by substitute"; the committee further resolved "that Captain George Stiles [and Captain Isaac Philips] be . . . hereby authorised to enforce the preceding order."[5]

George Stiles was honored for his role in the defense of the city. In 1816, he was elected mayor, cited for his eloquence in public office, and venerated wherever he went. He was reelected in 1818 by a substantial margin, 4,298 to 2,576. Dressing rather elegantly in silken fashions more in keeping with the turn of the previous century, his face smooth shaven, he seemed removed from the clatter of industry and the brawling world of ships and the sea.[6]

His official demeanor, however, was deceptive. He was, after all, a man of many facets. During the War of 1812, he set up a bakery on a little island then existing in the middle of Baltimore Harbor to furnish seaman's biscuits or "pilot biscuits" to ships entering or leaving port and to the defenders of the city. Even more surprising, during the same period, he busied himself with building a factory in partnership with his son, John. The factory had no assigned purpose; nevertheless, it developed many functions according to the whims of its owner.

George Stiles relished machinery. He found the new industrial flavor of the city exciting. In particular, on the waterfront of Fells Point near Lancaster and Wolfe Streets he discovered a shop in which a certain James Curtis labored, assisted at times by Royal Yeamans, a rather itinerant resident of Plymouth, New York, and Westfield, Massachusetts.[7] On February 8, 1812, these two men had patented a steam engine designed around an extremely novel idea.[8]

Their idea was in a sense revolutionary in that it rejected the design of earlier engines that depended on a cumbersome arrangement whereby a piston moving back and forth driven by steam in a cylinder would connect through a system of flailing connecting rods swinging about a crank and a number of cogwheels and flywheels to rotate the main shaft, which was linked to the lathe or the mill or the paddlewheel to be driven. In contrast, the concept of Curtis and Yeamans was simple enough. If the function of a steam engine was to rotate a shaft—and that seemed to be the principal reason for building steam engines at the time—why not attach a rotor directly to the shaft, surround it with a flat steam-tight cylinder, design the rotor with baffles to admit the steam at a certain point of rotation to use it for its pressure to develop power, and to discharge it when it had done its work? On this principle, the very simple rotary engine that they had patented had been put to the test by a company that mounted it in a small vessel at Georgetown on the Potomac to rotate the shaft connecting the paddlewheels; the experiment had been unsuccessful. Curtis had then set up shop in Baltimore very early in 1814, determined to put his invention on trial once again.

To George Stiles the simplicity of the rotary engine was appealing. It stood in sharp contrast to the reciprocating engines, previously described, being built at the time. Around Baltimore in 1813 and 1814, mill operators introduced huge reciprocating engines. Job Smith powered his sawmill by one on Chases Wharf. Charles Smith had one for a flour mill in a warehouse at the end of Commerce Street. A little later the firm of McElderry and Phoenix planned for the use of a steam engine to grind plaster of Paris to be sold in its store in Old Town. And other steam engines followed.[9] All of these were ponderous contraptions in which connecting rods driven by a piston in a cylinder swung about a crank on a shaft which, through cogwheels and other shafts, moved the grinding stones or the circular saws. The direct application of the Curtis-Yeamans engine to the rotation of a shaft struck Stiles as the practical answer to factory power, and he and his son decided to apply it.

Experimenting with the new engine and building it proved to be costly. Nevertheless, Stiles had one mounted in his factory near the glasshouse for the purpose of boring cannon. The end of the war brought that activity to an end. The engine was then used to power lathes in the shop.[10] In early 1818, George Stiles and Son advertised that their "Rotary Steam Engine [was] in full operation [running] a grist mill, with two run of stone; the engine . . . is only 14 inches in diameter and 12 inches deep . . . and can carry all the turning lathes in the factory."[11]

John S. Stiles, the son, declared that it had the power of 14 horses, that it weighed one-fourth as much as other engines of similar power and took up one-half the space, that it used one-third less fuel, that ordinary blacksmiths could build it, and that the one at the Stiles's factory was "under the care of a black man, whose chief qualities, as needful to its management, are sobriety and attention."[12]

George Stiles, seafarer, saw more pressing needs for the employment of the rotary engine. He had watched with intense interest the building of the first steamboat on the Chesapeake. It was easy for him to keep in touch with the progress of the boat. In spite of its blustering expansion, Baltimore in 1813 retained much of the social bonding that characterized the South. Its gentry were more than acquainted; they knew each other well through church and social contact and long association. Shipowners, shipbuilders, and those who managed the maritime enterprise of a busy port formed a group whose affairs were matters of common knowledge and thorough discussion.

A friend of Stiles was Lieutenant Colonel William McDonald, commander of Maryland's Sixth Regiment in the defense of North Point in 1814. Before his military renown, McDonald had enjoyed considerable financial success with his son in the operation of the Frenchtown packet line, which sent its fast sailing vessels laden with passengers and freight each day from Bowleys Wharf, at the lower end of South Street (not far from Stiles's factory), bound for Frenchtown on the Elk River in the upper Bay. There, passengers would cross by stage to Newcastle on the Delaware River for onward travel by sailing packet to Wilmington and Philadelphia. McDonald was an entrepreneur who profited from his commercial ventures in many fields; he lived expensively at his estate of Guilford just north of the city where his son kept a stable of the best Arabian racing horses in the state. The father and son were closely associated with Andrew Fisher Henderson, later to become a partner in the packet trade and cofounder of the Union Line. Through them, George Stiles knew of John Ferguson and John Owens of Cecil County, themselves owners of a packet line on the Elk River. And in 1812, he learned rather soon about the energies of Edward Trippe in enlisting the support of McDonald, Henderson, Ferguson, and Owens in a project to build a steamboat in Baltimore.

Edward Trippe was also a man of many facets. A sailing captain, owner of several vessels engaged profitably in the West Indies trade, he lived part of the year in Baltimore on South Charles Street near Camden, where the harbor waters lapped at his garden. When he wished to visit any of his vessels, a four-oared barge arrived at his garden gate to deliver him on board in state. A tall, courtly man, he was paid the ultimate compliment by John Quincy Adams who pronounced that he was "alike to gentleman and slave."[13] In addition to his Baltimore residence, he owned a large farm in Dorchester County. He possessed an undivided penchant for the sciences of the times and read everything he could obtain from abroad about the progress of physics, particularly mechanics, and its various applications.

He invested substantially in various maritime enterprises, and it was through these that he met Robert Livingston. The latter visited Trippe at his Eastern Shore estate, and Trippe went to Clermont, Livingston's home on the Hudson, where most certainly he met Robert Fulton. In 1807, Fulton, with Livingston's backing, had launched *North River Steamboat* (commonly known as *Clermont*).[14]

For some time, the ingenuity of a few American inventors had wrestled with the notions from abroad about the application of mechanics and steam power to industry and transportation. In particular, these men looked to the navigation of the vast waterways of the American continent. The relative contributions of John Fitch, James Rumsey, Oliver Evans, John Stevens, and Robert Fulton to the invention and practical development of the steamboat were matters of debate. Natives of the Chesapeake Bay country liked to advance the claims of Rumsey for pioneer work with his invention at Shepherdstown in 1785. As early as 1790, John Fitch had completed a working steamboat and, for a short time, operated it commercially between Philadelphia and Trenton.[15] But the first continuous commercial service began on the Hudson River in 1807 with Fulton's *North River Steamboat*. That Fulton deserved full credit for the invention of the steamboat remains questionable. Even at the time, it was clear that promises of exclusive rights of navigation, heavy financial backing, and greed for monopoly on the Hudson, possibly the Delaware, and especially the western rivers (the Ohio, the Illinois, and the Mississippi being early targets) were chiefly responsible for Fulton's success.[16]

The thirst for monopoly brought *New Orleans* from Pittsburgh to New Orleans by 1812; *Phoenix*, invented by John Stevens, had fled the Livingston monopoly on the Hudson to begin running on the Delaware, to be joined there by *Philadelphia, New Jersey, Eagle,* and *Camden,* the last replacing the Philadelphia horse-ferry. Livingston, through his acquaintances in Maryland, probably looked to the Chesapeake for an extension of his monopoly. His interest evaporated when a British fleet entered the Chesapeake Bay.

But Edward Trippe remained infected with Fulton's enthusiasm for steamboats. He set about to gain the support of McDonald and the others in building a steamboat for the Chesapeake. His enthusiasm was matched by that of McDonald; the others were vocal backers. He and Henderson—the pair having formed the Union Line—agreed to put up two-thirds of the money needed, under the condition that Trippe supply the remainder and apply his very considerable scientific knowledge to the project.

They engaged William Flanigan and his shipyard at 10 Pratt Street (at the basin) to build a steamboat modeled after its predecessors on the Hudson and the Delaware. Built at a cost of $40,000 and launched in 1813, *Chesapeake*, the first steamboat on the Bay whose name she bore, made her maiden voyage to Annapolis on June 13 of that year in spite of the threats posed by the war and the British fleet.[17]

Chesapeake resembled a sailing packet with an engine on deck; she carried a tiller aft and bowsprit, mast and sails as a visible precaution. A boiler amidships had a 20-foot stack; a crosshead engine through cogwheels turned uncovered paddlewheels 10 feet in diameter on either side; and with wood stacked all over her decks for fuel, she churned along at 5 miles per hour, enough to make her scheduled run to Frenchtown and return (120 miles) in 24 hours. Accommodations of sorts were provided in the men's cabin, used alternately as a dining room, and a women's cabin with berths. A swivel gun mounted on the bow signaled her arrivals and departures. It failed to impress the British.

Building a steam engine for *Chesapeake* was no mean feat. Employed at times in the U.S. Marshal's office in Baltimore in 1813 was one Daniel Large, age 31, sallow, 5 feet, 9 inches tall, with dark hair and blue eyes. He was an immigrant from England in 1807 and was the builder of a stationary steam engine for the Weatherhill brothers, local mill operators. Benjamin Latrobe of Baltimore fame saw this engine and, impressed by its quality, visited Large in his shop on Germantown Road, Philadelphia. One of Daniel Large's apprentices at the time was 26-year-old Charles Reeder, founder in 1815 of the prestigious engine-building firm that bore his name. Latrobe brought Daniel Large to the attention of Flanigan, McDonald, Henderson, and Trippe. During the spring of 1813, Daniel Large brought from Philadelphia the parts of an engine that he undoubtedly designed for assembly in the hull of *Chesapeake*. Much of the assembly work itself was performed by Charles Reeder.[18]

Chesapeake, making her regular runs to Frenchtown three days a week, was the only steamboat in Baltimore waters for two years, and she realized a profit for her owners of some 40 percent. During that time her voyages were interrupted by the proximity of the British flotilla (she ran an excursion on August 8, 1813, to the Patapsco entrance to view the enemy ships) and by the arrival of Vice-Admiral Cochrane's squadron off Fort McHenry in Baltimore Harbor one year and a month later. On September 13, 1814, the new steamer commanded by Captain Trippe stood in the line of blockade ships and presented her white paddlebox with the inscription *Chesapeake: Union Line* to the British men-of-war maneuvering toward Fells Point and access to the streets of Baltimore.[19] With the retirement of the British, she resumed her route with the same regularity as before.

Other steamboats followed. *Eagle,* which had operated on the upper Delaware from Philadelphia to Bordentown, became the second steamer (or perhaps, as some evidence indicated, the third) to sail the open ocean by running from Philadelphia to Baltimore in search of a charter. She was grabbed for charter by the competition to the Union Line, the firm of Samuel Briscoe, John Partridge, and others, which had started a packet line via Elkton (overland stage to Wilmington and steamboat *Vesta* to Philadelphia). The Union Line countered by building *Philadelphia* in Baltimore in 1816; Briscoe and Partridge answered a few months later by bringing *New Jersey* down from Philadelphia and continuing the Norfolk run started by *Eagle.* The Union Line built *United States* in 1818. At that point, Briscoe and Partridge surrendered to the competition and sold out. The bitterness of steamboat company rivalry had stung the Chesapeake.[20]

These early boats filled the residents of Baltimore, Frenchtown, Annapolis, Rock Hall, and other points on the Chesapeake and the Delaware with sheer consternation when they saw them for the first time.

At first glance, these boats looked like the sailing craft that Tidewater people understood. The lines of the hull, usually 100 to 150 feet in length, were those of a schooner—with a clipper bow and square or slightly rounded stern, with a tiller for steering, and with a bowsprit and a mast or two to carry fore-and-aft mainsail and jib and square topsail in case the engine failed. Cabins, not unlike those on the packets, were mostly aft and provided some sleeping accommodations and a dining area. But here the resemblance ended. Mounted amidships—or even slightly forward of amidships on some—were a boiler and engine. The former, of copper or iron mounted vertically some 2 or 3 feet above the deck to provide space for the firebox, was surmounted by a 20-foot stack. The crosshead engine consisted of a conspicuous T-bar riding up and down across the waist of the vessel. The vertical part of the T was a rod attached to the piston inside the vertical steam cylinder. The crossbar at the top of the T had a swinging rod at each end which turned a crank on either side of the vessel and caused each paddlewheel, port and starboard, to revolve. On some boats, the cranks worked through cogwheels to reconcile the difference between piston thrust and paddle speed. On the vertical cylinder moved a valve mechanism to regulate the input of steam from the boiler and the output of expanded steam to the condenser, a tank that used seawater to cool the steam to condensate and thus provide a source of fresh water relatively free of salt for return as feed water to the boiler—as well as a source of a vacuum, increasing the push and pull of the piston. Stacked on deck were huge piles of wood; the appetite of the firebox beneath the boiler seemed insatiable.

The sight of one of these boats clawing its way along, crosshead pulsing in its guiding rails, connecting rods flailing, paddlewheels (in some instances uncovered) throwing up spumes of water, and the stack belching smoke, was awesome in daylight to the uninitiated, but at night with wood sparks flying high from the stack (at times the top of the stack itself glowed red), the spectacle was unnerving to those who understood only the power of wind in a sail.

George Stiles, mechanic and practical engineer, looked critically at these square-engined boats docking with surprising regularity under his very nose at neighboring wharves. He compared their cranking cross-heads disdainfully with the little rotary engine he was developing to power his factory.

In 1815 he set about to complete the work of Curtis and Yeamans by building a small rotary engine in his shop and mounting it for trial in a little boat named *Antelope*.[21] The experiment proved costly in time, labor, and money. Nevertheless, the little boat with the small engine moved about the harbor with acceptable speed, and Stiles moved quickly to build a steamboat on the lines of a small sailing packet, with a rotary engine designed specifically to propel it.[22] By midsummer 1816, she was steaming about the harbor basin and in operation.[23] To the astonishment of observers, even of her owner and builder, she managed to circle *New Jersey* (then considered the fastest boat out of Baltimore) three times on a passage from the Baltimore basin to Fort McHenry, a distance of two miles, and set a record on the Bay.[24]

George Stiles and his son John were overjoyed. George especially savored success and strutted about the decks of the little vessel as her master, in spite of the pressure of other business awaiting him. Nevertheless, the practical employment of *Surprise*, as he named her, in the months and years ahead became a dominant issue, and George and John began the search for a profitable route (Appendix A).

Before the 1816 season ended, *Surprise* entered the Tred Avon River and astonished crowds of spectators at Oxford and along the shore. They marveled and shuddered at this strange apparition that belched fire yet moved against the current at a steady five miles per hour.[25] The press reported that "Captain Stiles, the respected and excellent mayor of Baltimore, has started his steam boat, Surprize [*sic*], as a packet to run to and from several places on the Chesapeake Bay. Her engine is propelled on the 'rotary motion, and she moves with more ease and swiftness than any other steam boat in the United States.' The construction is so simple that, it is said, independent of the boilers, the machinery will not cost more than one-tenth of the usual expence [*sic*] of machinery constructed in the ordinary manner."[26]

On July 3, 1817, in various Baltimore newspapers, George Stiles advertised the sailings of *Surprise* to Annapolis and Easton. From the advertising, it was clear that *Surprise* had run the Miles River and the lower Chester River through the winter of 1816–17.[27] The captain on board was Jonathan Spencer, engaged by George Stiles to replace him as master. Late in the summer season of 1817, advertisements proclaimed that *Surprise* would leave Commerce Street Wharf every Monday and Thursday at eight o'clock in the morning for Annapolis and

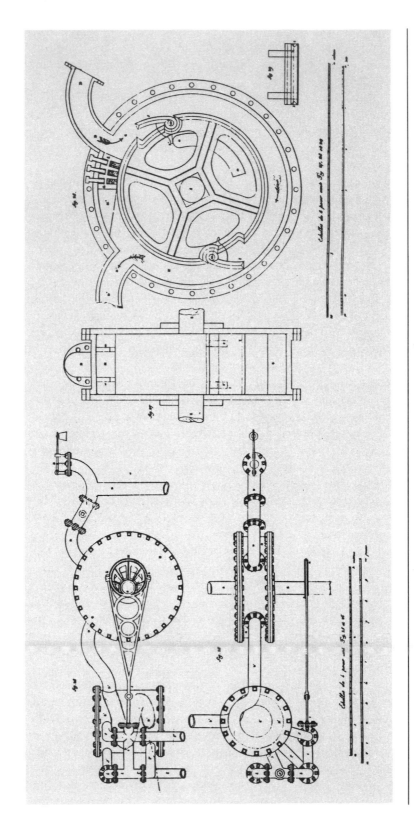

The rotary engine in *Surprise* is from [Jean Baptiste] Marestier's *Mémoire sur les Bateaux à Vapeur des États-Unis d'Amérique* (Paris, 1824)

Easton via Miles River Ferry and would depart every Wednesday and Saturday for Centreville at six o'clock in the morning to return the same day. Further, she would "take on board and land passengers to suit their convenience."[28]

Unfortunately, George Stiles knew too little about the people of the Eastern Shore. An insular and somewhat clannish society, hospitable and well endowed by the rich flatlands that produced tobacco and other produce in quantity, the residents of the long peninsula of Maryland and Virginia clung to the traditional patterns they had followed for generations. They viewed the arrival of *Surprise* with consternation and apprehension. Many feared the fire-breathing monster to the extent that George Stiles saw fit to advertise that "the *Surprise* boilers . . . will be proved every month to bear double the pressure at which they are worked."[29] Even then, many announced that they would not ride on her. Many planters, oystermen, sailboat owners, and shippers perceived the boat as a threat to their vital business interests. Some others, noting the movements of steamboats about the Bay, were more receptive.

She was, by standards of the times, well furnished. Dining room cuisine compared favorably with what was offered aboard other steamers on the Bay. Her rotary engine gave her a special distinction. The fact that George Stiles encountered considerable difficulty with the engine and laid her up for repairs during the winter suggested that the experimental phase had not yet been completed.

Surprise began the 1818 summer season, Jonathan Spencer as master, with Sunday and Thursday departures at 9:00 A.M. for Annapolis and Easton (to return the following day) and a Tuesday run to Centreville (to return the following day). The landings she visited were very much the same as before. By the end of the summer, however, circumstances surrounding *Surprise* had changed. Persistent difficulties with the engine, particularly with the motion of the interior rotor, intruded on the confidence that George Stiles held in its long-term performance. A mild explosion in early 1818 proved troublesome and somewhat alarming. George still waxed enthusiastic to any audience about the wonders of the engine; but privately, his misgivings multiplied. Even more private were his apprehensions about his health, which was clearly failing. His son John, burdened with the factory, displayed little inclination to operate a steamboat line.

Reluctantly, George decided to sell *Surprise*. Once he had reached that decision—onerous as it was—he stomped about, restless to find a suitable buyer.

At the end of that summer of 1818, another man with the given name of George stomped about restlessly. George Weems, at 26, shipowner and shipmaster and privateersman in the late war, watched the passage of the little steamboats back and forth in the nearby harbor and fretted to enter the steamboat business on the Chesapeake. At the time, he had a stake in several ships that turned a reasonable profit from their ventures abroad; he had served his stint as master aboard them, but now he hoped to settle down in his native Maryland and seek his fortune on the Chesapeake.

He savored the notion of operating some sort of shipping line, perhaps capitalizing on his seafaring background, but he wanted to add vessels for trade on the Bay from his vantage point in Baltimore. From the window of his house on Philpott Street, Fells Point, George Weems watched the steamboats come and go, winter and summer, fair weather and foul. Imaginative, innovative, impulsive, George immediately grasped their importance to tidewater Maryland and Virginia. All he sought was a way to enter the trade.[30]

In the maritime life of the port, George Stiles and George Weems, prominent as they were, certainly knew each other. Their meeting to discuss the sale of *Surprise* could scarcely have been an accident.

Both emerged jubilant. George Stiles, exuding enthusiasm for the little steamer, showered it with praise and forecast that all steamboats would soon be powered by rotary engines. George Weems could scarcely contain his eagerness. He wanted the steamer, and he wanted to buy her as soon as possible.

George Weems was a romantic adventurer, born with a yen for the sea. At the same time, he lived in the shadow of his heritage and his roots in the soil of southern Maryland.

His grandfather, David Weems, had arrived in Anne Arundel County in 1720, brought by his mother to live with her brother, Dr. William Loch, after the death of her husband William at the battle of Preston in 1715. Defender of the Stuarts, William was descended from the earl of Wemyss, lord high admiral of Scotland. In the New World David Weems spawned 19 children, one of whom was Mason Loch Weems, the colorful biographer of George Washington. Another son was David, the father of George (Appendix E).

The elder David, grandfather of George, spoke with the burr of Scotland in his teeth, but he brought to Maryland the vigor of his illustrious forebears. The tobacco trade beckoned. In 1732, Maryland and Virginia sent to England as much as 60 million pounds of the fragrant weed, and the Tidewater country thrived on the profits. Planters turned their wealth into extravagant purchases from abroad, into extended acreage and substantial manor houses at home as well as to ever-increasing numbers of slaves (averaging 30 slaves per 100 acres cultivated) to perform the required hand cultivation. At age 26, David Weems began his acquisition of land in order to become a planter himself. One of his first purchases, made in 1733, was a 150-acre tract called Marshes Seat on Herring Creek, which ran into Herring Bay on the western shore of the Chesapeake. His largest purchase was the 2,000-acre Mannour of Portland, acquired in 1740, on Lyons Creek, bordering the Patuxent River. At Marshes Seat, he built a manor house 100 feet in length, and he settled down to raise his numerous children and bask in the pleasures of the Chesapeake (Appendix E).

The younger David (born in 1751), father of George, smelled the sea at an early age. He ventured forth as a seaman from the landing at Town Point, which served Marshes Seat on Herring Creek, aboard ships bound for Europe. While a young man, with his father's encouragement, he designed and built on the shores of Herring Creek a vessel along the lines of a topsail schooner. The slaves of the plantation performed the actual labor. In the early 1770s, he sailed the ship for England and returned laden with furnishings and household treasures valued in colonial Maryland. In the gulf stream, on the return voyage, he came upon a large mahogany log, which he took in tow and brought back to Marshes Seat. There slaves sawed it up and turned it into a handsome table to become a family heirloom.[31]

Shortly after the American Revolution broke out, David Weems threw in his lot with three neighbors, John Muir, Isaac Vanbibber, and Charles Wallace, all seafarers, to outfit privateers for action against British shipping. On October 20, 1777, a letter of marque and reprisal was issued to Thomas Waters, master of the schooner *Williaminta* (also titled *Willy Minta*), owned by David Weems and his three compatriots, manned by 10 men, and armed with four swivel guns. Not quite a year later, on August 3, 1778, a letter of marque and reprisal was issued to John Burrows, master of the sloop *Washington* (60 tons burden), mounting eight carriage guns, six swivel guns, and 20 muskets, manned by a crew of 20 men, and owned by David Weems and his three companions.[32]

While he was outfitting the first privateer, David Weems courted Margaret Harrison and married her on April 15, 1777. He had six children, among them Gustavus (born April 2, 1779) and George (born May 23, 1784). In late 1818, David was suffering from infirmities that made an old man of him at age 67. Increasingly, he leaned on these two sons to support him in his declining years.[33] In a debenture dated January 7, 1819, David, Gustavus, and George entered into an agreement whereby the father granted to his two sons the 400-acre tracts of Marshes Seat and adjoining Pascals Purchase, provided that he could remain on one-third of the estate and in the manor house for the remainder of his life.[34]

Gustavus, in spite of his attachment to his father and to Marshes Seat, had made his fortune in neighboring Calvert County. He bought large tracts of land around Huntingtown, just north of Prince Frederick, the county seat; in all, he owned in excess of 2,000 acres in various parts of the county, some of which he farmed. In 1816, he was justice of the peace. In Huntingtown, he owned a general store and operated a warehouse in which he employed nine clerks for the shipment of tobacco and the handling of general merchandise arriving from Baltimore at the nearby Plum Point landing on the Chesapeake.[35]

George Weems, in contrast to the land settling of his brother, made his mark in the shipping world of Baltimore and sailed the seven seas in search of adventure. Early in life, with the encouragement of his seafaring father, he left the shores of the Chesapeake and put to sea. In his teens, he mastered his trade as sailor and learned the arts of seamanship and navigation. While still a lad, he had sailed from Baltimore with Captain James Norman (also spelled *Noonan*) to the East Indies. When the latter died in the tropics, George Weems assumed command and brought the ship safely to Baltimore. His taste for adventure on the high seas never flagged, and within a few years he had crossed the oceans of the world. During the War of 1812, he fitted out a fast sloop named *Halcyon* as a privateer and set out to harry British shipping. Surprised and out-gunned by a British ship, his vessel was captured, her cargo of flour seized; curiously, the British, after holding the vessel and her crew for a time, released *Halcyon* and allowed the crew to sail her away. After the war George managed to gain an interest in several vessels and prof-ited from their trade overseas.[36] He was respected on the Baltimore waterfront.

In 1808, he had met Sarah Sutton in Baltimore, married her after a whirlwind, three-week courtship, and bought a house at 47 Philpott Street, Fells Point, only a step from Weems Pier at the foot of the street and near the townhouse of George Stiles on Queen Street. The effect of family and city brought George to focus his maritime interests on the Chesapeake. His boundless energy and restless disposition, seemingly irrepressible, led him in search of novel enterprises and brought him to the purchase of *Surprise,* the experimental boat of George Stiles.

George and Gustavus, his elder brother, had shared a common bond through the years and had maintained a sort of partnership in a number of undertakings. This partnership was to be sorely tried in late 1818 and the months ahead.[37]

George's determination to buy *Surprise* from George Stiles was met with equal resolution from Gustavus to oppose it. The fire of excitement by George, fanned by the enthusiasm of Stiles for the rotary engine and his excessive eagerness to consummate a sale, induced only a cold cau-tion in the mind of Gustavus. He was torn by his loyalty to his brother and his own fear that *Surprise* would be the downfall of both of them. After evading several appointments with George Stiles, Gustavus finally joined George in a meeting with the seller of *Surprise* in the office of a Light Street wharf, where the brothers went into bond for $20,000 to consummate the sale. As he emerged from the meeting, Gustavus ob-served to everyone present, "This morning dates our ruin!" George Stiles responded, "Not so, Mr. Weems, your fortune." Gustavus coun-tered, "Not likely, Mr. Stiles."

Gustavus continued his grumbling. Finally, George Stiles agreed to take back $5,000. George was so certain of profiting from *Surprise* that he was ready to mortgage the property at Herring Bay to underwrite the remaining balance. However, when David, the father, heard of the pro-posal, he flatly refused to permit it.[38]

During the winter, the sale was consummated. On April Fool's Day 1819, *Surprise* was registered in the name of George Stiles, with George Weems as master. As required by law at the time, the registration of ownership by George Stiles was occasioned by his acceptance of a $6,000 note held by the Union Bank of Maryland against the $15,000 balance; George and Gustavus signed a note with the same bank for an additional $1,000. The remaining funds came from the property of George and Gustavus.[39]

Surprise began halting runs to the Miles and Chester Rivers and to Annapolis. Beginning on July 7, 1819, she was advertised to leave Baltimore for the Patuxent each Wednesday at 8:00 A.M. and to return to Nottingham each Saturday at 6:00 A.M., stopping at "Plumb" Point and Herring Bay each way.[40] Her trips were exploratory and sporadic (Appendix B).

On June 16, 1819, George Stiles, after a lingering illness that had withered him for months, died. The note for $6,000 had to be refinanced. George Weems scrambled for money and for backers.

The financial situation was abruptly aggravated by the halting performance of *Surprise*. All of the unstated fears of George Stiles became facts. The rotary engine broke down, again and again. With little experience on the part of George Weems, or for that matter among the fledgling ironworkers of Baltimore who had never seen a rotary engine, each effort at repairs required expensive reinvention and hand fabrication of needed parts. Innovation and redesign required testing; rebuilding the engine entailed time in the shop, and lost time meant lost revenue. *Surprise* broke down incessantly, often on her runs. In 1820, she was observed off Annapolis moving very slowly; she finally stopped on the open Chesapeake.[41] *Surprise* was seen far less on the waters of the Miles, the Chester, the Severn, and the Patuxent than she was in the repair yards of Baltimore.[42]

The strain between the brothers deepened as George moved from crisis to crisis with assured optimism, and Gustavus went more deeply into debt. For the latter, every Saturday was a day of reckoning to pay off laborers and to settle the cost of repairs.

The estate of George Stiles and the note he held on *Surprise* also required settlement. To his dismay, George found few conventional bankers ready to assume financing on any property as insecure as *Surprise*. In desperation he turned to Christopher Daushon and Solomon Etting, two speculators willing to take a risk for a price. They assumed financing and, as documentation required, titling in their names, with George Weems as master.[43]

Repairs ate up money as fast as George and Gustavus could find it. They borrowed an additional $4,500 on their personal accounts from the Union Bank of Maryland and then turned their attention to property that could be converted into cash. In his last days, David Weems, their father, had stood firm against proposals by George to mortgage the family home at Marshes Seat. After a debilitating illness, David Weems died on January 20, 1820, at the age of 69. Under the mounting pressure of debt, George Weems entered into a debenture with his sister, Sidney, on October 18, 1820, for the sum of $2,000, "against one-half part of the tract . . . of Marshes Seat . . . and Pascals Purchase."[44]

Creditors beset Gustavus. There began a drain on his business, a series of court suits against him, and the destruction of his credit for non-payment of debts. In 1823, he was reduced to the circumstance of signing a debenture for the sale of his "goods, chattels, stock, household furniture, one Negro man Tom, Negro man Perry, Negro man Isaac, Negro girl Polli, six horses, seven mules, 12 broken steers, 34 young steers and cows, 80 sheep, 70 hogs, nine feather beds and furniture, one clock, one sideboard, one bookcase and writing desk, four mahogany tables, four dozen chairs, three carpets, and two settees."[45]

Gustavus's judgment of rotary motion was summed up as follows: "I do not blame my brother George . . . It appeared to me that Stiles had not only driven it into his head but he had riveted it there. . . . I never heard any man . . . mention rotary motion . . . for it was just like a man running after his own shadow; . . . one was as easily caught as the other."[46]

George lost his investments in several ships and his house in Baltimore. But for the obstinacy of David, the father, the estate in Herring Bay may have been in jeopardy also.

George reluctantly agreed to dispose of *Surprise.* A Georgetown speculator bought her for $800 sometime before June 4, 1822, formed the Surprise Steamboat Company, and operated her (whenever she could be made to run) on the Potomac.[47]

In 1824, for the departure of Lafayette from the nation's capital, *Surprise* steamed down the river loaded with enthusiasts to accompany the country's honored guest riding aboard *Mount Vernon* to his ship *Brandywine,* awaiting him in the Chesapeake. Arriving first was a contingent from Baltimore aboard *Constitution.* Both steamboats hove to for farewell speeches on *Brandywine.*[48] Nothing official was heard from *Surprise* after September 20, 1826, and she was apparently abandoned in 1828 (Appendix A).

For George and Gustavus Weems, *Surprise* spelled catastrophe. However George looked at it, his dream of steamboating on the Chesapeake aboard a vessel so novel that it would revolutionize steam engine design was now no more than a costly and pain-stirring illusion.

But George Weems never lost his optimism. Even in the throes of financial debacle, he kept his faith in the promise of steam navigation on the Chesapeake.

The battle between the Union Line and Briscoe and Partridge intrigued him as it captivated the rest of the maritime audience of Baltimore. When, in early 1820, *Eagle* came up for sale by Briscoe and Partridge, George Weems thirsted for a chance to buy the little steamer with a soaring name.

In spite of his belief in the long-range value of the rotary engine in *Surprise,* he gave grudging acknowledgment to the endurance and seeming reliability of the crosshead (square) engines in the other steamboats running the Bay. And he was particularly captivated by *Eagle.* She was a vessel that had proved her worth not only on the Delaware and the Chesapeake but on the waters of the open Atlantic as well.

Eagle had been built in 1813 by J. & F. Brice on the shores of the Delaware River at Kensington in Northern Liberties Township, County of Philadelphia, just north of the city. She looked very much like *Chesapeake,* launched about the same time in Baltimore. Each was a 110-foot, flush-deck vessel, with a schooner hull and a mast carrying yards and square sail. An awning aft provided shade for deck passengers. Below decks were cabins, separated for men and women, the former doubling as a dining area. Amidships on *Eagle* were covered paddleboxes recessed into the hull and deck overhead. A 20-foot stack surmounted the iron boiler. Attached to the crosshead was a substantial green-painted wooden beam that pivoted to operate force pumps below. The crosshead engine was built by Daniel Large, the builder of the engine for *Chesapeake;* most likely, Charles Reeder had a hand in its construction. The first owners were Daniel Large and its new master, Moses Rogers.[49]

For two years, while *Chesapeake* steamed alone about the Bay, *Eagle* ran the Delaware River from Philadelphia to Bordentown, New Jersey. When other steamboats began to intrude on local waters, her master and prime owner, Moses Rogers, a romantic adventurer like George Weems, grew restless. Rogers decided to leave the Delaware and enter the Chesapeake in search of a charter.

Getting to the Chesapeake meant a voyage by sea around Cape Henlopen and down the Atlantic coast to Cape Charles, a considerable venture for an untried and rather small riverboat. But Rogers had done it before. In 1808 when George Stevens had rebelled at the monopoly that Livingston and Fulton imposed on the Hudson, he had engaged Moses Rogers to take *Phoenix* out of New York waters to the Delaware. *Phoenix* came around by sea from Sandy Hook, down the Jersey coast, and into Delaware Bay. Moses Rogers convinced himself that *Eagle* could go to sea also.

He succeeded. On June 19, 1815, he rounded Cape Charles, viewed the majestic Chesapeake stretching to the north, and sidled up to a dock in Norfolk. The small city of some 9,000 inhabitants at the mouth of the James River thrived on its trade with the West Indies. Its residents viewed with curiosity the arrival of *Eagle,* the second small steamboat to arrive within the month from the open sea. On May 23, 1815, the steamer *Washington,* commanded by Captain O'Neale, had arrived in Norfolk; it announced its destination as Washington, D.C. *Washington* was owned, so the press announced, by a company operating under a "patent of Messrs. Livingston and Fulton" for runs on the Potomac.[50] *Washington* for the Potomac River and *Richmond* for the James River were built in New York in 1813 by Charles Browne under the direction of Robert Fulton. That an interest on the Chesapeake was an unrequited goal by Fulton, backed by Livingston, is clear.

A few days after her arrival in the Chesapeake Bay, *Eagle* turned her prow to the north to make the first trip by any steamboat from Norfolk to Baltimore. In effect, she inaugurated a route that steam packets were to follow for generations. Captain Moses Rogers, conning the little vessel

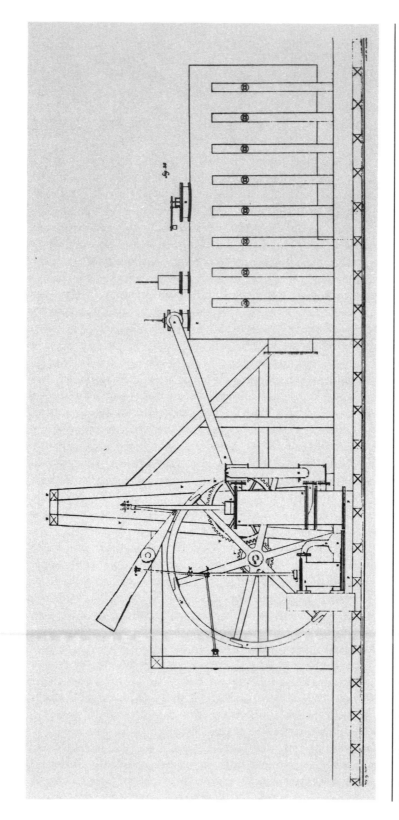

Engine and boiler of *Eagle* from [Jean Baptiste] Marestier's *Mémoire sur les Bateaux à Vapeur des États-Unis d'Amérique* (Paris, 1824). Note the crosshead engine and piston rod connected through cogwheels to the paddlewheels

from the top of one of the paddleboxes, shouting instructions to the man at the tiller aft, and stomping the deck to give his orders to the engineer below, savored the initial experience of steaming up the Bay.[51] He was no ordinary skipper, this Captain Rogers; he relished adventure. In his mind's eye was a sailing ship equipped with an engine—a ship to steam across blue water—a ship for him to skipper across the ocean. He was to realize his dream in 1819, when, as master of *Savannah,* he took the first steamship across the Atlantic to Liverpool and St. Petersburg.

After a 24-hour run up the Bay from Norfolk, *Eagle* arrived in Baltimore Harbor to the curiosity, skepticism, and cautious enthusiasm of the city's Bay-faring population. Rogers sought a charter, and he found one quickly. Samuel Briscoe and John Partridge, smelling immediate profit in starting a new line to compete with the Union Line's monopoly of the steamboat link via Frenchtown to Philadelphia, decided to engage *Eagle.* Her prime function was to sail three times a week to Elkton at the head of the Bay, where passengers could board stages for the Delaware River and for onward passage by boat to Wilmington and Philadelphia. This route was in direct opposition to the line of McDonald and Ferguson. So anxious were they to pursue this enterprise that Briscoe and Partridge forged ahead with a decision to buy *Eagle* in a corporate undertaking.

The Briscoe-Partridge line, with the backing of Elias Green, James Small, Alexander Scott, and others including John Partridge's brother, James, and the Hollingsworth brothers, Levi and William, purchased *Eagle* on August 26, 1817, and continued its operation under William Howell, master.[52] At that point, war raged openly between the rivals. It was waged in a costly blow-by-blow procurement of new boats by each side to elbow out the rival. It ended in 1819, when the Union Line built *United States.* At that point, Briscoe and Partridge, sensing that the continued competition would impoverish them, succumbed; they disposed of *New Jersey* to their rival and offered *Eagle* for public sale.

Just a year after the purchase of *Surprise,* George Weems, in partnership with an anguished Gustavus, was not in a financial position to consider the acquisition of another steamboat. Nevertheless, he looked longingly at *Eagle,* the blue-water steamer that journeyed back and forth with the regularity of the passing days. George lived under the shadow of his father's death and the adamant refusal of Gustavus to consider the use of his portion of the estate at Marshes Seat as collateral for further borrowing of money.

At that point, a neighbor, who owned property just to the south of Marshes Seat on Herring Bay, entered the life of George Weems. For George Weems, whether he knew it then or not, the interest of James Harwood in his affairs was of critical importance. Their discussions in late 1819 and early 1820 marked the beginning of an odd relationship that endured for nearly 30 years and punctuated almost every important decision that George Weems would make.

James Harwood, a contemporary of George Weems in age, was a

somewhat mercurial individual with a collection of conflicting traits. He was a money-making planter who fought the soil with righteous indignation. He was a speculator and a risk taker if the chances of success were better than even, but he was a hardheaded man with a balance sheet in mind. He was a survivor who was clever enough to escape when the business vultures circled over his head. He was somewhat of a scholar, known for youthful oratory at St. Johns College in Annapolis. He was a devout parishioner, who resided for a time with the Right Reverend James Kemp, bishop of the Protestant Episcopal Church, at the mansion on Saratoga Street in Baltimore. And he reveled in public service. But he was a tenacious and often critical—even acerbic—friend, who undertook to oversee the business ventures—and even the personal life— of George Weems, whom he considered visionary and impractical.

In 1819, James Harwood owned the large estate of Fair Haven on Herring Bay near its southern hook. His slaves farmed it for its worth in tobacco. His primary enterprise, however, was in Baltimore, where he profited from a business as flour merchant, wholesale grocer, and incipient commission merchant.[53]

James Harwood encouraged George Weems to gain control of *Eagle* as a way of offsetting his losses on *Surprise*. The way to the acquisition, in Harwood's view, was to obtain the investment of a number of backers who not only knew the reputation of *Eagle* as a dependable boat but also respected the skill of George Weems as a shipmaster. On April 5, 1820, *Eagle* passed to the corporate ownership of James Harwood, George Weems, Jeremiah Perry, and many others who shared their faith in the boat and in the future of her master.[54]

Eagle joined a half-dozen other steamboats departing Baltimore during each week for landings around the Bay. During late 1819, while Briscoe and Partridge settled her fate, *Eagle*, with George Weems as master, supplemented *Surprise* on runs to the Eastern Shore, to Queenstown, Centreville, and Chestertown along the Chester River and its tributaries. With the full acquisition of the vessel, however, George Weems sought other ports of call. He was hurried in this decision by the appearance in 1819 of *Maryland*, built by the new Maryland Steamboat Company (capitalized at $45,000), organized by a group of Easton men headed by Nicholas Hammond (Easton bank president), who demanded better service than could be provided by the hesitant and uncertain *Surprise* or the little *Eagle*.[55]

In 1822, the handful of little steamers leaving Baltimore each week had done little to displace the sailing packets on which the commerce of the Bay largely depended. Packets left on schedule for Philadelphia, New York, Richmond, Petersburg, Norfolk, Boston, Savannah, and Charleston, as well as Elkton, Annapolis, Washington, Alexandria, Havre de Grace, Port Deposit, and other points on the Bay from Smiths Wharf, Bowleys Wharf, the Light Street wharves, McElderrys and Dugans Wharves. Wharves surrounding the harbor were filled with sailing craft from landings all around the Chesapeake and its tributaries. If their owners felt any anxiety at the sight of these intrepid little vessels belching smoke and steam, the picture of masts and sails at the landings in Baltimore Harbor failed to reflect it.

The few steamboats ran with convincing regularity, even in the face of wind and sea. From Bowleys Wharf, steamers departed daily at 5:00 P.M. for the Union Line's triumphant run to the head of the Bay and connections to Wilmington and Philadelphia (alternately *United States* under Captain Edward Trippe and *Philadelphia* under Captain Spencer). At the lower end of Bowleys Wharf lay *Virginia* (Captain John Ferguson, partner of McDonald in the *Chesapeake* venture) and *Norfolk* (Captain Brown) departing Mondays and Thursdays at 9:00 A.M. for Norfolk. *Maryland* (Captain Vickers) left Commerce Street Wharf Wednesdays and Saturdays at 9:00 A.M. for Easton and Mondays for Chestertown and Queenstown. Within a year, *Constitution* and *Albemarle* would be leaving for runs in the upper Bay and Annapolis. In 1822, newspaper advertisements appeared announcing that "during the session of the legislature, the *Eagle*, Captain Weems, [would leave] Light Street Wharf on Sunday, Tuesday, and Thursday, at 9:00 A.M. [for Annapolis], and during the residue [*sic*] of the year . . . to ports in the Patuxent."[56]

Around the Chesapeake and its rivers, steamboats appeared. *Surprise* and *Eagle* became part of a growing procession.

In early 1822, *Surprise*, sold by Weems, departed for Washington to run the Potomac. Other steamers out of Washington greeted her on arrival. The steamer *Washington*, which had arrived in the capital in June 1815 after her trip by sea from New York, was joined by *Camden* in 1817 and thereafter by a succession of steamers: *Cygnet, Phoenix, Fredericksburg, Sydney, Salem, Paul Jones*, and others in the mid-1820s. They ran to Alexandria, Aquia Creek, and landings on the upper river.[57]

At an early date steamboats appeared on the James River. *Eagle* and *Washington*, after their brief stop, were followed by a series of steamers such as *Virginia, Richmond, Powhatan, Norfolk, Hampton, Seahorse*, and *Roanoke*. President Madison rode the last-named vessel when he came to Norfolk in 1819. In 1821, journalists reported that the river seemed "covered with boats," all crowded with spectators. Notables of all degrees enjoyed excursions aboard them, and ladies lost their fears of imminent elevation from exploding boilers. *Eagle* made a 90-mile trip to Richmond from Norfolk, thus inaugurating that route as it had initiated the Baltimore packet run to Norfolk.

On the Rappahannock, steamboats made a tentative appearance. In the summer of 1821, two excursion steamers from Norfolk, *Petersburg* and *Albemarle*, visited the Rappahannock as far as Fredericksburg. The Rappahannock was to await discovery by steamboatmen for a few more years.

George Weems had probed the Patuxent. In 1821, aboard *Eagle*—*Surprise* having been relegated to the Eastern Shore route whenever she could be persuaded to run—George Weems began in earnest his reach into the Patuxent River. He found that the patterns of life on the Patuxent were not easily changed. The routines of commerce were firmly established by the planters and the long-standing relationships with shippers, commission merchants, and markets in Baltimore.

The arrival of the steamboat, a disquieting novelty, did little to dispel the apprehension of crowds who gathered in curiosity at the landings. Without the engineer's knowledge of how to reverse them, the engines of early boats had to be stopped some distance from a wharf and the steamer allowed to drift alongside. Miscalculation could lead to violent collisions with the pier, and George Weems was known for standing on the bow and shouting to people to clear the dock if they valued their lives. The discovery that an engine could be reversed on an approach to a dock was made by accident when an engineer, believed to be named Yeager, unconsciously moved the lever admitting steam to the cylinder and—realizing his apparent blunder and terrified lest the boiler explode beside him—leaped to the dock and did not stop running until he had put the steamer well behind him. With that discovery, docking a steamer became a less hazardous undertaking.

The beginning of 1824 marked a time of assessment. In Calvert County, Gustavus began to consolidate what remained to him from the catastrophe of *Surprise*. In Baltimore, George Weems assessed what real progress he had made in gaining the support of planters on the Patuxent; he found it less than reassuring. Nonetheless, he was optimistic.

Tragedy struck with overwhelming suddenness. On Monday, April 19, 1824, *Eagle*, returning from Annapolis, stood in toward the Patapsco entrance. Off North Point, her boiler exploded. Captain George Weems was severely scalded about his legs and lower body. His son, Thomas Sutton Weems, age 11, who was standing near the boiler, was blown from the cabin through the skylight and inexplicably survived without injury. Several of the crew suffered burns and cuts. One passenger, District Attorney Henry M. Murray, like George Weems, was scalded (he lingered until April 28, when he died—the only passenger death recorded in the long history of the Weems steamboats).

Constitution, of the Union Line, was approaching the Patapsco entrance and rushed to the rescue. Her crew, discovering that *Eagle* was a shambles below decks and that her remaining crew were barely able to cope, extinguished the fires started by the explosion, took aboard *Eagle*'s passengers and crew, and towed the luckless vessel into port.

George Weems was carried overland by stage in an excruciating trip to Marshes Seat. At first, physicians despaired of saving his life. They decided that both of his legs would have to be amputated, but with what strength he could muster, George Weems revolted. "A man is nothing without his legs," he raged, "and I will go with mine and will not live without them." All or nothing, and the courage to see it through.

His wife, Sarah, who had been devoted to him since their breakneck marriage 16 years earlier, had an iron will of her own. She determined then and there to save this man by every means possible. She enlisted their 15-year-old daughter, Ann Margaret, to help. At Sarah's direction, George's scalded legs were immersed in cold water drawn from the well; bathing in this fashion went on continuously for days on end. In 1824, such a treatment was unheard of; the physicians threw up their hands and departed.

George's legs mended slowly while the patient lay flat on his back, deliberately regaining his strength and the will to contemplate once again the world of steamboats on the Chesapeake.[58]

The long recuperation marked dark months for George, who brooded over the failure of *Surprise*, the devastation that it had cost Gustavus, and the loss of *Eagle*. His maritime essays on the Chesapeake seemed doomed to failure. But George Weems was a stubborn man. He refused to accept defeat. And as 1825 and 1826 rolled by, he groped for ways to begin again.

With improvement in his health, George's exuberance returned. He resolved to try the steamboat business again with a truly new beginning. Both *Surprise* and *Eagle* had been passed to him by previous owners. Although both boats had captivated him at the time he had acquired them, George had not shared in the design and construction of either and, in fact, knew far too little about either of them when he took them from their moorings for the first time. Then an idea took form. George resolved to begin anew by launching a steamboat of his own design, built by a Baltimore shipyard in which he could observe the construction. The boat would be powered by an engine of local manufacture and fitted out to challenge the luxury of the best steamboats on the Bay. He would call her *Patuxent* to acknowledge the river patrons who had offered their sympathy at his loss of *Eagle*. He would start again, not as a tentative prober but as the manager of a steamboat line.

With his recovery nearly complete, George moved back to Baltimore. He had lost his home on Philpott Street from debts on *Surprise* and had been renting a house at Charles and Barre Streets until the explosion aboard *Eagle*. Now he moved into a dwelling on Conway Street east of Howard, only a block or two from the Light Street wharves.[59]

James Harwood, his self-appointed mentor, was living at the Saratoga Street mansion of the Right Reverend James Kemp. At the mansion Harwood met a member of the bishop's family, Edward D. Kemp, a lawyer, who was to become his lifelong friend. James Harwood had just purchased a lot at the corner of Union and French Streets on which contractors were building his home, and George Weems now turned to James for assistance.

To George's surprise, James vacillated. In the wake of *Eagle*'s loss, James steered around George's proposal to set up some sort of partnership on a second venture, suggesting instead the names of other men who might be interested in such an investment with its concomitant risks and rewards. James offered to help with operating costs, in the form of short-term loans, if and when the steamboat became a reality.

George Weems was undeterred. He turned next to Hugh McElderry, prosperous commission merchant and owner of the wharf that bore his name and which hosted a fleet of sailing vessels and some steamboats moving in and out of Baltimore Harbor. George also took his proposals to Charles Nichols, marine financier, who maintained an office and counting house on Fayette Street. Finally, he approached James Corner, commission merchant and aspiring shipping agent on Maryland Wharf. The eloquence of George Weems prevailed. To his utter delight, all three men agreed collectively to put up enough money to underwrite the initial construction of *Patuxent*. Furthermore, James Corner proposed that he become the agent for the new boat at Maryland Wharf.[60]

The pent-up restlessness of George Weems exploded in a burst of energy. He engaged the firm of Andrew Flanigan, successor to William Flanigan, builder of *Chesapeake,* to construct the new boat in the firm's yard on Pratt Street. There, in lofts above the yard, he and craftsmen pored over drawings through the autumn of 1826. The completed hull slid down the ways in the first hint of spring, and she was registered on May 5, 1827, by her new owners, Charles Nichols, Hugh McElderry, and James Corner, with George Weems, master. Because of difficulties in raising money, work on the outfitting proceeded slowly, and it was not until late summer of 1827 that *Patuxent* went through her trial runs and made ready for service on the Bay.

By the standards of times, she was a handsome boat, a step above *Surprise* and *Eagle* in size, with accommodations for freight and passengers, and cuisine. She was about 15 feet longer than *Eagle* and 20 feet longer than *Surprise*. At 123 feet she was still quite small. In appearance, her hull followed the lines of a schooner, not much different from the hull contours of her predecessors; but, most striking, she lacked bowsprit, mast and sails, a tribute to the dependability of the crosshead engine built by John Watchman and John Bratt, engineers and partners in a steam engine factory on Hughes Street, Baltimore. Cabin areas, still separating men and women, were somewhat more spacious. The men's sleeping area forward now contained small cubicles for berths, which could be curtained off. But male sleepers were aroused at an early and unconscionable hour to permit the conversion of their cabin into a dining room complete with white linen, silver service, and table decorations in season. George Weems advertised that "a first-rate cook and active, obliging attendants had been selected with great caution" by him for the new boat, and that "he hoped by these attractions and by his unremitting attention, aided by a sumptuous table, to merit and obtain for the boat a full share of public patronage" (Appendix A).

Patuxent was primitive in comparison with boats built just 10 years later. Nevertheless, she matched any of her contemporaries on the Bay, and she set a standard for comfort and bounteous hospitality by which the Weems steamboats were reckoned for years to come.[61]

Patuxent took her place in the small parade of steamboats running the Bay and its rivers—the vanguard of the steamboat era on the Chesapeake. The initial challenge to design and build steamers adapted to the environment of the Bay had led through several evolutions, from the geared-up engine of Daniel Large in *Chesapeake* and the doomed experimental Curtis-Yeamans rotary engine in *Surprise* to the crosshead engine of Daniel Large in *Eagle* and the masterful Watchman-Bratt crosshead engine in *Patuxent*. The evolution moved from the mounting of engines on schooner hulls equipped with masts and sails as a precaution against engine failure, as in *Chesapeake, Surprise,* and *Eagle,* to the construction of an engine so dependable in *Patuxent* that masts and sails were deemed unnecessary. *Patuxent* was a model for boats running the Bay at the time. In large measure, the tentative period was over. Adaptation, invention, and technical change would follow over the years, but the first quest for steamboats on the Chesapeake had been resolved.

CHAPTER 2

Probing for Trade: Risk and Frustration

In the late summer of 1827, when *Patuxent* completed her trials in Baltimore, one question plagued George Weems: where should he send his new steamer to earn her keep and secure a place in the steamboat trade on the Chesapeake? It was the fundamental question that had perplexed owners from the advent of the steamboat on the Bay.

Chesapeake had been fortunate. She had taken her place in 1813 among the sailing packets of the Union Line running to Frenchtown at the head of the Bay and providing a link to Wilmington and Philadelphia; her patronage consisted of regular Union Line passengers who were willing to risk their skins on the fire-breathing contraption rather than accept the uncertain schedule of the sailing packets. For the two years that she operated alone on the Chesapeake, she earned a healthy profit estimated at 40 percent.

Difficulties began with efforts to expand the Union Line by acquiring new boats and with the appearance of drastic competition from the Briscoe-Partridge line, which steamed in defiant opposition on exactly the same route in the upper Bay. Four steamboats vied for trade previously enjoyed by one. The open warfare between the rivals ended in

1819 when Samuel Briscoe and John Partridge caved in, realizing that they faced impoverishment.

The widespread financial panic of 1819, stemming from overextension of credit to purchasers of land in southern states where cotton was concurrently being overproduced, coupled with mismanagement of the national bank, may have contributed marginally to the debacle of Briscoe-Partridge.[1] More likely, however, there was insufficient trade on the upper Bay and the Elk River service to support more than one steamboat.

Early steamboat operators tended to miscalculate the readiness of the people of Tidewater to displace their traditional patterns of activity to accommodate the unknown steamboat.

George Stiles, when he dispatched *Surprise* to the Eastern Shore to solicit trade in 1816 and 1817, misjudged his targeted customers there. Around the shores of the Miles and the Chester and the Choptank and the other rivers extending through the peninsula of Maryland and Virginia, the settlers of several preceding generations had developed a discrete culture bred of relative insularity, clannishness, Englishness, and the largesse of a particularly hospitable and well-fed gentry. The rich flatlands, cultivated in large farms and plantations, consisted of heavy soil that tobacco did not deplete as rapidly as it did the lighter soil of the Western Shore; crop diversification and plenty of slaves for the handwork required produced not only a huge output of tobacco for export but a variety of produce for the markets of Baltimore.

Along these quiet rivers and shaded creeks the planters had built landings to accommodate the sailing craft that carried their tobacco and produce to Baltimore; more prosperous planters, who often bought the tobacco of smaller farmers to make up consignments and who just as often set up warehouses and general stores not only to handle these shipments but also to sell the goods returning by boat from the city to the local inhabitants, built larger wharves in these community centers. And oystermen and fishermen with their "buy-boats" built docks for handling their harvests of the Bay. Of the several hundred such landings around the Tidewater area of the Chesapeake, the Miles and the Chester and other rivers of the Eastern Shore certainly had their share.

Here, too, was a thriving boat-building industry, where generations of self-taught craftsmen had developed the skills to build the distinctive sailing craft that characterized the waters of the Chesapeake. The early settlers found soon enough that square-rigged oceangoing vessels were not practical craft for sailing the confined river channels of tidewater Maryland and Virginia. They were too bluff, too deep of draft, and most particularly, too unhandy in the often twisting and narrow channels of the upper rivers and in the capricious wind changes that frequently occurred. The Indians provided the model for a suitable boat in the hollowed-out log canoe, adapted by colonists to become a five-log, clean-lined craft with sharp bow, long bowsprit, narrow beam, and fore-and-aft sails, able to come about smartly and to speed in light winds.

Sloops and schooners followed, trim vessels suited to the cargo-carrying needs of Tidewater. From privateers and West Indian sloops out of Bermuda came the pungies in the 1700s, swift and rakish. Topsail schooners, slim hulled, with sharply raked masts, fore-and-aft foresails and mainsails and square topsails, proved that they could outsail almost any craft about. Many of the sailing craft on the Bay followed the needs of oystermen. From around the shores of tidewater Maryland and Virginia came the sailing vessels peculiarly identified with the Chesapeake. And from the rakish, clean-lined and overcanvassed schooners came the so-called *clippers* known to torment the British in the late War of 1812.[2]

The currents of change moved slow upon the land. The planters and the watermen of tidewater Maryland observed the seasons as they had done for 200 years. They sailed their boats from landing to landing, from wharf to town, as they had for generations. Their roots ran deep in family heritage and traditions of the land they tilled. And they measured their skill in the quality of the boats they built and sailed.

Planters, accustomed to their patterns of crop collection for consignment and shipment through accepted and understood channels of commerce, refused to allow the new steamboat to approach their landings. Oystermen, who sold their harvests to buy-boats for shipment to Baltimore, feared the displacement that might result from diverting their patterns of activity in the uncertainties of dealing with a steamboat owner who had few contacts with the commission merchants in Baltimore. And shippers and sailboat owners, immensely proud of the vessels they built, perceived an immediate danger to their very livelihood from the competition of a contraption that could run against wind and tide and maintain a steady schedule.

Nevertheless, there were many others who, more attuned to the movements of *Chesapeake, Philadelphia, New Jersey,* and *Eagle* along the packet routes of the upper Bay, awoke to the realization that *Surprise* could offer what they needed most: a dependable way to get their harvests to the market within a day. Furthermore, it was a means of comfortable and ready travel, free from the discomforts and uncertainties of sailing by slow packet or the travails of pounding over rutted roads by stage and attempting to escape unscathed from the leathery fare of local taverns or the welting stings of vermin inhabiting the overused beds of wayside inns. To a few of the more adventurous and enterprising, *Surprise* was a welcome arrival.

In late 1819 when George Weems skippered *Eagle* and in early 1820 when he bought her, she joined a handful of steamers operating out of Baltimore in direct competition to established packet routes that ran to Norfolk, Richmond, and Petersburg on the James; to Annapolis on the Severn; to Chestertown, Queenstown, and Centreville on the Chester; to Alexandria and Washington on the Potomac; and to points near the head of the Bay. These sailing packet lines did not bow to the steamboats; they continued to thrive in their accustomed channels of doing business. Attempts by steamboat owners to move into the packet routes met with limited success. The prospects for expansion seemed uncertain.

In fact, the continued persistence of the packet lines contributed to Weems's decision to remove *Eagle* and hesitant *Surprise* from service to the Chester River when *Maryland* appeared there in 1819.[3] There simply was insufficient trade left over from the packet route to accommodate more than one steamboat, and *Maryland* held the preference of the local shippers since her origins were also local.

In the early 1820s, Washington on the Potomac managed to bolster a few steamboats running to Alexandria and landings on the upper river. Some of these boats depended principally on pleasure excursions for their existence. Others, however, attempted to step into trade patterns long established by sailing vessels on the river. These patterns were remarkably similar on rivers of the Western Shore. From early colonial times, as settlers moved west, certain centers of commerce had developed. At the head of navigation, particularly at the fall line where vessels were stopped by rocks and rapids, transshipment centers for moving shipborne materials inland by wagon expanded into towns—Richmond on the James, Fredericksburg on the Rappahannock, Upper Marlboro on the Patuxent, Baltimore on the Patapsco, and Georgetown (adjoining Washington) on the Potomac. Sailing vessels in the 1820s served Georgetown, but, as in Baltimore, tradesmen and planters certainly eyed the steamboat as a viable alternative.

By contrast, Norfolk, which *Eagle* had served, had not fared as well. The city's dependence on the prosperity of trade with the West Indies had served it poorly; the steep decline of the importance of the Caribbean after the War of 1812 was felt in Norfolk just as the panic of 1819 beset the financial circles of the region; the city failed to recover. Merchants, also, were ill equipped to compete in a changing economy. Tobacco's depletion of soil in neighboring Tidewater country reduced Norfolk's importance as a port for shipment. Cotton planting moved from Virginia to the Deep South. Newly created industries found the coal fields and swift power-producing streams beyond the fall line compelling incentives for settling there. And the population moved westward. Whereas the population of Norfolk had expanded from 6,929 (2,724 slaves) in 1800 to 9,193 (3,825 slaves) in 1810, by 1820 it had decreased to a total of 8,478; and the decline continued.[4]

In contrast to Norfolk, Richmond, at the fall line of the James, had continued to prosper as a transshipment center; from a population of 9,235 (3,748 slaves) in 1810, it had grown to 12,067 by 1820. The city lay in the path of the railroad when it finally arrived; Norfolk was bypassed. Richmond loomed large in the eyes of steamboat men as they considered the future of water transportation in tidewater Virginia.[5] Fulfilling the dream was another matter.

Fredericksburg on the Rappahannock was to await regular service by steamboat for a number of years. Although the town had served as a transshipment point for sailing vessels coming up the river, the relative sparsity of people above the fall line and the wide spacing of plantations along the river and in the Northern Neck between the Rappahannock and the Potomac left Fredericksburg to grow very slowly, and in 1820 it counted only some 3,000 inhabitants.[6]

George Weems had probed the Patuxent and encountered an indifferent response.

In his first forays with *Surprise,* when elation outweighed caution, he had entered the river that he had known all his life. It lay to the south of Herring Creek, beyond the white cliffs rising a hundred feet on the Bay, along the shores of Calvert County, and it opened up as a wide and bending estuary at Cove Point. He had sailed up the river in his youth, even past the marshes where the channel narrowed to a tortuous stream, and reached Upper Marlboro, 40 miles or more above the river mouth. At that point, vessels could seldom sail in the constricted and silting channel but arrived and departed with the tide. At that distance from the Bay, the ebb tide, joined by the flow of fresh water draining from inland streams, produced a current so strong that boats using it to go downstream had to steer with care to escape the banks and shoals and eddies along the way.

He cherished the memories of those lazy, sun-filled days on the Patuxent. It was a river of many moods and tints, reflecting the blue of a summer sky in abject repose, swirling angrily in tidal wrath when the neap from the inland marshes met the spring tide from the encroaching Bay, turning a muddy green with darkening clouds and the change of the seasons, caressing with the softness of a Maryland spring when the marshes sang and the forests serenaded.

Running over little pebbles the Indians called it—*patuxent* in the language of the Piscataways. In its upper reaches, the description was apt enough. As it swept toward the Bay it carved out its channel between marshland and high banks and then swept majestically southward beside bluffs shadowed by deep forests, long expanses of open fields, and inlets or creeks opening to exquisite panoramas of tree-lined shores, laced with rippling water. Near the river's curving mouth, a mile or two in width, the channel deepened in places to a hundred feet. In the sheltered hook, a fleet could anchor in protected safety.

But the Patuxent had known its moments of history. Along its banks, the war between Puritan and Stuart beginning in 1642 in England had its counterpart in actions taken by the Puritan majority and the counteractions of the supporters of the Crown led by the proprietors, the Lords Calvert. Calvert County itself, carved from Anne Arundel County, came into being as a consequence. The disturbance to the tranquility of the region, exacerbated to some extent by the restoration of 1658, continued for some time. After successive Jacobite revolts, ending in the defeat of Bonnie Prince Charlie in 1715, waves of Scottish immigrants arrived in the Patuxent region, among them James and David Weems. In 1776, when the fires of revolt against the British, fanned by resentment in Massachusetts and Virginia against taxation by the Crown, reached the stage of demands for independence, many planters along the banks of the Patuxent—and indeed in other parts of Maryland—felt little resentment in paying money for their own defense; yet, when the war began, they trooped to the colors, and some—like David Weems—outfitted swift privateers to challenge British commerce on the high seas. As a response, the British sent a naval expedition into the Bay in 1780 and, among other depredations, marauded plantations along the Patuxent.

Then, in the War of 1812, the Patuxent witnessed both a naval battle and the advance of the British on the nation's capital. On June 10, 1814, in St. Leonard's Creek, off the Patuxent, a British naval force consisting of a ship-of-the-line, three schooners, a sloop of war, and 15 barges propelled by oarsmen and armed with cannon and rockets, attempted to bottle up Commodore Joshua Barney's Chesapeake flotilla, consisting of 13 barges invented by Barney. The barges were slim-bowed, shallow draft, oar-and-sail-propelled craft, armed with either 24-pounders or 18-pounders, which had successfully defied the British fleet in the Bay. The defeat of the British and their withdrawal from the blockade proved to be temporary. At Benedict, a little town on the west bank of the river some 20 miles from its mouth, the British landed more than 7,000 troops, supported by a contingent of heavily armed warships, for the advance on Bladensburg and Washington.[7] In spite of the activities of the British in the Bay, a number of the natives of the region, like George Weems, converted their sailing ships into privateers and put to sea against the British.

George Weems knew the history of the Patuxent and most of the planters along its shores. In 1821, aboard *Eagle*—*Surprise* having been relegated to the Eastern Shore route whenever she could be persuaded to run—George Weems commenced probing the Patuxent.

His object in bringing a steamboat into the Patuxent coincided with the aim of every steamboat operator at the time and for another generation: to divert planters from the use of sailing craft for transporting their tobacco and produce to market and to rent, lease, or buy their landings—or to build new landings—for steamboat wharves. The task was not easy.

Here on the Patuxent, where tobacco reigned supreme, planters shipped their harvests by log canoe, sloop, or schooner from wharves they built themselves—wharves constructed of rough oak or cypress piling driven into the river bottom and planked on top of stringers. Where the river shoaled offshore, the wharves were long; but in many parts of the Patuxent, the channel was deep close to shore, and docks simply buttressed the river bank.

Planters prospered. Some of the more speculative used the crops of their less well-endowed neighbors to ship large consignments and then became merchants themselves by opening stores and warehouses. A few independent merchants were quick to join the profits. Where these stores and warehouses appeared, wharves accompanied them, more

often well-built structures designed to handle seagoing vessels as well.
To these were added in colonial days the official ports of entry designated by the Crown to inspect, weigh, and most of all, to tax the lucrative cargoes passing under the eyes of the royal revenue collectors.[8] On
the Patuxent, the towns of Upper Marlboro, Lower Marlboro, Mount
Calvert, Selbys Landing, and Nottingham built warehouses and substantial wharves for these public purposes. Trading centers developed
not only there but at Whites Landing, Magruders Ferry Landing, Milltown Landing, Truemans Point Landing, and Benedict.[9] But along the
shore were scattered the landings of independent planters, whose yoke-
laced oxen pulled the hogsheads alone or by cart from the packing sheds
to the river for loading aboard the sailing vessels for Baltimore.

Dependence of planters, shippers, and merchants along the Patuxent
on the traditional channels of commerce was not easily broken. Friend-
ships, blood relationships, lifetime association, and generational habits
were all involved. And George Weems knew, from his standing among
the gentry of southern Maryland, that he had quite a task of persuasion
ahead of him.

But he also knew that he had a number of factors in his favor. Above
all was the indisputable fact that *Eagle* offered what sailing craft could
not; an assured one-day run from Patuxent landings to Baltimore, a two-
or three-day per week calling schedule, and, except for ice, hurricane,
or fog, a steady five-mile per hour speed from landing to landing, river
to the wharf in Baltimore. And, as far as the replacement of a commission merchant was a matter of concern, George Weems offered the alternative of James Harwood, even then expanding his grocery and flour
business at 113 North Howard Street into a full-fledged business as a
commission merchant.[10]

Within a year, his efforts and persistence were rewarded with a
modicum of success. By the time he and Gustavus had disposed of *Surprise*, George Weems was turning the prow of *Eagle* from her Light
Street wharf two or three times a week, depending on the season, for
landings on the Patuxent.

She steamed to Annapolis for her usual call going and returning, then
entered Herring Creek for a stop at the wharf adjoining the lands of
James Harwood, and, on the open Bay, tied up to the long and exposed
landing at Plum Point, serving the interests of Gustavus. Then she
rounded Cove Point and entered the Patuxent. Its mouth was marked
on the north by Drum Point and on the south, by Cedar Point. To the
south of the Western Shore lay Point Lookout at the entrance to the Potomac River. Local jesters renamed Cedar Point, called it *Point Again*,
and cast it with the points on the Western Shore in a little rhyme: "Point
Lookout, Point Look-in, Point No Point, Point Again" (Appendix B).

Crisscrossing the river, she visited Town Creek on the south shore,
Sollers and St. Leonards inside the serenity of St. Leonard's Creek, Sot-
terley in sight of the plantation manor house, Dukes and Parkers and
Trent Hall and Magruders Ferry, the towns of Benedict and Lower

Marlboro, and Green Landing above Jug Bay but below the shoals that rendered the river unnavigable except to small craft. Upper Marlboro (upsteam from Green Landing) had ordered the building of a wharf (cost not to exceed $150) in 1810 and had discovered its futility.[11]

The catastrophe aboard *Eagle* brought service on the Patuxent to an abrupt end. For three years, the river saw not a single steamboat on its waters. In that time, planters, shippers, and merchants forgot that *Eagle* had ever appeared.

For George Weems, the dilemma was real. In mid-1827, with *Patuxent* steaming about Baltimore Harbor, impatient to course the Bay, Weems faced the predicament of finding a place to send her. His beloved Patuxent River had extended only a tepid reception in the first place; and now, after the disappearance of *Eagle*, few planters and merchants seemed willing to disturb their reestablished arrangements with sailing captains to accommodate *Patuxent;* rekindling their interest and allegiance would take time. Only two landings seemed immediately profitable: Herring Bay, to serve his own immediate neighbor, and Town Creek, near the Patuxent mouth, to serve plantations in the vicinity and sailing skippers who brought down freight from the upper river for transshipment by other means to Baltimore.

Nevertheless, in the late summer of 1827, George Weems began the project of building local confidence in *Patuxent* and his enterprise. By midsummer 1828, however, he had reached the unpalatable conclusion that gathering a slim patronage on the upper Patuxent was not worth the costs of running his vessel there. Even as early as March, he had nursed his private misgivings. When *Maryland* of the Union Line (the boat that had driven out his *Eagle*) was laid up for repairs, he had swallowed his pride and chartered out *Patuxent* as a temporary replacement for runs to Annapolis, Easton, and the Choptank. By July 1828, no matter how he considered it, his dilemma was worsening.

He decided to investigate possibilities once again on the Eastern Shore of Maryland. As for the run to Chestertown, which he had made with *Surprise* and *Eagle*, the hope of revitalizing it had died with the appearance of *Maryland*, championed by the Maryland Steamboat Company and scheduled to operate to Easton, on the Tred Avon, and on the Choptank. In casting about for alternatives, Weems put aside the thought of entering the tributaries farther south on the Eastern Shore; the distances were great, and he knew precious little about the temperament of the people there and the vitality of their commerce. He settled on two possibilities: the Sassafras River, with Georgetown and Fredericktown opposite each other at its head, the crossing point for travelers northbound for Philadelphia and New York; and the Wicomico, fed by the rich agriculture of the surrounding flatland, with the rising town of Salisbury at its upper reaches.

He toyed with the notion of probing the Potomac River. It stretched for nearly 100 miles between Maryland and Virginia in a majestic sweep of open water and winding tributaries to Alexandria, Washington, and

Georgetown below the falls. Upon its waters a vigorous trade of sailing vessels served the plantations of Tidewater and, by transshipment, the land beyond the Piedmont. And upon its waters, also, ran nearly a dozen steamboats out of Washington, daily to Alexandria and weekly to Baltimore and to Norfolk, with intermediate stops at landings on the way. If *Patuxent* were to venture on the Potomac, a clash for trade by an outsider might be costly.[12]

To the south lay the Rappahannock River, separated from the Potomac by the Northern Neck. Along its shores spread the plantations in an ever-expanding clearing of the virgin forest to feed the voracious appetite of soil-depleting tobacco. There were lonely reaches along which trees shrouded the channel, and herons stood statuelike in the shallows. Among the trees and isolated fields leaned the huts of the poorer farmers living out their lives in a rural slum. But there were vast fields in which slaves toiled under a broiling sun to accomplish by sheer numbers and dawn-to-dusk labor the planting and cultivation of the pleasure-giving weed. At landings along the river, their chanting carried a haunting melody as they worked to ready the hogsheads for shipment. Great houses at the ends of meadows and parks bore the names of Tidewater gentry, names that rang in the annals of the nation's history. And little towns along the banks—Urbanna, Irvington, Port Royal, Tappahannock, and Fredericksburg—grew slowly in the valley. Oyster beds ripe for the tong and dredge extended for miles in the lower Rappahannock and along the nearby shores of the Chesapeake. Raising crops in warm weather and oystering in the cold was a way of life for countless residents of the Northern Neck and the lower shore of the Rappahannock. Their harvests vied with tobacco, produce, and goods crossing the river wharves.

Prosperity had come slowly and unevenly in this part of Virginia. In some areas, the population had actually declined with migration in pursuit of new fields for tobacco and the attractiveness of industry elsewhere; or it had remained stagnant. In the counties of Lancaster, Caroline, Westmoreland, Middlesex, Essex, and Spotsylvania, the population averaged 9,225 (5,418 slaves) in 1790, some 500 more in 1820, and 10,055 in 1830, an 8 percent increase in 30 years. But two counties, Essex and Spotsylvania, accounted for the growth; the remainder showed net declines. The exceptional growth of Spotsylvania County, especially in the vicinity of Fredericksburg, attested to the value of the trade in transshipment at the fall line.[13]

Sailing vessels made the 100-mile journey up the Rappahannock from its entrance. They could use the power of the wind to Tappahannock, near midpoint, and perhaps a few miles beyond; above, the river became a winding stream, with reversing bends, often cleaving hills clad with forests, and beset by a swift current that seemed to reverse the tide. Like the Chesapeake, which fed it, the Rappahannock was an estuary. A sailing vessel had to move with the tide, inbound and outbound, flood and ebb, except that the currents in the upper reaches were often stronger than anticipated and subject to variables not calculated in the tidal ranges of the Bay. In this respect, the Rappahannock and the Patuxent were similar.

George Weems found one aspect of the Rappahannock most appealing. In 1828, no steamboats traveled the river. In fact, except for a few excursions from Norfolk between 1821 and 1827, steamboats had not probed the river for trade. And yet the planters' landings along the shores, often lonely and separated by miles, saw the schooners and sloops come and go, laden with the harvest of field and stream or with goods from Baltimore. At Tappahannock, merchants stocked their warehouses with cargoes moving in or out by sailing vessels. And at Fredericksburg, the docks along the narrow river fairly bustled with commerce. Packets carried passengers for business and pleasure, and the social and economic life of the region surrounded the river. A dreamlike euphoria enveloped the countryside, as though the tapestry of plantation life would never fade or ravel. That the Northern Neck and the counties south of the Rappahannock stagnated in the depression that beset Norfolk in the 1820s—and for many of the same reasons—was not clearly understood, and certainly not by George Weems.

He decided to try his luck on the Rappahannock. In July 1828, advertisements in Baltimore newspapers and handbills posted on public wharves announced that "the *Patuxent,* Captain George Weems, [would] leave Baltimore every Tuesday morning, during the Season, at eight o'clock [to] arrive at Herring Bay at one o'clock, to land or take off Passengers [and] proceed to Town Creek, on the Patuxent . . . [to] arrive at five o'clock in the Afternoon; and at six o'clock . . . proceed from thence to the Rappahannock."[14]

For an unfathomable reason, the Fredericksburg newspapers were not included, and the shippers of that town learned of the forthcoming arrival by a chance reading of the Baltimore newspapers. Nevertheless, when the discovery was made, the local press extolled the event by declaring that the Rappahannock, with a river navigable for 100 miles, a commercial town like Fredericksburg at its head, and a rich backcountry near its banks, had at long last been discovered and accorded a steamboat run by some "spirited Baltimoreans."[15] Subsequent announcements in the press listed the schedule of *Patuxent,* noted that she would "stop at the several towns and public places on the Rappahannock . . . to land or take off passengers," and added that "in addition to the elegant accommodations for passengers, the *Patuxent* [was] constructed to carry the bulk of twelve hundred barrels freight."[16]

Patuxent's debut on the Rappahannock seemed auspicious. During the late summer and fall, Weems introduced day excursions downriver from Fredericksburg to titillate the town's fancy. "Parties of Pleasure" he called them, featuring feasts of "oysters, fish, and every luxury the season can afford," as well as "good music" and a round-trip fare, including dinner and supper, of two dollars. Most excursions went as far as Port Tobago. With occasional interruptions, *Patuxent* maintained her schedule of service to Fredericksburg (Appendix B).

But Weems had reason for a sense of disquiet: revenues had not measured up to expectations, particularly receipts for passengers and freight over landings on the river other than Fredericksburg. *Patuxent* had stopped at Port Royal, Tappahannock, Carter's Creek (for Irvington), and other landings and had served Urbanna by landing and taking off passengers in small boats. Nevertheless, in September 1828, he arranged to alter *Patuxent*'s departure from Baltimore to Wednesday and from Fredericksburg to Friday (arrival in Baltimore on Saturday evening), thus allowing three days (Sunday through Tuesday) for an experimental probe of the Sassafras River.[17] For a few weeks, *Patuxent* called at Georgetown and Fredericktown and a few other landings on the Sassafras without leaving a permanent impression on the economic or social life along the banks of the short but picturesque river. She turned away dejectedly (Appendix B).

There was another reason for disquiet on the part of George Weems with the scene on the Rappahannock, a reason more subtle but just as palpable. Although Virginians, on the one hand, lavished praise on *Patuxent*, on its service and its sumptuousness, on the other hand they could scarcely conceal their resentment at this invasion by Baltimore interests. Underneath was a rivalry between Virginia and Maryland which had smoldered for generations. For the most part the rivalry was friendly, but when tangible interests became involved, it accumulated a certain emotional content that was not always rational. At the outset, Weems had sought ways of meeting it. George Corner, now his agent in Baltimore and co-owner of *Patuxent*, had met quietly with various shippers and shipmasters in Fredericksburg. In January 1829, the local Fredericksburg press announced that "the owners of *Patuxent* [would] establish another Boat to ply between Baltimore and Fredericksburg . . . and they [were] desirous that a share of stock should be held by persons residing in this neighborhood." Lewis Parrish of Fredericksburg and Falmouth was designated to command the new boat.[18]

The scheme to involve local Virginia residents in the ownership of a sister boat to *Patuxent* never materialized. Instead, events took quite a different and dramatic turn, the depths of which stunned Weems and most of his partners. What occurred stemmed from jealousy at *Patuxent*'s apparent success and greed for the supposed markets on the Rappahannock. The idea was hatched in Baltimore and Fredericksburg: the creation of a new steamboat company to run in competition to *Patuxent*. It was called the Baltimore and Rappahannock Steam Packet Company. What confounded and overwhelmed George Weems was the sheer number (nearly 200 names) and importance of its stockholders—almost half from Fredericksburg and the Rappahannock Valley—the majority from prominent Baltimore commercial interests. When the company was incorporated and the list of stockholders published on February 1,

1830, Weems viewed with astonishment the names of John Bratt; John Watchman; Fielding Lucas, Jr., well-known Baltimore stationer and publisher, former resident of Fredericksburg; John Chew, a distant relative; Stuart and Bolton; Gerald T. Hopkins and Company; Gibson and Company; Conway and Armstrong; and a host of others, all leaders in the industrial and commercial life of Baltimore.[19]

What particularly astounded George Weems was the presence of John Bratt and John Watchman among the stockholders. Just a few months before, Corner, McElderry, and Nichols had concluded that the bills coming due from the construction of *Patuxent* would require infusing of additional capital or persuading the creditors to accept shares in the venture. They found four creditors willing to invest in the enterprise, along with George Weems himself, who put up his own savings. The four men were James Johnston, Duncan McCullough—and John Bratt and John Watchman, builders of *Patuxent's* engine.[20]

The new company brought the steamer *Rappahannock* to the river whose name she bore—a Baltimore-built vessel similar to contemporary crosshead-engined, schooner-hulled, one-deck steamboats on the lines of *Patuxent*. The captain of the boat was Noah Fairbank, a popular master of sailing packets that he had taken to Baltimore for more than 10 years. Along the Rappahannock, his name approached that of a legend.[21]

In the contest between *Patuxent* and *Rappahannock*, George Weems, and his son Mason L., who sailed as clerk and later as mate, were compared unfavorably with Noah Fairbank. As one observer put it, "Captain Weems appeared as a stern navigator [and] neither he nor his son was much given to urbanity. Indeed, the idea that they were unaccommodating, rude and illiberal generally extended, until they became quite unpopular. . . . Captain Noah Fairbank was of a different turn—polite and accommodating. . . . No doubt the unpopularity of the Weems enabled Fairbank to obtain subscriptions [for the construction of the larger *Rappahannock*, costing $60,000], but [he] did not have the systematic management of the Weems."[22]

The truth was that there was little room for two steamboat lines from Fredericksburg to Baltimore; the economy could barely support one.

Patuxent persisted through the summer and fall of that year, interspersing her service runs with day excursions from Fredericksburg replete with feasts, music, and fares reduced to 50 cents. She tried adding a stop or two on the Piankatank River but discontinued when they proved profitless. By early spring, Weems and the owners of *Patuxent* were dispirited. A brief fire from some packages in the cargo caused some excitement off Carter's Creek in late April 1830. It was the last event to stir any excitement in what was otherwise a moribund exercise in seeming futility.[23]

On May 15, 1830, a Fredericksburg newspaper announced that *Patuxent* would make no further trips between that city and Baltimore.[24] Some Fredericksburg businessmen and planters downriver urged Weems not to give up, to return to the Rappahannock. For the time being, however, he turned his back on the river, his disappointment as poignant as his memories of *Surprise* and *Eagle*.

Patuxent lay alongside Maryland Wharf in Baltimore while Weems pondered his options. The most tangible choice lay on the Patuxent. There, the extension of the route upriver from Town Creek to Benedict, and perhaps beyond, required only a painstaking labor of love, persuading his friends, even relatives, and the planters and scattered merchants to turn to *Patuxent* as a safe, sure, and scheduled link to Baltimore. But building a clientele amid the conservatism and entrenched patterns of life and loyalties in Calvert, St. Mary's, Charles, Anne Arundel, and Prince George's Counties looked like a lengthy process, and the immediate trade during the exploratory period would be unlikely to justify more than one trip per week for *Patuxent*.

The remaining choice rested in an area George Weems had considered when *Patuxent* was being outfitted. One river on the Eastern Shore, blessed by an outpouring of tobacco and other crops and by a thriving community at its head—but as yet untraveled by steamboats—was the Wicomico. It meandered through rich flatlands, marshes, and forested shores for 30 miles to Salisbury. The river at that point was so narrow that vessels had to be turned around by the use of spring lines and a helping current. But Salisbury, like Fredericksburg, stirred with new life, and George Weems opined that the town would welcome a steamboat. Downriver were the landings of planters and settlements, notably Whitehaven on the northern shore near the mouth.

In late 1830, *Patuxent* set forth on both routes, the Patuxent and the Wicomico (Appendix B). By March 1831, George Weems had advertised two sailings a week for *Patuxent* from the lower end of Dugans Wharf—a trip to Salisbury and Whitehaven during the first part of the week; a run to Benedict and other landings on the Patuxent (including the usual stop at Herring Bay) during the remaining days.[25]

In this new venture, Weems had the advice and active support of his neighbor and mentor, James Harwood, The latter, probably by self-appointment, became the agent for Weems and *Patuxent* from the Light Street wharf where he conducted his business as commission merchant. *Patuxent*'s bills, now for operating and maintenance expenses, kept coming due, and James Harwood began to lend his money to Weems to make the payments. At the same time, the need for capital to underwrite *Patuxent* as a viable company increased, and two shareholders were added. One was Walter Farnandis, a dry goods merchant at 141 Baltimore Street. The other was Edward D. Kemp, attorney-at-law, relative of the Episcopal bishop of Maryland. What escaped George Weems at first was that Kemp's share was held in proxy for none other than Kemp's friend, James Harwood.[26]

For 10 years, with a few interruptions, *Patuxent* churned up the waters of the Wicomico. For most of the period, she backed from Dugans Wharf late Monday afternoon, turned about, and headed down the Patapsco. By nightfall, she was in the open Bay and settling into the darkness, her prow plowing the little waves in scattered spray, her paddlewheels molding dim squares in a greenish wake. By first light, she rounded Hooper Island, lying low to port, crossed Hooper Straits on an easterly heading, and entered the confined waters of the Wicomico River. Where the river narrowed stood the little village of Whitehaven, a ferry crossing for travelers north and south. Her journey up the river to Salisbury followed a winding channel through ever-encroaching marshes and twisting bends, along river banks where flat fields seemed to stretch to the horizon or cypress swamps and thick forests seemed impenetrable—until the little town with its church spires, warehouses, and wharf emerged, nestled by the river.

During the decade of *Patuxent*'s journeys to the Wicomico, her schedule altered for various reasons. At the outset, in 1830, for example, Weems experimented with a scheme to have *Patuxent*, on her return trip, rendezvous with Union Line boats outbound for Philadelphia; the meeting was to take place at the mouth of the Patapsco; transfer of passengers was to be effected by maneuvering one steamer alongside the other—satisfactory in calm weather, hazardous in a chop. At a later period, *Patuxent* dropped, reinstated, and dropped Salisbury as a port of call; marginal profits and other reasons—distance and navigational—dictated operations only to Whitehaven. And then there were periods when the Wicomico River saw nothing of *Patuxent;* she was under renovation, or she had found other routes temporarily attractive (Appendix B).

Once again, the Rappahannock lured George Weems. Through the long months of 1831 and 1832, he had coaxed, cajoled, begged, and badgered the planters from Salisbury to Whitehaven and from Benedict to Town Creek to load their harvests aboard *Patuxent* and had nearly converted the boat into a floating hardware store, millinery counter, clothing rack, and soap dispenser to satisfy merchants on the river and in Baltimore and country housewives needing an errand performed for them in the city. Trade had improved, but profits by no means met the continuing drain for wood to burn, repairs, dining room fare, wharf rental, linen, the multitudinous costs of running a small floating hotel, and debt retirement. Labor—since all deckhands and engineroom helpers were Weems's slaves—was cheap, except for rations and rough clothing. What George Weems wanted was a margin of profit in order to rid himself of the other shareholders, to own *Patuxent* in his own name and for his son.

From the vantage of Baltimore, it appeared to him that *Rappahannock* was enjoying some success on her runs from Baltimore to Fredericksburg. With 100 miles of river to serve, a rich hinterland, innumerable plantations, and Fredericksburg beckoning, it seemed to George Weems that a place in the river commerce existed for *Patuxent*. His judgment was supported by James Harwood. He was encouraged further to try again on the Rappahannock by a number of Fredericksburg businessmen, planters along the river, and even some owners of resorts. And he was emboldened to try again by a Scottish obstinacy that refused to accept defeat.

Before he could venture forth on the Rappahannock—and indeed before he could continue any longer on the Patuxent and Wicomico—he had to overhaul *Patuxent*. She was ailing, she urgently needed repairs, and she had been built a bit too late. New steamers appearing on the Bay—the speedy *George Washington*, built in Philadelphia for the Union Line, *Columbia*, built in Baltimore for the Potomac River route, *Governor Wolcott*, serving the upper Bay and the Eastern Shore—all had more efficient and better-built boilers and a dramatically altered appearance. Gone were the schooner lines; a new hull design, with knifelike prow, flat bottom except for the keel, extreme dead rise at the stern, marked overhang of main deck to provide extended cargo space, an upper deck for public areas (called *saloons* for the French *salons*), and staterooms marked the transition to the style of steamboat that would run the Bay for many years. George Weems, knowing full well that *Patuxent* could not go much longer without overhaul and sensing the changes in the steamboats he saw arriving on the Bay, decided to contract for a major modification of the boat in yards in Baltimore. Because John Watchman and John Bratt held substantial shares in the boat—in spite of their stock in the Baltimore and Rappahannock Steam Packet Company—he turned to them for boiler and engine repairs and rebuilding. With others he contracted for work to be done—Godwin and Company (ship's carpenters) and Job Smith (lumber merchant) for deckwork and superstructure rebuilding; John McKim and Son (copper) and William Wallace (copper plate) for recoppering of the bottom, and many others. The bills for the undertaking, accumulating in 1835, amounted to $9,880.79, nearly the stock value of the entire boat.[27]

The actual work was completed in late July 1833. *Patuxent* had been reconstructed. She had been sawed in two and lengthened by 20 feet, and both her cargo and passenger accommodations had been rebuilt and greatly increased. Her boilers, while the superstructure was being altered, had been replaced, and her bottom had been recoppered.[28] Refurbished from bow to stern, embellished with new china and silverware and linen and other appointments, she was ready for the Rappahannock.

George Weems advertised in Baltimore and Fredericksburg that *Patuxent* would resume her runs to the Rappahannock on Wednesday, August 14, 1833, sailing from the Peoples Wharf on Light Street, rented for the service. She would stop on the way to Fredericksburg, according to the notice, at Merry Point, "where there is a highly respectable House of Entertainment kept by Mr. W. T. Jesse," and at Urbanna, Deep Creek, Tappahannock, and other landings (Appendix B). A column in the same Fredericksburg newspaper pointed out "that the Proprietors of the Steam Boat *Patuxent* were the first to navigate the waters of the Rappahannock by Steam Power, which they did for two successive seasons, when they were opposed and superceded. . . . In retiring from a contest on that occasion, it was done under full conviction that the route would not support two boats, but looking forward to an increase of trade . . . they determined to resume their original route . . . under a confident assurance that they will receive a share of the public favor or at least that portion of trade that cannot be carried by the other Boat."[29]

George Weems was supplicating for the attention and support of clientele. He failed to measure the trickle of trade on the river—constricted by the continued reluctance of planters to abandon their traditional arrangements with sailing vessels and merchants in Norfolk and Baltimore—at best enough even in 1830 to allow only one steamboat a meager living, and he underestimated the determination of the stockholders in Baltimore and Fredericksburg to see their steamer *Rappahannock* drive the rival *Patuxent* off the river.

He had reason to rue the day that he came back to the Rappahannock. During the rest of 1833 and the spring and summer of 1834, the owners of *Rappahannock* slashed their rates by half and waged a campaign on the landings to undercut *Patuxent*. Their challenge to Weems was painfully effective. In a letter addressed to the public on September 24, 1834, he declared that the return to the Rappahannock had been made at "great labor and expense" only to encounter *Rappahannock*, that he had offered to withdraw *Patuxent* "to wait an increase of the business which he had laid the foundation for," that his return was at the urging of "many respectable persons," that he would endure the rate cuts, if the "owners of the *Rappahannock* [would] give sufficient security not . . . to alter the present rates, otherwise . . . the *Patuxent* . . . [would] be immediately withdrawn."[30]

Patuxent continued bravely but dispiritedly until the end of the season. When winter came, she turned her back on the Rappahannock, never to return.

The experience of George Weems in searching for trade and probing the tributaries of the Chesapeake—in his case, the Miles, Chester, Sassafras, and Wicomico on the Eastern Shore; and the Severn, Patuxent, Piankatank, and Rappahannock on the Western Shore—was not dissimilar from the encounters of most steamboat owners and operators in the first two decades of the steamboat era on the Chesapeake. Trade was all too scarce; the economic framework of tidewater Maryland and Virginia was much too established for rapid change; and the fabric of rural society was far too traditional for quick acceptance of the steamboat as part of the way of life. During those first two decades, steamboat owners and operators tended to fight it out with each other for an elusive reward and often bloodied their heads in the process. Only as the two decades came to a close and the smudge from steamboat stacks became a familiar sight on the Bay did the travails of steamboatmen become more muted in the prospects of prosperity.

CHAPTER 3

Expansion: Acceptance of the Steamboat on the Bay

For George Weems, the adventure on the Rappahannock had ended. Saddened and embittered by the experience, he had now to lick his wounds and return to the Patuxent and Wicomico, hat in hand, to placate the farmers and merchants he had left stranded during his absence.

A mountain of debts from the overhaul of *Patuxent* and the feeble returns from the last season on the Rappahannock, together with a stubborn resolve to cleanse the title of the boat from the other shareholders, drove him to feverish efforts to build a profitable trade on the two rivers. He was successful not only because of his efforts to beguile shippers to use *Patuxent* but also because of the surge of acceptance of steamboats all over the Tidewater region. In the mid-1830s, little white steam packets were penetrating the tributaries of the Chesapeake from Port Deposit on the Susquehanna, and the Sassafras, Chester, and Miles Rivers and Pungateague Creek on the Eastern Shore, to the Potomac, Rappahannock, West, Severn, and lesser tributaries on the Western Shore. Nightly steamers ran to Norfolk from Baltimore; boats from Washington touched landings on the Potomac; and Norfolk saw regular steamboat service to Richmond and around the James River. In the mid-1830s, about the Bay and its rivers and creeks, some 35 steamboats journeyed, their trim white superstructures dotted with windows, their gilded paddleboxes glinting in the sun, and their tall stacks belching wood smoke becoming as familiar on the Chesapeake as the sails of schooners billowing in the breeze.

For the year 1835 *Patuxent* grossed $14,339.67 (far more than she was worth) and paid off her debts for overhaul.[1] For the times, this represented an extraordinary accomplishment. Steamboats rarely produced a yearly revenue of more than $10,000. In little more than a year, George Weems had reestablished *Patuxent* on the Wicomico, but, most important, he had created a firm foundation for a steamboat line on the Patuxent which would last for generations.

In a very real sense, the season of 1835–36 marked the beginning of the Weems line as a viable steamboat company. Until then, the failure of *Surprise,* the brief sojourn of *Eagle* on the Chester and the Patuxent, and the struggles of *Patuxent* on the Rappahannock had been the probings of a courageous but uncertain George Weems, attempting to find a place and a future in the rising tide of steamboating on the Chesapeake. With the establishment of a regimented and scheduled route on the Patuxent, with an ever-increasing clamor among planters and merchants along the river for the certainties and convenience of the steamboat's services, and with the warmth of a loyal clientele to hearten the prospects, the Weems line as an institution became a reality. The profits of the Patuxent route, its potential for expansion upriver, and its proximity to the Weems homestead outweighed the paucity of the Wicomico River route, and the Wicomico was abandoned at the close of the 1840 season.

The goal of Weems was to gain full ownership of *Patuxent*—to buy out the other shareholders—and to put his sons in charge. By the end of 1838, he had largely succeeded. James Corner, Hugh McElderry, and Walter Farnandis had relinquished their shares in March 1831, following the first debacle on the Rappahannock. Charles Nichols sold his one-fourth interest to George Weems for $3,000 on November 16, 1838. James Johnson sold his one-sixteenth interest for $700 on October 12, 1838. Then on December 12, 1838, George Weems experienced the grim satisfaction of paying $2,000 for the one-sixth share of *Patuxent* held jointly by John Bratt and John Watchman.[2] He now owned *Patuxent* with one exception. Remaining was a one-eighth share held by Edward D. Kemp. It was held in proxy for James Harwood, although George Weems did not know it.

In 1838, George Weems felt the infirmities of middle age and the physical devastations of past injuries coming upon him. He was only 46, but he suffered from lingering disabilities inflicted by *Eagle,* and he was tired. Years of pounding the decks of *Patuxent* in fair weather and foul, of navigating her through the narrows of the Patuxent, the Rappahannock, and the Wicomico, and of fighting seemingly endless and fruitless battles had taken their toll. He wanted a more settled life—some place to rest—either in Baltimore or on the banks of Herring Bay.[3]

During the past few years, he had prepared for this time of retreat. On board *Patuxent* he had taken his sons, singly or collectively: Mason Locke Weems, who turned 20 in 1834; Gustavus, age 18; Theodore, age 16; and George W., age 15. Assigned as mate, engineer, or clerk, they learned from their father—and through hands-on experience—the arts of navigating, handling, and maintaining a steamboat and the tasks of running a steamboat business. The Patuxent River—beautiful, sinuous, seductive, capricious—was their teacher and their mistress. At the end of the 1838 season, George Weems relinquished *Patuxent* to his son, Mason L., as master. The other sons continued to serve as engineer, mate, or clerk.

George Weems found himself preoccupied with the activities and proposals of James Harwood. Somewhat after *Patuxent* had fled the Rappahannock for the last time, James Harwood had withdrawn his status as agent for Weems in Baltimore. To Weems's utter dismay, Harwood suddenly emerged as president of the Baltimore and Rappahannock Steam Packet Company, owner of *Rappahannock*, the very enemy of *Patuxent*.

Harwood seemed to be ubiquitous, appearing everywhere in the affairs of corporations and the state. He was receiver in the bankruptcy proceedings of the U.S. Insurance Company in 1834; he became a judge of the orphan's court in 1838 and its chief justice in 1839; he was in line for the job of lottery commissioner for the state; and he was involved in a galaxy of enterprises in the commercial life of Baltimore.[4]

In late 1838, Harwood was engaged in a little minuet with George Weems and some other local residents on the banks of Herring Bay. They were dancing around the subject of a tract of land known as Fair Haven.

Ten years before, George Weems, with his brother Gustavus, had bought a small parcel of 21 acres of Pascals Purchase.[5] This tract extended south from Marshes Seat to the middle of Herring Bay. In contrast to the hilly, often ravined contours of the land around Marshes Seat on the north and near the lower hook of Herring Cove, the terrain surrounding the 21 acres rose gently from the shoreline in pastures and low-rising slopes. The sandy beach extended offshore in a gradual drop to a depth of 10 feet some 50 feet or more from the low-tide mark.

On this tract of land, George had built a house and a wharf. Here was the Herring Bay landing at which *Patuxent* called at first on her runs to Town Creek and elsewhere. On this land, there had been erected by lease from George Weems a public house called Fair Haven Tavern. Adjoining this land were several estates: that of George Sunderland known as "Ayres and Chews"; that of Robert Garner; and, most importantly, that of James Harwood. Harwood, to accommodate his own interests, had built a substantial wharf that *Patuxent* found convenient to use. Harwood's estate was known as Fair Haven. The name came to be applied to the area as well.

In 1837, George Weems rented his acreage at Fair Haven to Richard Houghy under the stipulation that the latter would feed and house any employees there from time to time and keep the icehouse filled for the steamer *Patuxent* in the summer.[6] Fair Haven, it seemed, had become something more than a way stop for *Patuxent* on her journeys south.

In September 1839, George Weems paid $573 to his neighbor Robert Garner for a tract of land at Fair Haven "where the ten pin alley stands." The place, sustained by passengers from Baltimore, showed the beginnings of an amusement park.

In the mind's eye of George Weems—and in the hardheaded calculations of James Harwood—was the creation of a summer resort on the site of this land on Herring Bay. With the rapid expansion of steamboat service up and down the Chesapeake and its principal tributaries, the pleasure-loving escapists of Baltimore and Norfolk had discovered the wonders of a trip by boat and a vacation, even for one day, in little resorts along the shore. Old houses became inns; farmers scrambled to cater to the city-weary for profit; and small communities became beach resorts.

Talks among Weems, Harwood, Sunderland, and Garner danced around the subject. In the meantime, Weems, impatient as ever in spite of his aches and pains, went ahead with plans to create a park from his small tract of land and some portion of the adjoining estates comprising Fair Haven. In the summer of 1838, *Patuxent* began to stop on her runs to Patuxent landings. Proceeds from the operations of *Patuxent* sufficed to buy out the other shareholders (except Edward D. Kemp) and to provide a living wage for Weems and his sons, but the proceeds were not enough to purchase any additional land of Fair Haven in time for the 1839 summer season. Harwood worked out a solution of his own, using the resources of none other than John Watchman.

"Dear Weems," Harwood wrote from Baltimore on May 13, 1839, "I have the satisfaction of telling you that I have seen Mr. Watchman and arranged fully with him respecting 'Fair Haven' for the present season, and I have know [*sic*] doubt before Jan I can put every thing perfectly straight if you do as you are advised by me—Mr. Watchman agrees that you may have the property on the following terms, his $500 for the House and ground and $500 for the Wharf making $1000 for the whole property to the 1st of Jan (1840). . . . You can therefore make any public notice you think proper and I can say you have rented it for the season."[7]

Fair Haven, as George Weems called it, began to function as a resort. For all practical purposes he moved there; the old house at the Marshes Seat estate had fallen on bad times, had been shortened from 100 to 50 feet in 1832, and suffered from disrepair in 1840. *Patuxent* called regularly, in the summer of 1839, on her runs to and from the river landings, many of her passengers arriving for a day of picnicking and bathing in the salty wavelets lapping on the sandy beach (George Weems had his slaves build bathhouses to accommodate them).

Fair Haven was now the resort envisioned by George Weems. He drew up plans for the conversion of a house near the wharf into a hotel. The structure was to be a 150-foot, three-story building behind a prom-

The front of the hotel at Fair Haven as romanticized in a somewhat primitive watercolor.
Courtesy of Alice Forbes Bowie

enade fronting the water. A wide porch would grace its entrance. To one side would be a dining room and a residential area, two stories high. To the other, would be a storage area. On the second floor, a bathroom would occupy the space over the storage area, and on the third would be 10 bedrooms and a washroom, with a wide porch overlooking the Bay. An extension on one side was to provide for five additional bedrooms with a fronting porch.[8] On the wharf, he sketched a warehouse and bathhouses, a row of cubicles to please the fastidious visitors from Baltimore.

Since 1837, Fair Haven as a park had catered to picnickers arriving by boat from the city; but with the 1839 season, it opened as a resort—a beach hotel, luxurious for the times with boasts of fine cuisine and splendid bedrooms, and various amusements.

In the June 1839 Baltimore newspapers notice was given that the "Steamboat *Patuxent*, Captain M. L. Weems, will leave the lower end of Dugans Wharf on Sunday morning the 26th instant for Fair Haven. . . . Passage to and from Fair Haven $1.50. Fair Haven presents to the citizens of Baltimore the most pleasant excursion that can be found so contiguous to this city, . . . and in a very salubrious district, commanding an extensive prospect of the surrounding country, and the broad waters of the bay. To persons desirous of enjoying the luxury of saltwater bathing, a very extensive bath house has been erected, with separate and distinct private apartments. Dinner will be served at the spacious Hotel, where all the luxuries of the season will be served up, together with an abundance of fish, oysters, and crabs . . . and with choice liquors. Persons fond of fishing and gunning can be particularly gratified at Fair Haven."[9] From his house nearby, George Weems could look at

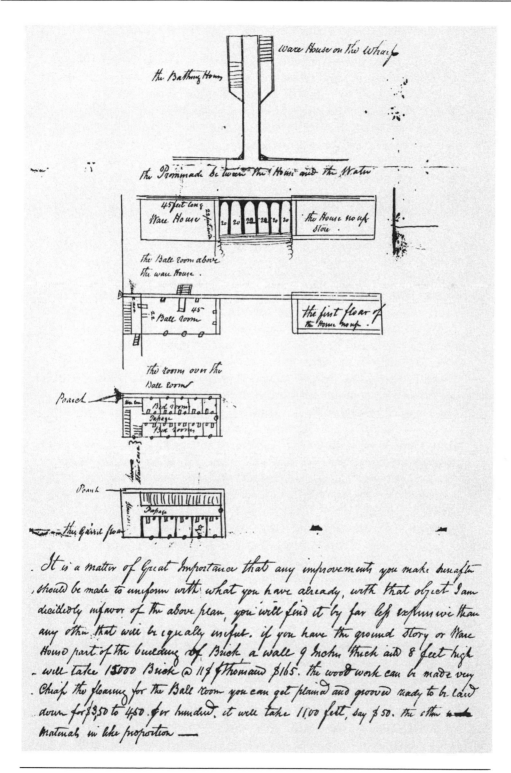

Plan, believed to have been drawn by George Weems, for the improvement of the hotel and other buildings at Fair Haven. Courtesy of Alice Forbes Bowie

the plans he had drawn up for Fair Haven and contemplate his accomplishments after a lifetime of struggle.[10]

At this time, James Harwood assumed almost a baronial attitude toward the administration of the estate of Fair Haven, and by conjunction with that of George Weems, of the latter's affairs as well. From his bastion in Baltimore, Harwood fired a continuous barrage of letters to George Weems on every subject related to their joint interests. The letters made clear that James Harwood perceived George Weems, semiretired at Fair Haven, as a convenient but not wholly responsible neighbor who would do Harwood's bidding in taking care of things at Herring Bay while Harwood continued to preside over his various functions in Baltimore. The letters also revealed that Harwood was an ailing man, frequently incapacitated and capable of ill-tempered diatribes. The letters invariably began imperiously with "Dear Weems" and proceeded with admonitions and peremptory instructions, rarely displaying much affection for his friend.

During 1840 and 1841, these letters, increasingly dictatorial, covered a wide range of subjects, demanding that Weems find a manager for Harwood's farm ("I don't want any more 'gentlemen' on my place—I mean to play gentleman myself") and that Weems supervise the distribution of clothing to Harwood's farmhands, oversee the planting of 160,000 tobacco hills ("every man must work 20,000") and the building of a house for Harwood's farm manager, arrange for the care of "a young Negro man" purchased by Harwood for his farm, settle some of Harwood's accounts in Anne Arundel County ("I am getting very tired of paying and receiving nothing"), and, finally, on April 27, 1842, in a stern statement prefaced by "Dear Sir," that Weems pay the rent due on some portion of the Fair Haven property and, also, the money awarded in arbitration as a result of an altercation between the two of them in the latter half of 1841.[11]

The arbitration referenced by James Harwood arose out of a longstanding dispute that grew more acrimonious. During the period when the Baltimore affairs of *Patuxent* were managed by Harwood, as agent, the transactions entered into by him never seemed to jibe with the accounts George Weems maintained on the boat which, in fact, seemed to show a continuing balance owed by Harwood to Weems. Furthermore, during the overhaul and subsequent operation of *Patuxent* on its costly Rappahannock venture and its uphill struggle to regain its footing and build its markets on the Wicomico and Patuxent, Harwood had tendered financial support. Throughout the period of promises, nothing tangible was forthcoming. As Weems saw it, Harwood had incurred indebtedness and obligations to him which required resolution. At the same time, Harwood—particularly when third parties were involved (like John Watchman)—had advanced money that Weems found himself obligated to pay. The exchange of charges and countercharges between the two men in 1841 led Weems to demand that their respective claims be submitted to a third party and that the two claimants each agree in advance to post a debenture of $10,000 and to abide by the arbitrator's decision. When Harwood suggested David Stewart, Jr., as arbitrator, Weems agreed reluctantly rather than stage another battle.

A formal agreement dated February 26, 1842, was exchanged between the two disputants.[12] On March 31, 1842, Stewart rendered his judgment: "I do award unto the said James Harwood the sum of fifty-six dollars and fifty-seven cents . . . it being understood . . . that the Interest and Claim of the said Jas Harwood in and to the Fair Haven property or the rent thereof . . . was not taken into the foregoing award. . . ."[13] Weems could not have been surprised at the adverse ruling; he knew, after all, that the arbitrator was Harwood's business partner.[14]

George Weems gathered his resources and the increased earnings of *Patuxent* to gain control of Fair Haven. Linked to any purchase of Harwood's land were the adjoining properties of Benjamin Sunderland and Robert Garner, both under a contract with Harwood for their use. By a system of 99-year leases of the Sunderland and the Garner tracts and the purchase of Harwood's Fair Haven tract for $2,090, Weems succeeded in his objective.[15] The domain of Fair Haven was complete, and George Weems could view with some satisfaction the fulfillment of his dream.

More than ever, he came to depend on Mason L. Weems, his oldest son, to manage his affairs. Mason, as master of *Patuxent*, and Gustavus and Theodore, still as engineer and mate, steamed out of Baltimore for Patuxent River landings and made Baltimore their home; George W., the youngest son, lived at Fair Haven with his parents. George Weems enjoyed the affection and loyalty of his sons.[16]

At age 60, George Weems felt conscious of his mortality. Accordingly, he celebrated that birthday by executing a bond with his four sons. By this agreement, the sons collectively posted $50,000, and the title of Marshes Seat was transferred to them by bill of sale. Further, it conveyed to them "all right and title to the Steam Boat *Patuxent* and all the negro slaves which are now employed in manning said boat as regular hands." But it also stipulated that "the said George Weems [hold] title to said property during his life [and that he not] be disturbed in any manner."[17] Thus the leadership passed to Mason L. Weems, but the legend remained with his illustrious father.

James Harwood in 1847 was a sick man, and he died on July 7 of that year. To recover the one-eighth share of *Patuxent* originally held in proxy by Edward D. Kemp and sold to Harwood for $2,000 in 1839, Susan Harwood, the widow, went to court to demand the auction of *Patuxent*. George Weems and his sons, who, by this time, owned the boat, shuddered at the thought. Through hasty prearrangement, *Patuxent* was bought on the block by Edward G. Leitch, their close friend, for $7,000 and subsequently returned to her rightful owners.[18] It was a tense period, and George Weems smoldered at yet another indignity at the hands of Harwood. On February 24, 1849, Theodore Weems transferred his one-fourth ownership to Mason L. for $5,000.[19] It was the start of a process to place the management in the hands of the senior brother.

George Weems continued to divest himself of responsibility. On April 5, 1847, he transferred his one-half interest in the steamboat line to Mason L., who owned the other half. At the same time, he sold the Fair Haven property to his eldest son for $10,000. In effect, Mason L. was left to control the destiny of the Weems interests. His brothers' interests were mixed: Theodore, in steamboats but also in substantial real estate holdings in Baltimore; Gustavus, in machinery and engines aboard the Weems boats; George W., in steamboats but also in a business as commission merchant on Light Street, Baltimore.[20]

In spite of her somewhat anachronistic appearance in the advancing steamboat pageant, *Patuxent* steamed on for many years, a stalwart boat used more and more by Weems as a spare. Her continued employment into her old age exemplified an aspect of the steamboat era on the Chesapeake which was so markedly different from the experience of steamboats on western rivers and on many other inland waterways around the country: advances in design and technology did not render boats obsolete, and old but sturdy boats continued to serve for decades as long as they were found useful.

George Weems did not see the denouement of his beloved *Patuxent*. After a lingering illness he died at Fair Haven on March 6, 1853. A biographical sketch of him stated that he "was remarkably kind and cheerful in his disposition, benevolent and public-spirited. It is said that his father bequeathed a larger amount of his property to him than to his son Gustavus, but George declined to receive more than an equal share. He was a sprightly and agreeable conversationalist and sympathetic in his nature. He had a great attachment for his kindred, and was fond of being with them. He was particularly courteous in the presence of ladies, and exceptionally neat in his dress and personal appearance."[21]

What the biographer failed to mention transcended his tinge of sycophancy: that George Weems was a man of indomitable courage, who rose above the worst of adversity, naïveté, bad judgment, physical injury, betrayal by persons he trusted, a bluff manner that sometimes offended, and considerable ill fortune to display an inconquerable spirit and a passionate will to succeed. Lesser men would have given up. Imaginative and idealistic, he was at the same time a man of extraordinary vision. He built for the future and for the fulfillment of a dream. Of such stuff dynasties are made.

Mason L. Weems inherited the adventurism of his father—and indeed, of his grandfather—but he was much more of a businessman than either of them. A rather stolid man, sometimes brusque in his response to strangers, even to customers, he viewed the steamboat enterprise with less sentimentality and more of the cold calculation of the counting-house. Like his father, he was a very determined man, but he turned his will to succeed into careful estimation of costs, likely profits, and future markets. He had carefully husbanded the profits that *Patuxent* had generated.

In his view, *Patuxent* approached senility in 1845; she was still busily engaged but better employed as backup for a more prestigious boat to carry the thriving Patuxent trade. As his father had done, Mason L. turned to the Flanigan shipyard in Baltimore, builder of *Patuxent* (and earlier, of *Cheaspeake*), for the construction of a new steamboat. She would be named *Planter*. That much he had decided.

The steamboats that began their maiden voyages on the Bay in the 1840s differed markedly from the pioneers of the earlier decades. The white-painted boats that steamed the length of the Bay and followed accepted routes on the Choptank, the Chester, the Susquehanna, the Severn, the creeks and rivers of Pocomoke Sound, the Potomac, and the James scarcely resembled vintage vessels like *Patuxent*. Their bows, unlike the schooner bows or spoon bows of their predecessors, were straight, vertical, and knifelike; their hulls lost the contours of sailing craft and became straight sided, flat bottomed (with a slight keel), and sloped upward under the counter above the rudder; the main deck on most of them was enclosed from the very stem to a point abaft the paddleboxes, thereby affording protection to cargo in the rougher waters of the Bay; the main deck enclosure, with its 10-foot overhang above the hull on either side, housed some cabin space, the paddleboxes, and usually a windowed dining room aft surrounded by a gallery wrapped around the stern. On the upper or promenade deck were a pilothouse (unknown on *Patuxent* or *Eagle*), a series of cabins and staterooms aft of the pilothouse, and open deck space surmounted by a canvas canopy. A single black stack was tall enough to carry sparks away from the decks below. But what most distinguished these boats and a flock of other steamboats on the Bay from *Patuxent* and her contemporaries was the walking beam seesawing amidships above the superstructure. A great vertical-mounted, diamond-shaped frame of iron, it pivoted from its center support. One end of it was thrust up and down by the piston rod from the steam cylinder in the engineroom; the other end had attached to it a monstrous connecting rod that rotated about a crankshaft moving the paddlewheels.

The vertical or walking beam engine diminished the difficulties engineers had encountered with the crosshead or square engine. In the latter were two connecting rods and two crankshafts, a set for each paddlewheel. The single piston rod forced a squared, horizontal T-bar to move up and down; attached to each end of the T-bar was a connecting rod, port and starboard, each turning a crankshaft for a paddlewheel. Friction (and vegetable and animal fats were poor lubricants), misalignment from uneven wear and tear, unequal stress from passing waves on opposite sides, and other problems were, to some extent, minimized by the single crankshaft of the vertical beam engine. The sight of the walking beam seesawing behind a tall smoking stack became a hallmark of the white steamboats on the Chesapeake.[22]

New steamboats, as they came along to serve the rivers from the James to the Susquehanna, modified their appearance to meet the challenges of the Bay. Their forward main decks to protect their cargoes

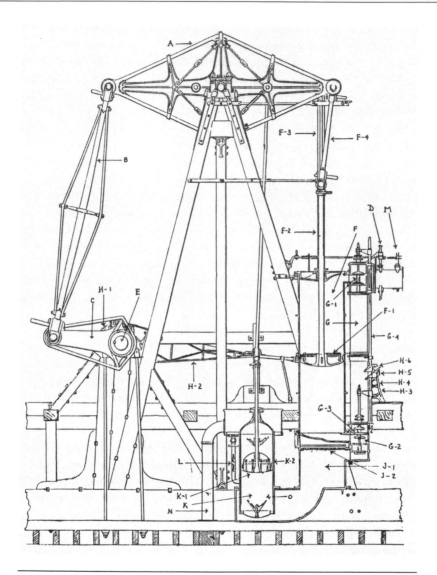

Schematic diagram of vertical (walking beam) engine. *A*, walking beam. *B*, connecting rod.
C, crank. *D*, cut-off. *E*, paddlewheel shaft. *F*, cylinder: *1*, piston, *2*, piston rod; *3*, track to
keep piston rod in alignment; *4*, connecting link (two rods to walking beam). *G*, steam
chest: *1*, upper steam chest; *2*, lower steam chest; *3*, double poppet valves (pressure of
steam assists in opening); *4*, example of lifting rod (one of four: two for live steam; two for
exhaust steam). *H*, eccentric: *1*, eccentric ring; *2*, eccentric rod; *3*, hooks engage crank on
rocker shaft and push and pull; causes shaft to rotate partially up and down; *4*, rocking
shaft (bar); *5*, toe attached to rocking shaft, swinging up and down, engaging wiper; *6*, wiper
attached to lifting rod, opens and closes either steam or exhaust valves. *J*, condenser:
1, intake for cold water from sea sprays a jet to condense exhaust steam and form a vacuum; *2*, perforated plate letting condensate escape to bottom. *K*, air pump: *1*, valve opens
on down-stroke, letting condensate flow above; closes on up-stroke, pulling vacuum and
bringing condensate into pump; *2*, valve opens and closes like teakettle top, pumping
condensate into hot well. *L*, hot well, reservoir for condensate, drawn off as feed water.
M, throttle. *N*, discharge pipe; *O*, force pump and bilge pump; *P*, A-frame, supports walking
beam. Redrawn from diagram in C. W. Bourne (ed.), *Treatise on the Steam Engine*, 3d. ed.,
(London: Longmans, Brown, Green and Longmans, 1849), 190

were even more enclosed, with entry ports for gangplanks; passenger decks moved to the upper or promenade level, with windowed staterooms running around the outside and elaborate saloons in the interior; pilothouses surmounted the entire superstructure, up forward; and the hull with its sweeping overhang gained a pronounced sheer, a safeguard against boarding seas.

Planter, built in 1845, stood in the middle of these advancements. She was a modest boat in many ways: 162 feet in length, 500 or so tons. Her main deck forward of the gilded paddleboxes was enclosed for cargo; a gallery aft of the paddleboxes surrounded cabin and dining areas; the promenade deck had a cabin running two-thirds of the length of the vessel containing staterooms and saloon; a covered deck encompassed the cabin aft of the paddleboxes; the pilothouse was a square box forward of the passenger cabin, with its roof raised sufficiently for windows fore and aft to give an all-around view. In the hull itself were the engine and boiler, cooking facilities, and berths and benches for Negro passengers and crew. Wood for fuel was stacked in huge piles on the main deck (Appendix A).

Mason L. Weems assumed command, with Gustavus as engineer, and relegated *Patuxent* to Theodore as master. George W., the youngest, boarded *Patuxent* with his brother when he was not engaged in helping the patriarch at Fair Haven. Both boats ran the Patuxent route, the older boat filling in when needed; however, during the summer season, *Patuxent*, under Theodore Weems, cleared Baltimore crowded with excursionists bound for Fair Haven.

Throughout the year, except when ice blocked the channel, *Planter* steamed up the Patuxent River to Green Landing. At this point— 45 miles from its mouth—the river was reduced to a narrow channel, not much more than 100 yards or so in width, sweeping in great loops through marshes filled with grass and inhabited by swans, geese, ducks, railbirds, and swarms of mosquitoes. Not far above Green Landing lay the county seat of Upper Marlboro, unreachable through the silted channel. At Green Landing, silting had begun by 1845. Runoff from the ruptured fields of tobacco began to encroach on the river far below Upper Marlboro. But the tidal current slicing back and forth had deposited the silt along the banks in such a way as to narrow the channel; it had also gouged out the river bottom to leave depths up to 50 feet in some areas. Rivermen, casting leadlines to gauge the changes through the years, noted with some apprehension, nevertheless, the steady process of shoaling and its movement downriver. Small, shallow-draft barges, drifting on the ebb tide, brought produce from Upper Marlboro down to Green Landing and returned on the flood tide, laden with goods delivered by steamer from Baltimore.

Beyond the marshes at Green Landing lay the fertile farms and gentle uplands of southern Maryland. Below Green Landing, in a south-leading valley, stretched the Patuxent. After an overnight stay at Green Landing, *Planter* started her journey down the river by first light. Turning in the confined channel meant thrusting her bow in the mud bank, throwing her rudder hard over, and going slow ahead on her engines, her paddlewheels throwing a wall of water against the turned rudder to kick her stern around. If the tide was right, the current assisted in the pivoting. Once partially turned, *Planter* backed clear of the bank, swung her bow downstream, and sought her way through the tortuous marshes to the open waters of the lower river.

Below Green Landing lay a succession of landings, carrying the names of planters who owned them or small towns whose wharves were leased for *Planter's* use. For half the distance south, *Planter* threaded her way in a twisting and narrow watercourse hedged in by expanses of marsh grass, which flooded in the incoming tide. Beyond the wetland, the hills forming the Patuxent valley rose in undulations, gently in some areas, abruptly and steeply in others. The headlands shadowed each other and on a misty morning seemed unreal, almost mystical. And then the river widened, a great arc of blue and silver curving to the east, its waters melding with the Chesapeake in a final hook around Drum Point. The drama of the Patuxent had spelled its magic on George Weems; its splendid vistas became the stage for the everyday lives of his sons (Appendix F).

On the trip down from Baltimore and on the return trip from the Patuxent, *Planter* stopped at Fair Haven. In the summertime, it disgorged its cargo of joy seekers. Baltimoreans in the 1840s had discovered the pleasures of steamboat excursions. In addition to their regular passenger and freight runs, a number of steamboats chartered themselves to Sunday schools and Hibernian societies and all sorts of organizations for daylong outings down the Bay: *Sydney,* to Annapolis; *Thomas Jefferson,* to the Chester River; *Rappahannock,* to Chestertown; *Maryland,* around the upper Bay with Professor Orlandt's Band to serenade; and *Patapsco* with the Cotillion Band to play for dancing (still looked on by some as scandalous).[23]

Fair Haven advertised in 1845 that new bathhouses offered excellent accommodations on the wharf near the sandy shore. Who used them remained a question. The Victorian reign had barely begun. The prudishness that accompanied it had just crossed the Atlantic, but the strictures of early Puritanism, Quakerism, and Catholicism, and the rising restraints of Methodism and Anglicanism had affected the mores of the times. Not one advertisement for bathing suits or beachside attire appeared in any newspaper. Bathing in public—particularly by the ladies—was simply not done in polite society, or so it seemed. If the more daring entered the water, they went fully clothed. For the ladies, not even an ankle was exposed. The bathhouses certainly hid the charms of the more audacious, but they offered a tempting reminder of the art of the possible.

From the decks of *Planter* and *Patuxent* streamed the excursionists down the dock to the beach and grove and hotel. The gentlemen in the hottest weather wore frock coats, vests, stocks, and stovepipe hats, some quite tall. And the ladies under parasols swept the ground in trailing muslins, lawns, balzerines, bereges, and cassimeres.

Immigrants settling in Baltimore—encouraged by the state of Maryland to stay rather than move on to the coal fields and iron mines of the West—tended to retain their ethnic identity, even to insulate themselves in neighborhoods within the city. At one time Germans outnumbered other Europeans, and they generally took care of their own interests.[24] German organizations frequented Fair Haven, their banners streaming, lederhosen slapping, and bands oompahing. In Baltimore, the concert halls echoed with the revolutionary thunder of Wagner's *Flying Dutchman* and the lilting strains of waltzes from Vienna together with melodies from the American heartland—songs like "The Old Oaken Bucket" and "My Old Kentucky Home." Hawthorne's *Twice-told Tales* excited some attention from local literati. Poe's "Raven" had just been published, and everyone was quoting "nevermore." And Longfellow's "Wreck of the Hesperus" and "Village Blacksmith" were taken up by local schoolmasters while everyone sang his "Stars of the Summer Night (Serenade)." Baltimore newspapers occasionally mentioned abolition, denounced the Mexicans, and dealt extensively with Mrs. Hanson's murder by candlelight and the troubles of a local blacksmith who got run over by a mule.

In 1845, events surrounding James Harwood and the Baltimore and Rappahannock Steam Packet Company riveted the attention of Mason L. Weems. As mentioned previously, Harwood, after severing his connection as agent for *Patuxent* following the latter's retreat from the Rappahannock, had manipulated his way into a position as president of the Rappahannock steamboat line. He had snooped around the edge of Rappahannock enterprises for much of his business career, apparently waiting for an opportune time to profit from the commercial opening of the region. From its offices on Light Street, the Baltimore and Rappahannock Steam Packet Company directed the operations of its steamboat *Rappahannock* out of Baltimore for landings on the river to Fredericksburg. *Rappahannock*, of the vintage of *Patuxent*, limped about in 1844 and 1845, suffering from an aging boiler and engine as well as a bottom that needed new copper. Another older vessel, *Fredericksburg*, acquired by the company to relieve *Rappahannock*, sank at the head of navigation in 1845 and was deemed unworthy of raising.

In 1845, the company under Harwood faced a crisis. *Rappahannock* had to be scrapped or sold or else given major and expensive repairs. Alternatively, to supplement or replace *Rappahannock*, the company could contract for the construction of a new steamboat, a costly venture at best. Two hundred stockholders—a bare half of them Baltimoreans, the remainder tidewater Virginians—failed to realize that the company was stone broke. To make matters worse, among the stockholders there was little love lost between Baltimoreans and Virginians, the former bent on taking full control and the latter determined to force the former out.

Mismanagement and barely suppressed internecine warfare had led to the crisis. Profits on the Rappahannock River had never soared, even after *Patuxent* abandoned the route to her competition. But the crisis of the Baltimore and Rappahannock Steam Packet Company was largely of its own making. Its bills went unpaid, funds were spent irresponsibly, and it delegated the expenditure of funds without backing them. For example, the board authorized Captain Noah Fairbank to issue notes for all sorts of expenses aboard the steamer—fuel, food for the dining room and help, wages to officers and crew, and wharfage—but the poor captain, popular with his crew and venerated along the river, was too naïve to realize that he was being left to hold the bag. He ended up bankrupt.

The directors, elected in June 1844, included James Harwood as president and other prominent Baltimore businessmen—Fielding Lucas, Jr., (publisher and stationer), John A. Robb (steamboat builder), John Bratt (engine builder), and Edward D. Kemp (Harwood's lawyer and compatriot). Only a few were Virginians—C. C. Wellford and Eustace Conway, for example.

On October 26, 1844, after hearing a report from a committee (Bratt and Kemp included), they voted unanimously to empower the committee to draw on the treasurer for construction of a new steamboat.[25] How they were to pay for it was not considered.

Accordingly, contracts were released to John A. Robb and his company (John A. and Eliakim K. Robb of Thames and Wolfe Streets, Baltimore) to construct the new boat and to John Watchman and John Bratt to build the engine. Numerous contractors were engaged for the enormous quantities of materials and hours of labor needed for the completion of the steamer. Work began about July 1, 1845.

On July 24 of that year, James Harwood as president, Fielding Lucas, Jr., John A. Robb, David Stewart, Jr. (the arbitrator), John Bratt, and Edward D. Kemp, together with a few Virginians, were elected as directors. Five days later, Harwood abruptly resigned—no reason given. Captain James Frazier of Baltimore replaced him.

Work progressed on the new boat. *Rappahannock* faltered and came to Baltimore for repairs, particularly on her ailing boiler. Problems developed on the new construction, as expected reimbursements for expenditures failed to materialize. John Bratt slowed up production of his engine; John Robb let his schedule lag. The new boat barely entered the water in time for the 1846 season.

She was a handsome boat—almost an exact replica of *Planter* in design and appearance although her dimensions were somewhat different (Appendix A). From her long enclosed main deck to her galleried dining room aft, from her squared two-windowed pilothouse to the cabins and awning-covered promenade deck, from tall black stack to graceful sheer, she looked like *Planter* underway. Her paddlebox decorations were different: *Planter* wore a lacy, gilded fan, and the new boat had an oval carving of a woman's head. Along each paddlebox was her name, *Mary Washington*.[26]

Mary Washington, with the amiable but unwitting Captain Fairbank as master, began her journeys from Baltimore to Fredericksburg in late 1846 under the most frightful auspices. For lack of money, the company neglected to insure her. And for lack of money, the company shuddered under the cloud of imminent receivership.

The thundercloud broke in a torrent. A flock of creditors began to join forces in a threat of suit. To forestall it and to produce some immediate cash to pay off the more predatory among them, the directors on August 17, 1846, agreed to sell off *Rappahannock.* Almost immediately, the suit of fieri facias was joined, and the creditors, led by Horace Abbott, proprietor of a forge, and some others, attacked the defendants, James Frazier, John A. Robb, and Fielding Lucas, Jr., all of whom represented the company. The suit before the Baltimore Court of Chancery was a bitter one, the complainants charging the defendants with contempt of court by violating its injunctions for the boats to remain in port, charging certain creditors with attempted circumvention by trying to sue independently in federal court (the boats having crossed state lines), charging the defendants with an effort to outwit the creditors by transferring the boats to a separate trust and hence new documentation, and scenting up the air with acrimony.

In the middle of it, Harwood, by deposition, declared that the building committee for *Mary Washington* had exceeded its powers in making contracts beyond a certain amount (Watchman and Bratt, $9,500 for the engine; John A. Robb, $10,000 for the hull; Thomas C. Morris, of the iron works for $5,300) and that he never agreed to these expenditures. He acknowledged, however, that the promissory notes issued to contractors could never be paid at maturity and that all of the contracts for *Mary Washington* "had been shamefully violated."

By order of the court and acceded to by the directors and defendants, *Rappahannock* and *Mary Washington* were sold at auction in Baltimore in early 1847. The former went off to the Delaware River for repair and a later life. *Mary Washington* was bought for $26,000 on February 3, 1847, by John Glenn, the attorney for the bankrupt Baltimore and Rappahannock Steam Packet Company, which had just ceased to exist.[27]

Astonishingly, John Glenn turned around on February 12 and leased *Mary Washington* to a newly formed company that had incorporated itself under the laws of Maryland on the very same day. Its name was the Maryland and Virginia Steam Packet Company (incorporated for $100,000). Among its stockholders were John A. Robb and John Bratt. Its president was none other than James Harwood.[28]

The new company, barely distinguishable from its predecessor, managed to acquire a new steamboat, *Mary Washington,* worth as much as $40,000, for the sum of $26,000—reward, indeed, for the mismanagement and ruthless indifference on the part of the directors, and particularly on the part of Harwood himself.

Mary Washington began her runs from Baltimore to Fredericksburg on March 14, 1847. On September 28 of that year, the company (J. S.

Shriver as president, Harwood having died) ended the lease and bought her.[29]

When Harwood's problems began to mount in September 1846 and the precariousness of the Baltimore and Rappahannock Steam Packet Company became public knowledge, Mason L. Weems decided to bring the name of Weems to the attention of the Fredericksburg and river shippers once again. He smarted under the indignity his father had suffered, and he vowed to try, and try again, if necessary, to rebuild the foundation his father had laid—the first steamboat route on the Rappahannock. In October, off he steamed in *Planter* to call at the landings and appear at the dock at Fredericksburg to challenge the fledgling *Mary Washington*. Their competition was direct and short lived; in December *Mary Washington* was prohibited by court order from leaving her pier in Baltimore, and for a short time *Planter* had the route to herself (Appendix B).

Then came the resurrection on February 12, 1847, in the form of the Maryland and Virginia Steam Packet Company. And with it came the return of *Mary Washington*. When the 1847 oyster season began, the two boats stood once again in head-to-head competition, even running the same schedule to gobble business from one another.[30] But *Mary Washington* had the advantage, the commitment of her owners exclusively to the Rappahannock (*Planter* was eternally bound to the Patuxent); and *Mary Washington* had the readiness on the part of her owners to play a rough game to monopolize the trade to Fredericksburg. Mason L. Weems retired to his usual haunts to await another chance.

Every day or so, *Mary Washington* steamed by, southward bound, a graceful apparition on a summer day. Every time he saw her, Mason L. Weems freshened with a smile. She was a natural running mate for *Planter*, and Mason L. relished her. Sometime, somehow—he would bide his time.

Planter resumed her runs on the Patuxent, staggering her weekly schedule with that of *Patuxent*. Both boats from Green Landing, at the head of navigation, to Drum Point at the mouth of the river enjoyed the hospitality of shippers along the way, and their profits increased, slowly but steadily. Nevertheless, Mason L. chafed at the number of days, particularly in the off-season, that *Planter* spent in Baltimore, and he cast about for opportunities to increase her yield.

He thought he saw a charter opportunity for a route to Norfolk and advertised that beginning January 1, 1848, *Planter* would leave Baltimore on Wednesdays at midnight for an overnight run to the city on the James; at her speed, she would arrive in the evening of the following day. That no further notices appeared indicated that the venture was not successful. Under George W., as master, *Planter* ran a charter to the York, East, and Great Wicomico Rivers in July 1859. That, too, was a single gesture. That *Planter* sought charters wherever she could find them found plaintive expression in a note dated August 21, 1859, from Mason L. to his wife, Matilda: "I leave in the morning to make the excursion from the River [presumably Patuxent] to Norfolk and I expect a large Company as all the State Rooms are engaged at double the usual price. I am almost worn out as I have never [been] more constantly engaged than I have since my return home."[31] On the very eve of conflict, *Planter* steamed on charter up the Potomac River to Washington; the year was 1861.[32]

For the most part, however, the life of *Planter* from 1847 to 1861 was that of faithful servant to the individual of the soil whose name she bore. In 1851, she underwent alterations that shortened her foredeck by some 14 feet and increased her maneuverability. The years raced by, the seasons wrapped her in comforting sequence, and *Planter* merged with the life of the Patuxent, as much a part of it as the toilers of the soil who gave it meaning.

She had her bits of excitement. She collided with a schooner or two, lost her bearings in a fog, sought escape from entrapment by ice, and weathered innumerable gales that swept the Bay. With *Thomas Jefferson* on January 15, 1848, she went to the assistance of *Columbus*, aground near the Magothy. One event was noted by a resolution drafted May 18, 1848, by no less than the passengers on board led by A. R. Sollers (Alexander Somerville, chairman; Dr. Richard Blake, secretary) in which it was resolved "that no fault [should] be attributed to Captain M. L. Weems . . . for [the grounding of *Planter*] on Whetstone Point . . . [which] under the circumstances was unavoidable."[33] The circumstances and mission of *Planter* were not recorded although the call for such an unusual and collective resolution by passengers suggests that they may have contributed in some fashion to the steering that led to the grounding.

Disaster struck on Thursday, May 17, 1855. About three o'clock in the morning, *Planter*, groping her way through the Patapsco entrance in rain and heavy fog, plowed into Fort Carroll, the round island of stoneworks and battlements guarding the approach to Baltimore Harbor. She drove her bow 20 feet into the outer works of the fort, stove in her stem and footing under the bow, and filled slowly with water. *Louisiana*, a Norfolk steamer, arrived on the scene and removed the passengers, who, startled from their berths, had scrambled to safety on the battlements of the fort. Some 18 in number, they consisted mostly of Barrett's Cornet Band, who had entertained an excursion group to St. Mary's on the previous day. *Planter* settled by the stern. Across her bow to the fort 30 hogsheads of tobacco were rolled to safety.[34]

The towboat *Edwin Forrest* with a draft of carpenters went out to Fort Carroll and determined that *Planter* was beyond repair, her keel broken and framing severely damaged. Mason L. rejected the judgment and vowed to restore her. She had undergone major overhaul recently and was in prime condition. Her loss was galling. Right then, a certain Weems stubbornness asserted itself. *Planter*, therefore, was patched temporarily from within, pumped out, and dragged off the seawall of the fort to the shipyard. In a few months, she was steaming out of Baltimore once again. Repair costs were over $9,000—half her price on the open market.

But the Patuxent River claimed the daily lives of *Planter* and *Patuxent* through all the years from the end of the Rappahannock episode through the 1850s. For Mason L. Weems and his brothers, it was a time of prosperity and contemplation.

In 1854, events on the Rappahannock River stirred Mason L. to action. The Maryland and Virginia Steam Packet Company, the 1847 phoenix rising from the ashes of the Baltimore and Rappahannock Steam Packet Company, was faring badly. Mismanagement once again beset it. But more importantly, competition was taking its toll. The Old Dominion Steamboat Company, owned totally by Virginians, had chartered *William Selden* in 1851 and built *Virginia* by 1854 to drive *Mary Washington* off the Rappahannock. The master of *William Selden* was Noah Fairbank. Shunned by the management of the new Maryland and Virginia Steam Packet Company (headed in 1847 by James Harwood), Fairbank had the satisfaction of becoming the nemesis to his old creation, the *Mary Washington*. Weakened by the vigor of the opposition, the threat of more steamers from Norfolk to compete, and dwindling resources, the management of the Maryland and Virginia Steam Packet Company simply succumbed in 1854. *Mary Washington* was advertised for sale. Mason L. Weems and his brother Theodore bought her for $17,000. They signed a mortgage for that amount on December 14, 1854, payable in six-month installments of $5,666.65. The vessel stood ready for operation by the Weems line on April 16, 1855.[35]

Two years earlier, George Weems had died. The purchase of *Mary Washington* came too late to symbolize an act of retribution. Yet in his later years at Fair Haven George Weems had spent long hours with his sons ruminating over the events long gone on the Rappahannock. He would have savored the moment when his eldest son stepped aboard *Mary Washington* as master. For Mason Locke Weems, the boat was truly a tribute to his father. It was also a fantasy realized; *Planter* had her running mate.

Mary Washington did not return to the Rappahannock. Instead, she joined *Planter* and *Patuxent* in serving the landings from Fair Haven and Plum Point on the Bay to Hills Landing at the head of navigation on the Patuxent. Green Landing—the name of the cluster of buildings that made up the small but busy fishing port and steamboat landing—was absorbed by William B. Hill, owner of the ancestral plantation of Woodland and operator of an adjacent boat landing, store, and warehouse. T. L. Gardner and George McCullough ran a steam-driven sawmill.[36] After 1855, when the purchase was finally consummated, the Weems boats advertised that their runs would terminate at Hills Landing rather than Green Landing. In 1852, William B. Hill began the construction of a toll bridge across the river from Pig Point to Hills Landing; its draw was sufficiently wide to permit passage of small craft, but it marked definitively the limit of steamboat navigation up the Patuxent.[37] Just below the bridge, after it was completed, steamboats seesawed their way to turn around in the swift current and tied up at the wharf at Hills Landing (Appendix B).

Trade along the river prospered in the late 1850s. At Pig Point, for example, a small town that had grown up in the first half of the century became a commercial center for the region. Several stores offered general merchandise, a lumber mill shipped sawn boards to Baltimore, tobacco warehouses emptied their stocks to arriving boats, a fishery packed every fish catch in ice for overnight transport to commission merchants in the city (and could be persuaded to pack the geese and ducks shot by hunters in the fall for shipment as well), farmers trundled their produce and livestock to the wharf, and, with the redesignation of the post office, the town called itself Bristol. Below the landing spread the great marshes of Jug Bay. At steamboat time, people for miles around came down to the landing to participate in the spectacle.

Planter or *Patuxent* or *Mary Washington* announced its departure from Hills Landing with a long shriek on the whistle.[38] It could be heard across the marshes to Bristol a mile or two away. As the steamer threaded its way through the narrow and curving channel, it seemed to the Bristol crowd like a white, windowed castle, with a tall chimney and two big bosomy humps on either side, but no bottom, skimming along, dreamlike, above the marsh grass. Then it emerged, its high, sharp prow and sloping decks aimed at the dock. Its whistle sounded once again to alert the line handlers and agent on the wharf. Its paddlewheels stopped, and it drifted toward the dock. Larger and larger it grew as it moved alongside, until its upper works towered white above the piling, and the crowd on the dock peered upward at the passengers clustered by the rail on the promenade deck. Then, at a gesture from the captain standing by the wheelhouse, bells were set to clanging somewhere below decks, and the paddlewheels began to back, throwing up a churning spume beneath the piling. Heaving lines, with monkey fists (tightly knotted balls, sometimes weighted) on the ends, thrown by deckhands fore and aft, were caught by line handlers on the dock, usually the young sons of the agent. Attached were hemp hawsers to be dragged to the dock, thrown over the bollards, and handled as spring lines until the steamboat had nudged against the wharf, then secured to hold the vessel against current and wind. Gangplanks came trundling through the sideports, the clerk appeared with tally sheets to meet the agent, deckhands jigged their way ashore, and the bedlam of loading freight and passengers began. Hogsheads of tobacco and heavy barrels of fish, produce, flour, and grain went over the gangplank to the foredeck, rolled by black men whose chants and shuffling dance came straight from the hinterland of Africa. Cattle and hogs and sheep driven from the livestock pen on the dock bellowed in terror at the gangplank, only to be projected by brute force and twisted tail aboard the boat and to crossbars to which they were tethered on the main deck. Off came the boxes and hampers and crates consigned to the storekeepers and artisans and tradesmen ashore from the merchants of Baltimore.

In the midst of the clattering freight emerged the passengers, some from the crude waiting room where they crowded by the potbellied stove to escape the river chill. Small scenes were reenacted: the last touch of a relative leaving for the city, the tearful reassurance of a mother to her son going off to boarding school for the first time, the boisterous farewells of a vacationing group returning to Baltimore, the first mate delivering a package of lace he had bought at Gutman's to a lady patron on the wharf who brought her shopping list to him each time the steamer docked. They milled about—the top hatted men and the homespun farmers, the long-sleeved and bustled and flower-hatted ladies, the rough-clad boys leering at simpering girls, and the slaves—deckhands and stokers aboard the boat and stevedores on the dock—setting up a din of song and chatter—until the captain, noting the end of loading and the time and the tide, gave the signal. Aboard came the gangplanks and the lines. The whistle deafened the spectators, and the steamer slipped away from the dock to resume its journey to a dozen other landings on the way to the Chesapeake.

In the 1850s, the Patuxent trade steadily grew. Bristol became one of the busiest landings along the river, and about a large wharf and warehouse flowed a volume of freight so heavy at certain seasons that all three boats were needed to handle the cargo. Steamboat time became a source of entertainment, almost a ritual, and country folk for miles around came by cart and carriage for the event.[39]

Weems prospered moderately. *Planter,* for example, earned net profits of nearly $4,000 in 1855, over $5,000 in 1856, more than $7,000 in 1857, and about $6,500 in 1858. And *Patuxent* earned a net profit of nearly $4,000 for freight alone in 1858. Placed against the expenditures included in the figures, Weems moved ahead, if not excessively, at least comfortably. Wood for *Planter's* boilers cost, on average, about $125 to $150 per month (a cord meant the expenditure of 90 cents) (Appendix C).

In the early months of 1856, *Patuxent* had her boiler rebuilt; the old one brought $400 on the market. She and *Planter* shifted from wood to coal, and costs for fuel diminished abruptly to something on the order of $750 for a nine-month period for *Planter.* Yearly wharf fees (rental or lease) extracted a toll ranging from $28 for Dukes and $145 for Bristol to $583.32 for the State Warehouse Wharf in Baltimore.[40] Marketing (food for the dining room and the crew's mess) and wages, funds paid directly by the captain, were substantial, averaging $295 to $400 per month. And there were constant bills for paint, glass, laundry, advertising, insurance, taxes, and repairs. Above these costs remained the monthly salaries paid to Theodore Weems, master of *Planter,* $75, and to Gustavus Weems, engineer, $65, and the dividends disbursed each year, $558.08 each to Theodore, Gustavus, and George W. from *Planter* alone. The accounts for *Mary Washington* and Mason L. Weems were handled separately.

Planter ran 32 regular trips on the Patuxent in 1855 (in spite of her disaster at Fort Carroll), another 30 in 1856, nearly 40 in 1857, but only 25 in 1858. During these years, she earned an average of $262 per trip from freight, $149 per trip from passenger fares in 1855; $253 per trip from freight, $195 per trip from passenger fares in 1856; $268 per trip from freight, $187 per trip from passenger fares in 1857; and $287 per trip from freight, $178 per trip from passenger fares in 1859. Bonus revenues came from the chartering of the steamer in 1855 for 18 days at $917.86 and in 1857 for a run to Norfolk at $1,025.71. In all, *Planter, Patuxent,* and *Mary Washington* probably netted on the order of $18,000 per year from 1855 to 1861 for the Weems brothers (above their salaries and dividends), not a princely sum but a respectable profit generally commensurate with the times.[41]

But these were troubling times around the shores of the Patuxent. Tobacco had proved to be a capricious mistress. Around much of the Patuxent basin the light, sandy soil, deprived of nutrients by continued production of the weed, progressively wore out. For a time, planters were successful in raising a leaf of a quality much desired on world markets, and the demand for the product kept the hogsheads moving by steamboat to Baltimore. But increasingly, farmers felt the bite of soil depletion, and the competition from tobacco growers spread all over the country for foreign and domestic markets. More and more, the shift to other crops and the move to soil replenishment became not only an agronomic requirement but an absolute economic necessity.

These were times of industrial change, when steam power revolutionized the very nature of manufacturing. The face of Baltimore, sooted and sweaty, reflected the change. Railroads reached out to the nation's interior and linked city to city, mine to factory, farmer and oysterman to merchant. The Baltimore and Ohio Railroad (construction was initiated by Charles Carroll of Carrollton in 1828) had reached Wheeling, West Virginia, in 1853 and looked toward extension to Chicago. Its effect on steamboats connecting Tidewater to Baltimore can only be a matter of conjecture in terms of produce and seafood packed for shipment to other cities and the country's interior, or tobacco handled by rail, or manufactured goods arriving by rail for distribution in Tidewater by steamboats. Tidewater Maryland and Virginia had lost claim to being the breadbasket of the nation or even a major supplier of food for regions beyond its own geography. How much the Baltimore and Ohio Railroad contributed to the prosperity of the steamboat industry can only be a subject for speculation. In Virginia, the Richmond and Petersburg Railroad (incorporated 1836; it was the start of the Atlantic Coast Line Railroad), the short line between Portsmouth on the James and Roanoke (begun 1832, the start of the Seaboard Air Line Railroad), and the City Point Railroad (started 1836, the parent of the belated Norfolk and Western Railroad) may have had some influence on steamboat trade to Fredericksburg and Richmond for steamboats in the 1850s, but the effect was difficult to measure and not marked.

These were times of transition. The counties around the Patuxent stagnated; Baltimore bulged with growth. Whereas the counties of Anne Arundel, Calvert, and St. Mary's totaled only about 40,000 inhabitants in 1860 and showed only a miniscule 8 percent growth in 20 years, Baltimore City and County had six times that number, representing a doubling of the population in the same 20 years. Almost 400 occupations swelled its ranks. Eighty churches and synagogues functioned. There were 20 temperance societies and a hundred times as many saloons and taverns. A number of theaters and music halls (some a bit naughty) flourished, and the newspapers and city directories advertised several public baths, open every day in summer and only Saturday and Sunday in winter—all equipped with reading rooms, no less.[42]

These were days of social unrest. Around the shores of the Patuxent, the news arriving aboard the Weems boat stirred hot blood. The planters of southern Maryland, slaveowning, bred to plantation life, echoed the fire of rebellion coming from the South. On the other hand, the merchants, small manufacturers, and professionals—more often linked to the economy and society of the city—found their loyalties divided. Aboard *Planter, Patuxent,* and *Mary Washington*, slaves continued to serve as deckhands and stokers, and their owners joined hands with the planters.

The savings from the profits of the three boats persuaded Mason L. Weems and his brothers in late 1857 that a new boat should be built to replace the aging *Patuxent*. Twelve years before, *Planter* had been launched for that purpose, but *Patuxent* had successfully defied obsolescence and continued to serve effectively, carrying both freight and excursions. But prestige demanded something better.

The four brothers decided to build a memorial to their father. The new steamer, launched in 1859, was an elegant counterpart to *Planter* and *Mary Washington*. She cost $41,384.55 (Appendix A and D). Her furnishings were lavish; even a William Knabe piano graced the saloon. Below the lacy fan of her gilded paddleboxes were emblazoned the letters, *George Weems*. She took her place on the Patuxent, even as the storm clouds gathered across the land.[43]

This was a time of celebration for Mason L., Gustavus, Theodore, and George W. A splendid new boat—a triumphant symbol of the Weems name on the Chesapeake—steamed out of Baltimore to Fair Haven and the Patuxent. She was one of four boats, part of a Weems fleet. In fact, the steamboat world in Baltimore pointed to them as "palace boats," famed for their superb appointments and excellent cuisine. To call the fleet the "Weems Line" seemed comfortably appropriate, even though the name had no legal standing.

In the decades between the 1830s and 1850s the steamboat had become part of the way of life on the Chesapeake, and steamboat owners and operators prospered. The open waters of the Bay and the channels of its tributaries accepted the comings and goings of white-sided steamboats as a part of the routine of economic and social life. The expansion of established steamboat lines was its inevitable consequence. Among these lines, prosperity was unevenly distributed according to the profitability of routes and distances traveled. The Weems brothers had not known much wealth from their enterprise, but they had created for themselves an established place in the steamboat world of the Chesapeake. The brothers, particularly the eldest, viewed the prospects with optimism.

They were a close-knit group, bound together by success, devotion to family, and a patriarchal symbol. They had much to celebrate in 1858. Then, just as the celebration subsided, the blow struck. Gustavus, who had stood shoulder to shoulder with Mason L. aboard *Patuxent* and *Planter* and *Mary Washington* through the years, died on July 6, 1859.

A shadow lay long on the stilled decks that afternoon.

CHAPTER 4

Civil War:
Disruption and
Rebuilding

The flames of rebellion engulfed the tidewater Chesapeake. North and South divided at the Potomac; Washington and Baltimore lay to the North; Richmond and Norfolk, to the South. But passions spilled over, and in southern Maryland loyalty to the South ran deep. The broad waters of the Bay and its long tributaries became highways carrying the weapons, the supplies, and the men of war. For either side, the Chesapeake held the key to grand strategy. In its southern reaches, it linked Richmond and the Northern Neck to Hampton Roads and access to Albemarle Sound and the South. In its northern reaches, it connected the industrial strength of the North through Baltimore to armies in the field. For both contestants, it spelled access to the sea.

The role of steamboats on the Chesapeake assumed critical importance. Richmond and Norfolk were not as well favored as Baltimore. Fewer than 15 steamers operated exclusively out of Norfolk and were available for seizure. Nearly twice that number docked in Baltimore, and, in addition, steamboats on the Delaware River could be brought down to augment the boats ready for plucking by government forces. Locust Point, at the foot of Baltimore Harbor, became a great depot for

66

stocking and distributing the supplies of war—a logistical center for the Union.

Baltimoreans watched—with mixed sympathies—as their beloved steamboats were commandeered, their services regulated, and their missions transformed into those of transports and carriers of munitions and military supplies. Almost immediately affected by the outbreak of hostilities were the steamers of the Baltimore Steam Packet Company (the Old Bay Line), which had started operations in 1840 between Baltimore and Norfolk. Its steamers were turned back at Old Point Comfort (Hampton Roads), the route disrupted, and its boats seized (one was later captured and burned by the Confederates). The Merchants and Miners Transportation Company, a line serving the coastal trade since 1852, lost a boat to torching by rebels in Savannah even before the war began and the company found its vessels seized by the federal government as hostilities mounted. One by one, the steamboat lines in Baltimore lost their boats to compulsory charter or outright confiscation—the Eastern Shore Steamboat Company, the Slaughter line, the Individual Enterprise Company, and most others.[1] The boats were driven hard, abused, left without adequate maintenance, released occasionally and immediately seized again, and turned back, in the end, to their owners in a decrepit state that nearly defied rehabilitation.

The Weems line suffered more than most. The first to go to Union seizure was *Patuxent* on December 18, 1861, in Baltimore. She served at $125 per day (reduced to $100) until May 1, 1863. Discharged, she sat for 10 months until bought by the U.S. Quartermaster Department for $16,000. At the end of the war, the government sold her off to S. & J. Flanagan in Baltimore for a mere $3,200.

The next to go was *Planter,* seized on January 1, 1862, either on the Patuxent or in Washington (the record is not clear on the place of seizure). She ran for the government until June 12, 1865, earning from $66 to $175 per day, depending on her duties. A week after the initial seizure of *Planter* went *Mary Washington;* she served under enforced charter intermittently until April 1, 1865, at $148.47 to $175 per day. *George Weems* continued to operate for Weems only until August 14, 1862, when mandatory charter kept her in government service off and on until May 11, 1865, at rates from $87.83 to $200 per day.[2]

In effect, the Weems line, except for periods before and in between charters, had to accede to the management of the USQMD during the war years. Except on special operations when military personnel took charge, its officers ran the boats. The final authority over the movements of the boats and their functions rested with the government.

Mason L., Theodore, and George W. bore the brunt. However, from the early 1850s, Mason L. had recruited young men to serve as clerks, pursers, or quartermasters to learn the steamboating business. His hope was that some of them would become mates and masters with the skills needed to skipper the boats and even manage the company. He found an answer in a lad of 16 years, fresh from Ireland, who eagerly applied himself to a job as purser aboard *Patuxent*. Five years later, on July 19, 1857—the lad's 21st birthday—Mason L. proudly presented to him his master's license. On the certificate was engraved the chap's name, James Russell Gourley, a very special protégé, whose Irish intuition suggested a portentous future. He was one of many trainees engaged by Weems.

Gourley became relief skipper, alternating with Mason L. and his brothers on the schedule exacted by the government. At first, before the demands of the battlefield took charge, the vessels were sent off to Fair Haven, to landings on the Patuxent, and up the Potomac as far as Washington to provide freight and transport services, and even to carry general passengers. The run up the Potomac and back was particularly hazardous where the river narrowed.

Rebels on the Virginia side did not learn immediately of the Southern sympathies of the Weemses and gave their snipers free license to fire on the passing pilothouses. The only answer for the Weems skippers was to fashion some sort of boilerplate that could be lugged from one side of the pilothouse to the other as needed. Passengers—with excessive amiability—moved to the Maryland side of the boat, also.

The Potomac River at the outset became the stage for intensive military activity not only because of its strategic juncture between North and South but also because of the surreptitious but incessant nocturnal flow of munitions, personnel of opposing persuasions, and intelligence information across its waters from southern Maryland to the Northern Neck of Virginia, and vice versa. An established route across the Patuxent to Millstone Landing, thence overland to Point Lookout or Mathias Point or Leonardtown on the Potomac provided the linkage by fast boat under a moonless sky to Coan or Bundicks on the Coan River or Kinsale on the West Wicomico River, both intricate waterways off the Potomac. In 1861 at Coan, a Tennessee regiment took station to cover the clandestine traffic. Kinsale, early on, became the link in smuggling operations from Leonardtown; it gained a decided reputation and a certain flavor from the speculators, shady merchants, spies from both sides, northern sympathizers trying to go north, southern sympathizers arriving by nightskiff with muffled oars from across the Potomac, even ladies of the night gathering pillow secrets. During the same period, Leonardtown, on Breton Bay off the Potomac, was the northern terminus of the would-be secret route to Kinsale, and its streets and hotel and rooming houses and docks developed the same cosmopolitan, sleazy, and bizarre flavor as their southern counterparts in the otherwise orderly town of Kinsale.

Both Confederate units on the south shore and Union forces on the north mounted shore batteries at various strategic points, and Union naval units attempted to establish a blockade and patrol force from Point Lookout to Washington.

At the onset of hostilities the Weems boats were permitted to run, were even dispatched, on trips up the Potomac to Washington and also permitted operations on the Patuxent, just across St. Mary's County from the Potomac; inevitably they found themselves in jeopardy. Contributing to their precarious situation were the sympathies of the Weems family, slaveowning and plantation oriented, facts known to the rebels and Union authorities as well.

The Weems steamers, except for officers (masters, mates, pilots, engineers), quartermasters, clerks, and pursers, were manned by slaves—deckhands, roustabouts, stokers, oilers, dining room waiters, chambermaids—all Weems-owned slaves. As long as the boats operated under Union direction on their own, prior to confiscation by USQMD, no issue arose. Even after enforced seizure by USQMD, the lack of any federal or state law of abolition—and even the predilection of some local army commanders to consider slaves the undisputed property of their owners—would suggest that the Weems boats continued at least for a time with slave crews on board; there is no evidence to indicate when the practice ended; but certainly the activities of the Weems steamers, particularly of *Planter* and *George Weems* in later campaigns of the war, would suggest that manumission had occurred or that paid crews had been hired.

But from the start of hostilities, the Weems boats were viewed with suspicion. They were often boarded at their Baltimore wharves, stopped at Fort McHenry, and searched for contraband such as weapons, medical supplies, and money. They were always eyed with a question even after they were seized by USQMD.

An incident aboard *Mary Washington* on July 8, 1861, electrified the news on both sides of the Potomac. It had all begun a month earlier in a series of events that captured the fancy of romanticists everywhere.

It seemed that the USS *Pawnee,* a gunboat patrolling the Potomac to the great annoyance of Southern operatives crossing the river, was supplied regularly by a steamer from Baltimore, *St. Nicholas,* of the Alexandria, Washington, Georgetown, and Baltimore Steamboat Company. *St. Nicholas* had run the Potomac out of Baltimore from the mid-1850s and in 1861 was engaged in provisioning government blockading and patrol vessels in the river. Confederate observers were quick to note that on her frequent visits *St. Nicholas* went alongside USS *Pawnee* without the slightest challenge, her arrival accepted as routine.

The notion of capturing USS *Pawnee* by capturing *St. Nicholas* first and using the latter in a surprise boarding of the former seemed to have occurred to several Confederate naval officers simultaneously.

In June 1861, Lieutenant H. H. Lewis, CSN, observing the movements of USS *Pawnee* and *St. Nicholas* from the vantage of Aquia Creek, proposed to Brigadier General Thomas H. Holmes, his superior, that a force of 300 men from the Tennessee regiment be used to capture *St. Nicholas* downriver. The general thought the plan too risky. An appeal to Captain M. F. Maury, CSN, at Fredericksburg brought approval from the Confederate secretary of war, L. P. Walker; but General Holmes refused to accede.

On June 18, 1861, Commander George N. Hollins, CSN, left Baltimore aboard *Mary Washington* for the Patuxent, where he left the steamer to cross the peninsula to the Potomac and thence by small boat to the Virginia shore. He, too, had conceived the notion of seizing USS *Pawnee* via *St. Nicholas* and approached the Confederate secretary of the navy with his plan. In the office of the secretary, he met Lewis, Maury, and others. He was told that the secretary would not approve the plan but that Virginia governor John Letcher would. Letcher, according to Hollins, produced a draft for $1,000 and introduced him to Colonel Richard Thomas, the man who was to procure arms and arrange the details of the adventure. According to Lewis, he had returned to his post on the lower Rappahannock after being rebuffed by General Holmes; there he was surprised by a visit from Hollins and Thomas who informed him that they were on the way to Baltimore to work out the details for the capture of *St. Nicholas*. Returning to Fredericksburg, he found in readiness part of the Tennessee regiment and some maritime officers, who embarked on *Virginia* for Monaskon and marched overland to Coan to await the arrival of *St. Nicholas*.

In the meantime, Hollins and Thomas recrossed the Potomac, stayed over for a day awaiting the arrival of *St. Nicholas* at Point Lookout, and in a pouring rain Thomas boarded the boat for Baltimore. The instructions given him were to use the $1,000 draft to buy arms, secrete them in trunks, and return aboard *St. Nicholas* for Point Lookout, where Hollins and a party of men would board for the fateful trip up the Potomac.

Hollins was well aware of the identity and reputation of Colonel Richard Thomas. His father, Richard Thomas, Sr., was one of the most respected men in St. Mary's County and had presided over the Maryland House of Delegates for years. Richard, Jr., educated at Charlotte Hall and Oxford on the Tred Avon, attended West Point briefly; he went to the Far East to fight piracy on the China coast, and then he arrived in Italy to join the rebel forces of Garibaldi. There he assumed the name of Zarvona, which he had legally attached, by Confederate government authority, to his given and family name. At 21 he was utterly indifferent to danger, thrived on swashbuckling adventure, shaved his head, wore the red oriental-flared uniform of the Maryland Zouaves with casual flamboyance, and broke the hearts of women wherever he went.

In Baltimore, Richard Thomas gathered together a few stalwarts in whom he could confide. All of them booked as passengers on *St. Nicholas* bound for the Potomac on Friday, June 28, and dispersed themselves about the boat. Also boarding was a rather demure lady, tossing her fan about and animatedly speaking French or heavily accented English.

About midnight, *St. Nicholas* docked at Point Lookout at the mouth of the Potomac. Two passengers boarded. One was a rather elderly looking man, who took up a position on deck near the ladies' cabin, apparently to observe the weather. The French lady, who had boarded in Baltimore, floated about and then retired to her cabin. The *St. Nicholas* got under way and proceeded up the Potomac.

A mile or two upriver, the outer window of the French lady's cabin opened, and climbing from it to the pilothouse was a resplendent officer, sword and pistol at the ready, in the full uniform of a colonel of the Maryland Zouaves. The elderly passenger suddenly transformed himself into the person of George N. Hollins, late captain USN, now captain, CSN. And most of the young male passengers abruptly descended on the trunks the French lady had brought aboard and disgorged a quantity of arms which they turned upon the officers and crew of *St. Nicholas*. The seizure ended immediately and quietly. Passengers and crew were treated with great courtesy, and the bow of *St. Nicholas* under Hollins was turned toward rebel territory at Coan, where Lewis and the detachment of Tennessee militia and other personnel awaited. Under way again, *St. Nicholas* left the Coan River, reentered the Potomac, and headed upriver in search of USS *Pawnee*. Hollins soon learned that the skipper of a sister gunboat had been killed during an engagement at Mathias Point, and *Pawnee* and other gunboats had gone to Washington for the funeral.

Frustrated, Hollins drove *St. Nicholas* into the Chesapeake and sought compensatory prey. Near the mouth of the Rappahannock, Hollins seized the schooner *Margaret* and used her cargo of coal to refuel *St. Nicholas;* then he captured the brig *Monticello*, laden with 3,500 bags of coffee, and the schooner *Mary Pierce*, loaded with 200 tons of ice. At Fredericksburg *St. Nicholas* was purchased for $15,000 by the Confederate government under court decree and became CSS *Rappahannock;* she was burned in the evacuation of Fredericksburg in April 1862 to prevent capture by Union forces. Hospitals in Richmond in July 1861 welcomed the ice and coffee.[3]

Worries about the prospective movements of Richard Thomas, other audacious rebels, and small vessels that might carry predatory forces nagged at Union authorities in the Potomac and Chesapeake in the first weeks of July following the capture of *St. Nicholas*. Noted one memorandum addressed to the secretary of the navy in Washington: "a man of notoriously bad character . . . has formed a plan for the capture, during the present week, of one of the steamboats plying between Baltimore and the Patuxent River, either by putting his men on board the boat at Baltimore, or at Millstone Landing . . . a position whence more smuggling of men and provisions is carried on than any other place in the Chesapeake waters. Small vessels are constantly plying between that position and the Rappahannock and Coan Rivers, chiefly to the latter, where a Tennessee regiment is posted." On July 9, the captain of USS *Pocohontas* in the Potomac reported that "a pungy had come over from Coan River and landed crews of the three vessels captured by the *St. Nicholas*. The crews proceeded by land to Millstone Landing . . . and the pungy went up the Chesapeake Bay. She was manned by well-armed men, variously estimated from eighteen to thirty. . . . The overland men arrived safely and had taken passage in the steamer *Mary Washington* for Baltimore. . . . The notorious Thomas went up in disguise, the idea of him and the armed party . . . is to capture the next steamer from Baltimore, which will be the *George Weems*."⁴

On July 4, strange characters had been observed circling about *Columbia*, a likely target for Richard Thomas where *Columbia* was lying at Fardy's Shipyard (Federal Hill) in Baltimore. Then the authorities learned that several chartered omnibuses with certain parties had left Baltimore for Fair Haven, and suspicion arose that Thomas had arrived there under disguise, with further depredations in mind. Accordingly, an expedition consisting of Provost Marshall John R. Kenly, Lieutenant Thomas H. Carmichael, John Horner, and a small company of police officers set out in the steamer *Chester* (or possibly a sloop) for Fair Haven. To cover its purpose, the expedition arrested a vacationing barber by the name of Neale Green on the charge of fomenting assault on a Massachusetts regiment passing through Baltimore on April 9, and the entire detachment with Green in tow boarded *Mary Washington* for return to Baltimore.

Shortly after departure, Lieutenant Carmichael, from casual conversation with a number of more talkative passengers, confirmed what he suspected. First, Captain Kirwan and two other officers of *St. Nicholas*, released after capture, were aboard *Mary Washington* enroute to Baltimore and certainly could identify their captors. Second, seven or eight of the men who captured *St. Nicholas* were also aboard *Mary Washington*. Third, Richard Thomas Zarvona himself was on board, bound for Baltimore to effect his next escapade.

When *Mary Washington* cleared Annapolis on her way north, Lieutenant Carmichael directed Captain Mason Locke Weems to dock the vessel at Fort McHenry, now a Union prison in Baltimore Harbor. On hearing of the order, Richard Thomas appeared and demanded to know by what authority Carmichael had diverted the steamer; Carmichael invoked the orders of Colonel Kenly, provost marshall. Immediately, Thomas drew his pistol, called some of his men around him, and threatened Carmichael. Confusion reigned, women screamed and ran about, and some of the men passengers tried to stand between the adversaries and bring calm.

Mary Washington docked at Fort McHenry. General Banks, commanding at the fort, when apprised of the situation, ordered a company of infantry to board the boat and arrested all of the men identified by Carmichael, Kirwan, and other passengers—all, that is, except Colonel Richard Thomas Zarvona. He had vanished into thin air.

Some conjectured that he had jumped overboard. But others vouchsafed that he would have been seen if he had made the attempt. For an hour and a half the soldiers searched *Mary Washington* from mast to keel, stem to stern.

Then they found him. He had been fitted into a bureau or dresser in the ladies' cabin by some of the more "afflicted" among the female passengers. The bottoms of the drawers had been removed to provide space, but the little "lady" colonel, cramped and drenched with perspiration, made a sad spectacle as he was dragged off to prison.[5]

Another man on board *Mary Washington* that day added to the dismay and confusion, and undoubtedly the distress, of Captain Mason Locke Weems. The man was none other than his protégé, James Russell Gourley. There are two accounts of his role in the action involving Colonel Richard Thomas Zarvona. One account places Gourley on board *Mary Washington* serving under Captain Weems and recalling the incident later as an eye witness: "When Colonel Thomas stepped on board the steamer . . . I, who knew him personally, warned him against remaining on board, telling him he would certainly be recognized and arrested. He laughed my warning to scorn, but when it became whispered about who he was and the boat, according to police orders, was headed for Fort McHenry, he realized his mistake." Gourley observed the armed confrontation between Zarvona and Carmichael; he was present when some frightened ladies betrayed Zarvona and the authorities dragged him from his hiding place in the bureau "as though he was emerging from a Turkish bath." He reported that Zarvona was taken ashore and imprisoned in Fort McHenry.

Another version of Gourley's role came to light more than a half-century later, when newspaper accounts of his death reported that he was much more involved in the activities of Zarvona than his observations on board that day had indicated. According to these reports, Gourley, as a young and ardent Confederate sympathizer, was captivated early on by blockade running and contraband smuggling. He entered enthusiastically into Zarvona's wild scheme, along with some 20 other young men from southern Maryland, to capture the Union gunboat. Gourley was a member of the party that captured *St. Nicholas*. According to these reports, all of the men were subsequently captured, including Zarvona, who tried to conceal himself on a Baltimore-bound steamboat. Also, according to the report, Gourley himself was held prisoner at Fort McHenry for a brief time, although the list of prisoners at Fort McHenry in 1861 does not include his name. He may have been held at another of several Baltimore detention centers administered by the military authorities at Fort McHenry.

If indeed James Russell Gourley was aboard *Mary Washington*—or perhaps boarded it with Zarvona's group at Fair Haven—he confronted Mason Locke Weems with a painful dilemma. The latter was no actor, and playing a role of knowing but not knowing must have taxed his skills. Buffeted by police, the military, a potential battle between decks, sudden orders to Fort McHenry, boarding by the infantry, a search for a flamboyant pirate who had disappeared, and the near destruction of his boat, he had also to dissemble somehow. With the knowledge that Gourley knew Zarvona and of his recent escapade with *St. Nicholas*—enough to warn him—and, indeed, if Gourley came on board with Zarvona's men, who were readily recognized, then Weems faced the task of hiding both his knowledge and his affection for the boy, a difficult role even for a stoical captain.[6]

At the time of the *Mary Washington* incident the Weems boats were regarded with particular suspicion. In a report dated July 3, 1861, to Gideon Welles, secretary of the navy, Commander S. C. Rowan, senior officer in the Potomac, wrote, "It is reported that the steamers, *Patuxent, Planter,* and *Mary Washington* are in the habit of carrying numbers of men from Baltimore and landing them at some point on the Patuxent from whence they cross to the Potomac and so enter Virginia."[7] His words barely reached the secretary when *Mary Washington* made her spectacular journey from Fair Haven to Baltimore. Nevertheless, the boats were not yet under the absolute jurisdiction of USQMD, although the action was imminent.

After the incident, exchanges between army authorities and Captain Mason L. Weems were politely stilted. On July 15, the provost marshall decided to search *George Weems* before she was allowed to sail.[8] On July 18, it was reported that "*Mary Washington* and *George Weems* have been inhibited from making any more trips to the Patuxent River until it shall please General Banks to remove the inhibition." The steamers were charged with "giving aid and comfort to the enemy by landing supplies of men and munitions to St. Mary's County which are transported across the county to the Potomac and then boated over to Virginia at night."[9] On August 17 General Dix demanded that Captain Weems send up the witnesses (one of whom was the cook) "in regard to the secreted arms" to Fort McHenry. And, finally, on August 28, the provost marshall laid down specific restrictions on freight and baggage and passengers allowed to travel on the Weems boats.[10] At this point, the Weems steamers were in the process of seizure by USQMD and rapidly lost control of their own management.

George Weems steamed about the Bay on supply and transport missions for most of the war, interrupted by her frequent need for repairs. She spent most of June through December 1861 undergoing boiler repairs by Charles Reeder, Jr.; March through July 1862, in engine repairs; April through May 1863, having boiler repairs repeated; July through December 1863, in boiler renovation; and June through August 1864, in further major boiler repairs.[11] That *George Weems,* a new boat, required extensive and exceptionally frequent boiler work could not be denied. In fact, she spent as much time in the repair yard as she did under way during the war years. The conclusion could be reached that rough handling and hard running by Union forces led to her misfortunes; damage and injury were excessive from inexperienced crews, as many steamboat owners learned. Another hypothesis could be advanced: that Southern sympathizers in the Weems crew saw to it that she sailed as little as possible for her Yankee managers (Appendix C).

However, as a sample of the profits from government charter, in one eight-month period, total repairs (including boiler repairs) on *George Weems* amounted to less than $2,000. In contrast, in the same period, her net earnings were $28,058.78. The charter rates applied whether she sailed or not. During the same period, the combined net earnings of *George Weems* and *Planter* were $43,298. Surprising, indeed, that *Planter* did not enjoy some arranged yard time during the same period! She was much too occupied for the luxury.[12]

Suspicions about *George Weems* could be raised by the fact that neither before nor after the war did she suffer from such boiler irregularities. Impatience with her behavior by USQMD prompted the dispatch of a letter dated April 10, 1863, which peremptorily required the Weems brothers to take possession of their boat forthwith.[13]

Such releases from contract were inevitably short-lived. In spite of her wartime infirmities, *George Weems* managed to be the conveyor of supplies in late 1864 and early 1865 up the James River to City Point at the mouth of the Appomattox River; the occasion was the seige of Petersburg.

In early 1862 *Patuxent* found herself in operations against rebel positions on Roanoke Island in Croatan Sound. These operations were part of the efforts of the North Atlantic Squadron to blockade Pamlico and Albemarle Sounds and of the campaigns of Generals Burnside and Foster to wrest the region from the hold of Confederate forces. In January and February 1862, a prime objective of the Union forces was Roanoke Island, resting astride the channels connecting Albemarle and Pamlico Sounds and a key, therefore, to access from the South to Norfolk and Hampton Roads. In January *Patuxent* served as a tug to tow vessels through the swash (narrow channel between the sandbars) near Hatteras and to pull a few off the bars when they grounded.

Reconnoitering in the vicinity of Nags Head and Roanoke Island on February 6 revealed the presence of 15 Confederate steamers and 10 sailing vessels, in the Roanoke Marshes and in Croatan Sound, protected by piling and sunken vessels. With these, the Confederates could slip northward, outflanking the Union blockading force and threatening the southern approach to Norfolk. Accordingly, the decision was made to launch an assault on Weir's Point, the northernmost promontory of Roanoke Island, above the positions of the Confederate forces and ships.

The attack began at 3:00 P.M., February 7, led by *Patuxent* and *Union* and followed by other troop-laden transports, including *Pilot Boy*, well known on the upper Chesapeake, towing a large number of boats and a pontoon bridge. The assault beginning at Ashby Harbor and driving north to Weir's Point sent the rebel defenders reeling to the northern tip of Roanoke Island, where they were pursued, cornered, and captured.[14]

One month later, *Patuxent*, along with *Pilot Boy* and *Alice C. Price*,[15] were dispatched to the Neuse River, which emptied into Pamlico Sound. On March 13, 1862, the same steamers, with launches and boats in tow, entered a creek on the south shore near the mouth of the river and began an assault against Confederate forces there. The beachhead was secured within a day.[16]

Patuxent's subsequent movements remained undocumented. USQMD found her useful enough, however, to buy her outright, in Philadelphia on July 1, 1864, for $16,000. At the end of hostilities, she was auctioned off, bought by S. & J. Flanagan of Baltimore for $3,200, redocumented as *Cumberland* on April 12, 1866, and abandoned in 1868. On that July 1, 1864, when she became the property of the government, *Patuxent* bid farewell to the men of Weems who had nurtured her and to the haunts of the river whose name she bore (Appendix A).

Planter began rigorous duties as a troop transport in 1862 and 1863 on runs from Baltimore to the James River and from Hampton Roads up the James River to the line of battle.[17] At one point, she carried passengers on the Potomac to Washington and at another time ferried prisoners of war to camps near Annapolis and Baltimore and wounded to hospitals. For a time, she ran up to Whitehouse Landing on the Pamunkey as a transport.

But *Planter* earned a place in history and in the affections of the Union army as "Grant's Apothecary Shop." She became a floating medical supply house, moving up the James River to replenish field hospitals and medical units as she went. In January 1865, under Captain Norris and Dr. Brinton, she reached a point about a mile above City Point, where she tied up to a pontoon bridge. On the opposite bank, part of the Bermuda Hundreds, were General Butler and the army of the James, encamped after the failure of their advance on Richmond. Rebel forces repeatedly attempted to destroy the pontoon bridge but were driven off by Union gunboats. There *Planter* remained until April 9, 1865, the date of surrender at Appomattox.[18]

During the war years, the landings along the Patuxent saw little of the Weems steamboats. Sporadic service, a month at a time, occurred when the government released a boat from contract. Planters and merchants adjusted to the loss with some difficulty. Over the years, the Weems boats had exercised a virtual monopoly on the Patuxent, and they did not brook any attempt to break it. In 1860, a fledgling Patuxent Steam Express Company had set out to challenge Weems, acquired the old steamer *Express* (built in 1841), and began calling at Patuxent landings. The enterprise had been short-lived; the Weems boats had squeezed out the so-called Opposition Line, and *Express* had conveniently burned at her wharf in Baltimore.[19]

But along the Patuxent, the landings saw the Weems boats infrequently during the war. When, near the end of the war, a few other steamers appeared on the river, they were met not with resentment and fierce opposition by Weems but by readiness to allow them to use landings and to approach customers, with the hope that the Patuxent trade could be revived. In 1864, for a very brief period, *Phoenix* visited the Patuxent.[20] On January 1, 1865, *Commerce*, a new 188-ton propeller-driven steamer built in Wilmington, Delaware, advertised that she would commence service from Light Street to Fair Haven, Plumb [*sic*] Point, and Patuxent landings to Bristol on the 21st; the advertisement was repeated only in March. Weems had no way of countering the service.[21] But the tenure of *Commerce*, like that of *Express*, was short-lived. For a brief time after hostilities ended and before the Weems line could resume its stance on the Patuxent, *Juniata* of the D. G. Tubman Company ran a weekly schedule to Hills Landing.[22]

The most sensational entry on the Patuxent in the war years was that of *Harriet Deford*.[23] Just launched (October 5, 1864), a handsome boat—fast, propeller driven—she captured the fancy of residents from Fair Haven to Hills Landing. The Weems brothers welcomed her with an invitation to call at Fair Haven and their usual landings on the river. She arrived in late October 1864, advertising, "For Patuxent River, stopping at Fair Haven and all the landings . . . leave wharf foot of South Street every Friday morning at 6 oclock, permission having been obtained to land at all Weems's wharves . . . Pardon & White."[24]

She was a small but graceful boat and excited the interest not only of river residents but also of the Confederate underground, which maintained a well-established channel of communication across the Patuxent, through St. Mary's County, to the Potomac.[25]

Arriving in Calvert County on April 3, 1865 was Captain Thaddeus Fitzhugh and a band of some 27 Confederate guerillas, late members of Mosby's band in the valley of Virginia. With an appraising eye, Captain Fitzhugh targeted *Harriet Deford*, in spite of the drab paint that had been applied to disguise her. On the night of April 4, 1865, he moved his men to the woody groves of Fair Haven, where *Harriet Deford* lay overnight on her runs in and out of the Patuxent. At 2:00 A.M., he stormed aboard with his troops and seized the boat. In the dead of night, it was an easy capture. He put ashore the mate and captain—first relieving the latter of his wallet—and all the white passengers. Retained as captives were the engineer, firemen, and some 60 Negroes, including many children. *Harriet Deford*, with Fitzhugh in command, steamed off down the Bay as a prize of war. On the way she plundered *St. Mary's*, a schooner.

A report of the steamer's capture sent to the secretary of the navy by Commodore T. A. Dornin in Baltimore resulted in telegrams sent regionally ordering a search for *Harriet Deford*. Foxhall A. Parker, commanding the Potomac Flotilla, reported that he had dispatched 10 patrol vessels in pursuit and followed his report with a general order to trap or sink *Harriet Deford*.

The following day, April 6, 1865, a telegram from Commander Parker announced that the steamer had been located by several gunboats in Indian Creek, Virginia, and vowed "that she will be recaptured or destroyed." He added to his assault force several ships, each drawing less water than *Harriet Deford*. He warned that desperate men aboard *Harriet Deford* might attempt to carry a gunboat by boarding and thus escape. On the envelope of the telegram to Acting Volunteer Lieutenant Commander Edward Hooker, commanding the First Division of the Potomac Flotilla (in charge of the assault), he added a note: "I have just learned that the *Deford* is in Diamond (Dimer's) Creek. I have this from the engineer of the *Harriet Deford*, who says that the vessel is partially destroyed. Be careful that you are not deceived with regard to their situation and recapture or destroy her without delay."

On April 7, Commander Parker in gunboats *Coeur de Lion* and *Heliotrope* met *Jacob Bell* and took aboard Simon Brown and James Hudson, two of the crew of *Harriet Deford*, who informed him that *Harriet Deford* was indeed in Dimer's Creek. He proceeded with his gunboats inside the creek and found the wreck of the captured steamer. She had been set on fire by the rebels and "was still burning when we boarded." The gunboats fired into her machinery and effectively destroyed the vessel. He reported that the 60 or so Negroes captured with *Harriet Deford* had been taken to Kilmarnock, Virginia, and sold at auction on April 6, 1865. He ended his report with the observation that "there were rebels around who could be seized as hostages for those Negroes."[26] Officially the war ended on April 9, 1865, only a day or so after the devastation aboard *Harriet Deford*.

During the long four years, the Weems brothers perforce had endured the sacrifice of their boats to government service. In 1864, they had decided to try a new venture to outflank the government and maintain some minimal service on the Patuxent. In effect, they set about to build a new boat.

She had been launched in April 1864, a much larger boat than *George Weems*, longer, heavier (more than 900 tons), with greater capacity for passengers and freight.[27] The design on her huge paddlebox was remarkably similar to that of *Mary Washington*. But the bust carved in the oval frame on each side was notably buxom, attributable to the person for whom she was undoubtedly named. Beneath the carving was the vessel's name; *Matilda* (Appendix A). Mason Locke Weems had named the steamer for his wife, Matilda Sparrow, whom he had married in 1844. Their lives had been saddened by the childhood deaths of four of their six children, including all three sons in whom the hopes of Mason L. for shipmasters had rested. Matilda had died on September 26, 1861, leaving him with two surviving daughters and a void that seemed impossible to fill (Appendix E).[28]

Hardly had *Matilda* cleared the launching ways when USQMD seized her on charter at $500 per day and dispatched her as a transport to the James River. Just before the enforced charter, Mason L. had advertised her widely for an excursion to Fair Haven, but the government forced its cancellation, the bitter protestation of Weems notwithstanding.[29]

Spring 1865 touched the land with mortal sorrow. A breath of life only deepened the tragedy of death. The tenderness of new beginnings shuddered before the vastness of destruction and the chaos of a society rent by the tortures of war.

The Weems family began the task of rebuilding its future. Scarcely had their sights been set when still another tragedy occurred. On July 26, 1865, George W., the junior of the brothers, died.[30] Corn merchant, commission merchant, and part-time steamboat master, he had been the namesake of the revered patriarch, had stood by him at Fair Haven in his declining years, and had labored with his older brothers through the decades of painful growth and disappointment. Mason L. and Theodore faced a perplexing world, with only each other for counsel.

The difficult days of reconstruction struck hard at tidewater Maryland and Virginia. Abolition of slavery meant an abrupt and dramatic change in economic and social patterns that had been the underpinning of life in the region for generations. Blacks left the fields in multitudes, beckoned by the prospects of employment in urban industry. White owners abandoned their farms when the lack of labor or its sudden cost drove them from their livelihood. Plantations were sold off into smaller tracts. And the rural landscape changed in appearance, as the fields of labor-intensive tobacco gave way step-by-step to grain and truck farming or to the dreariness of abandonment.

Population shifts after the war marked the decline of the rural regions of the Patuxent, the Potomac, and the Rappahannock. In Maryland, the counties bordering the Patuxent and the Potomac suffered a 3 percent decline in population (89,404 to 86,142) from 1860 to 1870. In Virginia, the drop in inhabitants in the Northern Neck and counties along the south shore of the Rappahannock (79,480 to 71,013) was an even more startling 10 percent. In harsh contrast, Baltimore City and County (238,655 to 330,741) rose 38 percent in population (Baltimore City alone 25 percent). Norfolk in 1870 stood at 19,229; it had taken 20 years for the population to double.[31]

The shift from tobacco to other crops was far reaching in Maryland. It was necessitated by shortage of labor, land division, and soil depletion. Growing the weed was abandoned altogether on the Eastern Shore. On the Western Shore, harvests dropped dramatically from 41,029 hogsheads in 1846 and 51,247 in 1860 (the largest ever produced in Maryland) to 25,479 in 1865. For a few years, the use of cigarette-making machines and the growing of prime crops to feed them brought some improvement, but the volume dropped to little more than 20,000 hogsheads by the 1880s and remained at that level. The tobacco-raising counties of Virginia had similar experiences.[32]

Diversification to truck farming, fruit growing, corn and wheat production, and livestock raising required experimentation, capital investment, and ready access to markets. Such shifts in agriculture tightened the link between the city and the countryside. For most of tidewater Maryland and Virginia, the link was the steamboat.

Watermen on the Chesapeake were a stubborn lot. Many farmed as best they could in the months of planting and harvest, in spite of the ravages of armies moving about, and they oystered or fished or clammed, depending on the seasons, in defiance of Union patrol boats that questioned their activities and their motives. Some did slip past the blockade and, in larger boats, smuggle contraband through the lines. But, for the most part, they harvested from the Bay unmolested by the war, and they looked toward a steady growth in business with the hungry cities. Claims of proprietary rights over oyster beds, rivalry between Marylanders and Virginians, hatred between those who tonged and those who dredged flared up into open warfare, exacerbated by the growing demand for oysters, craved wherever they could be shipped. Fishermen, too, in spite of the hard life they—like the oystermen—led, looked forward to prosperity. Many watermen still brought their fish and oysters in their own boats or in buy-boats to the city for sale to commission merchants, but just as many shipped by steamboat. The packing houses along the shores of Tidewater, thriving on the watermen's labors, iced their products in tins, crates, and barrels and packed them off to Baltimore by steamer. The war had disrupted the steamers, and the watermen used their own sailboats; but they awaited the return of the steamers with their dependability and overnight delivery of perishable products to the markets in Baltimore.

After 1865 Baltimore darkened its skies with the smoke of smelters, mills, shipyards, chemical plants, and belching furnaces. Its streets ran with sewage, and its harbor reeked with offal. Along the narrow streets, row after row of small houses were jammed together in monotonous mediocrity to shelter the laborers and skilled workmen who poured into the city in ever-increasing numbers. Only the well-to-do could escape the stench by establishing residence in the surrounding suburbs. In the aftermath of the Civil War, once the pangs of adjustment wore off, Baltimore exploded with industrial energy. It reached outward for its markets, to overseas commerce (and the ships flocked to its harbor), and to trade with the farmers, merchants, watermen, and small manufacturers of Maryland and Virginia.

Norfolk did not fare as well. Given the factors that would indicate a strong economic potential, the city should have prospered. George Alfred Townsend, the celebrated Civil War correspondent who used the pen name of GATH, summed up the prospects for Norfolk a few years after the war ended.

Will Norfolk become a great city? . . . Norfolk has the best harbor in the South and some think the best in the country. . . . Measuring by straight lines, Norfolk is twenty miles nearer Chicago than is New York. New York is further from Cairo than Norfolk by 150 miles . . . further from St. Louis than Norfolk by 80 miles . . . further from Louisville by 120 miles . . . further from Atlanta by 250 miles . . . Hampton Roads is to Norfolk what the Lower Bay is to New York. . . . The commercial life of Norfolk has hitherto been of no consequence except by the incidental associations of a navy yard and a roadstead. . . . Prior to the war, in Madison's administration, Norfolk dealt a great deal with the West Indies. As a naval station Norfolk has been famous from earliest times. . . . Norfolk might have been Baltimore in the race for commercial prominence had her merchants been enterprising and had the state of Virginia not encouraged Richmond to the prejudice of Norfolk. It was not until three years before the War of the Rebellion that the best of Chesapeake seaports was connected with the West by rail. It has, therefore, had no opportunity, compared with New York and Baltimore, to derive advantage from the grain, sugar, livestock, and cotton trade of the West.[33]

Both Baltimore and Norfolk shared in a basic dilemma. The problem centered on the fact that in the postwar period neither Maryland nor

Virginia seemed destined to become an industrial giant; the focus had moved northward and westward. Although Baltimore bustled with commercial activity, the city could claim no dominant industry, and it yielded across the board to the weight of growth in the key steel, coal, copper, and chemical industries in other areas. Norfolk's predicament was similar but exacerbated by its isolation from the mainstream of commerce. Both Maryland and Virginia suffered, too, from the fact that, crop diversity notwithstanding, neither could lay claim to contributing heavily to the agricultural needs of the nation; the breadbasket, the corn and wheat production centers, had moved to the Middle West.[34] The development of a regional economy, sustained by the potential of a rich Tidewater country, newly emerging entrepreneurial venturing, and the weight of Baltimore as a burgeoning port and a locus for a wide spectrum of industrial growth, from canning to shipbuilding, from clothing manufacturing to machine construction, became a cumulative process of adjustment.

Paradoxically, the years of depression and evolution that beset tidewater Maryland and Virginia in the postwar period tended to favor the steamboats. Not that getting started again was not difficult for the steamboat lines—most of the owners found their vessels nearly wrecked by the government agents who had seized and operated them. Not that getting back in business was not complex and disappointing—steamboat operators discovered that their clients were not the same, the trade had vanished or shifted, new markets had to be created, new landings visited, new cargoes hauled, new schedules accommodated, new needs met. And yet, in spite of these obstacles, the steamboat became the very means by which recovery could occur. In the absence of all-weather roads for long-distance hauling, of railroads (the Western Shore from Annapolis south had virtually none, and the Eastern Shore had a skeleton system but little service along the tributaries and the Bay itself), and of rapid, efficient, and scheduled transport by sailing craft, the steamboat even more than ever was the economic lifeline connecting Tidewater with the city, and the city with its markets in the countryside. Tidewater itself would have stagnated without the steamboat; the commercial life of the city would have moved slowly without its markets in Tidewater.

From 1865 to 1870, the steamboats operating out of Baltimore jumped from a low of 20 at the end of the war to nearly double that number. Some of the steamers seized by the government returned to their prewar haunts. But many others appeared on the scene. Around the sweeping bend of the Sassafras River, bound for Georgetown and Fredericktown, came *Cyrus P. Smith* and *Van Corlaer the Trumpeter* (happily known as *Trumpeter*). The latter, to be renamed *Kitty Knight* in later years for the gallant lass who, in the War of 1812 extinguished the flames of the British at Georgetown as fast as they ignited them, was destined for a long and colorful history on the Bay. *Balloon*, newly purchased from the auction of government vessels, ran up the Miles River to St. Michaels and Miles River Ferry near the head of navigation.

Wilson Small, carrying the name of an obscure but highly competent manufacturer of walking beam engines, ran the tortuous Choptank all the way to Denton, until she met with disaster and sank in August 1867. Screw-propelled vessels went through the locks of the narrow Chesapeake and Delaware Canal to the Delaware River and to Wilmington and Philadelphia—steamboats like *W. Whilldin* and *Florence Franklin.* Steamboats probed the rivers and creeks of Pocomoke Sound; *Massachusetts* went up the Pocomoke River to Snow Hill, called at Crisfield, and ventured into Onancock Creek. The Eastern Shore Steamboat Company sent *Sue* and *Maggie* on a scheduled route to the same landings. From Baltimore the Powhatan Steamboat Company ran boats up the York River; the Maryland Steamboat Company operated boats along the Western Shore from Annapolis and the West River to the Piankatank and Great Wicomico Rivers; and the Chester River Steamboat Company ran *Chester* and *George Law* up the splendid expanse of river to Chestertown. The *Maggie Saffell,* commanded by Captain Joseph White, attempted a route to Fredericksburg from Baltimore. Excursions gained in popularity; *Samuel J. Pentz* and *Champion* carried teeming hordes to Holly Grove (Sparrows Point near the mouth of the Patapsco).

Among the more prestigious, even glamorous, steamboats were the packets leaving Baltimore on widely advertised schedules for Washington and the Potomac River. The end of hostilities in 1865 saw the emergence of three steamboat lines serving the landings along the river and Alexandria, Georgetown, and Washington. The Potomac Transportation Line, controlled by Thomas Clyde, operated the *C. Vanderbilt,* a 205-foot vessel of some luxury, the *W. Whilldin* an 186-foot, propeller-driven steamer also useful in the Chesapeake and Delaware Canal, and the 172-foot *Express* (predator on the Patuxent and harbinger of forthcoming disaster). Another line, the Washington, Alexandria, and Georgetown Steam Navigation Company, ran *Columbia* and *Diamond State.* Somewhat later appeared the People's Accommodation Steamboat Company with *Isaac P. Smith.* Along the river, planters, merchants, villages, towns, and the steamboat companies themselves erected wharves where the steamers could dock. Washington, which no one up until then seriously considered to be a commercial port, became the hub of a steamboat trade, thriving as the postwar economy sloughed off its doldrums and adjusted to the demands of a new era.

The packets to Norfolk, rebuilding the broken link between North and South as soon as hostilities ceased, carried with them a special aura. Their saloons and public rooms were intended to impress passengers with Old World elegance, their dining rooms boasted a lavish cuisine unsurpassed by the finest hotels, and their schedules were followed with pride and precision. The Leary Line operated *George Leary* and *James T. Brady* from Baltimore to Norfolk with connections aboard *City Point* and *Dictator* for Richmond. At the same time, the New Peoples Line ran *Ellie Knight* directly between Richmond and Baltimore. But the historic Old Bay Line (Baltimore Steam Packet Company) made the Baltimore-

Norfolk route famous with its celebrated overnight packets, the standard of luxury on the Bay. *Adelaide, Georgeana, Louisiana,* and *Thomas A. Morgan,* with a pageant of steamers to follow, reigned as queens of the Bay.

Norfolk itself, in February 1867, spawned the Old Dominion Steamship Company, created from the ashes of the disbanded Atlantic Coast Mail Steamship Company, which had maintained service between New York, Norfolk, and Richmond. In June 1867, the new company absorbed the New York and Virginia Steamship Company, competitor for the Norfolk trade. The Old Dominion operated in three dimensions. A major thrust was coastal trade with the New York market. A second and major endeavor developed with the opening of the postwar Tidewater to the movement of truck farming products, livestock, fish, and oysters to Norfolk for transshipment to New York. Finally, a third but viable activity encompassed steamboat service to Richmond and the James River, to Mobjack Bay and the York River, to the Eastern Shore, and to other communities in Tidewater or below Norfolk, accessible only by water. Many of the early steamers, like *Hatteras, Albemarle, Niagara, Saratoga, Yazoo,* and *Creole*—large and commodious—started their voyages in Richmond or other landings, called at Norfolk, but then became oceangoing ships, which they were, for the coastal journey to New York.[35] As time went on, small steamers began to serve as feeders, connecting the Tidewater country with transshipment docks in Norfolk. The Old Dominion, in spite of its reverses in the 1870s, contributed immeasurably to the emergence of Norfolk as a major port for tidewater Virginia in the postwar years.[36]

As the years of reconstruction moved along, often haltingly and painfully, the Chesapeake and its tributaries became even more than ever the water highways for the region's commerce. It seemed that on the channels leading in or out of Baltimore or of Norfolk, the hour was rare on a given day when the smudge from a steamboat stack could not be seen.

There was something about a steamboat that smacked of a time before the war, of an age of gentility, and days of leisure and quiet abandon. Tidewater lived aboard the steamboats of the Chesapeake. In the years after the Civil War the boats came to symbolize a way of life—elegant, pretentious, self-indulgent, class conscious, but exquisitely attuned to the beauties and vagaries of the Chesapeake.

In the spring of 1865, Mason Locke Weems and his brother Theodore began the task of rebuilding the line to the Patuxent. One by one, USQMD released the steamers: *George Weems* on March 31, *Mary Washington* on April 1, *Matilda* on May 11, and *Planter* on June 12.[37] With scant refurbishing or repairs, they were ushered into service, any renovating relegated to off-season shipyard time. Mason Locke Weems was a man in a hurry, impatient over years lost to the war, stirred by the prospects of acting quickly in the moving tide of reconstruction.

Several problems confronted him. The first and most immediate was the slow pace of recovery on the Patuxent. Shattered by abolition and the migration of labor northward as well as the collapse of a plantation and tobacco economy, southern Maryland nearly stagnated in the summer and fall of 1865. Related to the condition of economic somnolence was a second problem for Weems: what to do with four steamboats that represented his livelihood and stake in the future. In spite of the abuse the boats had suffered at the hands of the army, the profits that had accrued from USQMD contracts were substantial. How to continue profiting by judicious investment and skillful management of the four steamboats became his consuming preoccupation.

All consuming, too, had been his lifelong obsession with the Rappahannock River. He burned with the memories of his own misfortunes and the troubles his father had encountered at the hands of competitors on that river, and he bridled at the thought that the pioneering of his father with *Patuxent* on the Rappahannock had not endured through the years. He noted with keen satisfaction, in the spring of 1865, that the disruption of war had left the Rappahannock without any steamboat service whatsoever.

Accordingly, in May, on the release of *Matilda* from government charter, he advertised the start of service from Baltimore to Fredericksburg, with calls at the Rappahannock wharves served long ago by *Patuxent*. When *Matilda* blew her whistle for Irvington in Carter's Creek and stirred up the mud at Urbanna, Mason L. savored each moment. Returning to the Rappahannock and to Fredericksburg marked a day of triumph after an absence of nearly 18 years.

Almost immediately his exuberance was tempered by sobering rumor. The Baltimore and Susquehanna Steam Company (parent company of the Baltimore and Susquehanna Steamboat Company and the Baltimore and Susquehanna Towing Company), according to the intelligence bandied about, was contemplating putting a steamer on the Rappahannock route. This company, incorporated in 1850, was owned principally by Jacob Tome (Robert Taylor and William S. Gittings, associates), its purposes being the navigation of the Chesapeake Bay.[38]

According to the information, Jacob Tome intended to introduce his steamer *Wenonah* to the Rappahannock. This vessel, completed in 1864 for the use of Tome's towing company in hauling stones on the upper Bay, had been converted into a transport while in wartime government service. It had carried troops from Baltimore to Cape Hatteras. Then in June 1864 *Wenonah* had appeared with other transports at White House on the Pamunkey River. There, at the site of McClellan's old headquarters before the battle of Cold Harbor in the Peninsula campaigns, the vessels with *Wenonah* among them were discharging troops and supplies in mid-1864 for Grant's drive to force Lee to Richmond and to win the war by attrition. At the end of the war, *Wenonah*, equipped as a transport, could be readily converted for passenger and freight service on the Rappahannock (Appendix A.)

Mason L. decided to approach Tome directly. At age 55, only a few years older than Mason L., Jacob Tome (or *Thom* in the original family spelling) bore a formidable reputation. He was known as a self-made man, pulling himself from a humble German background in York, Pennsylvania, to part ownership of a lumber business, succeeded by partnership in a vast lumber company comprising 50,000 or more acres of timber in Pennsylvania and Michigan, large holdings in grain and agricultural trade in Port Deposit on the Susquehanna, directorship in several railroads and the Susquehanna and Tidewater Canal Company, principal ownership of several banks and financial institutions, and holder of principal ownership in the Baltimore and Susquehanna Steam Company, operator of *Portsmouth* plying between Baltimore and Port Deposit, and later purchaser of *Lancaster* and *Juniata*. During the war, he had given distinguished service as a member of the Maryland legislature and adviser to the state on finance. Largely unknown was his philanthropy—to the Episcopal Church and its charitable undertakings and to the Tome Institute, a private school for boys, founded on the bluff high above the town of Port Deposit on the Susquehanna.[39]

To his surprise, when Mason L. Weems met Jacob Tome, he discovered a humble man—gray bearded, very small, square jawed, gentle eyed—who listened attentively to a narration of the Weems primordial interest in the Rappahannock. In 1865, Tome's empire spread over several states and in innumerable and vastly profitable undertakings. A monopoly on the Rappahannock—far from his interests on the upper Bay—scarcely whet his appetite.

With a decided bent toward retiring from the Rappahannock, Tome proposed that Weems join him in the formation of a new company to operate vessels on the Rappahannock and suggested that his share be *Wenonah* and Weems's share be *Matilda*. Mason L. demurred, offering instead a price for a half-share of *Wenonah* and the use of *Matilda* under the name of the company to supplement *Wenonah* as the trade on the river required. Recognizing that Tome's interest focused on the Susquehanna rather than the Rappahannock, he advanced another stipulation: that he be given the option of purchasing the share of Jacob Tome (and that of any other shareholder who might enter the corporation) and thus of gaining sole ownership of the new company. To these rather unusual demands—under the circumstances of his disinclination to pursue the Rappahannock trade—Tome acceded.

The new company, incorporated in 1866 under the laws of Virginia,[40] was called the Baltimore and Virginia Steamship Company. Its prime owners were Mason L. Weems and Jacob Tome (Alexander K. Phillips, John S. Gittings, Robert A. Taylor, George H. Williams, Joseph James Taylor, and James S. Murphy, associates, two of whom were associated with the Baltimore and Susquehanna Steam Company). Its legal object was the navigation of the Rappahannock River and the Chesapeake Bay. Even before the act of incorporation was passed, *Wenonah*, under joint ownership, began her runs from South Street Wharf in Baltimore to the Rappahannock under the popular and advertised name of the Fredericksburg Line. Later, when *Matilda* was ushered on the route, the name of the same line covered her sailings. For limited purposes on the Rappahannock, it seemed that Tome and Weems were indistinguishable.

Mason Locke Weems vowed then and there, with the arrival of *Wenonah* at Fredericksburg followed by *Matilda*, that as long as Weems steamers survived, there would always be Weems boats on the Rappahannock. Never again would he capitulate to competition. He began the task of buying out the half-interest of Jacob Tome in the Baltimore and Virginia Steamship Company. By February 15, 1869, he was able to state—quite unofficially—that although he had not completed the liquidation of Jacob Tome's share, he held control of the company. In a few years, he expected to have complete ownership.[41] The Fredericksburg Line, or the Baltimore and Fredericksburg Line, as he now called it (the name had no legal significance without an act of incorporation), was his to run, and he intended to keep it that way.

On the Patuxent, steamers *Planter, George Weems,* and *Mary Washington* turned in a consistent profit. In 1868, for example, *Planter* made an impressive 69 trips and earned $12,172.69, not including $1,308.69 spent in recoppering the bottom, $666.66 taken from the profits by Mason L. Weems, and certain other payments to merchants. Her net profits for the year totaled $11,505.16. In 1869, she made an astonishing 86 trips to the Patuxent and netted $17,431.70, half her total estimated worth. During the two years, freight receipts per trip far exceeded passenger ticket sales. For most of the trips, total receipts more than doubled expenditures, which probably included fuel, wages, food for the dining room and crew, wharfage, and some underway maintenance. *Planter* faithfully earned her keep and filled the coffers of the Weems brothers (Appendix C).

George Weems was less successful than *Planter.* In 1868, for example, she netted $9,001.11 in 28 trips to the Patuxent and 13 charters. In 1869, she earned only $2,944.19 for 10 regular trips and 33 charter excursions. The fees charged various organizations, from the Pocohontas Tribe and the Waiters Association and the Iron Molders to various Masonic lodges, Catholic groups, and other church and civil clubs, varied from $150 to $300, depending on the length of the trip. Of the three boats serving the Patuxent route, *George Weems* spent the most time on charter.

Mary Washington, like *Planter,* earned her way by calling at the river landings and hauling freight and entertaining passengers. In 1868, for 30 trips she netted $11,825.96, not including $1,412.39 to Charles Reeder for repairs and to other merchants for renovation, as well as $666.67 to the personal account of Mason L. Weems. In 1869, she earned a net total of $11,753.30 for 41 trips to the Patuxent. Like *Planter,* the steamer *Mary Washington* was a workhorse of the fleet.

The newest of the boats, *Matilda,* spent 1868 and 1869 running the Rappahannock between Baltimore and Fredericksburg. Her net profits in 1868 were $15,307.92, but that figure omitted money spent for minor repairs and most particularly some $5,436.31 transferred to Robert A.

Taylor of the Baltimore and Virginia Steamship Company to liquidate his share in that company (except for Jacob Tome no other stockholders held significant ownership). The net figure of $8,340.99 was reduced further to $4,162.17 by payments to Jacob Tome. *Matilda* on the Rappahannock became the means for Mason L. Weems to regain a position of dominance on the river through the purchase of *Wenonah*. Some of the earnings of *Matilda* were derived from her service in carrying the mail and in handling so-called "money packages," pouches between banks and individuals, and country residents and stores in the city, which were carried in the safe in the purser's office. In 1869, *Matilda* earned $10,780.23. On the account sheet an entry "amt. due on joint receipts" increased the net to $13,194.47, probably an addition of the Weems share of net receipts from *Wenonah* (Appendix C).[42]

In all, Mason Locke Weems, with the support of his brother Theodore, took in nearly $27,000 in 1868 and $44,000 in the following year. Many costs, such as wharf maintenance and repairs, overhead, depreciation, and endless expenditures incidental to operating four floating hotels, were undoubtedly not deducted. Nevertheless, in the immediate postwar period, when trade on the Patuxent and the Rappahannock languished, the profits were significant. Each year, following a general trend of growth, brought more incentives and increased the yield. In 1871, Mason L. Weems leased the wharf at Pier 8, Light Street, for the Patuxent route and turned the second story into a headquarters office. He began to use a title for the route, the Weems Transportation Line, and he displayed it in advertising opposite the caption for the other route, the Baltimore and Fredericksburg Line. Neither title had legal significance.

By mid-1870, indications pointed to the need for expansion. Steamboat lines around the Bay were prospering, and the Weems boats were doing well. On both rivers, they remained unchallenged. Their comings and goings in the channels and creeks, their plaintive whistles sounding at the landings, their white and graceful shapes and smoking stacks appearing around the bends were taken as part of the scene, an accepted skein in the pattern of tidewater Maryland and Virginia. Life seemed to surge in the land, and many steamboat owners on the Chesapeake sensed the tide of growth.

At age 56, Mason Locke Weems, comfortably placed in his home at 6 North Carey Street, where he had lived for 12 years, could contemplate his achievements since the retirement of his father with some satisfaction. He had brought the steamboats back from the disasters of the Civil War and built two promising lines—the Patuxent and the Fredericksburg—among the most respected on the Chesapeake. Fair Haven, as a resort for Baltimore vacationers, flourished on Herring Bay. Around Anne Arundel and Calvert Counties, his estates yielded a substantial income. And one daughter, Georgeanna, was married on June 11, 1868, to an upcoming and ambitious young attorney named Henry Williams; they lived in Prince Frederick, county seat of Calvert County, where

Williams was developing a lucrative practice. Mason L. could imagine the pride of his father, George, in these events. The old patriarch had suffered much for what little he had gained. At this point Mason L. could point to the steamboats on the Bay—the cherished dream of George. The old man's defeat on the Rappahannock had been vindicated; the Weems line ran uncontested on the river; and all the sons of George Weems had stood loyally together, holding firm to the traditions of the family and to each other (Appendix E).

One nagging worry was the health of Theodore. At age 50, he suffered from a chronic illness that seemed to drag him down month by month. At Mason L.'s insistence, Theodore had given up skippering any of the boats about the Bay. Until George W. died, Theodore had lived with his younger brother and the latter's daughters, Gustavia and Rachael, in their home at 506 West Fayette Street. Then he had moved in with Mason Locke at 6 North Carey Street, where he had all the care that his older brother and his niece, Matilda Sparrow Weems, could provide.

In the midst of these worries over Theodore, sudden disaster struck in Baltimore Harbor. On the night of Saturday, June 10, 1871, the steamer *George Weems* caught fire and burned to the water's edge on Light Street. The steamer had arrived in Baltimore from the Patuxent River at 2:00 P.M.; the boiler fires had been banked; and only Captain Baden and a clerk, J. Peterson, remained aboard. During the night, the captain inspected the boat. However, an hour or so later, passersby on Light Street saw fire surrounding the boiler of the vessel and licking at the upper woodwork. When the alarm sounded, the captain and clerk barely escaped with their lives by boarding a small boat at the stern; firemen arriving viewed the boat totally enveloped in flames. The stern line of *George Weems* parted, and she drifted alongside *George Law* in the adjoining slip, threatening that boat with destruction. Then the burning vessel drifted back and threatened the adjoining pier structures. Firemen were able to save both the pier and *George Law*, but *George Weems* was totally burned out, leaving only the metal of her engine and boiler standing in the debris. Her worth was estimated at $45,000, some portion of it insured.

She had just been overhauled to begin her summer excursions to Fair Haven. Mason L. announced that she would be replaced on the excursions by *Matilda*. The loss of the steamer freshened once again the memory of the father (and indeed the younger brother) for whom she had been named.

Theodore's condition abruptly deteriorated in the summer of 1871, and he elected to complete his will. Dated July 26, 1871, it bequeathed $300 to his sister, Margaret Jones of Baltimore ($5,000 of his estate to be invested to produce the revenue); $100 to one Alexander Franklin, in token of esteem; $10,000 to Mason Locke Weems; one-half of the remaining estate to Mason Locke Weems in trust for the latter's daughters, Georgeanna Williams and Matilda S. Weems, in equal proportions; the remaining one-half to Gustavia Weems and Rachael Weems, daughters of the late George W. Weems, in equal proportions; and the stipulation that "I direct that as to steamers and other vessel property in which I may be interested at the time of my death . . . said brother Mason L. Weems shall during his lifetime have the whole control, management and direction thereof in every particular.[43]

Theodore Weems died on September 13, 1871. His death was not unexpected, but its effect on his brother was profound. They had been inseparable through the long years. They had shared each other's thoughts, they had wept together through each tragedy, exulted in every triumph, built steamboats together, skippered and managed them together. Every decision they undertook had been made together. Mason L., the oldest of the four brothers, stood alone, with only his daughters to share his loss and his burden.

In the poignancy of the moment, Mason Locke Weems decided to replace the burned boat with a new one to be named *Theodore Weems*. She would be built by William H. Skinner and Sons, thereby carrying on the tradition of building Weems boats in Baltimore.[44] The engine of the old boat, the very heart of *George Weems*, was pulled out of the wreckage and installed in the hull of the replacement. The new boat, resembling in many particulars the vessel she replaced, was somewhat longer, with increased tonnage and draft, but she was designed to do what her predecessor had done—serve the Patuxent River and carry the pleasure-loving crowds to Fair Haven.[45]

From the very start, *Theodore Weems* captivated her excursion-bound passengers with her spacious, airy decks and holiday hospitality. Her hurricane deck, unlike that of most Bay steamboats which terminated just ahead of the pilothouse, swept forward to the very bow, thus affording passengers a huge sun-swept area on the upper deck and an equally large shady and breeze-swept space on the bow of the passenger deck. In a short time, her dining room had won a reputation for the sumptuousness of its fare and the attentiveness of its service. Among Bay steamers, such publicity was enviable.

To mask his grief and loneliness and sense of advancing years, Mason L. turned to the management of his steamboats with consuming intensity. He drove hard, with a fixed determination to end the link with Jacob Tome and to expand the service offered by both the Patuxent and the Baltimore and Fredericksburg lines. In the midst of his preoccupation, he gave his daughter Matilda in marriage to Sydney Hume Forbes on April 15, 1873.[46]

But the single-minded intensity of his work and the endless brooding over the loss of his family contributed to his undoing. Overwrought by events, Mason Locke Weems died on October 15, 1874. His death was attributed to "softening of the brain" (a stroke).[47]

In utter shock were his daughters—bereft of a father on whom they had completely depended—beset by the ownership and management of a steamboat line about which they knew nothing.

CHAPTER 5

Red Ball on the Three Rivers

The end of 1874 almost brought an end to the Weems steamboats on the Chesapeake. With the sudden and unexpected death of Mason Locke Weems in October, effective management of the lines on the Patuxent and Rappahannock virtually disappeared. Mason Locke Weems was not a man to delegate responsibility, and except for Theodore in later years, he kept his own counsel, reached decisions based on his own aspirations, and issued orders and directives. His brain was a vast storehouse of details—a file unavailable to his subordinates and his heirs.

Steamboat schedules were met, operations continued on the Rappahannock and the Patuxent, at Fair Haven, and in Baltimore on a day-to-day basis by the improvisation of wharf agents, steamboat masters, and employees who continued working as they had in the past. But new schedules had to be set for the forthcoming seasons, plans had to be made for Fair Haven, charters had to be arranged, and major decisions had to be reached about pressing issues.

The two sisters, Georgeanna and Matilda, now owners of the steamboat lines, had no training for business, knew very little about their father's activities in the steamboat trade, and stood behind the barrier of the times which generally excluded women from participating in the man's world of transportation and commerce. Furthermore, they were some distance apart in both geography and circumstance. Georgeanna, who had married Henry Williams on June 11, 1868, was now the mother of four children (Appendix E).[1] They lived in Prince Frederick, county seat of Calvert County, where they had built a sumptuous new home and where Henry Williams practiced law with James T. Briscoe.

Born October 9, 1840, at the parsonage of All Saints Church in Calvert County, where his father was the rector, Henry Williams came of old Maryland stock. Educated by private tutors and at Toppings School in Baltimore, Henry read law under the guidance of Charles J. M. Gwins, later attorney general of Maryland. During the Civil War, Henry won election to the House of Delegates and then in 1871, to the State Senate. In 1874, he still served as senator from Calvert County and maintained his law practice in Prince Frederick. His roots in Calvert County ran deep. In 1874, his experience in the business world of Baltimore and with steamboats in particular was nonexistent.

Matilda had married Sydney Hume Forbes on April 15, 1873. On July 18, 1874, almost coinciding with the death of Mason Locke Weems, Matilda's son, Theodore Weems Forbes, was born.[2] Sydney Forbes turned from one line of endeavor to another, not finding a future in any. He seemed to lack both drive and aptitude for business. At the time of Mason Locke's death, Matilda and Sydney were physically in residence in Baltimore at the seat of the Weems business, and Sydney was unhampered by other occupations. They had taken up residence at 6 North Carey Street when her father died. Initially at least, on the shoulders of Sydney Hume Forbes fell the mantle of control over the destinies of five working steamboats, an empire of wharves along the Patuxent and the Rappahannock and in Baltimore, a hotel resort at Fair Haven, and nearly 200 employees from senior captains and agents to the lowliest of deckhands and stokers. Dutifully, Sydney Hume Forbes arrived at the old office of Mason Locke Weems in the upper story of the rather dowdy rat-infested Pier 8, Light Street, and assumed the title of superintendent. It was immediately obvious to him that he was unsuited by interest and temperament to exercise the necessary responsibilities of exclusive management.

The call to Prince Frederick was answered. Henry Williams and Georgeanna cast aside a life in the gentle countryside of Calvert County, for the competitive and tension-filled confusion of commercial Baltimore. In the sedate and class-conscious society of Calvert County, Henry Williams held the respect and admiration of his colleagues and political supporters. He belonged there, and the connotation was an important one in southern Maryland. In departing, he was breaking subtle ties that had bound him to the land of his birth and tradition. Leaving was difficult and painful.

Nevertheless, in early 1875, Henry Williams, Georgeanna, and their children took up residence at 6 Waverley Terrace, Baltimore, and Henry opened an office at 41 St. Paul Street, just up the hill from the Light Street wharves.[3] He set himself up as attorney and agent for the Weems Transportation Line.

The title held important meanings. As attorney, Williams held the key to the finances and legal position of the enterprise and, in particular, to the problems, first, of ending the involvement of Jacob Tome in the Baltimore and Virginia Steamship Company and second, of resolving the ownership questions raised by the terms of the will of Theodore Weems. As agent, in fact principal agent, he became the manager of day-to-day operations.

Particularly significant—and perhaps ironic—was his early dropping of the title Weems Transportation Company. Mason L. had used it to distinguish the Patuxent route from the Baltimore and Fredericksburg Line (his name for the Baltimore and Virginia Steamship Company, inconveniently incorporated in Virginia). For almost a half-century, since George Weems had first experimented with *Surprise*, there had been no special name to identify the steamers or the organization with the name of Weems. Even with Mason L.'s invention of the title, he had not formalized it in any suggestion of ownership. In fact, all documents of ownership, including enrollment certificates for all of the steamboats, simply showed the names of the persons who actually owned the boats, Weems family members or, in some instances, joint shareholders. For now, with the entanglements of the Baltimore and Virginia Steamship Company and other matters confronting him, Williams was content to leave the property in the names of Georgeanna Williams, Matilda S. Forbes, and the estate of Theodore Weems. Ironic was the fact that the name of Weems had never been coupled legally with the line of steamers which the name connoted and was erased at the very time when no one with the last name of Weems owned or controlled it.

With the settling in of Williams, there was a sudden awareness that a new era had arrived for the Weems enterprise. Sydney Hume Forbes remained for a time as nominal superintendent. But total responsibility shifted to the new arrival, and it was clear that Williams was a force to be reckoned with. He was a remarkable individual—highly intelligent, articulate, skilled in encompassing new information and putting it to work efficiently, persuasive, an accomplished diplomat, and a courtly gentleman. He was slight of build, but his presence commanded immediate attention; kindly, quiet-spoken, thoughtful, he missed little of importance. In a remarkably short time, he had learned what he needed to know of the steamboat business and the inner workings of the Weems interests. He had journeyed up and down the Patuxent and the Rappahannock listening to the bleatings and pleadings of farmers and merchants and watermen; he had studied the day-to-day functioning of Fair Haven and its promise as a resort; and he knew by name every employee of the Weems line from captain to clerk to roustabout. About the steamboats and the wharves, there was a renewed sense of confidence. The heritage of George Weems and Mason Locke Weems now rested in capable hands.

Some of Williams's immediate decisions, before he learned the ropes, were disastrous. For example, in June 1875, he advertised in the

Baltimore newspapers that during the summer the steamers *Theodore Weems, Matilda, Wenonah, Planter,* and *Mary Washington* would be available for charter. In sheer consternation, the masters of these vessels demanded to know how the schedules on the Patuxent, the Rappahannock, and Fair Haven routes were to be met if the entire Weems fleet fetched up on charter. Hastily, the advertising was amended.

At the very outset, Williams resolved to use whatever resources he could muster within the Weems estate to liquidate the remaining interest of Jacob Tome in the Baltimore and Virginia Steamship Company. In short order, he succeeded in his endeavor. For $30,000, Jacob Tome transferred to Georgeanna Williams and Matilda S. Forbes *Wenonah* together with other assets of the Baltimore and Virginia Steamship Company,[4] a company that, for all practical purposes, ceased to exist with the transfer of Jacob Tome's interest. With ownership of *Wenonah* came possession of Pier 9, Light Street, home of the so-called Baltimore and Fredericksburg Line; the two lines were now consolidated.

It was the contingency of the estate of Theodore Weems that troubled Williams. It was not that he questioned the rights of Gustavia and Rachael Weems, the nieces of Theodore Weems, to half of their uncle's interest in the steamboat line, but the drain on the company's income to the tune of roughly one-fourth of the yearly profits had no time limit, if the nieces' successors were considered. Settlement, to the exclusion of further rights, meant paying these heirs the equivalent of one-half of Theodore's share in the steamboats and related property, valued at the time of his death. A schedule for such a settlement, drawn up and agreed to, meant allocation of earnings over an extended period, thereby precluding incorporation (with the two sisters and their husbands as prime owners) until the liquidation was complete—a continuing and nagging matter for Williams.

As a new decade approached, Williams decided to promote Fair Haven as a resort. There were good reasons for doing so. In the late 1870s resorts and amusement parks had caught the fancy of the American public. The notion had started much earlier in Europe, but in the United States by the 1850s Coney Island (Konijn Eiland or "Rabbit Island" as known by the Dutch settlers) had its bathhouses and Ferris wheels operating and steamboats ferrying huge crowds by the day, fast steamers ran on the Delaware to Long Beach, New Jersey, from Philadelphia and Wilmington in the 1870s, and boats from Cincinnati plunged down the Ohio in the middle of the decade to Parker's Island (Coney Island of the West) with its bowling alley, dance pavilion, shooting gallery, and merry-go-round powered by a mule. The Philadelphia centennial in 1876 brought miniature railroads to intrigue both children and grandmothers. And the roller coaster—a Russian invention perfected by the French—came to America, complete with little cars equipped with longitudinal seats facing each other, gentle slopes instead of dips, and not enough speed to dislodge the cartwheel hats of the lady passengers. Daring dips and curves were not far behind.

The idea of building resorts and parks had caught around the Chesapeake Bay in the late 1870s. Bay Ridge on the Severn, Tivoli on the Patapsco, Sandy Grove (Bay Shore), Rockway Beach, Fairview Beach, Brown's Grove, and others were in various stages of planning. And on the Eastern Shore, an odd pair of Quakers, Calvin and E. B. Taggart, propelled by a vigorous and enterprising young employee by the name of William C. Eliason, were in the process of throwing aside their religious and traditional restraints and establishing on the Chesapeake shore of Kent County the most prestigious resort and amusement park of them all, Tolchester.[5]

The way to get to most of these parks was by steamboat. *Pilot Boy* and *Nelly White* journeyed back and forth from Baltimore to Tolchester Beach in summertime, their open decks crammed with hundreds of picnickers bent on a day of fun splashing in the salty water—picnickers clad from head to toe in black bathing suits, eating enormous quantities of fried chicken and baked ham in the shady groves, and riding the "flying horses" (carousels) and the elevated roller coaster connecting the hotel and the amusement park. The Maryland Steamboat Company ran *Samuel J. Pentz* and *Champion* to Holly Grove at the mouth of the Patapsco, and as time went on steamers began ferrying pleasure seekers by the hundreds to popular resorts within short distances from Baltimore. From Washington and Norfolk, excursion lines prospered as well.

Excursion boats differed considerably from the overnight packets delving into the reaches of Pocomoke Sound or the winding rivers of the Eastern Shore or running the length of the James, the Rappahannock, the Potomac, the Patuxent to the ends of navigation. These overnight boats, like the Baltimore to Norfolk packets, carried large numbers of staterooms for first-class passengers, considerable sleeping accommodations for second-class passengers, and operated like floating hotels during the periods of transit. In contrast, excursion steamers had few if any staterooms, virtually no sleeping facilities, and provided huge areas of open or sheltered deck space, where day passengers lounged, ate from their hampers, and reveled in the briny air of the Bay.

Many, if not most, of the excursion boats performed dual or even triple functions. They shuttled picnickers back and forth from resort areas; they carried excursion crowds on special or chartered runs around the Bay; and they ran a scheduled route to certain river landings with the transport of freight and passengers as a regular service, often carrying at the same time a collection of picnickers, pleasure-bent day-trippers, converting the routine progress of the steamer up the river from landing to landing into a holiday.

Such a vessel was *Samuel J. Pentz* of the Maryland Steamboat Company. For years this steamer visited Annapolis and made the rounds of the landings on the South, West, and Rhode Rivers, carrying freight and travelers. But on these trips, she catered to the day-trippers, advertised the healthful benefits, and even carried on board Professor Emmerich's Band and Orchestra for concerts and dancing. In 1891 her place on the route was taken by the beloved *Emma Giles* of the Tolchester line, which ran not only shuttle service to Tolchester Beach but also freight, passenger, and excursion trips at various times to the Miles, Little Choptank, South, West, and Rhode Rivers—day voyages complete with the colorful tumult of river landings and the serenading of Professor Webber's Orchestra or the chorus of passengers on the afterdeck at sunset.

Such a boat also was *Theodore Weems*. Unlike *Samuel J. Pentz* and *Emma Giles*, she carried staterooms and second-class sleeping arrangements for overnight passengers on the Patuxent run, or, when called upon, the Rappahannock run. But, in contrast to other steamers of the Weems line, she had expansive deck space, open to the sky from bow to stern on the hurricane deck and, except for the cabin area, open from side to side on the passenger deck. Hundreds of passengers could lounge in shady and breezy comfort on the lower deck or bask in the sun on the upper. Inside the cabin, her appointments suggested Victorian luxury; in the dining room, her bill of fare matched the best restaurants in Baltimore. Professor Itzel's Fifth Regiment Band furnished music for listening and dancing, both on board and at Fair Haven.[6]

Matilda, her deck space increased under Henry Williams's direction, ran tandem with *Theodore Weems* to Fair Haven in peak season. Even *Wenonah*, when crowds overwhelmed the two boats, assisted in ferrying the overload. Williams perceived Fair Haven as a hotel resort, a retreat south of Baltimore on the Chesapeake where the Bay and the sky and the countryside would revive the city-weary, where the trip by steamer for several hours each way would constitute in itself a short vacation by water, and where superb cooking and service would develop a reputation and create a loyal clientele. Fares were minimal: $1.00 round trip for adults, 50 cents for servants and children. He saw no need for a roller coaster, miniature railway, or midway. And he saw no reason to follow the Anti-Saloon League lead of Tolchester; fine liquors were served aboard the Weems boats and at Fair Haven.

In 1879, James H. VanSant, owner of the Annapolis-Bay Ridge Hiring and Livery Stables and energetic leader of the Bay Ridge Company, bought Tolly Point, where the Severn River met the Bay, and built a large hotel overlooking the Chesapeake. By subsequent negotiations with Henry Williams, agreement was reached that the Weems line would begin service from Baltimore on a modest scale in the summer of 1880. At the start of that season *Theodore Weems* was engaged in trips to Fredericksburg and the Rappahannock, but when the resort opened, she coupled her seasonal runs to Fair Haven with stops at Bay Ridge. Beginning in 1881 and lasting for eight years, during the summer months *Theodore Weems* held to an arduous schedule; she ran daily excursions to Fair Haven and Bay Ridge; at certain periods of the season some of the runs during the week included extended trips to Patuxent landings; her decks rang with merriment and music (Appendix B).

At Bay Ridge, the sound of the whistle of *Theodore Weems*, as the seasons passed, carried the same excitement; she slid alongside the piling at the end of the long wharf and disgorged hundreds of passengers. And Bay Ridge opened its doors to them. "The Queen Resort of the Chesapeake," as local newspapers called it, enticed travelers from far and wide by rail and boat to enjoy the luxuries of the grand hotel, the restaurant pavilion, and many forms of entertainment, including concerts, dances, and variety shows. In July 1881, *Theodore Weems* brought 4,000 visitors for a jousting tournament and evening fireworks and dance. Other steamboat lines discovered the profits of service to Bay Ridge and either scheduled stops by their steamers or arranged for charters to handle the crowds headed for the resort from Baltimore or the Eastern Shore.

Columbia, a big 262-foot two-stacker, acquired by the Bay Ridge Company itself, began service in May 1888. Other boats included *Jane Moseley, Tred Avon*, the deep-draft two-stacker *Empire State* (it often embarrassingly ran aground within sight of the Bay Ridge pier), *Tockwogh, Emma Giles*, and others. In spite of the competition, *Theodore Weems* held a place in the loyalty and affection of its clientele. Bay Ridge, however, suffered cycles of financial misfortune. As a result, its prospects were not conspicuously bright.[7]

By mid-1879, Henry Williams had succeeded in retiring a substantial portion of the obligations due the heirs of Theodore Weems. Through the trustees of the estate, D. W. Crain et al., he negotiated for the direct sale of the shares held by the estate in four steamers, *Theodore Weems, Planter, Mary Washington*, and *Matilda*, to the two sisters, owners of the Weems line. As for the fifth boat, the sisters held clear title to *Wenonah* as a result of the transaction ending Jacob Tome's interest in the boat. Through the negotiations with the trustees, Henry Williams acquired title to *Planter* for $23,500, to *Theodore Weems* for an equal amount, and to *Mary Washington* and *Matilda* for undisclosed but lesser amounts. His reason for forcing the issue of ownership was a sad one. Except for *Theodore Weems*, the boats were venerable and nearing the point of exhaustion.[8]

Planter had been steaming for 34 years; she had wandered about the Bay in the trials of Mason Locke Weems; she had suffered through the tribulations of government service in the Civil War; and she had performed valiantly on the Patuxent, season after season. She was beyond repair, and Henry Williams needed a clear title to dispose of her. With the title in hand, he would be able to sell her to wreckers in Baltimore. There were many who remembered the plucky steamer—sniped at by rebel friends from a hostile shore, shouldered aside on competitive ventures, and abused but venerated as Grant's Apothecary Shop on the Appomattox (Appendix A).

Matilda, also, suffered from obsolescence. Built hastily at the end of the war, she had few of the amenities of *Theodore Weems*, and Williams found her useful primarily as a spare boat to haul produce in season or to carry overloads of passengers from Fair Haven. He hired one William R. Lewis as her master in later years—the father of several seafaring sons from Onancock, Virginia. One of the sons, Charles R. Lewis, was fated to cross the path of Henry Williams at an important juncture in the subsequent history of the Weems line. On one occasion, Henry Williams chartered the boat for Negro excursions. William R. Lewis was a stuttering man; his engineer was nearly deaf; unable to vent their frustrations on their uncomprehending passengers, they locked themselves in pilothouse or engineroom and stayed there throughout each voyage. In spite of the shortcomings of her master and engineer, *Matilda* performed valiantly, but Henry Williams perceived the liability of the old boat. Accordingly, as in the case of *Planter*, Williams gained title and made plans for the disposition of *Matilda*.[9]

These plans coincided with a much more ambitious project. Williams wanted to build a fleet of new steamboats, as replacements not only for *Planter* and *Matilda* but also in the longer term as replacements for *Wenonah* and *Mary Washington*, both becoming increasingly decrepit. From the shipyards around Wilmington and Philadelphia on the Delaware, out of New York and New Jersey building ways, and indeed from the yards around Baltimore, a flock of new steamers was taking to the water. Their construction, engineering, and appointments far exceeded the most extravagant expectations of the builders and owners of the years before and immediately after the Civil War. These new boats were more commodious, spacious, had more staterooms, provided more deck space, carried more freight for their size, boasted rich saloons and public rooms heavy with Victorian decor, used boilers and machinery of a superior and more efficient design, and impressed the steamboat world with their beauty. The packets being built for overnight service on the various rivers and sounds from New England and New York to the Delaware and Virginia capes moved with elegance and grace.

The first step in building a new fleet for the Weems line was the replacement of *Planter* (Appendix A). Accordingly, Henry Williams sold her to junk dealers in Baltimore at the start of 1881 and began the making of urgent plans with William Skinner and Sons for the building of a new packet. No contract was drawn up; none was needed among these men who trusted each other. Henry's concepts were ambitious, and he was willing to pay to realize them. At the very start, there was little question about the name of the steamer; she would be called *Mason L. Weems* and would be sponsored by the daughters. In contrast to existing boats of the Weems line, *Mason L. Weems* would be much larger, 222 feet long, with a hull width of 33 feet and an overhang at the paddleboxes of nearly 12 feet on either side, thereby accommodating wider and larger paddlewheels. Her gross tonnage at 1,200 and net at 829 meant more than double the capacity of any previous Weems vessels. Her interior furnishings—panelings handcrafted by Morris, great stairways and galleries, stained-glass skylights, and (for the times) comfortable staterooms—were designed to emulate the best accommodations in Baltimore. Like *Theodore Weems*, her hurricane deck was carried to the very bow, providing a shaded deck area forward on the passenger deck. But Henry

Williams had still another specification in mind: speed. He envisioned stepping up the schedules on the Patuxent and Rappahannock, with more landings visited in less time and more passengers and freight carried with greater efficiency. To this end, his injunction to James Clark and Company, Baltimore engine builders, was to design a vertical beam engine, which, coupled with a sleek hull (7:1 ratio of length to beam) and large paddlewheels, would propel the boat at speeds up to 18 or 20 miles per hour. The engine placed in the new boat would have a stroke of 11.5 feet but a massive cylinder diameter of 56 inches, an engine powerful enough to meet the designated speed. The total cost of the new steamboat exceeded $100,000 (Appendix A).[10]

Mason L. Weems was launched with great fanfare on June 13, 1881. The official party celebrated in state. Unofficially, in the yard, near the launching way, two groups of caulkers, white and black, toasted each other with kegs of beer and ate from tables loaded with crackers and cheese. Her great engine was installed. True to expectations, her trial runs on the lower Patapsco in the fall of 1881 proved her speed. In March 1882 she began her runs from Pier 9, Light Street, to wharves on the Rappahannock and to Fredericksburg.

At the outset, *Mason L. Weems* created problems. Although her depth of hold at 12.3 feet was not much more than that of other steamers of the line, when the boat was loaded her hull sank deep in the water, largely because of the slim lines of the hull in relationship to overall beam (over the guards). Heavier loads, which could be carried because of the greater length and beam, only succeeded in increasing the draft to a point at which navigation in Urbanna Creek or Carter's Creek or the upper reaches of the Rappahannock River near Fredericksburg or, for that matter, the narrow and shoaling channels at Hills Landing on the Patuxent, became risky. To increase the problem, the enormous thrust of the paddlewheels backing down or clearing a wharf or steaming over a shallow bottom created a large surge under the counter and caused the stern to sink even lower in the water. Stirring up the mud in these creeks and narrow channels was a commonplace experience for all Weems boats, particularly at low tide. But for *Mason L. Weems*, going in or out of these shallow areas meant tailoring a cargo to an acceptable draft and adjusting a schedule to high tide. Her speed no longer became an important factor except on open stretches of the Bay and the broad reaches of the lower river.

On August 14, 1882, enroute to Fredericksburg, she went hard aground in Urbanna Creek. A week later, she was still there. Unloading, an exceptionally high tide, and much straining of the engines managed to free her. She seemed to be hard to handle and ran into repeated difficulty. In attempting to turn around at Fredericksburg she struck the paddlebox of *Mary Washington*; she developed a reputation for slamming into piers and jarring the piling and warehouse and the tempers of her masters as well. Another bleak statistic about *Mason L. Weems* confronted Henry Williams: her fuel costs were prohibitive, and she was expensive to operate. Disappointment sharply curbed his enthusiasm.[11]

Nevertheless, Williams moved quickly to implement the next stage of his plans to replace the aging and obsolescent steamers. In late 1882, he sold *Matilda* for conversion into a barge to Wesley Ricketts of Baltimore (Appendix A). After the enormous expenditure for the building of *Mason L. Weems*, Williams looked with considerable satisfaction on the fact that *Matilda's* walking beam engine, constructed 17 years before, was in excellent condition and could be salvaged. He had the engine removed from the hull and reserved for the new boat under design at William Skinner and Sons.

The new boat was to be shorter than her predecessor by some 20 feet, lower in tonnage and capacity (horsepower and likely speed limited by *Matilda's* engine), but fitted out with the same luxuries and interior lavishness and equipped to cater to passengers in the style long established aboard Weems line boats. Her staterooms surrounding the saloon on the passenger deck were arranged in two banks, the more expensive on the outside with shuttered windows overlooking the river or Bay scene, the inexpensive on the inside, connected to the saloon by interior corridors and offering neither view nor ventilation. Like *Mason L. Weems*, the paneled saloon seemed overstuffed with upholstered furniture, dark carpeting, and, up forward, the linen-covered tables of the dining room. Illumination still was by gas light, tankards of the dangerous material under pressure being loaded aboard and connected up to piping running through the ship (oil lamps were still being used on older boats). Running water, with small washbasins in first-class staterooms, was an advertised amenity, auxiliary steam pumps being used to force the water from the tanks through the boat. She was an impressive sight under way; her great paddleboxes displayed a carved eagle at the center of a golden fan on either side, and another carved eagle perched aggressively atop her pilothouse ornamented a shapely superstructure and a hull with a pleasing sheer. Although delighted with her appearance, Williams was less than happy about her performance. She was far slower than expected, but in most respects, the new vessel met the critical specifications of her new manager, in spite of his misgivings about her speed. In arranging for the design of the new boat, Williams had listened attentively to James Gourley, Dan Davis, and other masters as well as the engineers of William Skinner and Sons. She was launched in midsummer 1883 and began service on the Rappahannock to Fredericksburg in September.

She was welcomed along the river landings and at Fredericksburg for several reasons. First, she was a handsome, rather stately looking vessel, and residents were pleased by her comely appearance. Second, after the misfortunes of *Mason L. Weems*, she was dependable. Third, she arrived at the very time that planters and merchants along the shores of the Rappahannock had begun to raise their voices once again in disgruntlement at what they perceived as unfair treatment by the Weems line. And fourth, she bore on the golden fan of her paddlebox a name that portended another trend in the life of the Weems steamboats.

After *Mason L. Weems*, Williams resolved that the practice of naming steamboats to memorialize Weems family members should end, not only because there seemed to be no one else to memorialize but also because he felt that the line had good reason to link itself to the regions that it served. The new boat carried in red Old English letters the name *Westmoreland*. She was the first of the Weems line boats to be named for counties neighboring the Rappahannock River in Virginia or the Patuxent River in Maryland. The move was not just one of diplomacy; the names themselves carried the sonorous ring of history (Appendix A).

Westmoreland began her service on the Rappahannock in a season of rising complaints from farmers, merchants, bankers, and newspaper editors along its banks about the indifferent quality of service of the Weems line, as they perceived it. From 1828, when George Weems nosed *Patuxent* up the river to Fredericksburg and came scuttling back to Baltimore, bruised by the battering he received, to this year 55 years later, the Weems steamboats had endured an odd experience on the Rappahannock. On the one hand, the residents were profuse in their praise of the Weems line boats, particularly in the post-Civil War period and especially during the regime of Henry Williams, whom they credited with contributing enormously to the economic development of the region. They were lavish in their expressions of affection for the man himself, as a loyal friend and benefactor, as a listener who attempted to solve their difficulties, and as a gentleman who lived up to a code of honesty and fair dealing. At the same time, they castigated the steamboat line for what they saw as poor service, extortionate rates, unreasonable schedules, and unwillingness to link the Rappahannock with markets and transshipment facilities in Norfolk. Despite whatever means Williams used to counter the charges and meet the demands, he never seemed to quell the criticism or to do quite enough to please everyone. A good part of the restiveness stemmed from an underlying resentment at the intrusion of alien Baltimoreans and from the long-standing unstated but trenchant rivalry between Virginians and Marylanders.[12]

Over the years, competitors had attempted to break the Weems postwar monopoly of the Rappahannock trade. *Maggie Saffell* in 1866 and *Massachusetts* in 1868 had operated briefly between Baltimore and Fredericksburg. Several day boats owned by Fredericksburg interests or lower Rappahannock river residents ran on local routes or to Norfolk. From July 1874 to April 1875 *Eliza Hancox*, Civil War veteran and venerable steamer on the Delaware and along the coast out of Savannah, ran on charter by the James River Steamboat Company between Rappahannock landings and Norfolk.[13] The residents of the Rappahannock cheered *Eliza Hancox*, supported her with their trade, and stormed their disapproval when she left for warmer and more propitious climes.

In October 1883, William R. Lewis, father of the brothers from Onancock, Virginia, who interested themselves in steamboating, was master of record of *Lady of the Lake*, a 204-foot veteran of the Potomac owned by the Inland and Coastal Seaboard Company of Washington. In that month, he chartered *Lady of the Lake* and attempted to establish a place for her on a Washington to Rappahannock River run. His essay into the territory of Weems met with no success. His son also served as master of *Lady of the Lake* at one time or another; his name was Charles R. Lewis, and he had a long and sour memory for the first and fruitless bout with Weems and Henry Williams. [14]

To answer the incessant demand for service between the Rappahannock and Norfolk, Williams dispatched *Mary Washington* to Fredericksburg in October 1883 to inaugurate a new route. During the season, she was to leave Fredericksburg twice a week in the morning (after the arrival of the morning trains) for a daylong journey down the river, calling at Port Royal, Tappahannock, and other landings and an overnight run to Norfolk in order to connect with Old Dominion Steamship Company vessels bound for New York the following morning. First-class passage was $1.50; second-class, $1.00. [15] Variations on this schedule were to occupy the worthy but aging *Mary Washington* until 1885 (Appendix B).

In spite of this attempt to meet their demands, the Rappahannock valley residents continued their clamor for service to Norfolk and threatened all sort of reprisals, including the creation—source unknown—of a rival line. Williams decided to build another boat, not only to ameliorate the public beating he was suffering but also to replace *Mary Washington*.

Once again, the firm of William Skinner and Sons was called upon to produce a steamboat in record time. On this occasion, however, Williams departed drastically from designs of the past. *Essex*, as the boat would be named, would be propeller driven, the first screw boat of the Weems fleet. The forward portion of her passenger cabin or saloon would be completely surrounded in windows transforming the appearance of the steamer into that of a day boat. There were fewer staterooms (accommodations for only 50 first-class passengers), and the whole design coincided with a plan to operate the steamer on shuttle service from the Rappahannock to Norfolk. She was designed to carry about 250 tons of freight. Less than 150 feet long, with a 25-foot beam, she was well powered by a compound (two-cylinder) engine designed and built by James Clark and Company. Her estimated cost was $40,000 (Appendix A).

The keel was laid on February 14, 1885, and she was launched at the end of July. Her first runs to the Rappanhannock, however, were from Baltimore. With the opening of the 1886 season, she commenced her overnight trips twice a week from Fredericksburg to Norfolk and return. She docked at the Norfolk pier of the Baltimore Steam Packet Company by prior arrangement, and coincided her arrival with the schedule of the Old Dominion Line for freight transshipment and passenger transfer to New York, connecting with north and southbound trains at Fredericksburg at each end of the trip. Six months of the year, *Essex* maintained the schedule (Appendix B). To the protests of local residents that it should be longer, Henry Williams answered that he would be glad to extend it if he could get her expenses paid.[16]

On the night of September 1, 1887, *Essex* caught fire at her Light Street wharf. The blaze was extinguished before the hull or superstructure was materially damaged. Repairs cost from $15,000 to $18,000 and *Essex* was back in service quickly. *Essex* should have been a fleet and fancy boat; she was not. Her lines were not particularly graceful, and her general appearance was awkward. Nevertheless, over the years, she served as a workhorse, running the Bay in the worst of weather, shuttling faithfully at the peak of the season when cargoes were heavy, and appearing at landings up and down the Rappahannock in the small of the mornings or the full of the moon to perform her chores. At one time or another, most of the Weems line masters skippered her, including James Gourley, James B. Sanford, J. M. H. Burroughs, W. H. Van Dyke, Daniel M. Davis, John A. Clark, A. M. Long, and Herbert A. Bohannon.

In 1886 *Mary Washington* said farewell to the Bay and the rivers she had served for 40 years. She was no longer needed and was too weary to compete. In 1887 she was turned over to the wreckers to be dismantled (Appendix A).

The Weems fleet now consisted of the old steamer *Wenonah*, serviceable as a spare boat in the heavy oyster season or harvest seasons; *Theodore Weems*, running the Fair Haven and Patuxent route; *Essex*, shuttling from Fredericksburg to Norfolk six months of the year and from Baltimore to Fredericksburg in the remaining months; and the new steamers *Westmoreland* and *Mason L. Weems*, serving the Rappahannock route from Baltimore to Fredericksburg and assisting on the Patuxent. Because of her draft, the movements of *Mason L. Weems* were circumscribed by time and tide; because of her age and condition, the usefulness of *Wenonah* was reduced; because of her excursionlike configuration, the overnight value of *Theodore Weems*, particularly on long Rappahannock hauls, was constrained. These factors led to schedules on the Fredericksburg run which in turn stirred up a renewed irritability on the part of the clientele ashore and calls for an independent steamboat line to challenge the Weems monopoly (Appendix B).

To aggravate matters even more came the catastrophe on the night of September 10, 1889. *Theodore Weems* caught fire and burned at Pier 8, Light Street. When Williams arrived to view the boat the next morning, he found her sunk in 20 feet of water, her bow at the surface almost intact but her superstructure aft of the pilothouse a mass of blackened wreckage.

On his rounds at 2:30 A.M., the watchman, by the name of McCreedy, noticed smoke pouring from the engineroom ventilators. He roused the men on board, and they played the steamer's firehose on the blaze until they believed they had extinguished the flames. But the fires broke out again, licking their way aft along the upper decks. The crew turned in the alarm, but when firemen arrived they found they could do little, as the stream of water they could direct fell short of the after part of the steamer. The best they could do was fill the hull with water and allow the boat to sink. Two bulls, two cows, nine calves, and a dozen coops of chickens and ducks perished and were later hauled off to a local glue factory. Sixty out of 70 hogsheads of tobacco were salvaged; a cargo of grain and produce was lost. Total damage was estimated at $50,000, covered partially by insurance. Some engineers believed that her engine could be salvaged—the engine that had been pulled from *George Weems*. Ironically, *George Weems* had burned on June 10, 1871, on the very spot at which *Theodore Weems* now lay, a smoldering wreck.

To Williams, the fire constituted more than the prospective loss of *Theodore Weems*: it meant increased difficulty in meeting the competing demands on the Rappahannock, the Patuxent, and at Fair Haven. All over the Chesapeake, steamboat lines were expanding their reach into rivers and creeks and along the shores of the Bay, until, like railroads (where railroads went), they had become the accepted and indeed, in most instances, the only means of transportation and communication. They were the very lifelines for those who lived and prospered along the Bay and its tributaries. Steamboat lines were growing and thriving; Williams felt the pulse of the times, and he was determined to keep the Weems boats in the lead.

As his first move, he contracted for the urgent reconstruction of the burned boat. Recognizing the importance of Fair Haven, he kept the design as an excursion boat very much as it had been before September 10. The rebuilt boat, almost indistinguishable from the vessel that had been launched in 1872, emerged from the yard at Skinner's on May 1, 1890. Carrying the engine of *George Weems* and *Theodore Weems*, she bore a new name, *St. Mary's*, for the county on the south shore of the Patuxent (Appendix A).[17]

In the interim, during the midseason of 1889–90, Williams contended with the circumstance that he had few steamers to operate and a vociferous crowd of Rappahannock editorialists, setting forth all sorts of proposals for the improvement of service on the river and to Norfolk. Those with the most bite wanted to lessen, or even sever, the dependence on Baltimore and Maryland interests and cultivate a link with Norfolk and transshipment opportunities to New York and Philadelphia. They were indeed troublesome for Williams, and they created ideas he had to counter.

Even while he was engaging William Skinner and Sons in the project of rebuilding *Theodore Weems* as *St. Mary's*, Henry Williams set about to overcome his disappointment and chagrin at the shortcomings of *Mason L. Weems*. In Kingston, New York, he negotiated for the sale of his fast but incompatible boat to the Romer and Tremper Steamboat Company (owned by the Cornell Steamboat Company) for service out of New York. At the same time he laid on Skinner's drawing board the specifications for a replacement. The sale of *Mason L. Weems* was consummated in April 1890; her name was changed to *William F. Romer*, and she held the record, except for that of the *City of Kingston*, for the fastest run from New York to Stony Point (she reportedly made 24 miles per hour). Her speed led to her undoing; on her way to Kingston-on-Hudson one June day she ran at full speed onto a bank of solid clay; at low tide her paddlewheels were five feet above the water, and an observer could walk around her without flooding his boots. She had to be dredged out of her predicament (Appendix A).

In Baltimore, at the Skinner yards, two Weems boats were on the ways at the same time, one being rebuilt, the other under construction.

Richmond, as the new steamer would be named (for the Virginia county in the Northern Neck), would be equipped with the latest advances in steamboat design and engineering. James Clark and Sons proposed to place aboard two steel Scotch boilers of recent patent which would furnish sufficient steam independently to power the engine and auxiliary machinery. Although she would measure 205 feet in length, 33 feet in hull width (56 feet overall), with a depth of hold at 11 feet, *Richmond* would draw even less water than *Westmoreland* by virtue of her hull configuration. Her hull was built of wood (she would be the last Weems boat to have a wooden hull). With a cylinder diameter of 48 inches and stroke of 11 feet, her indicated horsepower at 952 nevertheless exceeded that of *Mason L. Weems*. Aside from certain qualities of engineering, *Richmond* boasted superior accommodations for 125 first-class and 175 second-class passengers. The main saloon, designed by Charles Morris, was finished in oak, sycamore, and cherry, a mosaic of artistic paneling and carving. The ladies' cabin was in cypress. Staterooms forward were reached through alcoves; those aft were fitted out as bridal suites. All of her cabin space would be heated by steam. Nothing was spared in the planning for plumbing facilities, brassware, table silver, linen, glassware, and other amenities. Designated officers were James Gourley, master; Thomas Massey, first officer; Richard Shenton, second officer; William O'Donnell, chief engineer; Robert Carr, purser, and John Dare, steward. Most newsworthy of all was the information that she would be lighted throughout by electricity powered by a steam generator in the engineroom and that on her bow would be mounted an electric 5,000-candlepower searchlight controlled by the lookoutsman at the direction of the master in the pilothouse (it would be reinstalled atop the pilothouse and controlled by a hand-operated mechanism through the roof). Most of the shipping world in Baltimore turned out for her launching on June 26, 1890. By the first week in August, she had taken her place with *Westmoreland* on the route to Fredericksburg and Rappahannock landings (Appendix A).

The Weems line prospered. Although admonitions still came from the shores of the Rappahannock, the journalists and merchants and shippers were no more strident and, in fact, seemed eminently pleased with *Westmoreland* and the rather palatial *Richmond*. On the Patuxent, the seasons passed in a blissful routine of profitable trade. Fair Haven attracted large crowds to its groves and beaches in summertime, and even off-season visitors came to stay in the pleasant old hotel. The year 1891 boded well for the health of the Weems line. In view of the growing demand, Williams looked ahead to the building of an expanding fleet. As far as he could see, the prospects were unbounded.

At the end of 1891, he and Georgeanna, together with Matilda S. and Sydney Hume Forbes, felt that they were in a position to undertake a major legal decision. In 1879, through the trustees of the estate, they had paid to the heirs of Theodore Weems the value of the steamboats included in his estate. By these means, the owners, through Henry Williams, were able to hold title for the sale of these boats in final disposition. By mid-1891, all of the obligations that held Georgeanna and Matilda to the estate of Theodore Weems had been absolved. The decision they reached, therefore, arose from their financial independence and the legal realities of the times, when personal ownership of enterprises engaged in public service carried palpable risks. They undertook to incorporate the line under the name of the Weems Steamboat Company of Baltimore City. The company was incorporated on December 14, 1891, by the Baltimore City Superior Court acting under the general laws of Maryland; its directors were Henry Williams, Sydney H. Forbes, Mason L. W. Williams, John H. C. Williams, and Henry S. Beal; its aggregate capital (paid in full July 26, 1892) was $600,000 in 6,000 shares of $100 each. Stock was not sold to the public, and the two sisters retained their de facto ownership. Total property value, including the steamboats, wharves, and other real estate, totaled $541,400 with an outstanding mortgage of $60,000. On January 1, 1892, the new organization took possession of the property in the name of the Weems Steamboat Company (Appendix G). All of the steamboats were redocumented under the new house name, and Henry Williams assumed the duties of president and general manager.[18]

In a sense, the ironic circle was complete. The name of Weems was irrevocably linked to the line and to the steamboats after more than 70 years during which the linkage had been mouthed but never consummated, and it was done at a time when no one by the last name of Weems controlled or managed the company.

To formalize the event, the steamboats carried new insignia; on the stack appeared a red ball with the letter *W* cut out or painted black; at the masthead flew a blue flag with a red ball at its center. As the packets of other lines passed in the morning or evening pageant of departure from Baltimore and displayed their flags—a white field with blue propeller, for the Ericsson Line; a white field with red arrow, for the Chester River line; a red field with black *B*, for the Old Bay Line; and a red and blue field with white *T*, for the Tolchester line—the handsome packets of the Weems line could break out a new house flag at the masthead and move in the parade with justifiable pride.

In 1891, the Weems line had much to celebrate.

At the beginning of the decade, the steamboats of the Chesapeake were staging some tentative measure of recovery from the local depres-

sion of the late 1880s which they had helped create. Because they had
linked the farmer to the city and the urban manufacture to his rural con-
sumer by overnight service, local dependence on small tradesmen and
manufacturers and on regional produce had weakened; competition
from large manufacturers and city commission merchants, made possible by extensive steamboat service, had put little producers out of
business, and a regional recession had resulted. But the persistence and
farsightedness of some steamboat operators, even at lower rates and
increased costs, had given business between the city and tidewater
Maryland and Virginia a sense of possible stability, soon to be shaken in
widening depression.

In the climate of 1891, Henry Williams decided to build still another
steamboat to augment his fleet. Under no pressure, as he had been in
the past, he chose to make the erection of the new boat an event in the
history of steamboat building around the Baltimore waterfront.

For this boat he chose the Maryland Steel Company of Sparrows
Point as the builder. The hull, therefore, was to be made of steel. The
company, only a few years old, had spent more than five million dollars
in developing a large industrial complex near the mouth of the Patapsco.
Four great furnaces turned out daily more than a thousand tons of iron,
and a steel plant produced nearly the same tonnage in steel; a shipyard
rang with business, and a work force of 4,000 created virtually a new city
nearby. The new boat proposed by the Weems line would be the largest
the yard had yet to undertake. Henry Williams, with the engineering
staff of the steel company, laid out the design and specifications; James
Gourley, senior captain, superintended the construction for the Weems
line, as he had done for most of the recent boats built for the company.

Lancaster was launched on Friday, April 15, 1892. More than a thousand spectators, half of whom were ladies, gathered in the early morning
hours to watch the launching. About 500 had boarded *Westmoreland* at
Light Street; she left her pier at 8:45 A.M. bedecked in bunting and
hosted by genial Captain James Burroughs and Henry Williams. At the
side of Williams was Jennie D. Forbes, the 16-year-old daughter of Sydney Hume Forbes. She was the steamboat's sponsor.[19]

On the ways stood *Lancaster*, a line of pennants streaming from a
makeshift mast amidships. She glistened in white paint but was missing
her machinery and superstructure, her paddleboxes only white half-
spheres awaiting the gold trim of decoration. At ten o'clock, Miss Jennie
Forbes, with other dignitaries, moved to a high stand at the bow. As
soon as the blocks had been knocked out from under the vessel on the
ways and the hull began to move, Jennie swung mightily at the bow with
a gaily trimmed bottle of champagne. At 10:10 A.M., *Lancaster* entered
the water to the plaudits of the crowd and the shrilling of whistles around
the point. After outfitting at the Maryland Steel Company, she went on
the ways at Skinner's for a final bottom painting and made her trial run
on August 16, 1892. Captain Gourley declared, "She is the completest
boat with which I ever had anything to do. There is nothing shoddy

about her, and every detail in her construction received the closest attention of her builders."

James Gourley and Henry Williams had good reason to be proud of *Lancaster* when she began her journeys to the Rappahannock in late August 1892. She had been built at a cost of $113, 307.37, a sum being paid off within the year from current earnings (Appendix G). She was a handsome boat. Some 205 feet long, with a beam of 32 feet (57 feet over the guards) and hold depth of 12 feet, she resembled *Richmond* in many respects. But her hull, unlike that of *Richmond*, was of mild steel throughout; the keel was of dished plate, forming a waterway; and the stern post and rudder frames were cast steel. Heavy framing, spaced 22 inches apart and connected by seven keelsons, provided rigidity; three-eighths-inch steel plating surrounded the hull; and a steel deck extended aft of the engine and boilers. The main deck of four-inch white pine ran from bow to stern. Steel enclosed the engine and boiler casings and the framing of the paddleboxes. Wheels 30 feet in diameter, a beam engine with 48-inch cylinder and 11-foot stroke, and two Scotch boilers with working pressure of 50 pounds per square inch were designed to propel the boat at the speed of *Richmond*. Edward Weems was designated chief engineer (Appendix A).

The interior of the boat awed the first passengers. The saloon, its joiner work in bass and sycamore with carving and molding and ornamental alcoves and paneled doorways and its ceiling in white and gold, ran fore and aft with 40 staterooms opening to port and starboard, accommodating 80 first-class passengers. Staterooms aft—large, equipped with brass bedsteads, painted in pastels of blue, white, and gold—were designated as bridal suites. Staterooms and saloon were carpeted in body Brussels; furniture was oak framed, upholstered in dark green leather; gold mirrors hung in the saloon.

On the main deck aft lay the ladies' social cabin, paneled in hardwood; oak chairs upholstered in dark green leather stood around the sides. Like the saloon above, the smoke-stained chandeliers were lighted by electricity. A ladies' washroom, with hot and cold running water and marble plumbing fixtures, opened to the rear of this cabin. Also on the main deck were the barroom, furnished in walnut like a British pub; the mailroom; gallery; and quarters for officers and crew. Just forward and aft of the engineroom spaces in the hold were cabins holding 97 second-class passengers.

A broad stairway with carved balustrade in cherry and bass connected main deck and saloon deck forward; a similar one was aft. On the hurricane deck, which ran from bow to stern as on other recent Weems line boats, stood the pilothouse, finished in tongue-and-groove hardwood and the latest navigational equipment; the captain's cabin, finished in bass and sycamore and featuring a built-in bedstead, of the same materials; and quarters for the first and second mates.[20]

Lancaster was a magnificent boat, and she entered the steamboat world of the Chesapeake with the adulation due a queen. The attention given her originated not only in the excellence of her construction and appointments but also in the care Henry Williams had taken in publicizing her debut. All of the prestigious owners of steamboat lines knew that the old Weems line, which had struggled through the long years to succeed, had joined the vanguard of the pageant of packets.

In the early 1890s, steamboating on the Chesapeake was a splendid spectacle, not yet sullied by the specter of spreading economic depression. More than 45 steamers hailed from Baltimore Harbor. In the morning and evening procession out of the harbor could be counted the little packets bound for landings along the far recesses of tidewater Maryland and Virginia, the overnight vessels bound for Philadelphia or Norfolk, and the day boats laden with excursionists and with cargo and passengers for rivers within ready reach of the city.

Chowan and *Choptank*, small vessels with accommodation for perhaps 30 overnight passengers but ample freight decks, set out for the winding and shallow course of Nanticoke River. The old *Chester* on the Sassafras and the *B. S. Ford* and *Emma A. Ford* and *Gratitude* (which named a landing and a town) on the arching watercourse of the Chester River and its tributary, the Corsica, began their journeys across the Bay. For the Eastern Shore Steamboat Company departed *Maggie*, *Tangier*, *Pocomoke*, and the bulky but faithful *Eastern Shore* bound for the Pocomoke River, Crisfield, and the landings on the lower Eastern Shore. For the Piankatank on the Western Shore headed *Avalon* and *Kent*. *Enoch Pratt* ran the Wicomico. *Ida* and the swift and popular *Joppa* of the Maryland Steamboat Company headed for the Choptank on the long run to Denton. On the same run, they were challenged by two comely propeller steamers of the Choptank Steamboat Company: the fast but overrated *Cambridge* and the slim boat with the graceful sheer, *Tred Avon*. There were many others of the same type. These were all overnight packets, remarkably similar in general appearance in spite of their differences, traveling long distances up remote and winding channels to serve landings and small communities scattered on the shores of Tidewater, bringing excitement and a note of glamour with the sound of their whistles and the touch of their guards against the piling.

Then there were the often faster and larger overnight boats, connecting the cities. To Philadelphia through the Chesapeake and Delaware Canal were the narrow *Richard Willing* and *General Cadwalader*; and building on the ways was the big three-decker *Anthony Groves, Jr.* To Norfolk and to Richmond and the York River were *Charlotte*, *Danville*, and *Baltimore* of the Chesapeake line, as it was called, or *Carolina* and *Virginia* of the Old Bay Line. There were others like those that ran the Potomac to Washington, and between the cities were vessels on overnight service which appeared and disappeared with the fluctuating fortunes of their owners and the vicissitudes of trade on the Chesapeake.

And there were the excursion boats. Some like *Louise* devoted themselves entirely to catering to huge picnic crowds bound for the beaches and roller coasters of amusement parks and resorts such as Tolchester and Bay Ridge. Others like the venerated *Emma Giles* turned the business of carrying freight and passengers into an excursionists' holiday, complete with bunting, bands, and dancing. Into this scene of pageantry fitted the Weems line boats bent on their excursions to Fair Haven and Bay Ridge and intent on their heavy schedules up and down the Patuxent and the Rappahannock.[21]

Baltimore did not march alone in the steamboat pageant of the early 1890s. Norfolk participated, but the penetration of the railroad into some parts of tidewater Virginia tempered the prospects of prosperity. The Old Dominion Line, for example, was adversely affected. When the venerable line began operations after the Civil War, its coastal freight to New York consisted of fish products, lumber, cotton, rice, tobacco, and other agricultural products brought for transshipment by steamboat from North Carolina via Albermarle Sound with its connecting tributaries and from the Eastern Shore, the York River, and the James River country. The railroad, built in 1881, from Norfolk to Elizabeth City punctured the steamboat trade to North Carolina. Steamboats of the Old Dominion in Virginia waters, however, were far less affected and continued through the 1890s to ply their way through the tributaries of the southern Chesapeake to bring the produce and lumber to Norfolk for transshipment to New York. The oceangoing ships of the line, carrying passengers as well as freight, constituted the major activity of the Old Dominion, but its steamboats contributed enormously to the economic development of tidewater Virginia.

Northampton steamed in service to Cherrystone on the Eastern Shore; *Luray* ran to Richmond; *Washington, Beaufort, R. L. Myers, Virginia Dare,* and *Albemarle* ran to landings in North Carolina. The last, not to be confused with the schooner-rigged sidewheeler built in 1865 as a sister ship for *Hatteras*, carried the engine of *Pamlico* and a tall, thin stack, immediately identifiable at landings awaiting her arrival. *Isle of Wight*, until she burned in 1895, ran to destinations in Gloucester and Mathews County, along with the misshapen *Accomac*. Many of these boats, and others, doubled at times in service; patrons knew them in various divisions of the Old Dominion from Richmond to Cherrystone, Mobjack Bay to Ocracoke.[22]

In early 1893, a new boat appeared in Norfolk waters and turned the heads of spectators along the shores. Built at the shipyard of Harlan and Hollingsworth in Wilmington, Delaware, for the Virginia Navigation Company at a cost of $150,000 and launched on April 25, 1893, *Pocohontas* arrived in the splendor and accoutrements of a princess. Intended to supplement the thrice-weekly trips of the old *Ariel* up the James and its 30 or more landings to Richmond, *Pocohontas* quickly established a place of her own in the affections of the region. A steel-hulled vessel, 204 feet in length, 57 feet in beam overall, driven by a vertical beam engine (cylinder 46-inch diameter, 10-foot stroke) she advertised a top speed of 20 miles per hour and an elegance unsurpassed on the Chesapeake. Her interior accommodations boasted a social hall, sunporch, and ladies' parlor apart from the saloon, which in itself was an ornamental master-piece in ivory and gold. There were also private cardrooms and small intimate parlors draped in silk; grand stairways; and an expensive electric "orchestrion" with the effect of 30 instruments playing popular music. Her trips became something of a legend, her voyages part of the fabric of steamboat history. Most of the residents along her route could not imagine the river without the graceful, thrilling, and comforting presence of *Pocohontas*. [23]

On the Potomac, steamboats in the early 1890s flourished, also. Packets, many of them as elaborate as those out of Baltimore or Norfolk, provided overnight service between Washington, Potomac landings, and Norfolk. The Inland and Coastal Seaboard Company, representing a branch in the reorganization of the New York, Alexandria, Washington, and Georgetown Steamship Company engaged in shipping between Washington and New York, operated several venerable but stately boats to Norfolk: *W. W. Coit* (173 feet), *Jane Moseley* (200 feet), *Lady of the Lake* (210 feet), and *John W. Thompson*, shortly to be sold to an up-and-coming shipowner, Ephraim Randall; *John W. Thompson* would be renamed for Ephraim's son *Harry Randall* and used to carry freight on the lower river. Also, the Potomac Steamboat Company ran *Excelsior* (240 feet) and the palatial *George Leary* (237 feet) on the same route. In 1892, with the imminent arrival of the modern packets of the Norfolk and Washington Steamboat Company, these lines saw their trade endangered on the river and between Washington and Norfolk. Active in shuttling overnight between Baltimore and Washington via the lower Potomac landings was *Sue*, owned by the Potomac Transportation Company, in the process of transfer to a new owner. Many other steamers sailed down the majestic expanse of the Potomac for its historic landings; some ferried passengers between Washington and Alexandria and local river ports, and others loaded excursionists to the tolerable limits and headed for riverside resorts not far from the city. One of the last was a little vessel by coincidence named the *Mary Washington*, a completely flat-bottomed, 154-foot craft, with twin funnels athwartships, side-wheels, and the anomalous configuration of a Mississippi steamboat. Her saloon deck was one long expanse of dance floor, where the more stately of the passengers danced the quadrille and the lancers, and the more sprightly showed an ankle with the polka, the schottische, and the waltz. [24]

Certain minor events on the Potomac in 1893 were destined to have enormous consequences for the Weems line. The events surrounded the enterprising activities and personality of one Charles R. Lewis, who had come lately into the steamboat business. In 1888, he, with his father (William R.) and brothers (Franklin C. and Andrew I.), had bought a small steamer named *John E. Tygert* from her owner, John E. Tygert, president of the Philadelphia and Smyrna Transportation Company, Philadelphia. They had purchased the rather awkward-looking propeller-driven steamer, only 109 feet in length, with a 22-foot beam, with the apparent intention of starting a steamboat service from Baltimore to landings in the lower Potomac river. The vessel burned on October 12, 1890 and was redocumented on February 21, 1891 after having been rebuilt and reregistered under the names of the four Lewises and John A. Ketcham (master). All four Lewises claimed Accomac County, Virginia, as their place of residence and Onancock as the homeport of *John E. Tygert*.[25] Charles R. Lewis and William R. Lewis had been masters of *Lady of the Lake*, sailing for the Inland and Coastal Seaboard Company in the early 1880s. Charles R. Lewis, in addition, had been engaged for some time in the canning business at Lewisetta, at the mouth of the Coan River, in Northumberland County, Virginia. He became the first postmaster when the post office was established there on January 9, 1888. Lewisetta itself had been named in 1753 for a forebear, Etta Lewis, daughter of a local landowner.[26]

On March 19, 1891, Charles R. Lewis, as the principal, consummated arrangements for the incorporation of his steamboat interests in a newly titled Maryland and Virginia Steamboat Company. It was incorporated by a certificate issued by the Baltimore City Superior Court acting under the authority of the general laws of Maryland.[27]

In March 1891—coincident with incorporation—Charles R. Lewis bought *Sue*, a comely but aging 175-foot paddlewheel steamer, from the Potomac Transportation Company and registered the owner as Charles R. Lewis of Westmoreland County, Virginia, and the home port as Tappahannock (Essex County, Virginia). Now fully occupied in developing trade on the Potomac and the Baltimore-Washington route, Charles R. Lewis, emerging as the real owner of the line, had two vessels, *John E. Tygert,* home ported in Onancock, and *Sue*, home ported in Tappahannock (Appendix A). He lived in Baltimore but still operated his canning factory at Lewisetta.[28]

In early 1893, residents of the lower Potomac from both sides of the river exploded in resentment at the quality of the steamboat service they were receiving. Various groups met from time to time, communicated with each other, and decided to appoint a committee to represent them in Baltimore. Accordingly, a select committee descended on the offices of various steamboat companies. Having heard that Henry Williams was a man of some foresight and empathy, they approached him first to solicit his advice on how to proceed with their quest for better steamboat service. When the subject of *John E. Tygert* and *Sue* came up, Williams stated that he would be willing to comply with the expectations of the Potomac residents if the two steamers could be bought "at a reasonable and proper figure," although he added that "he preferred the route rather than the steamers."

A subcommittee then visited the offices of the Maryland and Virginia Steamboat Company to ascertain if the company would discuss the possibility of selling the boats. But neither Charles R. Lewis, who held the title of general manager, nor Thomas S. Flood, a former pharmacist from Elmira, New York, who acted in the role of president, was available. An underling by the name of McPlynceon vouchsafed the opinion that the boats and "good will" could be bought for $125,000. Some members of the group observed that the value of *John E. Tygert* could be placed at no more than $15,000 and the *Sue* had been purchased from the Potomac Transportation Company for $17,000, leaving an exceedingly high price to be paid for "good will."

The committee moved to the office of the Choptank line, delivered their grievances, and gained a courteous but fruitless hearing. Without a tangible conclusion to their efforts, members of the full committee returned to their home on the Potomac to await some move on the part of the steamboat companies.[29] They had little reason to know that one man—Henry Williams—had digested what they had to say.

The erratic plunges of Charles R. Lewis into the steamboat market seemed even more perplexing when he acquired *Lady of the Lake* from the Inland and Coastal Seaboard Company and applied for her enrollment as temporary in Baltimore on July 7, 1893. What surprised the steamboat world and river residents alike was his proposed running of the boat from Alexandria to landings on the Rappahannock.[30] Even more astonishing to them was his October announcement of his intention to inaugurate a route from Baltimore to Tappahannock beginning in December. His agent in Baltimore proceeded to secure wharf privileges at the Light Street Bay Ridge wharf and began soliciting freight for *Lady of the Lake*.[31]

Here was a clear challenge to the monopoly of the Weems line on the Rappahannock. Here thrown in the face of the splendid new packets flying the red ball flag was a rather tawdry old boat claiming few wharves and grasping for trade wherever dissatisfaction with Weems could be stirred up. Rumors immediately began to circulate that if Charles R. Lewis contemplated an invasion of Weems territory on the Rappahannock, there would be a counterinvasion by Weems on the lower Potomac. The rumors gained some substance when apparent overtures for wharf privileges at Potomac landings were being made by Weems agents, and *Lancaster*, the newest and most prestigious of the Weems line boats, was being readied for other than her route on the Rappahannock.[32]

Reactions around the Rappahannock and Baltimore were varied. Some held the view that a line with only one boat could not succeed: what shipper would wait for that boat's arrival if several steamers of the Weems line appeared on schedule?[33] Others held that the Rappahannock was served by the most accommodating line with the most gentlemanly manager: why change?[34] Still others welcomed competition but commented on the "modest" appearance of the *Lady of the Lake* and doubted that its managers could afford to be as forthcoming as Henry Williams in meeting the needs of the local shippers.[35]

The venture of *Lady of the Lake* to Tappahannock barely feathered the waters of the Rappahannock. As a commercial endeavor, it was described as "unremunerative."[36] Charles R. Lewis allowed her to languish and then on August 25, 1894, sold her to J. W. Patterson, president of the People's Transportation Company of Washington, a black-owned excursion company.[37]

The adventurism of Charles R. Lewis on the Rappahannock ended in debacle. What it had done, however, was to excite the interest of Henry Williams in the Potomac. His appetite was whetted by rather obvious circumstances. In late 1893, the Weems line enjoyed an exceedingly prosperous monopoly on the Patuxent and the Rappahannock; separating each of these rivers from the Potomac was a peninsula only a county or two in width; the economies of these peninsulas or necks leaned as much to the Potomac as they did to the Patuxent or Rappahannock; the Potomac, it seemed, should be brought into the fold of the service provided by the Weems Steamboat Company. In addition, the Potomac River, particularly the landings and settlements in the lower regions, suffered from the lack of adequate steamboat service; *John E. Tygert* and *Sue* were not enough; delegations from both the Maryland and Virginia shores had made their complaints, dissatisfaction, and pleas for new and better service forcefully clear to several steamboat companies, and particularly to Henry Williams. Finally, the Maryland and Virginia Steamboat Company, led by Charles R. Lewis, was in disarray after the Weems threat of intervention on the Potomac; some of its officers had hinted that the two operating boats and certain wharf facilities could be bought; newspaper articles speculated that negotiations for the sale of the Maryland and Virginia Steamboat Company were actually under way although Charles R. Lewis vehemently denied the reports.

Charles R. Lewis was stung by the events on the Rappahannock and smarted from what he perceived as peremptory treatment by the Weems people both in 1883 and in 1893 to Lewis ventures with *Lady of the Lake*. Although mercurial and seemingly unpredictable, Lewis was nevertheless a brooding and stubborn man who would not brook being overrun by a competitor in this fashion. In 1893, he decided to counter any implied threat from the palatial Weems boats on the Potomac by building a new and handsome steamer of his own. It would be the finest of its class. With it, he would, even yet, demonstrate that the Maryland and Virginia Steamboat Company and Charles R. Lewis were forces to be reckoned with.

He placed the contract with the Neafie and Levy Ship and Engine Building Company of Philadelphia, one of the most prestigious shipbuilding firms bordering the Delaware.[38] *Potomac*, as he planned to name the boat, would be designed specifically as an overnight packet for the Baltimore-Washington route—a vessel of moderate size, 177 feet in length, 36-foot beam, 11-foot depth of hold, shorter by 30 feet than *Lady of the Lake*—a handy steamer, propeller driven, powered by a compound (two-cylinder) engine of the latest design. She would be a commodious vessel with 37 comfortable staterooms surrounding a well-decorated saloon. She would be a gracious ship with a dining room aft on the main deck encompassed in windows looking out on vistas of the Bay and facilities for the preparation of the finest cuisine, a well-staffed boat with quarters for a crew of 30. And, most noteworthy, she would be a seakeeping vessel, trim and gracefully sheered, able to negotiate the narrow creeks and little rivers feeding the Potomac and at the same time breast the roughest seas of the open Chesapeake in the worst of weather. The marine architects at Neafie and Levy believed that *Potomac,* a lovely apparition as she appeared at trials on a misty morning in June of 1894, was one of the finest boats they had ever built. Their pride was justifiable (Appendix A).

Financing the building of *Potomac* taxed the ingenuity of Charles R. Lewis. Much depended on the income derived from the operation of *John E. Tygert* and *Sue. John E. Tygert,* because of her small size and awkward configuration, was of limited value; the costs of rebuilding her after the fire in 1890 and the lease of an interim replacement (*W. W. Coit*) offset her profits in succeeding years.

Sue alone earned substantial profits. She was built in 1867, on speculation with no clear buyer in sight, by Harlan and Hollingsworth in Wilmington when the firm was idle in post war doldrums, and she bore the name of Sue Harlan, daughter of one of the firm's partners who held an interest in the Eastern Shore Railroad and hoped that the company would buy the vessel. A steamer similar in dimension to the prospective *Potomac, Sue* had appealed to hoped-for buyers. During a rather checkered career, she had steamed about the Bay for a number of companies, concluding with her sale by the Potomac Transportation Company in March 1891 to Charles R. Lewis (listing himself as a resident of Westmoreland County, Virginia) and, in turn, for $50,000 to his own corporation, the Maryland and Virginia Steamboat Company.[39] Overworked through the years, *Sue* in late 1892 showed signs of age and fatigue. By necessity, Charles R. Lewis placed her in the Woodall yard in Baltimore for overhaul. She emerged on May 3, 1893, repainted, refurbished, with main and passenger decks torn out and rebuilt, a new Scotch boiler installed, machinery repaired (boiler and engine work by James Clark), main saloon rebuilt and redecorated, recarpeted and refurnished throughout, and a searchlight and a new electric generator added for illumination (Appendix A). Under command of James Geoghegan (John Kirwan, first officer), she had immediately resumed her calls on the Potomac to Washington.[40]

Sue's repairs and her absence from the Potomac, leaving only *John E. Tygert* to provide a meager schedule, had been costly, both in money and in the anger generated among the residents along the Maryland shore and in the Northern Neck.

The issue of financing the construction and outfitting of *Potomac,* therefore, presented a major dilemma to the Maryland and Virginia Steamboat Company, owned almost exclusively by Charles R. Lewis. The building costs in advance of completion approximated in excess of $100,000, much more than the resources available to Lewis. His solution was to sign four promissory notes to the Neafie and Levy Company for the anticipated shortfall: $2,206.63 plus interest from December 14, 1984, due February 12, 1895; $8,333.33 plus interest from January 3, 1895, due March 7, 1895; $13,333.03 plus interest from June 30, 1894, due January 3, 1896.[41] Neafie and Levy agreed to hold these notes under the stipulation that the shipyard would retain title until all the notes were repaid.

Without a notion on how these obligations were to be met, Lewis advertised the forthcoming sailings of the new and splendid steamer *Potomac* to begin on July 3, 1894, from Pier 18, Light Street. In a blaze of bunting, *Potomac* took her place in tandem with *Sue* and began her runs to Washington and Potomac landings.

By October, if he did not know it sooner, Lewis had reached the conclusion that his bold gamble for a stake on the Potomac was doomed to failure. The payments due on *Potomac* could not be met from current proceeds of the company, and neither *John E. Tygert* nor *Sue* was worth enough to raise a mortgage. In the wings stood Henry Williams, attuned to the plight of Lewis and impelled to some action to appease the vociferous merchants and shippers of the Potomac valley. Lewis swallowed his bitterness and capitulated.

Fruitless negotiations on price continued for some time in a climate of veiled hostility, with periodic announcements that no negotiations were in progress at all, or that if there were such undertakings, no deal had been struck, or that all attempts at negotiation had failed. In the middle of the confusion, unconfirmed rumors spread that the Baltimore, Chesapeake, and Atlantic Railway Company was attempting to buy a controlling interest in the Weems line. Denials only added to the turmoil. The general confusion stirred up a hotbed of gossip on the Baltimore waterfront.

In this instance there was substance to the rumor. The Baltimore, Chesapeake, and Atlantic Railway Company (BC & A) had just triumphed in overrunning and buying out the major steamboat companies serving the Eastern Shore and some areas on the opposite shore. On March 9, 1894, the Choptank Steamboat Company sold out to the Eastern Shore Railroad Company; on July 18, both the Eastern Shore Steamboat Company and the Maryland Steamboat Company sold out to the same railroad company. The Eastern Shore Railroad Company, successful because it paid a good price at a time of financial instability on the part of the steamboat companies it acquired, redocumented itself on October 20, 1894, as the Baltimore, Chesapeake, and Atlantic Railway Company. Its rail tentacles spread over the Eastern Shore and brought it into conflict with the New York, Philadelphia, and Norfolk Railroad (known as the Nip 'n N) running down the spine of the Delmarva peninsula. With the new acquisitions, it gathered 15 steamboats to its fold, a virtual control over some of the best steamboat routes in Maryland and Virginia and a voracious appetite for monopoly over the entire Chesapeake Bay. The BC & A made no secret of its policy to absorb as many rival lines as possible by purchase (in fact, all of the steamboat lines out of Baltimore) and was in the process of approaching each line with a query on the price for its sale. It was reaching out now for the Wheeler Steamboat line; Henry Williams had good reason to be apprehensive about its intentions toward the Weems line and, especially, about the possibility of its approaching Charles R. Lewis and the Maryland and Virginia Steamboat Company.

Rumors of the intended takeover by BC & A of the Weems line spread to the Rappahannock. Where just a week before the local press castigated Weems for one fancied shortcoming after another, it suddenly reversed itself and called upon Henry Williams to resist the sale.

Praise was suddenly heaped on Henry Williams and the Weems line: "It may be said that this company has a monopoly of the trade and commerce of the Rappahannock river . . . but it is seriously doubted if there is another transportation company in the United States, having such a monopoly and possessing such opportunities for charging exhorbitant freight rates, that has been as just, as fair, and even as liberal in dealing with its defenseless patrons as this old and reliable company has always been."[42]

Henry Williams listened to the blandishments of the BC & A syndicate concerning the possible purchase of the Weems line and named a price so high that no reasonable capitalist would accept it. As independent owners, even though incorporated, Georgeanna Williams and Matilda S. Forbes, with Henry Williams at the helm, still had many options and considerable resources to support them. On the other hand, Henry Williams would not brook the insidious intervention of BC & A on the major Western Shore rivers, and he moved rapidly to preempt any moves by BC & A toward the tottering Maryland and Virginia Steamboat Company. Quickly, he drove to finalize the purchase of the latter by Weems.

Abruptly, on January 4, 1895, Charles R. Lewis resigned his office as general manager, transferred his controlling interest to Thomas S. Flood, president, and fled to Lewisetta, with the excuse to the press that his canning business there at the mouth of the Coan River demanded his full attention.[43] In fact, unable to face the final act of sale of his company to his nemesis, the Weems line in the person of Henry Williams, he had left to the absentee president from Elmira, New York, the execution of the distasteful task.

Potomac, which had never belonged to Charles R. Lewis and had remained under the ownership of Neafie and Levy, together with *Sue*, *John E. Tygert*, and certain wharves, became the property of the Weems Steamboat Company on January 30, 1895, for $150,000. Deducted from these proceeds were the promissory notes plus interest owed by Charles R. Lewis. The Weems line suddenly increased its indebtedness to $175,000 as a result of the purchase, some $53,000 of which it paid off in the current year, the remainder from earnings in the following year (Appendix G). Under an understanding signed on January 29 by Jacob Neafie, president, the Neafie and Levy shipyard agreed to transfer *Poto-*

Charles R. Lewis (1856–1937), general manager of the Maryland and Virginia Steamboat Company when the Weems line bought it in 1895. Courtesy of Alice Taylor

mac directly to the Weems line on payment of the amount due from Lewis in view of the contract of sale between Thomas S. Flood and Henry Williams.[44] The price paid by Henry Williams for the Maryland and Virginia Steamboat Company was more than fair. It covered the costs of building *Potomac,* and it generously compensated Charles R. Lewis for the transfer of two boats, one of questionable value, and some wharves.[45]

Henry Williams acquired *John E. Tygert,* a rather useless boat that he sold within months to the Laflin and Rand Powder Company in New York for $7,000, to carry the ingredients of gunpowder; *Sue,* an old but solid boat rejuvenated and embellished by rebuilding in 1893 and good for many years on the Potomac route; and *Potomac,* the newest, most sturdily built, and best equipped overnight packet on the Chesapeake (Appendix A). He also gained virtual control of the overnight steamboat trade on the three great rivers of the Western Shore—on the Patuxent and the Rappahannock, where he held an understood monopoly, and now on the Potomac, where his steamers provided services offered by no other company to river landings, particularly in the lower reaches.

With the entrance of the Weems line on the Potomac, Williams could bask in the pleasure of presiding over one of the major packet lines on the Chesapeake and one of the oldest and most respected transportation companies in the United States. With its capital conservatively estimated at $600,000, its personnel numbered at 250, and its seven steamboats—*Lancaster, Richmond, Westmoreland, St. Mary's, Essex, Sue,* and *Potomac*—reckoned among the most luxurious on the Bay, the

Weems Steamboat Company dominated travel on the Patuxent, the Potomac, and the Rappahannock. The prospects seemed undiminished by the clouds of growing depression settling over the region.

With the acquisition of a stake on the Potomac, Williams could look to a goal he frequently stated: to contribute to the economic development of the Potomac valley as he had helped develop the Rappahannock and the Patuxent. Unstated was the fact that the grand design came from the lips of another man who had expressed it, laid it out, but could not execute it.

That man was Captain Mason L. Weems.[46]

CHAPTER 6

Coping with the Nineties: Catastrophe, Confrontation, and Adjustment

The temper of Baltimore in the 1890s until the turn of the century was a curious mixture of elation and depression. The elation carried over from having survived the hazards of previous decades and showed in the building of lavish hotels, extravagant forms of entertainment for the well-to-do, the settling-in of established industry and commerce with a clear eye to the future, and the implied divisions of society into those who could afford the material pleasures and those who could not. The depression was economic; it afflicted the city and environs for a prolonged period, and it spread to the entire Chesapeake and Tidewater region. It was different from the sharp dips and troughs of the 1870s and 1880s. It was persistent. Its effects were devastating to those who could least afford deprivation, and it cast its shadow over the steamboat industry as it did over other forms of enterprise.

The prolonged depression of the 1890s dropped Baltimore among the industrial cities from a position of 8th place in 1880 to 11th by the turn of the century; industry began to move out of the city, some plants relocating in other areas of the country, some settling in smaller communities such as Frederick, Hagerstown, Cumberland, Cambridge, and Salisbury. Around the Bay area, producers found a slackened market in Baltimore, and, with lessened revenues, they bought less from the city. The depression adversely struck Norfolk—itself struggling with its own commercial woes—and to a lesser extent, Richmond.

Baltimore's industry, in spite of the economic doldrums, went through a period of consolidation into clothing factories, canneries, fertilizer plants, meat-packing houses, foundries and machine shops, tobacco factories, steel mills at Sparrow Point, and new oil refineries. The export of grain, raw cotton, and canned foods, among other products, through the port of Baltimore for overseas markets held its own. The trunk lines of the Baltimore and Ohio Railroad and the Pennsylvania Railroad together with local lines connecting the port with the heartland brought the city to the point of emergence as a major railroad center on the eastern seaboard.[1]

The plight of the laboring class in Baltimore was only aggravated by the layoffs and slow growth of the 1890s. Around Fells Point, the fetid slums lined with wretched rows of 1½-story houses dating from early days reeked with overhabitation. In 1900, Baltimore was the only major city in the United States without a sewerage system. Waste drained into cesspools; the ground became increasingly saturated; dirt-packed foundations of old houses softened; and densely packed streets became untenable from the stench. Open sewers and manufacturing plants delivered offal to the harbor until the smell became unbearable, and steamboats turning their paddlewheels or propellers churned up black and noxious sludge. It so discolored the white paint on the hulls below the guards that some steamboat lines elected to paint the entire hulls of their boats with the same red antifouling paint used for the bottoms of the boats, thus eliminating the white color and waterline below the rubrail. Laborers' wages were pathetically low. Earning from $1.25 a day unskilled to $2.50 a day skilled, laborers spent a half to three-quarters of their pay on food alone and found themselves increasingly exploited and suffering under nearly inhumane conditions.[2]

The blacks in the city, enduring the highest rate of unemployment and having little to sustain them except each other or retreat to the farm, which offered little more than seasonal labor, suffered most. Ethnic groups, increasingly of Irish, Polish, Italian, Scandinavian, Czech, Lithuanian, Greek, and Russian extraction, furnished part of the labor force, although many immigrants avoided the city and headed west on landing at the Baltimore and Ohio Marine terminal.[3] The German population, numbering over 150,000 and accounting for more than one-fourth of the city's population, contributed to the supply of skilled labor and also to the artistic and musical life of the city; but pride in their origin, stemming from the martial emergence of the German empire after the Franco-Prussian War, kept them largely apart and culturally unassimilated.[4]

Nevertheless, above the squalid slums and sewage-laden harbor, there flourished a cultural and social life of sharp contrast. The wealth that had accumulated from Baltimore's industry and commerce also provided the means for its pleasure. The mansions surrounding Mount Vernon Place or Lafayette Square at Lanvale Street or spreading northward into Guilford from upper Charles Street attested to the growth of an affluent upper class. Its members belonged to fashionable clubs, rode to the hounds from country estates, entertained royally at receptions and balls, and closed ranks on interlopers. They presented their daughters to society at the yearly Bachelor's Cotillon and held their boxes at the opera, season after season, in order to be seen in all their opulence.

Under their sponsorship Baltimore earned a respectable reputation as a center for the arts. The Walters Art Gallery—a repository for an astounding collection of European art—opened. Theaters drew crowds for every performance. The old Holliday Street Theater, originally built in 1794, rebuilt in 1813, and built again in 1874, had a long and distinguished history for its Shakespearean performances and, much earlier, as the setting for the first playing of "The Star Spangled Banner." The Front Street Theater remembered Jenny Lind's concert in 1850 and a long succession of concerts by artists from abroad thereafter. The stage at Ford's Theater resounded to the theatrics of every major actor of the times, including Otis Skinner, Ethel Barrymore, James O'Neil, and the lovely courtesan of Edward VII, Lily Langtry. On Howard Street, the Academy of Music boasted a huge electric chandelier in its ceiling and the claim of being one of the finest theaters in America. In October 1894, the Lyric—a majestic theater capable of staging *Die Walkure* and the heftiest Brunhilde—opened, with a concert by the Boston Symphony and no less than Nellie Melba as soloist. Puccini lovers shed sentimental tears over *La Bohème* in 1897 and *Tosca* a few years later. At the Howard Theater, box holders enjoyed the unlikely double billing of *Pinafore* and *Cavalleria Rusticana*. Great hotels, such as the Rennert and the Belvedere, catered to the wealthy and fashionable. Amusement parks such as Riverview, with its dangerous roller coasters, and Gwynn Oak, with Farson's Band, appealed to the middle class. A great university with emphasis on graduate education in the German model opened its doors; it was named for Johns Hopkins, wealthy benefactor. The Enoch Pratt Free Library came into existence through the generosity of still another prosperous entrepreneur. Sportsmen engaged in lacrosse, curling, footracing, boxing, baseball, and cockfighting, and the Baltimore Orioles, who started up in 1882, won the National League championship in 1894. A little-known English teacher by the name of Lizette Woodworth Reese won national acclaim for a one-verse sonnet called "Tears."

Department stores such as Hutzler's new "palace building" attracted crowds. People rode electric streetcars on Sunday just for the fun of it, particularly when the streetcars towed open "summer cars" designed to catch the breeze. And they clapped to the marches of Sousa in the park and hummed some catchy tunes of a young composer of light opera—his name was Victor Herbert.[5]

Baltimore in the 1890s and at the turn of the century was the economic and social magnet of the Chesapeake. In tidewater Virginia, the pull of the city was felt inexorably and resisted resentfully. Virginians, around the Rappahannock in particular, leaned strongly toward Norfolk with an eye to its potential growth and its facilities for linkage to New York and the Northeast. They pointed to the fact that the Old Dominion Line in the early 1890s was dispatching nine ships weekly to New York and planned to add *Princess Anne* in 1897 and *Jefferson* and *Hamilton* afterward. With such a fleet and such exceptional service, the tie of tidewater Virginia to Norfolk by steamboat would mean the outlet of produce to the market of New York and direct communication with the major trade centers of the eastern seaboard.

However, Norfolk did not prosper as predicted. In 1900 its population stood at 46,624. It had doubled since 1870, just as Baltimore's population had doubled; but in absolute figures, Baltimore's doubling to 508,957 by 1900 offered a stark contrast in sheer size. Furthermore, whereas the immediate countryside around Baltimore had increased sharply in population, the county surrounding Norfolk had decreased nearly 35 percent in 10 years. Sustaining Norfolk was not its commercial or industrial establishment but the naval base and transshipment facilities. And the depression of the 1890s left its mark on the city with the same telling force as it had done on Baltimore. Richmond as the state capital and a railroad center held its own with a population of 85,050. Fredericksburg at 5,068 had grown little since the 1870s. Washington (population 278,718 in 1900), at the head of the navigable Potomac, was neither an industrial city nor a commercial hub.[6] Virginians of Tidewater earnestly searched for an economic focal point of their own and inevitably found themselves in the orbit of Baltimore.

The Tidewater counties of Maryland bordering the Patuxent and Potomac grew unevenly in the depression years; except for Baltimore County, close to the city, growth was less than 13 percent. In Virginia's Tidewater counties along the Potomac and Rappahannock, the population growth was perceptibly more uneven, averaging less than 1 percent; Spotsylvania County alone suffered a loss of 34 percent. In absolute numbers, the growth in rural Tidewater during the decade remained consistently low. It reflected the continued flight from the farm to the city and the economic uncertainties of the times.[7]

Steamboat activity on the Chesapeake in the 1890s reflected to some extent the economic doldrums of the decade. In the first few years, the number of steamboats operating out of Baltimore increased from 45 to 49, but it declined precipitously to 37 by 1895, reflecting boats laid up or services discontinued for lack of trade.

After launching *Lancaster* with great flourish and embarking on the

Potomac enterprise with such drama, Henry Williams decided to take the measure of the economic landscape before proceeding with other plans for expansion. In these years of plateau, he sought to consolidate his gains, adjust his scheduling to seasonal needs, and meet as best he could the chronic bleatings of merchants and shippers.

Gross receipts of the Weems Steamboat Company grew slowly during the decade, from $231,747.49 in 1892 to $292,989.89 by 1895 and $299,742.02 by 1896. Earnings for 1897 and 1898 stood about $324,000 and at $340,000 in 1899. The spurt in prosperity began in 1900 with gross receipts of $380,601.93; in 1901, of $403,263.31; and in 1902, of $459,611.57, nearly double the receipts of a decade before. Net earnings, however, were another matter. They changed very little through the decade. From 1892 through 1894, they actually dropped from $66,289.35 to $60,054.37, the consequence of the fruit crop failure in one year but overwhelmingly the hammering result of the economic slowdown in the region. The Patuxent and Rappahannock routes produced net earnings of a similar amount in 1895, but the new Potomac route earned only $8,940.43. One year proved to be an exception; in 1897, the company reported net earnings of $91,875.26. It was enough to inspire the company to absolve all of its indebtedness, complete needed wharf and steamboat repairs (some of the steamers were showing their age), raise the annual dividend paid on capital stock held exclusively by the two sisters from the 2½ percent paid through the decade to a dramatic 5 percent, and plan for the building of new steamboats. Net earnings for 1899 through 1902 held at a range from $70,000 to $77,000, reflecting rising costs for fuel, repairs, increased number of scheduled trips demanded by the trade, and overwhelmingly the urgently needed procurement of new and expensive boats to complement the old, all of which were paid for from current earnings of the company. For the Weems line the doldrums of the mid-1890s were not dispelled completely until the turn of the century (Appendix G).

In the 1890s steamboat life on the Patuxent was not much different from the way it had been for many decades except that the river had shoaled. In the spring of 1879, *Planter* and *Wenonah* encountered difficulty at Hills Landing; the river had silted, and taking a steamer alongside the landing was virtually impossible except at very high tide; turning around was treacherous. With reluctance, Henry Williams notified the residents that Weems steamboats would go no farther up the river than Bristol, a mile or two below Hills Landing on the opposite shore. For those who depended on the steamer, it meant hauling produce, cattle, and passengers across the toll bridge above Hills Landing and down the dusty roads for five miles or so to the village of Bristol and its busy wharf. No alternative existed. The river ever so slowly continued to silt, aggravated by the increase in truck farming along its shores, and the shippers at Bristol and Lower Marlboro and Lyons Creek watched it apprehensively, year by year. Even at Bristol during the 1880s, steamers were often delayed by low water over the bar, extending 800 feet from shore, or at Swann's Bar, three miles below Bristol Landing.

A survey conducted by the U.S. Army engineers in 1886 resulted in the excavation of channels and turning basins at both Bristol Bar and Swann's Bar, enabling steamers to approach and clear Bristol Landing and to turn around in low water.[8]

Fair Haven, in spite of the best publicity Henry Williams could muster in the local press, failed to attract the enormous crowds he had hoped for. His choice not to make of it an amusement park had been deliberate; he wanted instead a peaceful hotel resort and picnic grove by the Bay, with the pleasant boat ride on a comfortable steamer, fine dining and dancing on both the boat and at the hotel, and a genteel atmosphere at the beach, away from the boisterous crowds, as inducements for patronage by a somewhat more sedate clientele. The patronage, however, came from all levels of Baltimore society which could afford the $1.00 fare; ethnic societies, church groups, labor unions, and beer-drinking German organizations stomped aboard the boats in about the same proportions as well-to-do matrons, with their servants to handle the children and luggage, and as family picnickers bent on a day at the beach. The resort earned a comfortable income, but by no means did it compare with the experience of Tolchester.[9]

The placid life of the Weems company on the Patuxent and at Fair Haven during most of the period was not matched by other experiences it endured. The decade of the 1890s seemed fraught with unforeseen difficulties, stemming from the worst storms to plague the region in years, from a succession of collisions and groundings and burnings, and from tension-filled encounters with would-be competitors.

Storms in the 1890s rivaled the worst on record on the Bay. In 1893 and 1895, ice gorges formed on the rivers above the fall line and burst on the sheet ice already extending from shore to shore at the head of navigation. The resulting mass on the Patuxent and Rappahannock thundered down the river valleys carrying with it wharves, warehouses, and barges. On the Bay, ice clogged the shipping lanes and left steamers stranded for days or even weeks. The ferocity of gales and torrential flooding nearly matched that of 1889, when the upper Bay was choked with logs and debris brought down from Johnstown and the Susquehanna. Late in the decade, a howling storm of hurricane force devastated Calvert and St. Mary's Counties. The storm followed the course of the Patuxent, leveling buildings in its path; the warehouses at Jones, Forrest, Parkers, and Sotterley were blown away; some deck crewmen on *St. Mary's* were hurt; and many residents were killed or injured. *St. Mary's* survived at a landing; *Essex* made Deep Creek Landing and found herself pinned to the wharf by the wind. Some excursionists at Parkers Wharf, when the warehouse in which they had sought shelter disintegrated, lay flat on the wharf, their fingers clinging to the cracks between the planking. When the storm abated, they found that the wind had turned their bodies completely around, feet to head. At Broom's Island and at Sotterley, some visitors were blown into the water and drowned. The Weems steamboats visited the wharves, brought back the injured and dead, and provided solace for the distraught.[10]

The winter of 1895 developed into one of the coldest on record. Steamers remained in port for weeks on end, and *Potomac* got stuck in the ice on the open Bay, unable to move and reduced to being a home for its crew who used the ice as a playing field for improvised hockey matches. Mail could not be delivered by boats, and local residents berated the line for the lack of service. Finally, after beating her way through ice 10 to 12 inches thick—a feat impossible for a lesser vessel to perform—*Potomac* reached Leonardtown to the admiration of the populace, who blessed her for reestablishing communication with the outside world.[11]

The ice created other problems. Before her dismissal from the Weems fleet, *John E. Tygert* performed one useful service: on February 27, 1895, she arrived at her Light Street wharf with *Essex* in tow. *Essex* was disabled by breaking her rudder and damaging her sternpost while crunching through ice in Carter's Creek. At North End *John E. Tygert* had received a message to turn back and assist *Essex* and towed the latter to the Patuxent mouth, laying to until the wind abated. *St. Mary's* arrived and took the *Essex* passengers to Baltimore. *Essex* went to Skinner's for repairs; *John E. Tygert* returned at once to the Rappahannock and to scenes of damage. Several Weems landings, including Wellfords, were scored by the ice, and the wharf at Monaskon in Lancaster County had been completely devastated.[12] The winter conjured up the image of December 1893, when steamboats stopped running, ice filled the Bay from shore to shore, and record temperatures, below the zero mark, stayed for weeks on end. It seemed that the winters of the 1890s were the cruelest that steamboat men had known.

Then, on the afternoon of February 14, 1895, as *Potomac*, between runs, lay at her berth at Pier 8, Light Street, several mattresses caught fire in the after cabin below the main deck on the starboard side. Before the blaze could be contained, a number of mattresses and four berths were destroyed, $400 worth of damage was done to woodwork, and Captain Lindsay of the fireboat *Cataract* suffered a cut on his scalp from a hose nozzle. It was supposed that the fire was caused by the ignition of matches that were carried into the berths by rats.[13]

Collisions seemed to plague the Weems line steamers. In mid-February 1895, the large steamer *Danville* of the York River line collided with *St. Mary's* (Captain James Gourley) in a heavy evening fog off Fort Carroll. Whereas *Danville* was virtually undamaged, the starboard side of *St. Mary's* was wrecked, her paddlebox carried away, hurricane deck splintered, saloon skylight left in shards, staterooms and galley shattered. No one was injured; one woman fainted. A corpse in transit was unshaken in his coffin.[14]

St. Mary's (formerly *Theodore Weems*) seemed to have a penchant for collisions. Some years later, again commanded by Captain James Gourley, she met the Old Bay Line steamer *Georgia* in a resounding crash

Steamer *Potomac* locked in ice on the Chesapeake. From the collection of Captain J. D. Davis. Courtesy of the Mariners' Museum

between Fort McHenry and the Lazaretto. *Georgia,* inbound from Norfolk in the early daylight of a snowy morning, rammed *St. Mary's,* outbound for the Patuxent. *Georgia's* bow plunged into the port paddlebox of *St. Mary's,* broke the housing, shaft supports, and several buckets, entered the galley within three feet of a blazing stove, smashed the dishes in the pantry, collapsed the ladies' toilet (no occupants!) and the adjoining cabin, and split the headrest of a sofa in the latter on which the wife of State Senator Charles L. Marsh was reclining (she raised up just in time). *St. Mary's* had to be towed back to Light Street.[15]

Then, in a heavy rain squall on the morning of September 18, 1897, *Westmoreland* came upon the bugeye *Seabird* of Dorchester County in the midst of tacking across the harbor from Broadway Pier to Locust Point. She struck the bugeye a glancing blow on the starboard side and cut a great gash near the bow. The vessel began to sink, and Captain Davis of *Westmoreland* ordered lines thrown to her, warped her alongside, gathered her crew of five aboard, and attempted to tow her to the Weems pier on Light Street. But the lines broke, the bugeye rolled over on her side, and would have sunk had the fireboat *Cataract* not spied her and brought her into Commercial Wharf. Captain Davis was commended for his seamanship.[16]

In the same year, *Potomac,* inbound to Baltimore, cut pungy *Three Brothers* in two off Seven Foot Knoll. The accident occurred at 4:00 A.M. in clear weather. *Potomac,* with *Three Brothers* close aboard, shifted her helm slightly to make room for a vessel on the opposite side. The pungy, seeing this maneuver, then attempted to cross *Potomac's* bows. Struck amidships and divided in half, the sailboat sank so quickly that her skipper, Thomas Hart of York Street, Baltimore, was unable to escape and drowned. Captain William Geoghegan had *Potomac*'s boats lowered to circle the sunken wreckage. Four men were rescued from the rigging. Aboard *Potomac*, the shock of the collision was so slight that passengers were not awakened.[17]

Lancaster collided twice with schooners in Carter's Creek and sank both of them. One night the schooner *Morning Light* of Irvington was lying off the channel at anchor when struck by *Lancaster*. She was raised, placed on the ways at Weems, Virginia, and refloated; damages were $325 and were paid by Henry Williams. Schooner *Nancy Hanks* of Irvington dragged anchor in heavy wind as *Lancaster* attempted to pass her on her way out of the creek; although the engine was reversed, the steel prow of the steamer caught the stern of the schooner and sank her; the Weems line made no offer of compensation or repairs.[18]

When two Weems line boats collided with each other, they made a bit of steamboat history. Off Point Lookout in a heavy fog at night, *Essex*, under Captain Daniel M. Davis, ran into *Potomac*, causing extensive damage to both steamers. *Essex* was bound down the Bay; *Potomac* was enroute to Baltimore. The fog was so dense that lookoutsmen could see only a few yards. Before anyone aboard *Potomac* was aware of the proximity of another vessel, she was struck amidships on the starboard side by *Essex*. Captain Davis, just a second before the crash, had rushed out on deck by the pilothouse and was knocked senseless. Passengers and crew on both boats were badly shaken. Aboard *Potomac*, joiner work on the superstructure above the waterline on the starboard side was shattered. The bow of *Essex* was heavily damaged, and she put into Solomons to examine her wounds. *Potomac* continued to Baltimore. Bruised but conscious, Captain Davis was given the luxury of a ride by cab to his home on Lafayette Avenue.[19] Both boats were consigned to the shipyard for repairs while Henry Williams and his attorneys tried to figure out how insurance worked in such unusual circumstances.

Groundings took curious turns. One Sunday at 5:00 A.M. *Potomac* went hard aground in the Coan River off Cella Cove Point, leaving her bow high on the mud and the bottom of the river plainly in sight from the after gangway. No amount of backing by the engines or fishtailing with the rudder prevailed. Her passengers were landed by small boats. She stayed there for several weeks until a spring tide and monumental engine effort freed her. Shortly afterward, Henry Williams received a bill for $25 from a gentleman claiming to be the guardian of the young lady who owned the riparian rights to the land (river bottom) on which *Potomac* sat during her grounding. The bill was for "ground rent." Baltimoreans, of course, understood; renting one's land to another person on which he could build a house and own it harked back to the manorial system. But the idea of applying the notion to a grounded steamboat startled Henry Williams. When confronted with the fact that the state of Virginia owned the bottom of the river, the lady's guardian then claimed that the $25 was intended to cover damage to his oyster bed. Rather than continue an unwanted altercation, Williams paid.[20]

Most of the Weems boats went aground at one time or another in the 1890s. In 1896 *Richmond* landed in the shoals twice. One incident occurred in Urbanna Creek, when she managed to free herself. On the second occasion, in Mill Creek, *Essex* made an attempt to pull her free, failed, and called in a dredging tug to assist. *Essex* herself went aground opposite Williams Wharf near the mouth of Battle Creek in the same year. And *Sue* grounded in the same area.

Late in the decade *Potomac* backed into shoal water near one of her creekside landings and lost her rudder. Rumor around the Baltimore waterfront had it that *Essex* had taken her in tow for a tortured run to Baltimore. *Essex* had indeed begun the towing operation when an ingenious mind aboard *Potomac* conceived the idea of fastening a long pole to a gangplank and, by a bit of wedging in the guards, using the assembly as a kind of rudder. It worked. *Potomac* came home to Baltimore under her own power with her improvised tiller.[21]

Aside from the depredations of storms, collisions, and groundings, the directors of the Weems Steamboat Company, with Henry Williams as president, had to deal with a succession of problems arising during these years.[22]

Open secrets bruited about caused worries. In March 1895, the press in Fredericksburg reported such a secret in disclosing that Connecticut "capitalists" had acquired a charter for the building of a railroad connecting West Virginia with the Chesapeake via the Northern Neck. Such a railroad, linking not only the West with Tidewater but tying the Northern Neck in rail service by transfer to Baltimore, would immediately affect Weems on the Potomac and Rappahannock. No clear forecast on the railroad's prospects seemed to be available.[23]

The idea of building a railroad down the length of the Northern Neck to the Chesapeake Bay surfaced at various times in the late 1880s, 1890s, and even until the turn of the century. At one time, every county in the Northern Neck voted $30,000 to assist a Connecticut syndicate in building such a rail line, and, in fact, one mile of track was laid from Fredericksburg. As reported by one newspaper, "at that time the Weems Steamboat Company of Baltimore bought the company off, and that was the last heard of the enterprise." Some land was cleared for track near the Great Wicomico River at the proposed eastern terminal, and that too was abandoned. Clamor in the press for a Northern Neck railroad never succeeded; a rail line was never built. Whether or not he had anything to do with squelching such clear-cut competition on both the Rappahannock and the Potomac, Henry Williams never disclosed.[24]

The irritations took an ugly turn as competitors asserted themselves on the lower Potomac. In May 1895, *Sue* and *Potomac* of the Weems line confronted *Wakefield* and *T. V. Arrowsmith* of the Washington Steamboat Company in a rate war. The latter company had been operating the two steamers on the Potomac for a number of years and in the first part of 1895 ran in tandem to landings on the Nomini, the Coan, and the Yeocomico on the Virginia side and to Leonardtown, St. Clement's Bay, and Piney Point on the Maryland side. *T. V. Arrowsmith*, a trim craft of 201 feet, and *Wakefield*, a boat of 160 feet built by Pusey and Jones in Wilmington in 1885, enjoyed an established trade out of Washington. The Weems steamers out of Baltimore, using the wharves inherited by ownership or lease from the Maryland and Virginia Steamboat Company, threatened that trade. Weems announced a reduction in freight rates; tobacco would be hauled at $1.00 per hogshead. The resulting rate war was severe but short.

"The opposing steamer lines carrying freight on the Potomac," reported a local journalist, "are each fighting to control freight on that river. When informed that a steamer of each line was at a wharf recently, the crews were soliciting freight for their steamers. Each cut its rate until finally one steamer offered to take freight from that wharf free and did so." Loyalty tended to focus on the Washington Steamboat Company. "If our people ever forsake the steamers of [that company], as faithful and true as they have ever been to us through the storms, cold and ice of winter, the storms and heat of summer . . . I shall think them very ungrateful," prated one commentator. [25]

In fact, the wharves owned by the Maryland and Virginia Steamboat Company and transferred to Weems extended up the river to Washington but coincided with the rights of the Washington Steamboat Company in only a few instances. An uneasy truce developed in which both companies maintained their services and their rates since no other solution seemed practicable. In a way, Henry Williams had the upper hand with *Potomac*, a new and impressive boat, and *Sue*, since the two boats were able to offer four trips a week instead of the two under Charles R. Lewis. And *T. V. Arrowsmith*, her age and condition showing, went off to be rebuilt in 1895 leaving *Wakefield* alone to compete with Weems.

The following year another altercation developed between the Washington Steamboat Company and Weems, when the latter proposed that as a service to merchants and farmers near Mount Holly on the Northern Neck, any goods ordered by them from Baltimore could be brought down on *Potomac*, transferred to *Wakefield*, which called at the wharf in question, and delivered at the cost of only one freight charge. The Washington Steamboat Company demurred, pointing to the Baltimore and Ohio Railroad terminal at Shepherd's Landing (on the Maryland shore above Alexandria), where *Wakefield* could pick up freight consigned from Baltimore to the residents of Mount Holly. The snub indicated that the standoff continued between the two companies. [26]

Then in the summer of 1895 came *Tarpon*. She was a sturdy vessel built in 1887 by Pusey and Jones as *Naugatuck* for the Naugatuck Valley Steamship Company to run between Derby, Connecticut, and New York City. But Henry Bradley Plant bought her in 1890, lengthened her to 160 feet, renamed her *Tarpon*, and placed her in service along the west coast of Florida. Her main deck was enclosed fore and aft to meet the weather and protect the freight, but her passenger deck, with wheelhouse forward of its deckhouse, had, for most of its length, staterooms, some of which opened out on deck rather than into the saloon. Many steamboat operators in the Florida coastal trade leased their boats in the summer off-season to operators up north. In the summer of 1895, *Tarpon* was leased from the Plant Line, accommodated at Pier 12, Light Street, and advertised as initiating a line to operate between Baltimore and landings on the Potomac. Furthermore, it was expressly announced that the boat would run in opposition to the Weems line on its Baltimore to Washington route.[27]

The opposition "line" centered around one Alvin P. Kennedy, whom most people along the Potomac considered to be no more than a front for Charles R. Lewis, late owner of the Maryland and Virginia Steamboat Company. In fact, Alvin P. Kennedy had been one of the "directors" of the Maryland and Virginia Steamboat Company when it was incorporated by Charles R. Lewis. *Tarpon* was skippered by a Captain Beatley, late master of *John E. Tygert*, who had resigned in protest at its sale to the Laflin and Rand Powder Company, New York, as a conveyor of gunpowder. Disgruntled, he had joined forces with his old boss to retaliate against Henry Williams and the Weems line. For a time, some shippers along the river patronized *Tarpon* and saw in the boat a counterpart to the absent *John E. Tygert*. But very quickly the gamble failed, and the venture scarcely ruffled the rumor mill in Baltimore. *Tarpon* dutifully returned to Florida to resume an eventful career lasting for many years and eventually ended in a watery grave.[28]

In 1893, there appeared a new personality on the Potomac steamboat scene—Ephraim Randall. He had bought *John W. Thompson*, an old boat of the Inland and Coastal Seaboard Company, renamed her *Harry Randall* (after his son, born in 1875, the same year the boat was launched), and set her up as a freight carrier to continue such service on the lower Potomac. When she continued on after 1895, she was no more than a minor but rather incessant irritant to Henry Williams. Shortly after the turn of the century, however, Ephraim Randall acquired the Washington Steamboat Company and began building a line of packets to serve the freight and passenger requirements of both shores of the Potomac. At 51 years of age, he was a rough-shod, self-made New Yorker who had arrived the hard way. Beginning his career with the Union army at the age of 11, he became a pool hall operator. His steamboat life began as an agent for various lines, including that of the little bargelike, two-stack excursion boat *Mary Washington* and its connection to Riverview. By one means or another, in a matter of years, he became a steamboat operator and began packet service to the lower Potomac. With his acquisition of the Washington Steamboat Company, he gained *Wakefield* and *T. V. Arrowsmith*, both handsome vessels, the latter having undergone hull alteration and extensive refurbishing in 1895. Added to this fleet could be counted *Estelle Randall*, a 111-foot steamer built in 1898, and little 45-foot *Lovie Randall*, built in 1892, both for Ephraim Randall.

He owned also *Samuel J. Pentz*, an old but renowned excursion boat bought from the Maryland Steamboat Company.

Ephraim Randall proceeded to divide his steamboat service into three routes: upper river, middle river, lower river. It was the last route that brought him into collision with the Weems line. The challenge was not a serious one. In fact, at the outset, Henry Williams was determined to accommodate the Randall interests in the lower river. A newspaper editorial stated that "the man with a large generous heart Mr. Henry Williams, agent of the Weems Steamboat Company, has arranged with Mr. Randall, owner of the *Harry Randall*, so that if you live near any of the wharves that the *Harry Randall* stops at you can order from Baltimore anything you want to be shipped on the steamer *Potomac* in the care of the *Harry Randall* to your wharf at a moderate freight. Encourage this kind effort to accommodate you and show this big hearted man you appreciate it."

Wakefield offered more systematic service on the lower river segment, and both Henry Williams and Ephraim Randall agreed that short of engaging in a rate war from which neither would benefit, a division of trade would be in order. Accordingly, *Wakefield* shifted her interest to Colonial Beach and certain landings on the Virginia side, leaving the Maryland side of the lower Potomac to Weems. Landings below Colonial Beach on the Virginia side continued to be served by Weems, whereas the Randall line concentrated its interest in the middle and upper river. A gentleman's understanding had prevented a costly confrontation.[29]

Not so an altercation that developed on the Patuxent! There, the dispute was not between two competing steamboat lines but between Weems and a blundering railroad. Earlier, in 1891, an enterprise called the Washington and Chesapeake Railway launched an ambitious project to build a rail line 28 miles long from Washington to a proposed 3,000-acre resort to be called Chesapeake Beach, on the Bay in Calvert County. The prospectus announced that a great drawbridge, the largest single-span plate girder bridge in the United States, had been constructed to cross the principal obstacle, the Patuxent River. The announcements were overblown, financial arrangements miscarried, and a new enterprise was formed under the name of the Chesapeake Beach Railway to complete the project. With fits and starts and much mismanagement, the railway progressed on its route, and the resort began construction. Otto Mears, well-known railroad builder from Colorado, now brought into the corporation, was instrumental in its progress.

The bridge at the Patuxent River remained the major problem, as construction proceeded in 1898. The initial charter of the company, passed by the Maryland General Assembly, outlawed the construction of any obstruction to navigation downstream from Bristol, served by the sidewheelers *Richmond* and *Westmoreland* of the Weems line. *St. Mary's* also went up to Bristol. Disturbed citizens of Bristol and vicinity circulated a petition requesting the legislature to reconsider and require the railway to build its own bridge north of Bristol. They feared that the Weems line would withdraw its steamboat service if the bridge was completed as contemplated. Under its plan, the railroad planned to cross the Patuxent from Mount Calvert (just below Hills Landing) to Jug Bay (just below Pig Point or Bristol), thus isolating Bristol above the crossing. A bill was introduced in each house of the Maryland legislature; the bills differed materially. A conference committee met to reconcile the differences. Henry Williams appeared before the committee to plead for relocation, the conference committee failed to agree, and the bills died.

The "great drawbridge" advertised so much earlier had, of course, never been built. A contract for a new drawbridge, which would have to gain the approval of the U. S. Army Corps of Engineers since navigation of the river was entailed, was awarded to the Youngstown Bridge Company. It called for the installation of a 183-foot plate girder drawspan to swing from a center island with its attendant machinery. In 1899, the span was generally in place, but the machinery for rotating the span had yet to be installed. This condition required, at the convenience of the bridge builders, the use of cables to haul the span around to allow passage of the steamers past the draw. On other occasions, when the status of construction work ostensibly precluded such action, the Weems line was forced to delay service to Bristol. At one point, the construction of bulkheading appeared to reduce the channel past the draw to such an extent that the Weems line questioned whether its broad-beamed sidewheelers could make the transit, thereby requiring the use of *Potomac*, screw driven and narrow, at considerable rescheduling difficulty for the company. Finally, tempers broke, and Henry Williams and Captain James Gourley complained angrily to the corps of engineers, accompanied by a threat of suit. As a result, the Chesapeake Beach Railway was forced to change its plans and its priorities, complete the drawbridge quickly, and provide for access past the draw wide enough to accommodate the sidewheelers with room to spare.

At the beachside resort, construction of boardwalk, pier, bathhouses, midway, and amusements continued haltingly, with financial disasters rearing up intermittently in 1900. On the opening day, June 9, 1900, the steamer *J. S. Warden* disgorged hundreds of excursionists on the half-finished pier. In the previous summer, with some of the beach facilities barely completed, Henry Williams had tried to prod the resort developers by routing *St. Mary's* to the Chesapeake Beach landing on a Wednesday and Saturday run to Fair Haven. He continued biweekly service through the winter and into the next summer season. But with the chartering of regularly running steamboats by the Chesapeake Beach Company itself and the tentative prospering of the railway to Washington, he dropped the service (Appendix B).

In the years ahead, Chesapeake Beach was to have off-and-on-again success, and *Dreamland*, the largest excursion steamer out of Baltimore, carried 3,000 picnickers at one time to revel in the surf, eat enormous meals in her dining room, and drink beer at five cents a glass. On her moonlight cruises, couples danced on a huge floor to one of the sweetest-sounding bands known in Baltimore and finished the evening to the theme song "Meet Me Tonight in Dreamland." Carousels at the beach honked away, and crowds shrieked in mock terror aboard the roller coaster. The train chugged back and forth to Washington, crossing the Patuxent River below Bristol, occasionally stopping to allow the drawbridge to swing open to allow a stately steamboat to pass through.[30]

During the decade of the 1890s the Weems line encountered stiffening resentment among shippers and farmers along the Rappahannock. Part of it came from inbred distaste for Yankee intrusion, part stemmed from the hammering effects of the post-Civil War depression among the farmers and their perception of the Weems line as a monopoly bent on extracting their very blood in the form of high freight rates, and part of it emerged from the beginnings of the Farmers' Alliance groups, organizations established to address the problems of the regional planters. In contrast to some groups that looked to Norfolk as the outlet to major markets in the Northeast, some of the leadership, particularly in the organizations residing in the upper river, looked to the railroad terminal at Fredericksburg as the point of transshipment for their produce. Some of the merchants of Fredericksburg wanted a way of encouraging local commercial activity along the river to bolster their own businesses. All of these objectives looked to the starting up of local steamboat service on the Rappahannock: first, for the upper river residents, to develop a local steamboat trade centered on Fredericksburg; second, for the lower river residents, to work out some arrangement for local steamboat service and transshipment through Norfolk; and, third, to counter the monopoly of Weems, whether or not it was fair in its rates and services. Oddly enough, as in the past, the residents eulogized Weems and Henry Williams and in the very next breath denounced the company for its perceived misdeeds. One of the themes of criticism was that Weems tailored its services to favor commission merchants in Baltimore at the expense of local services that would benefit merchants and rail transshipment possibilities in Fredericksburg.

Stormed one newspaper correspondent from Port Conway, "we have been for the past twenty-five or thirty years at the mercy of that . . . extortionate combine called the Weems Line . . . and we should discover some means by which the noble river . . . may be used by . . . all good citizens so as not to offend . . . the steam magnates of Baltimore who have waxed fat and grown rich, chiefly at our expense." Declared another from Laretto (near Saunders Wharf), "we pay double railroad rates . . . cattle today are brought from Chicago to Baltimore, nearly one thousand miles, as cheaply as we can ship from points on the Rappahannock to Baltimore."[31]

Influenced by this editorializing in the local press and the Rappahannock Transportation Committee, formed from Alliance groups, the little steam barge *Mattie,* under one Joseph Colbert, began day service from upper Rappahannock landings to Fredericksburg, not only to meet the Fredericksburg trains for forwarding the farmers' produce to northern markets within a day (an overly optimistic assumption) but also to link his dry goods store in town to the river trade (a more realistic proposition). *Mattie* served to disclose the fact that the Weems steamboats did not have much trade on the upper river and that the rates charged were not incommensurate with the costs. She had started her run in the summer of 1891; *Mattie*'s stay was brief. However, she made her presence felt in Baltimore, where Henry Williams and the directors of the Weems line wondered when other ventures of a similar sort would respond to the criticism and clamor on the Rappahannock.[32]

Henry Williams tried to earn the respect of the farmers on the Patuxent, the Potomac, and the Rappahannock. On many occasions, he fought their battles for them. In 1893, for example, he stood in the office of Secretary of Agriculture Rusk in Washington to protest a quarantine imposed on all cattle south of the Potomac because of aplenetic or "southern" fever, when in fact no cattle in Virginia had been infected. His plea was heard, and the quarantine was lifted.[33] Williams listened patiently to complaints, responded to suggestions, and tried to meet the demands of the shippers. One lady took the steamer to Baltimore for a confrontation with the president of the company in his office over freight rates to the city: "Seventy cents on a coop with nineteen turkeys and ducks too much." Frequently at the height of the harvest or oyster season he dispatched extra steamers loaded with nothing but barrels. Said one shipper: "vote for Henry Williams for president of the United States."

In spite of Williams's efforts to meet the demands of shippers in scheduling and rate setting, the barrage of criticism from the newspapers and various organizations of the Rappahannock valley continued unabated throughout the decade. By the turn of the century, it had turned vitriolic, and Williams found himself sorely pressed to placate his detractors and maintain a viable relationship with the trade on the river.

The decade of the nineties had been a time of trial and a time of settling-in for Williams. He had studied the steamboat horizon of the Chesapeake and had learned to deal with its vagaries. Although the unusual severity of storm and ice had taken their toll and a series of accidents and groundings had chalked up sizable costs in repairs and lost steaming time, these were part of the price of steamboat management, and Williams, along with the owners (his wife and Matilda S. Forbes), took them in stride, just as other steamboat operators all over the Bay were doing. He met confrontations with competition—whether on the Potomac or the Rappahannock—with decisiveness and a gambler's instinct for the winning card. It was the way of the steamboat world on the Chesapeake.

But the economic appetite had lagged throughout most of the decade, reflecting in steamboat activity a continued lethargy in agricultural Tidewater and a persistent plateau in the sectors of industrial activity supporting the steamboat trade. Williams's decision to build no more boats after the launching of *Lancaster* in 1892 was predicated on his caution in the economic climate.

In 1895, however, he threw caution to the winds in two climactic decisions. One paid off handsomely; the other ended in humiliating defeat.

The defeat was the result of miscalculation, even ineptitude, in the rough-and-tumble game of Baltimore City politics. In 1895 Williams decided to run for mayor, counting on the Democratic machine of Arthur Pue Gorman and Isaac Freeman Rasin, which had dominated Maryland politics for 20 years, to give him victory. Instead, the Republican reform movement, capitalizing on the slums and sweatships of the city, swept the Democratic slate from power in a bloody election in which the Democratic contenders tried to run roughshod over the voters. Humiliated, Williams vowed to try again for mayor, this time relying on the Democrats to initiate an uproar over the failure of the Republicans to make good on their promises of reform. In 1897 he was defeated for a second time. As a result, neither the economic nor the political landscape, given the thrust of the elections, must have seemed overly attractive to Williams (Appendix E).[34]

But 1895 also marked the year during which Williams plunged into the venture on the Potomac. When presented with some unpalatable choices—watching the insolvent company of William R. Lewis with its link to the splendid new *Potomac* being swallowed up by the railroad syndicate, or enduring ever-encroaching competition from other boats of the syndicate, or surrendering himself to the railroad's blandishments—he had acted boldly, even impetuously, in grabbing preemptively the boats of Charles R. Lewis and his steamboat interests on the Potomac.

In spite of periodic competition on the Potomac, producing little more than annoyance for him, the venture in purchasing the Maryland and Virginia Steamboat Company, and particularly *Potomac*, had paid off handsomely, even after an uncertain and unprofitable start (Appendix G). Coupled with the steady income from the Patuxent trade and the certain but tempetuous fiscal return from the Rappahannock, the Potomac route joined to produce a mounting flow of wealth to the coffers of the two sisters and, by conjunction, to their husbands and offspring. Henry Williams himself was a wealthy man.[35] His personal portfolio included stock holdings in railroads, real estate, banks, and other enterprises (Appendix E).

He and Georgeanna, the latter grown matronly and portly, saw to it that their daughters lived a prominent social life as well. Introduced at the appropriate age to Baltimore society at the Bachelor's Cotillon, Elizabeth Chew Williams (December 5, 1872–March 19, 1959) and Matilda Weems Williams (January 3, 1878–December 20, 1952) drew around them the social elite of the city. They entertained lavishly, and in return whirled away their time at balls, receptions, theater and opera parties, and endless benefit functions of one sort or another.

At the Williams home flush times shone on the glitter of entertainment. Stated one press clip, "one of the handsomest receptions of the winter was given at three o'clock yesterday by Miss Elizabeth Chew Williams and her sister Miss Matilda Weems Williams at their home at 407 W. Lanvale Street [with] several hundred guests." A certain fascination for visiting European nobility attended the functions of Baltimore society. A ball for a countess here, a reception there for Admiral His Serene Highness Prince Louis of Battenberg—the social register fairly outdid itself on bended knee and an accompanying gesture of noblesse oblige.[36]

As the decade drew to a close and a new century shone on the calendar, the economic depression weakened its grip, and business began to boom. Farmers and merchants sensed the improvement; industry took its stride; and wealth poured once again into the pockets of corporate ownership.

The Gilded Age had stepped upon the stage. Its opulence reached into the steamboat world, and new steamers coming down the ways attempted to match in splendor all its supposed grandeur.

CHAPTER 7

The Gilded Age: Palace Packets, River Conflict, and the Railroad's Grasp

The advent of a new century, with a burst of prosperity, brought the steamboat era on the Chesapeake to its peak. In the first few years, an average of 50 or more steamboats plied out of Baltimore to several hundred landings on the rivers and creeks of the Bay. Out of Norfolk, nearly 20 steamers and out of Washington a similar number—depending on the particular year—headed for the regions they served. The steamboat pageant swept the Chesapeake and its tributaries in a wave of nostalgia and romance. It had started three-quarters of a century before, had swelled with each passing decade, and showed no signs of ever ending.

New steamboats joined the parade around the turn of the century. For the Ericsson Line in 1903 the sister ships *Penn* and *Lord Baltimore* steamed for daylight runs through the Chesapeake and Delaware Canal to Philadelphia. So slim (because of the width of the canal locks) that an observer waited for a breeze to capsize them, they were capable of making better than 20 miles per hour, a speed necessary on the open Bay and the Delaware River in order for them to reach their destination in daylight hours. In spite of their lack of girth, they boasted luxurious appointments.

Augusta, built by Neafie and Levy in 1900, added to the fleet of the newly named Chesapeake Steamship Company for runs to Norfolk. To steamboat fanciers, *Augusta* was a strange-looking vessel with two very tall stacks, but she offered first-class overnight accommodations. A few years older but remarkably handsome were the companion steamers *Alabama* and *Georgia,* carrying the elegance of the Old Bay Line on their service to Norfolk and presaging the superb packets of the next generation.

The old *Chowan,* rebuilt as *Nanticoke* at a time when its old owner, the Maryland Steamboat Company, found itself swallowed up by the Baltimore, Chesapeake, and Atlantic Railway Company (BC & A; owned by the Pennsylvania Railroad), emerged from the William E. Woodall yard with the accolade of being one of the most palatial boats on the Bay—"a main saloon in white and gold with velvet carpet of olive green, and several large mirrors of French beveled glass."[1]

For the BC & A (often called "before Christ and after" or "black cinders and ashes" by its satirical and irreverent public), two vessels were built: *Maryland* in 1902 by Harlan and Hollingsworth for the Pocomoke River route, and *Virginia* in 1903 by the Maryland Steel Company for the Wicomico River route to Salisbury. These were splendidly equipped overnight paddlewheelers, distinctive for the glass-enclosed house perched on the hurricane deck of each of them to cover the walking beam.[2]

Others appeared and swelled the ranks of the steamboat parade. Around Light Street in 1900, the congestion of wagons and drays and carts during the day while steamers were loading and unloading reached what, in contemporary times, would be viewed as a traffic gridlock. Light Street itself and Pratt Street intersecting it were little more than 30 feet wide, jammed between cavernous warehouses of commission merchants on one side and the board-fronted steamboat wharves on the other. Ranked on either side—backed into position by the mules or horses that drew them—were the drays delivering or receiving goods or produce. At the wharf, each rig stood vertical to the street, horse or mule with its nose in the traffic; hundreds of such rigs lined the length of the wharves. Waiting—and jammed together in a vast mass of confusion—stood a mile-long length in both directions of other drays, driven by harassed drivers who vented their frustrations on their animals and in a pungent vocabulary developed for such occasions. In the midst of the line inched along a street car here and there, channeled to the tracks on which it rode. The cobblestoned streets reeked with crushed garbage, occasional dead rats, and the dung of horses and cattle. In the air, there was the aroma of roasting coffee and spices, mingled with the smells of cattle, smoke from the steamer stacks, and the stench of harbor water. For the pedestrian, the attempt to cross to the wharves required a particular fortitude and considerable agility (the Old Bay

Top, Light Street piers about 1900 (before the Baltimore fire of 1904). *Bottom,* Group of steamers clustered at Light Street wharves about 1900: *Enoch Pratt, Joppa, Avalon, Cambridge, Ida,* and *Virginia.* Both illustrations from the collection of H. Graham Wood. Courtesy of the Steamship Historical Society, University of Baltimore library

Line even built a bridge over the street to protect its patrons). The scene at steamboat time was one of pure bedlam. Oddly enough, those who engaged in it—steamboat men, draymen, stevedores and shippers—thrived on it. It was a way of life, colorful and zestful, that they understood and loved.

Around Norfolk, new steamers graced the harbor. *Virginia*, sleek, fast, and groomed, appeared in 1902 to run between Norfolk and Newport News for the Chesapeake and Ohio Railroad Company. Just as graceful under way, the twin-funneled *Pennsylvania* began service between Cape Charles and Norfolk, thus linking rail connections on both sides of the Chesapeake entrance. The Old Dominion Line sent *Princess*

Anne, Jefferson, and *Hamilton,* all launched before the turn of the century, on its oceangoing service, with transshipment for Tidewater produce and passenger connections to New York. *Hampton* came along in 1901. In 1902, two overnight packets, *Berkeley* and *Brandon,* propeller driven, with hotellike comforts, ran the night line on the James River from Norfolk to Richmond. One boat in particular carried with her, year after year, the sentiment of the people of Gloucester and Mathews counties. Built in late 1899, the Old Dominion Line scheduled her to be named *Western Shore,* but the local residents earnestly enjoined the company to call her *Mobjack.* Under the name, the revered paddlewheeler steamed back and forth from Norfolk to Mobjack Bay, across Hampton Roads to the Chesapeake and around to the Mobjack's landings, a link for watermen and farmers to Norfolk—an excursionist's one-day paradise and an object of affection through the long years.[3]

Between Norfolk and Washington ran the overnight packets of the Norfolk and Washington Steamboat Company and, with much pride and fanfare, the 246-foot *Norfolk* and *Washington,* presaging, as in the case of the Old Bay Line steamers, a class of luxurious, swift packets operating with almost railroad scheduling in service between the major cities of the Chesapeake region. The Potomac seemed filled with steamers around the turn of the century, many of them excursion boats bound for resorts and holiday grounds within reach of Washington. *River Queen,* a venerable and venerated excursion boat, ran Negro excursions to Notley Hall. *Charles Macalester,* a popular and beautiful 195-foot sidewheeler, entertained several generations of passengers, shuttling from Washington to Mount Vernon (to tie up at the pagodalike wharf below the mansion) and Marshall Hall, the amusement park on the Maryland shore below Mount Vernon.

The flourishing of the steamboat industry at the turn of the century and the prosperity of the Weems line induced Henry Williams to consider the possibility of building some additions to the fleet. He was impelled to this decision by the clamor for additional service, particularly from vociferous and sometimes unruly patrons on the banks of the Rappahannock, by the aging of *Sue,* which, in 1900 showed her age of 33, and the disappointingly slow speed of *Westmoreland,* which relegated her to the shorter Patuxent route.

The qualities of *Potomac* impressed Henry Williams, and to her builders, Neafie and Levy, he now turned for the construction of a new steamer that would be equally impressive. In a sense his contract with the Philadelphia firm broke with the past; this would be the first boat built under contract by the line away from Baltimore. She was built at a cost of $127,256.49, paid in cash from the company coffer. The hull of *Northumberland* slid down the ways at 3:00 P.M. on March 3, 1900; the bottle of champagne was wielded by Elizabeth Chew Williams, and the applause came from a crowd of friends and well-wishers transported by train from Baltimore that morning by Henry Williams. Two months later she took her place on the Potomac route, for which she had been designed and where she would steam for several decades. With a length of 190 feet, overall beam of 41 feet, and depth of hold of 12 feet, she was somewhat longer and heavier than *Potomac*, with a greater net tonnage, but she resembled her in general appearance. Steel hulled and propeller driven, she was fitted with a triple expansion engine (30-inch stroke and cylinder diameters of 18, 25, and 45 inches) and two gunboat-type boilers (9.10 by 20 feet). Her interior appointments surpassed the finest: saloon paneled in carved oak, 43 staterooms boasting unusual comfort and furnishings, a social hall for music and dancing, and a pub-style smoking room in which gentlemen could drink and play cards (Appendix A). Her initial officer list included Captain William Geoghegan, master; Charles Goeghegan, first mate; John Douglas, second mate; Thomas J. Young, chief engineer; William Young, assistant engineer; Alexander Beale, purser; and David Crockett, lookoutsman; a certain obvious nepotism dominated the list. As a new packet on the Bay, for a time *Northumberland* was reigning queen.[4] But by the time *Northumberland* hit her strike on the Potomac, a new steamer was on the ways at Neafie and Levy. Persuaded by his friends and patrons around the Patuxent River that he was bestowing too many Virginia county names on his steamboats, Henry Williams agreed that the name of the new boat would be *Calvert*. During 1901, construction of the new boat moved along on schedule.

Then, near the end of 1901, a major disaster shocked the Weems line. On the afternoon of November 14, *Richmond* caught fire alongside the wharf at Fredericksburg and burned to the water's edge. Originating in the forward cabin from the careless throwing of a match among papers in a trash can, the fire spread so quickly that there was little hope of saving her. Preparing to leave for Baltimore, she had on board a large cargo and a long list of passengers. The latter were able to escape with clothes and baggage, and the purser grabbed up the boat's papers and money, but Captain Burroughs, his officers, and crew lost all of their possessions. At the height of the fire, a flagpole fell across the whistle cord, and *Richmond* expired with a long and mournful wail. The insurance paid on the steamer (some $70,000, her market value) stood at half the estimated cost of replacement (Appendix G). Her burned out hulk blocked the river channel for months.[5]

Even carping critics on the Rappahannock were moved to sympathy for Henry Williams. Sang one editorialist,

the public has long recognized that under the management of Mr. Henry Williams the Weems Steamboat Company has been the one monopolistic enterprise which gives 100 cents worth of first-class service in cash and throws in courtesy and a spirit of accommodation as *lagniappe*. Nowhere is a man better fed, better or more luxuriously sheltered, and waited upon with greater courtesy, than upon the steamers which ply between Baltimore and Fredericksburg and Norfolk. Therefore, when it was announced a few weeks since, that the palatial steamer *Richmond*—named, in graceful compliment to our shippers, after our own county—had been completely destroyed by fire at her dock at Freder-

Steamer *Richmond* on fire at Fredericksburg, Virginia, November 14, 1901. Photo by A. D. Alexander. Courtesy of the Library of Congress

icksburg, there was a unanimous expression of regret at the disaster and a feeling of wide-spread sympathy . . . . When it was known that Mr. Williams would pay for the goods destroyed sympathy was merged with admiration.[6]

Richmond's loss was catastrophic, particularly in view of the demands placed on the line without her. Henry Williams was galvanized into making almost extreme demands on Neafie and Levy to ready *Calvert* for launch. The company responded gallantly.

Calvert was launched on November 23, 1901, christened by Henry's other daughter, Matilda Williams. It was a difficult christening: three times she hurled the bottle at the steel hull, increasing the power of her stroke at each attempt, gasping out "I christen thee Calvert" with each shot. She succeeded on the third mighty fling, deluging the retreating bow, President Seddinger of Neafie and Levy, and most of the spectators with the foaming liquid.[7] *Calvert* went down the ways as though shot out of a cannon.

When outfitted, *Calvert* had certain superficial similarities to *Northumberland*. Equally palatial in her saloon, stateroom, and dining room accommodations, she had a power plant that was somewhat different. Her engine was compound (two cylinders, 20- and 40-inch diameter, 28-inch stroke) and inclined, a radical departure from *Northumberland*. She had one single-end Scotch boiler. Most observers remembered *Calvert* for the height and placement of her smokestack: an extremely high, black, thin funnel extending 30 feet upward from the hurricane deck and rearing up considerably aft of the midships position aesthetically accepted by steamboat connoisseurs on the Chesapeake. Nevertheless, *Calvert* was fairly fast, an immediate competitor in speed to *Potomac*. A friendly but understood rivalry developed between the two, and when they left at the same time in the evening from their Light Street wharves, a race inevitably developed. Belching smoke in the air, they sped side by side down the Patapsco toward Seven Foot Knoll, to the delight and exhilaration of crew and passengers alike (Appendix A).

Henry Williams received *Calvert* from Neafie and Levy on March 11, 1902, and dispatched her to the Patuxent to relieve *Westmoreland*, laid up for repairs. She was greeted by the entire population of Solomons on her arrival, a speech by the state's attorney, and a bouquet of flowers for Captain William C. Geoghegan, to his embarrassment. He responded by a tuneful display of the steamer's whistle before backing her clear of the wharf for her rounds of Patuxent landings. But *Calvert*'s destiny lay on the Potomac, a route she would serve for a number of years.[8]

Even while work on the building ways in Philadelphia was under way, speculation began among Rappahannock shippers and newspaper columnists about the purposes of the new boat and future plans of the Weems line. Most feared that the new boat would be, like *Potomac*, another screw-type vessel, with neither the girth nor the number of staterooms to accommodate the expected Rappahannock trade. The implication was that Henry Williams should consider revamping *Calvert*'s design to a sidewheeler or build a new paddlewheel steamboat. Another correspondent, assuming *Calvert* would steam on the Rappahannock, requested that Henry Williams mount a very large illuminated clock on the hurricane deck so that residents could set their clocks day and night as she went past. Henry Williams replied that he feared that the rolling of the boat and exposure to the weather would prevent such a clock from keeping time, but that he would try to comply with the request; he never did.[9]

As *Calvert* began her weekly voyages, another steamboat's skeleton stood on the ways at Neafie and Levy—a further replacement for *Richmond*, the weary *Sue*, and the slow-paced *Westmoreland*. Rumor of the new construction reached the Rappahannock, where tempers had reached a seething point over various grievances with the Weems line. One prominent contributor to a local newspaper suggested that Henry Williams name the new boat *Fredericksburg* to placate and compliment the local citizenry and, furthermore, bring her to the Rappahannock instead of *Calvert*, a not too subtle rejection of the Maryland connotation.

Henry Williams decided to adhere to his policy of naming the steamers after Maryland and Virginia counties bordering the rivers that served them. He wanted to name this boat for a Maryland county; however, to help quell the incipient quarrel with residents of the Rappahannock, he chose to call the new boat *Middlesex*. Furthermore, he decided to bring out the new boat with as much flourish as the presentation of a new debutante to society.

Built during 1902 and received by Henry Williams on March 26, 1903

Top, Evening race to the open Chesapeake. Steamers *Potomac* (*left*) and *Calvert* (*right*) in company down the Patapsco after departure from Baltimore. Photo by A. Aubrey Bodine (c. 1931). *Bottom, Calvert* as a Weems line steamer about 1902. From the collection of J. S. Bohannon. Both illustrations courtesy of the Mariners' Museum (some eight months behind schedule at considerable embarrassment and loss to the Weems line), *Middlesex* nevertheless was a striking and very lovely addition to the Weems fleet. To the appreciative eye of steamboat lovers on the Bay, her sleek and graceful sheer set her apart —an exquisite touch of artwork on the waters of the Chesapeake. More than 200 feet long with a 59-foot overall beam, she had the sidewheeler's capacity to carry freight and the staterooms to accommodate passengers, just as recommended by the residents of the Rappahannock (Appendix G).

Her propulsion system departed radically from the other Weems line boats. *Middlesex* had a compound inclined engine (cylinders of 24 and 53 inches in diameter with an 84-inch stroke) driving small sidewheels (13.2 feet in diameter), the nine curved buckets of each wheel mounted by a system of levers so that they would feather and strike the water perpendicularly when operating. The piston rods driving back and forth to rotate the crank of the paddlewheel shaft resembled nothing less than the flailing of the driving rods of a train locomotive. Two single-end Scotch boilers supplied steam. Connecting the paddlewheels was a "stick-shaft," unable to separate the wheels for the maneuverable "go ahead on one, back on the other" operation. At 1,300 indicated horsepower, 125 pounds of pressure (very high for Bay steamboats), and 45 revolutions per minute, her engineering represented a radical shift in conventional Bay boat design.[10]

Because her paddlewheels were small, great gilded paddleboxes to cover them were unnecessary, and *Middlesex* underway—each side showing one continuous windowed expanse of white—could easily be mistaken for a propeller-driven vessel. With a 4.6-foot sheer forward and a 2-foot sheer aft, clean lines, and a properly raked, well-proportioned stack, she earned the admiration bestowed copiously on her around the Bay.

Her interior design was even more luxurious than that of her predecessors, marked by unusually comfortable accommodations and an oak-trimmed social hall for second-class passengers, a saloon paneled in richly carved woods and surmounted by a dome crowned in gold leaf, first-class staterooms finished in cherrywood and handsomely furnished, and a dining room seating 42 under a second dome above the saloon (Appendix A).[11]

With *Middlesex* taking her trials in the Weems fleet, Henry Williams cast about for a buyer for *Sue*. Built in 1867, the old boat no longer appealed to passengers who compared her unfavorably with the sumptuous packets steaming on the Bay. On October 24, 1903, *Sue*, which had lain idle for a time at her Light Street wharf, was conveyed for $990 to Peter Hagen, who in turn transferred her to Herman Schell. *Sue* steamed out of Baltimore for the last time for Camden, New Jersey, underwent some repair work, and emerged finally under the name of *Bristol*, to sail for another 20 years for the Delaware River Navigation Company under the ownership of Henry L. Brown and Henry B. Massey.[12]

In spite of the acclaim attending the launching of *Middlesex, Calvert,* and *Northumberland* and his reception as a distinguished elder statesman in the steamboat world of the Chesapeake, Henry Williams found himself sorely tried by the events of the first few years of the new century.

A political venture of his turned out to be a sorry one. In 1901, he cast a bid for a return to political power in Baltimore, met with initial success in gaining election as president of the second branch of the city council (hence serving in the seat of mayor in the latter's absence), but lost his seat in 1903. The newly elected Robert McLane appointed him city collector (of taxes). The death of McLane in 1904 brought to office E. Clay Timanus, a Republican opponent who sought to squeeze Henry Williams from his post as tax collector by demanding that he physically occupy his office in City Hall from 9:30 A.M. to 3:00 P.M. each day, a tormenting requirement that Henry Williams endured for four years rather than submit to his nemesis (Appendix E).[13]

Henry Williams was in office in the last days of Mayor McLane when the great fire of February 7, 1904 engulfed the financial and harbor district of Baltimore. Beginning on a quiet Sunday morning, when few people were around the financial and manufacturing areas a few blocks back from the harbor, the blaze, starting from a discarded cigar or match thrown into the basement of the drygoods firm of John E. Hurst and Company at Hopkins Place and Liberty Street,[14] erupted into an inferno. Driven by a wind from the southwest, the fire spread quickly through the garment, drug, and sundries manufacturing and warehouse areas into the financial center of the city, destroying even 16-story steel and masonry "fireproof" buildings in its path. Leaping from building to building and overcoming the efforts of more than 1,200 firemen (some came from Washington and other cities) to extinguish it, the fire raged for 30 hours. Seventy city blocks were leveled, 1,526 buildings were burned out, 2,500 businesses were gutted, among them 20 banks, eight hotels, nine newspaper offices,[15] and most of the transportation offices in the city, including the central office of the Baltimore and Ohio Railroad. The fire swept northward from Pratt to Fayette Street, eastward to Jones Falls, then with a shift in the wind, southward to the harbor, destroying the waterfront from the intersection of Pratt and Light Streets through McClures, Dugans, and Smiths Wharves, and Commerce Street, Frederick Street, Long, and Union docks to Jones Falls. The worst fires in the harbor area occurred in the vicinity of Philpot and Thames Streets, where George Weems had begun the Weems enterprise 85 years earlier. At the peak of the fire in the financial district, when large buildings were erupting like volcanoes, the temperature was estimated at 2,500 degrees Fahrenheit. Chunks of burning debris and flying embers ignited buildings many blocks from the source, and wooden buildings at some distance from the fire itself were scorched and saved only by what worn-out firemen and valiant volunteers with small streams of water could do.[16]

Such was the case with the Weems wharves and other steamboat piers along Light Street. Some were scorched but not burned. All stood when the fire ended on Monday. Destroyed, however, were the warehouses of commission merchants, the business establishments that dealt with the steamboat lines and which shipped their products aboard their vessels, and the offices of the financial institutions that supported them.

About midnight on Sunday, when the flames began to lick at Pratt Street, all the steamers at wharves in the basin, along the docks off Pratt Street, and at the Light Street piers got up steam and moved down the harbor in a melee compounded by so many boats milling about in a narrow space at once, the eery spectacle of the enormous conflagration, and rescue boats like fireboat *Cataract* and tugboat *Oriole,* trying to go against the exodus and extricate people trapped on the docks. At one point *Potomac* assisted *Windom,* revenue cutter, in storing bags of coffee dragged from a B & O warehouse about to go up in flames.[17]

In the weeks after the fire, Henry Williams had the Weems boats back on schedule from Piers 2, 8, and 9, Light Street. He counted himself fortunate that his wharves were still standing. Only the Ericsson Line docks at the intersection of Pratt and Light Streets stood between Pier 2 and the fire on Pratt Street. But the devastation extended beyond the waterfront. It reached into the financial fabric of the city and its ability to pull itself together for the enormous task of reconstruction. The death of Mayor McLane left a politically motivated and disorganized city government in place, and the initiatives for rebuilding had to come from responsible business leaders, among them Henry Williams.

Losses were estimated from $50 million to $150 million; five Baltimore insurance companies promptly failed. But within two years, the area of devastation was transformed. New buildings were constructed and occupied, streets were widened and clutter reduced, sewers were laid, and a new wave of optimism about the future of Baltimore was felt. Light Street at the wharves was widened from 41 to 126 feet (the clutter around the wharves was only nominally reduced, it seemed). But, in the absence of an effective administration, the reconstruction of the city followed no plan, and the result reflected, in large measure, the interests of the individual business enterprises.

Fire and its peripheral effects must have been on Henry Williams's mind throughout much of 1904. The *General Slocum* disaster in New York had the potential, as Williams knew, of wreaking devastation on steamboat lines from the stringent safety requirements likely to be passed by state legislatures and the Federal government as a consequence. On the morning of June 15, 1904, the excursion steamer *General Slocum,* with 1,300 members of St. Mark's Evangelical Lutheran Church on board, bound for an amusement park, suddenly burst into flames north of Hell Gate. The fire, starting in the galley in the forward lower deck, spread to the wooden upper decks in minutes. The captain tried to beach the boat at North Brother Island, but the fire swallowed the superstructure like a tinderbox before the boat grounded; frantic women and children scrambled to reach the top deck and stern, and these decks collapsed into the inferno below. The strong current was filled with drowning people shoved overboard by the struggling mass of humanity at the stern. At least a thousand people died in the disaster. Subsequent investigation disclosed serious deficiencies aboard *General Slocum*: defective fire hoses, broken fire mains, inadequate fire drills, poorly trained crew, and other critical shortcomings. Her holocaust brought the wrath of the country to the state legislatures and to the halls of Congress.[18]

Demanded was legislation to stiffen safety requirements aboard steamboats. For some steamboat lines, marginally successful, the levying of such requirements would be financially disastrous. Williams wondered how the weight of regulation would fall on the Weems line.

The first few years of the new century had come to spell uncertainty for Williams. Events had not matched his optimism.

On the Rappahannock, he had dealt with a condition of nearly open warfare that climaxed in a bitter standoff. Farmers, businessmen, shippers, politicians, and newspaper editorialists had taken up verbal and physical cudgels against the Weems line. All the familiar complaints and demands of the past had been intensified, and the leadership in the region threatened to join forces in a determined opposition to the Weems line. No amount of diplomacy or compromise on the part of the Weems management seemed enough to quiet the rising cacophony. For the first time in his steamboat career, Williams felt deep-seated anger at his clients from Fredericksburg to Tappahannock.

In Baltimore, his political career had landed on the shoals prepared for him by Mayor Timanus, and there was no graceful way of backing off. He smoldered under the injustice that had come his way and resolutely subordinated his pride and his daily administration of the Weems line to a stubborn compliance with the demands of Timanus. But the intractable situation sorely tested his certainty about the political future.

Then the great fire and the resulting upheavals in business circles diminished his confidence in Baltimore finance, of which he was substantially a part. The possibility of legal stricture on vessels and the levying of requirements for safety equipment as a result of the *Slocum* catastrophe tempered his judgment of the prospects of steamboat operations.

Mounting expenditures for fuel, high costs of steamboat maintenance and repairs, and increased wharfage fees worried him. The capriciousness of the weather added to his woes; the Bay had frozen over at times, and wharves on the rivers had been heavily damaged. The summers were some of the coldest on record, and excursion trade had fallen off. At times Fair Haven welcomed only a sprinkling of its usual patronage.

On the Eastern Shore, the Pennsylvania Railroad, through its tentacles of control, reached for a monopoly of steamboat lines to complement its rail service; for independent steamboat operators the view was disquieting.

But it was the Rappahannock controversy that plagued him most. It was persistent and pernicious, and it stood on the edge of open warfare. Part of the criticism arose from scheduling. When the shippers in the upper river focused on the necessity for having through-service between Norfolk and Fredericksburg, Williams worked out a schedule, as best he could, to meet these often conflicting demands. Conflicting they were, since the farmers and merchants of the lower river, who relished the notion of having the Norfolk route but continued to prosper in their dealings with Baltimore, had far different shipping requirements than those of the residents of the upper river and Fredericksburg. To complicate matters further, about 1901 there began a serious proposal to press for service between the Rappahannock and Crisfield, Maryland, on the Eastern Shore, the steamers to connect with a branch railroad line linking to the New York, Philadelphia, and Norfolk Railroad to Wilmington, Philadelphia, and New York.

Scheduling assumed an importance that Henry Williams never expected. The resulting pull-and-tug produced schedules that shifted with unwanted frequency and seemed to satisfy no one. One local Rappahannock wag in 1901, attuned to the dilemma of Henry Williams, wrote,

I beg leave to submit the following schedule for the careful, prayerful consideration of the President of the Weems line of steamers. It may seem a little one sided, but is just about as reasonable as some of those already proposed. . . .

Leave Fredericksburg daily at 7:00 A.M. for Baltimore direct, arriving at 7:30 A.M. same day. Leave Fredericksburg daily stopping at all landings 3:00 P.M., arrive in Baltimore 3:45 P.M. same day. Leave Blandfield for Baltimore direct every half hour arriving in Baltimore every 15 minutes. Leave Baltimore for Pratts direct every 5th Sunday arriving at six o'clock next summer. Leave Tappahannock tomorrow at 3:00 A.M., arrive in Baltimore at 4:00 P.M. day before yesterday. Leave Port Royal 4th of July, arrive at Easter. Stop at Pratts Thanksgiving Day. All steamers stop on signal at Wilmington, Philadelphia, and New York, Crisfield, Norfolk, Cape Charles, Richmond, and Pauls X Roads. Fare one way 37 cents, including meals and stateroom. Round trip one-half price. Between 6 and 60 years of age free. All tickets include transportation to Buffalo Exposition, admission to grounds, hotel bills, hack hire, and a pilot, a novel by Lama Jean Libbey, a paid-up life insurance policy, and a photograph of President Williams, a lock of Capt. Davis' hair, and a year's subscription to the Tidewater Democrat. Cigars, "High Balls," Mint Juleps and "small beers" free upon application to the steward. — Anonymous

Planters on the upper river (Tappahannock seemed to be an accepted dividing line between upper and lower) bore the brunt of the scheduling difficulty, particularly between late spring and early fall. In April 1901, one Port Royal correspondent, supported by planters all along the upper route, commented, "In shipping our produce to the Baltimore markets, under the present schedule, it has to stay on board two nights and a day, so one can readily see what condition our livestock and perishable goods must be in when they are offered for sale."

His lament was justified. On the other hand, as with most of the residents of Fredericksburg and the upper Rappahannock valley, he had overlooked some essential factors: the length of the route up the Rappahannock to Fredericksburg, the relative paucity of trade in the upper region, and the costs of running steamboat service with sufficient frequency to fulfill ideal shipping schedules for stock and perishables. Williams met frequently with businessmen, farmers, and community leaders in an effort to explain his position and to reach some acceptable compromise. He pointed out at various times that his company had lost heavily in attempting to operate a steamer all year round from the upper river to Norfolk or through to Baltimore and that no steamboat line could carry freight at a loss for half the year. He squelched the idea of running a boat to Crisfield, saying that there would be little to carry and that the rates from Crisfield (a way station) were higher than from Norfolk. He assured the farmers on many occasions that ample facilities would be provided on the upper Rappahannock to ship fruits and truck farming products as soon as they had enough to ship to justify the running of additional boats.

A local editorialist, rising in support of Williams, stated,

From our observation it does not appear that the Weems Company has increased its riches to any unmerited extent within recent years. They have been put to extraordinary expense, have sustained some heavy losses and been forced to make great outlays for new boats. A personal inquiry, that would probably have been denied by the officials had they known the purpose in view, reveals the fact that on a recent trip of the steamer *Essex* from Norfolk, where she was loaded and had to reject a small portion of freight, her cargo netted less than $250. When it is stated that it took nearly $100 worth of coal to make this trip and more than that figure for payroll and provision bill, to say nothing of agents and wharf hire and percentage, it will be seen that there is no great profit in such trips. . . . Let us not abuse the bridge that has carried us safely for so many years.[19]

The editorials waxed venomous in their charges against Williams for alleged extortion in the rates he charged and for enriching himself and Baltimore capitalists at the expense of poor farmers and merchants on the Rappahannock. Williams denied all of these allegations. In contrast to the continuing barrage of criticism, there were voices extolling the history of the Weems line on the Rappahannock and saying that, of all the institutions surrounding the river, the old steamboat company had most likely contributed the most to the economic development of the area. It indeed was the lifeline, long standing and long tested. For Williams as a person, there was seldom anything but praise. He was perceived as a genial, energetic, sympathetic man—a manager, capable, and strong—and as a public-spirited gentleman of the traditional school, with whom Virginians could do business.

In the first years of the new century, the controversy centered increasingly on the need for a day steamer to serve the upper river, with Fredericksburg as its commercial hub. It was true that the small city had assumed an important place in the region. It boasted a number of stores, warehouses, and various manufacturing ventures. Its population of around 5,000 included a substantial professional and well-to-do business class as well as a lengthy list of landed gentry. And its railroad facilities linked it to the main line north and south, with connections west. The use of a smaller day boat, visiting the upriver landings and terminating in Fredericksburg, would bring produce from the farms to the local markets and to the railroad and transshipment to the major cities much more expeditiously than the service provided by the Weems packets out of Baltimore. Residents along the river could use Fredericksburg as a center for shopping. Fares could be cheap in view of the smaller size of the vessel and the shorter distances run. And by venturing such a boat, the monopoly of the Weems line, and the evils of such a syndicate, would be broken.

In late 1902, the Business Men's Association in Fredericksburg, led by its energetic president, William D. Carter, decided to locate a small steamer and charter it for an experimental month or two. Local businessmen and the association itself put up enough money to initiate the project. With little or no knowledge of steamboats and their management, the group began a search for a suitable vessel and discovered one on the market.

Tourist was a 284-ton twin-screw vessel, 116 feet long with a 21.5-foot beam, and 6.5-foot depth of hold; she was built by Tom Pitt in 1894 in Nyack, New York, and owned by the Rock Creek Steamboat Company for excursion runs to Rock Creek out of Baltimore. She was available for charter and seemed to fit the needs of the Fredericksburg seekers. On November 20, 1902, the new charter having been consummated, *Tourist* began runs as advertised out of Fredericksburg to Urbanna and return. As specified by William D. Carter, her owner was shown as the People's Steamboat Company. To show that he meant the venture to be permanent, Carter raised the money to purchase her in January 1903 and incorporated the company.

At the very outset, *Tourist,* under Captain A. E. Craddock, made clear that the People's line intended to use some 13 wharves of the Weems line—two owned, the remainder leased. *Tourist* began to off-load and board passengers and freight at these landings as if they were her own. At this point, Henry Williams reached the flash point. He had his agents serve notice on Carter that his action, if continued, would result in litigation.

On December 19, 1902, just before Christmas, the first incident occurred. As reported by Purser Archer of *Tourist,* the steamer arrived at Port Royal with 35 passengers, freight, and a horse and buggy to unload, only to discover that "a fence had been built across" and "the rails smeared with tar . . . . There were several ladies, and it was impossible to land with these conditions confronting us. I asked Mr. Askins, the agent, by whose orders that fence was put there, and he replied by the orders of President Williams. . . . Several passengers said, 'Tear down the fence', and it was immediately done. Then another difficulty confronted me—The warehouse was locked, and it was impossible to land freight, but the passengers could get on the wharf, after which they had to pass by the side of the warehouse in a space of two feet, running great risk of falling in the water. There was no other course for me to pursue but to draw the staple, open the door and let the horse and buggy through, as under the law as public carriers, we are entitled to do."

For a time *Tourist* enjoyed the patronage of the upper Rappahannock and Fredericksburg. But the owners and their supporters failed to count on the anger of Henry Williams. Thoroughly aroused over what he considered to be the high-handed and illegal activity of the People's line, he resolved to force *Tourist* off the river. He shopped around for a boat to challenge her.

In March 1903, he purchased *Emma Reis* for $17,905 from the Milford and Philadelphia Transportation Company, operating out of Wilmington on the Delaware. Only a few years old, *Emma Reis* matched *Tourist* in many ways: length, 114.6 feet; beam, 21 feet; depth of hold, 6 feet; gross tonnage, 187; net tonnage, 102; twin screw. Williams had hoped for a speed advantage over *Tourist*, but in this characteristic he misjudged *Emma Reis*. Williams promptly honored a Virginia county by renaming the boat *Caroline* (Appendix A). He just as promptly advertised her schedule, three times a week calling at the same wharves and at the same times as *Tourist*. And at the same time he dropped fares to unheard-of levels: from Port Royal to Fredericksburg, 10 cents; from Tappahannock, 15 cents; freight hauled at giveaway rates. Such rates cost the company some $7,722 (Appendix G). Residents of the lower river (they were not engaged in the fracas) complained that he raised rates there to compensate. Williams blamed the rates on increased costs. Even before *Caroline* began service, William D. Carter threatened various forms of retaliation.

The contest between the rival steamers began on April 1, 1903, with crowds at the landings to watch the race. To the chagrin of Henry Williams, *Caroline* proved to be slower than *Tourist*, but he counted on his rates, which the People's line could ill afford to match, to win patronage. Loyalties, avarice, and anger competed. *Tourist*, to the surprise of Williams, held her own, and in spite of the magnet of cheap rates posed by *Caroline*, *Tourist* fared reasonably well at first. Side by side, the two little steamers raced, blocking each other in the channel, outmaneuvering each other for wharf space, dancing about in the narrow upper river to the glee of spectators and betting sportsmen.

Henry Williams took his battle to another arena. At considerable expense he entered a lawsuit against the People's line in U.S. District Court, Judge Edmund Waddill presiding, claiming that the wharves he owned or leased were private property and that the owners and managers of *Tourist* were trespassing. In defense, the People's company argued that the wharves in question occupied the river termini of public highways, that post offices accompanied their functions as landings for freight and passengers of entire communities for which no other public transportation facilities existed, that many vessels, other than steamboats, used the wharves upon payment of the requisite 10 percent of fares and freight charges to the agents in charge, and that the wharves could not, therefore, be converted from public to private, indeed exclusive, use by the Weems line. George Weems Williams, the son of Henry Williams, and H. St. George Fitzhugh represented the Weems line; William D. Carter and A. Thomas Embry, the defense. Both sides to the legal contest and the general public waited expectantly for the decision of Judge Waddill.

In the meantime, *Caroline* and *Tourist* continued their bout on the river. Each time one strove to reach a wharf before the other, those who observed the minuet solemnly predicted the inevitable. It finally occurred on the afternoon of May 15.

Tourist, with *Caroline* trailing a few hundred yards, came downriver on an approach to Port Conway on the left bank and Port Royal, just below, on the right bank. Captain Craddock, master of *Tourist*, knowing that *Caroline* carried the mail and would normally stop at Port Conway, decided to try a bold maneuver by skipping Port Conway altogether and heading for Port Royal directly, thus gaining the larger freight shipments from that landing. To this end, he swung his vessel on a wide turn across the narrow river, not much more than a quarter of a mile wide, to go alongside the wharf at Port Royal. Noting the swing of *Tourist*, Captain Richard Shenton of *Caroline* immediately steamed right past Port Conway and headed directly for the Port Royal landing. Both vessels arrived off the wharf at about the same time, *Tourist* very slightly ahead, but *Caroline* on a better approach to the piling. Seeing that *Caroline* would not give way, Craddock backed his engines, but not before *Caroline* clipped the stern of *Tourist*.

The newspapers in Fredericksburg headlined the affair as a disastrous collision, claimed that it was a flagrant example by the Weems line of harassment, and demanded justice in the matter. But *Tourist* showed up at the landings as usual, and the damage was scarcely noticeable. In June, a local board of U.S. steamboat inspectors, having examined the circumstances of the collision, came to the conclusion that neither party was at fault. The decision brought forth a diatribe from the local newspapers and silence from Henry Williams.

About the same time, Judge Waddill refused to grant the injunction requested by the Weems line to restrain the People's line from using the wharves in dispute but, citing his inadequate knowledge of the law governing such cases, deferred a decision in the matter to the opinion of one Ernest Long, attorney.

William D. Carter threw down the gauntlet at the feet of Henry Williams by acquiring a small vessel named *Sunbeam;* Carter's idea was to link *Tourist* and *Sunbeam* at Tappahannock for freight transshipment by the new boat, an allegedly fast vessel, to the markets in Baltimore. Such activity was an open challenge to the Weems line and its service on the Rappahannock.

However, the fortunes of the People's line were on the wane. More and more, the shippers of Fredericksburg and the upper river found the service of *Tourist* wanting, the schedules unsatisfactory, and the connection with *Sunbeam* for Baltimore inadequate. The decision of Waddill hung in the balance, but lawyer Long's opinions seemed to favor Weems. Little by little, the business community of Fredericksburg and the valley deserted Carter. Both *Tourist* and *Sunbeam* disappeared from the Rappahannock by the end of 1903, and the monopoly returned once again to the Weems line and Henry Williams. *Caroline* continued the day service on the upper river which *Tourist* had initiated.[20] Unfortunately, the court case over the wharves lingered on for years—even beyond the point of relevance—to the utter frustration of Henry Williams.[21]

The first few years of the new century had sorely tried the patience and fortitude of Henry Williams. Nevertheless, there was an ebullience and stony determination about the man which carried him into the future. In 1900, he had launched *Northumberland; Calvert,* in 1901; and *Middlesex,* in 1903, all queenly packets that were called "palatial" by steamboat connoisseurs on the Bay. All of them had been built to meet the growing demands of the expanding trade on the three rivers. Still looking optimistically at the future, Williams decided to build still another steamboat, perceiving the company as making still another—and expensive—gesture to meet the needs and complaints of its patrons.

In the first week of January 1904, Williams signed a contract with the Baltimore Shipbuilding and Drydock Company to build a steamer, the first contract placed after 1900 for a boat to be built in local waters. Bids on the contract had excluded Neafie and Levy, which was embroiled in a damage suit over a boiler explosion aboard *City of Trenton.*[22] Also, Henry Williams had registered his dissatisfaction with the firm by holding up the last payment of $12,000 due on *Middlesex* because the boat was eight months late in delivery. He displayed some pleasure in returning his shipbuilding business to Baltimore where for many decades most Weems boats had been constructed.

The keel was laid on January 13, 1904, and work moved along rapidly under the prodding of Henry Williams; James Gourley, who was commodore of the Weems line (and who superintended construction); and John McGoldrick, chief engineer, who watched over the building and installation of machinery. She was ready to go down the ways on schedule in mid-May. A slight controversy developed over her name. There was no question but that the boat would be named for a county in Maryland bordering the Patuxent or the Potomac; only three counties remained unacknowledged, since *Calvert* and *St. Mary's* carried the names of two. The choices rested among *Charles, Prince George,* and *Anne Arundel.* Again, the Weems family quickly made its selection, Anne Arundel, the county so closely identified with the early history of the family. The question was one of spelling. The Maryland Historical Society vouchsafed the opinion that the correct way to spell the name, as used by its original owner, was *Anne Arundell,* and Henry Williams promptly ordered that all name plates on the boat be painted in that spelling. Strong local sentiment, stirred up by the rumor of the impending name and loyal to the spelling given the county, prevailed, and in deference to the tide against him Henry Williams at the last minute ordered the second *l* dropped and the nameplates repainted.

Anne Arundel was launched on Saturday, May 14, 1904. That the date just missed the ill-omened Friday, the 13th, seemed never to have entered the minds or disturbed the sensibilities of the builders, owners, or sponsors. At 2:06 P.M., Elizabeth Chew Williams, the 31-year-old daughter of Henry Williams and sponsor of an earlier Weems boat, broke the traditional red-white-and-blue bedecked bottle of champagne over the bow. The boat, high on the ways at Locust Point, close to Fort McHenry, glided obediently into the water, amid the cheers of a substantial crowd and the whistles of tugs and steamboats. [23]

In a little over a month, *Anne Arundel* was fitted with her engines, completed from keel to pilothouse and stem to stern, and readied for her trial runs. On Thursday, June 30, at 1:00 P.M., she left her berth at the Baltimore Shipbuilding and Drydock Company with colors flying and headed down the Patapsco, receiving an ovation from every passing ship. She turned about at Thomas Point Lighthouse, off the South River entrance, and returned to the builder's yard, having developed the contract speed of 12 miles per hour without a falter in the machinery. In the dining room aft, spirited toasts celebrated the success of the boat, the builders, and the owners. [24]

Anne Arundel resembled *Potomac* in many respects: length, beam, and depth of hold were nearly the same; gross and net tonnage were similar. But in one external feature *Anne Arundel* differed from *Potomac*. On the former, the joiner or cabin work surrounding the dining room aft on the main deck extended out to the guards all the way around the stern; on the latter, a gallery encompassed the dining room, thereby bestowing a more traditional and graceful note of elegance to the older steamer. But the dining room on *Anne Arundel* held more tables as a result of the added space. And in another aspect *Potomac* and *Anne Arundel* differed. *Potomac* drove her propeller by a compound (two-cylinder) engine; *Anne Arundel*'s engine was a triple-expansion engine (three-cylinder). As time was to prove, *Anne Arundel*'s engine scarcely measured up to the performance expected of it; many rumors held that the engine originally had been designed for a tug. Certain it was that she was slow in clearing a dock, steady in a seaway, but no runaway in a race. [25] Like her predecessors, *Anne Arundel* was handsomely caparisoned (Appendix A).

On July 7, 1904, *Anne Arundel* made her first run from Baltimore to Washington under the care of William C. Geoghegan, master; John McGoldrick, chief engineer; William Marshall, assistant engineer; and Henry Williams (no relation), steward.

To many steamboat lovers on the Bay at the time, *Anne Arundel* and *Potomac*, near sister ships, represented the finest in overnight packet travel. In their view, these boats—and they sometimes included other recent additions to the Weems fleet—symbolized that class of steamers that trundled the freight and catered to the passengers on the long stretches of the tributaries of the Chesapeake. Their machinery had developed from the state of the art in steamboat design. Their enclosed main deck, transporting freight through the roughest weather, provided security similar to that of oceangoing vessels. Their sumptuous appointments rivaled the finest and most palatial of steamboats on the Eastern Seaboard. Their size, not as long or decked or heavy as the Baltimore to Norfolk packets, fit precisely the needs of overnight service to the landings and communities of tidewater Maryland and Virginia. Their sturdy construction and seakeeping qualities, among the best on the Bay, recommended them even for future generations. And their appearance, clean, lithe, and sheered, with their white sides glistening, their funnels amidships raked to a satisfying angle, and their bows curling back the seas with the keenness of a blade, painted a picture on the waters of the Bay and its rivers of beauty and utter grace.

Henry Williams and the Weems descendants reveled in the handsome fleet that seemed to climax the 85 years of their heritage, the longest continuous history of any steamboat line in the United States.

In July 1904, Williams could view the events of the new century with mixed emotions. His magnificent fleet was the envy of the Bay, and his pride in having built it was justified. His efforts to serve the public, to develop the regions of the Patuxent and the Potomac and the Rappahannock where his steamboats provided the principal if not the only means of shipping and travel, and to cultivate the public interest had brought their own rewards. He was respected, admired, and reasonably well-to-do. But in mid-1904, a certain restiveness overtook him. Recent events had not been kind. A harsh winter had frozen the Bay and closed the routes on the three rivers for many weeks. Baltimore's heart had burned in one of the greatest fires in American urban history and shaken the financial center of the city to its foundations. Mayor McLane had died in a matter of months and stranded the city administration in a mire of politics. In New York, the *General Slocum* disaster had presented the legislatures, state and federal, with a whiplash to alter steamboat design and management. And on the Rappahannock, the backlash from the *Caroline-Tourist* war continued to rage, with no sign of abatement in spite of its ignominious ending.

Two other series of events troubled Henry Williams.

During the year, his steamboats had delivered several gasoline-driven "horseless carriages" to landings along the rivers, and automobiles, some outfitted to carry goods, were puttering about the streets of Baltimore. In the newspapers, reports showed that 4,000 automobiles had been sold in the United States in 1900, more than 11,000 in 1903, and the number was growing geometrically. During 1904, the federal Office of Public Roads reported that 154,000 miles of paved roads, mostly concrete, had been built in the United States, substantially reducing the nearly two million miles of unpaved roads. The burst of construction had been necessitated by the rapid increase in automobile traffic. Although there seemed to be little change in the back country roads along the Patuxent, Potomac, and Rappahannock, Williams knew instinctively what the statistics portended.[26]

The other troubling series of events was the emergence of the Pennsylvania Railroad as a dominant, if not overweaning, force in steamboat life on the Chesapeake. In 1894, the Choptank Steamboat Company, the Eastern Shore Steamboat Company, and the Maryland Steamboat Company had been absorbed by a syndicate shadowed by the finances of the Pennsylvania Railroad (PRR); the resulting corporation, the Baltimore, Chesapeake, and Atlantic Railway, had its management under that railroad's control. With these acquisitions, the PRR held in its grasp, not only most of the transpeninsular rail service on the Eastern Shore, but also most of the steamboat passenger and freight service crossing the Bay from Baltimore. In 1904, there were rumors that the PRR had its sights set on the New York, Philadelphia, and Norfolk Railroad (NYP & N) running down the spine of the Delmarva peninsula and connecting by ferry at Cape Charles to Norfolk. Although the PRR had never financed the building of the line up to its completion in 1882, it had supported its construction with various understandings and agreements, and PRR Vice President Alexander J. Cassatt had been instrumental in its planning and initial financing. In 1904, gossip flowed that the PRR was looking for a way to gain complete control of the line, thereby giving it undisputed dominance over rail traffic on the Eastern Shore and a throughway from Philadelphia and New York to Norfolk.[27]

Even more disturbing was evidence that the PRR was engaged in sounding out other targets for acquisition. One was the Queen Anne's Railroad, founded in 1894 to run from Queenstown and Love Point, Maryland, to Lewes, Delaware. It was, in 1904, a financial disaster. Another was the Chester River Steamboat Company, a small but prosperous line running four old steamers, *Gratitude, Corsica, Emma A. Ford,* and *B. S. Ford,* from Baltimore to Chestertown and Centreville and in season hauling peaches stacked to the overhead to the commission merchants in the city. And, it seemed, the appetite of the Pennsy (as the PRR was called) went far beyond the Queen Anne's Railroad and the Chester River Steamboat Company. These were small pickings.

Henry Williams was not surprised when he was approached by Nicholas P. Bond, Baltimore attorney, and Henry Scott, of the Wilmington banking house of Scott and Company, both representing a syndicate tied to the PRR. Their proposal had a simple objective: a package purchase of the Queen Anne's Railroad, the Chester River Steamboat Company, and the Weems Steamboat Company, lock, stock and barrel. The terms were attractive, and the price generous. The directors of the Queen Anne's Railroad and of the Chester River Steamboat Company snapped at the offer. Henry Williams hesitated.

For Georgeanna Weems Williams and Matilda Weems Forbes, sale of the Weems line would mark the end of a dynasty begun by George Weems 87 years earlier and brought to a magnificent climax in their own era by Henry Williams. They owned the company, even though it was incorporated with a body of directors, and they would have the final word about selling it. For the heirs apparent, the children of George-anna and Matilda, the prospects of running the line in the future were less attractive than the money to be gained by the sale. For Henry Williams, putting aside the dreams and labor of a lifetime cut to the quick.

On the rational side of the argument, Henry Williams reckoned with the adversities of the past few years. And he speculated very thoughtfully about the future prospects. Automobiles and trucks and roads—sooner or later they would stifle the steamboats. What would happen if he refused the offer? Would the Pennsy, with its grasp reaching for most of the steamboat service on the Bay, stand still and let the Weems line go unchallenged? Would it allow the Weems line to function as the Old Bay Line and the Chesapeake Line were left to operate in their independent runs to Norfolk? Or would the Pennsy by rail or steamer encroach on the monopoly enjoyed by Weems on the three great rivers of the Western Shore?

And then there was the question of age. Nearing 65, Henry Williams now stood at the stage in life when many men retired. He was weary; the last few years had taken their toll.

After an anguished debate, the two sisters and Henry Williams agreed to the sale.

The entire transaction involved nearly $2.5 million. With respect to the Queen Anne's Railroad, the agreement called for the absorption of $330,000 in 5 percent gold bonds, $1.4 million in mortgage bonds, and $600,000 in income mortgage bonds, together with $1 million in common stock held by the bondholders. The property of the Chester River Steamboat Company, unencumbered, was sold for about $200,000; it included the steamboats and wharf property.

When the directors and the stockholders met on October 10, 1904, the fate of the Weems Steamboat Company had been decided. Henry Williams resigned and would be succeeded by William Thompson (an interim appointee of Scott and Company), the exchange in office to take place at noon on October 12, 1904. Arrangements for the two sisters (virtually the only stockholders) to assume the assets and claims against the company for resolution and transfer were consummated (Appendix G).

The directors of the Weems Steamboat Company—Henry Williams, his sons (Mason Locke Weems Williams, Henry Williams, Jr., and George Weems Williams), and General Agent Henry S. Beal—met in the office of George Weems Williams, counsel, and received payment from the syndicate for the sale of the company. The two sisters, as owners, received $1,030,966.13. The date was January 3, 1905. In exchange, the syndicate received all the wharves owned by the Weems line (except Pier 2, which was conveyed back to the two owners); scows; transfer of leased property; and the older steamers *St. Mary's, Westmoreland, Lancaster, Potomac,* and *Essex;* the newer steamers *Caroline, Northumberland, Middlesex,* and *Calvert;* and the new *Anne Arundel*[28]

(Appendix G). The sale did not include Fair Haven, nor did it include Pier 2, Light Street.[29] They continued with a history of their own.

As a final gesture, Georgeanna Williams and Matilda Forbes suggested at the meeting of the directors on October 10, 1904, that $25,000 of the proceeds be distributed to the oldest and most deserving employees of the company—for example, to Captain James Gourley, with more than 40 years of service, and Henry S. Beal, general agent, with 39 years—to insure them in the event that they could not continue with the new owners. When the news of this action leaked to the public, some editorialists hailed it as a milestone in labor relations.

By the transaction involving the Weems line, the Queen Anne's Railroad Company, and the Chester River Steamboat Company, the new Pennsy subsidiary, named the Maryland, Delaware, and Virginia Railroad Company (MD & V), together with its sister subsidiary, the Baltimore, Chesapeake, and Atlantic Railway Company, gained control of most of the rail network on the Eastern Shore. Except for a few independent vessels and excursion lines such as the Tolchester company, the MD & V owned the steamboats out of Baltimore which served the tributaries of the Eastern Shore or connected to terminals of the rail network. And the MD & V owned a large fleet of handsome steamers plying the waters of the Patuxent, the Potomac, and the Rappahannock in a highly profitable and colorful trade on the great rivers of the western Chesapeake.

The red ball with the cutout *W* came off the stacks, and the flag with the red ball on the blue field came rattling down the flagpole. In time, the hulls of the steamers lost their white paint to the ruddy hue of antifouling paint (often called "Pennsylvania red"), and in time the red keystone (symbol of the PRR) shone on both sides of the smokestacks.

Along the Patuxent and the Rappahannock, residents who had known the steamboats of the Weems line for generations mourned the end of the name. The Weems boats were institutions; they were the very lifeblood that encouraged the country to develop and to share in the economic and social growth of the city; they carried the harvest of soil and sea and the products of industry on their sturdy decks; they sheltered passengers from the storm and entertained them in the beauty of the Bay and the sumptuousness of hotel comfort; and, with their plantation hospitality and simple beauty, they won the affections of everyone for their accomplished grace.

CHAPTER 8

Steamboat Life through the Years

During its near century of life, the Weems line reflected the will and temperament of three men: George Weems, Mason Locke Weems, and Henry Williams. The visionary, somewhat impractical, occasionally brusque, but Scottishly stubborn George was the progenitor—whimsically taken by the novelty of *Surprise*, captivated by the notion of retreat in his Bayside resort at Fair Haven, courageously rising above his grievous injury in the explosion of *Eagle*, adventuring with *Patuxent* in the byways and long reaches of the rivers threading their way from the Chesapeake, and ultimately launching his family in a dynasty of steamboating on the Bay. His brother Gustavus, stricken with fear at the price to be paid for George's ventures, provided the practical foil in the early drama of the beginnings. The heritage was carried on by George's sons— Gustavus, Theodore, George W., and, most importantly, the eldest son, Mason Locke Weems.

Inheriting his father's tenacity, Mason L. fought years of adversity and opposition with a determination that was not always gracious and a business sense that was not always compromising.[1] However, to his daughters he left the framework of a steamboat empire on the Chesapeake and a broad vision of a monopoly as the means for developing the entire Western Shore surrounding the Patuxent, the Potomac, and the Rappahannock.

Realization of that dream came to pass in the calm diplomacy, skillful amiability, and practical perspective of Henry Williams. When the

Weems line came to an end in 1905, with a large fleet of the finest steamboats on the Chesapeake, Williams could look with enormous satisfaction on the fruition of 87 years of steamboat history—the longest continuous chronicle of any steamboat line in the United States. The name of Weems had been linked as a symbol, even as a synonym, with steamboat life on the Chesapeake.

Aboard the steamboats themselves, a life existed far removed from the boardrooms and the machinations of competition. The years traced their course in the men who manned the steamers—the masters and mates, the pilots and quartermasters, the engineers and their helpers, the pursers and clerks, the stevedores, the stewards, and the dining room waiters. Time measured its passage in the people who gathered at the wharves and gaped at the white-clad steamers from Baltimore or who rode their decks, gorged on the food, and slept in the natty staterooms or the cluttered berths below decks. Youngsters, eagerly learning the skills of steamboatmen or diving off the ends of wharves to show off for gawking passengers, became old men; faces appeared and faded away in the memory of nearly a century.

Well before the Civil War, Mason L. began the practice of training bright young men with an aptitude for a seafaring life in the skills of steamboat navigation, engineering, and management. Through the years, the practice continued. Captains were brought in from other lines. In 1905 the Weems line could claim with considerable conviction that it had produced the finest crop of steamboat captains on the Bay. The list was long: James Russell Gourley, Mason Weems Gourley, Daniel Moncure Davis, John D. Davis, William C. Geoghegan, Herbert A. Bohannon, J. M. H. Burroughs, James B. Sanford, W. H. Van Dyke, John A. Clark, Arch M. Long, and others. The names suggested that sons carried on after their fathers.

Among the most revered of them was James Russell Gourley. For 61 years he served as master of steamboats on the Bay, most of the time spent with the Weems line. Born in Ireland on July 19, 1836, he came to Baltimore before he was 16 years old, found a job as purser aboard *Patuxent* under Captain George Weems, under whose tutelage he began to learn the Bay and its tributaries. Captain Mason L. Weems saw to it that the young but enthusiastic Irishman obtained his master's license on his 21st birthday. He had married his bride of 16 at the age of 18, and they honeymooned together on the anniversary every year thereafter. During his long years with the Weems line, James Russell Gourley commanded *Planter, Mary Washington, Theodore Weems* (and mourned her loss as skipper of *St. Mary's*), *Essex, Mason L. Weems, Richmond, Potomac,* and *Westmoreland.* After the sale of the line in 1905, he continued as master of *Anne Arundel.*[2] James Russell Gourley, called the "nestor" of the Bay, died on April 17, 1912.

Venerated at every landing on the Patuxent, Potomac, and Rappahannock, Gourley held the longest master's license in actual service on the Chesapeake Bay. Commodore of the Weems fleet, he was remembered in his later life as a small, frail-looking, quiet man, with the calm self-assurance inculcated through decades of skill in shiphandling and of unsurpassed knowledge of the Bay and its vagaries.

Through the years, Gourley had been associated with the story of the celebrated rebel spy, Colonel Richard Thomas Zarvona. Gourley's role in the escapade aboard *St. Nicholas* and later on *Mary Washington* became part of the Civil War legend of the Weems line (Chapter 4).

James Russell Gourley won affection from the ladies. In 1895, on a run of *St. Mary's* to the Patuxent via Fair Haven, Governors Run, and Plum Point, she stopped at Bay Ridge for several hours to allow excursionists to try out the thrills of the Ferris wheel, merry-go-round, and the midway's razzle-dazzle. When ready to leave, *St. Mary's* sounded a series of blasts on her whistle. But a large group of ladies on the outing failed to hear or heed the whistle. *St. Mary's* got under way. After she had gone about 200 yards from the pier, the score of ladies discovered they had been left behind. At the end of the long wharf, they vented their consternation and despair. Genial Captain Gourley relented and turned back. "I cannot ignore the plaintive wail of ladies," he said. Declared the ladies, "He is the most gallant mariner that ever trod a deck."[3]

The offspring and relatives of James Russell Gourley continued in his path. Under his father Mason Weems Gourley gained his master's license and skippered a number of the Weems boats, particularly the so-called "training boat" *Essex*, on which he served for many years. Thomas B. Gourley, brother of James, was purser aboard the Weems line boats and continued on the same steamers after their sale in 1905. Like his brother and nephew and a number of other senior employees of the Weems line, he shared in the $25,000 extended to them by Georgeanna Williams and Matilda Forbes.[4]

The career of Daniel Moncure Davis almost matched that of James Russell Gourley. Owner and master of a schooner that was destroyed at Fredericksburg in order to keep it out of the hands of the Union army, Daniel joined the Weems line after the Civil War and served as master of *Mary Washington, Wenonah, Theodore Weems, Mason L. Weems, Essex, Westmoreland, Richmond,* and *Lancaster*. He was identified with the Rappahannock route during his long career and died aboard *Lancaster* on January 20, 1910, while on a run to Fredericksburg. His son, John D. Davis, started a steamboat career as lookoutsman on June 2, 1896, aboard *Essex*, against the wishes of his father. In 1901, at age 22, John earned his first-class pilot's license, but because he was the most junior officer on the list, he failed to find a berth as master aboard the Weems line boats before the company went out of business. Nevertheless, the former Weems line steamers knew him as master under later management—aboard *Middlesex* on her Rappahannock runs for 20 years, during which he rescued passengers and crew from the burning *Three Rivers* in 1924, aboard *Potomac* until her final days, and aboard *Anne Arundel* when the saga of the former Weems line boats as overnight packets came to an end in 1937.[5]

Like John D. Davis, many of the skippers of former Weems line boats under the MD & V and BC & A learned their skills aboard the school-ships of the Weems masters. Among these were Mason Weems Gourley, Robert Horsman, and Emerson Harding on the Patuxent; Herbert Bohannon, Joseph Smith, and Robert Hart on the Potomac; James Burroughs and Arch Long on the Rappahannock.[6]

Not all of the Weems line masters began their careers aboard its boats. William C. Geoghegan, portly and genial master of *Northumberland, Middlesex,* and *Calvert,* in later years transferred his allegiance to the red ball flag from the Maryland and Virginia Steamboat Company of Charles R. Lewis. As master of *Sue* for the Potomac Transportation Company in 1890, he brought that steamer to the Weems fleet in 1895 with her sale by Charles R. Lewis; in 1896, he steamed off as master of the new and comely *Potomac,* pride of the fleet. Predating his experience with the Potomac Transportation Company, he was master of *Sue* when she served the York River line in 1874, rammed Fort Carroll in a fog on November 8 of that year, and, when she emerged from repairs, ran the Baltimore-Norfolk route in opposition to the Old Bay Line.

Captain Geoghegan was an Eastern Shoreman who somewhat anachronistically became a Unionist, an allegiance brought on by the seizure of a boat he ran by the Confederate raider *Alabama.* His affiliation later brought him into stentorian argument with Captain Daniel Moncure Davis, whose zeal for the Confederate cause was almost religious. Davis was not known for violent expletives, but when he exploded with "Jeem's River!" or "Sugar and mo-*Lass*-es!" all his fury poured out at once, and Geoghegan was often on the receiving end.[7]

Many years later, aboard the *Anne Arundel* on January 14, 1909, Geoghegan received from the secretary of the treasury a medal for a brave rescue performed on December 10, 1876, when he saved Midshipman James J. Smith and 16 men of the flagship *Hartford* in Hampton Roads. In an open boat, the men had dropped their oars in the bitter cold of a wintry gale and were drifting out to sea; Geoghegan, skipper of *Sue,* brought the steamer alongside, slipped on the ice of his own deck while going to the rescue, but held to the steamer's molding and pulled himself along to snatch the men from an icy grave.[8] Captains were heroes to many.

In the eyes of the little boy in knickers, gazing upward at the gold-braided figure on the upper deck of the steamer as it coasted in to the dock, the resplendent captain—moving his hand to order the quarter-master in the pilothouse to throw the wheel hard over, yanking the bell-pulls to clang and jingle the engine bells far below decks, and to send spume flying from the reversing paddlewheels—was little short of omnipotence itself. To hang around the doorstep of the pilothouse by the hour for a glimpse of the captain conning the boat around the bends and along the banks of the narrow rivers or setting her on course for long reaches of the Bay was a private joy for a young passenger; and actually being invited inside the pilothouse (by a captain who grew tired of tripping over the little figure on the doorstep) was little short of heaven itself.

Understanding the captain's orders to the man on the wheel required initiation into a special language: *Let 'er come to port* (or starboard) meant turning the steering wheel three or four spokes in the direction indicated while watching the swing of the jackstaff on the bow; *midships* meant centering the wheel; *steady* meant turning the wheel in the opposite direction just enough to stop the swing and put the vessel on a straight course; *hard over* required instant labor to rotate the wheel as far as it would go in the direction indicated by hand-over-hand pulls on the spoke handles and then fastening the rope becket to a spoke handle when the wheel had gone as far as it would turn. And there were the brass bellpulls to the engineroom: one, an open hook, for the "gong"; another, a closed triangle, for the "jingle" (the shapes designed to differentiate them in the dark). The captain snapped these pulls to signal his orders to the engineer; from *stop*, one gong meant *slow ahead;* followed by a jingle, *full ahead;* another gong, *slow ahead;* still another gong, *stop;* two gongs, *slow astern;* followed by a jingle, *full astern;* and one gong, *stop.* For the gaping youngster, hearing the special language and understanding the engine orders marked his entrance into the rites of brotherhood.

Snuggled in the upper berth of his stateroom down below, the lad would perhaps listen to the sounds of the steamboat—the faint whoosh of the walking beam engine, the creaks and little rattles of the timbers with each pulse of the engine, the lowing of cattle and bleating of sheep far forward on the freight deck, someone singing softly on an upper deck—and the swish of the waves past the latticed window, the sudden deep sound of the whistle to signal a passing ship, the call of the lookoutsman on the bow. He would envision the darkened pilothouse and the men there who searched the gray waters for the turning by a spar buoy in the night. And he would feel the comfort of his destiny held in the hands of this omniscient captain. Growing up never changed that veneration for a captain. Men and women traveling the boats of the Bay gave him the respect and social standing demanded by his dominance over the life aboard the boats.

Captains were hosts. Some were genial and cordial, mixing with the passengers. Others were more reserved, even austere in their demeanor, but they could not forget that the reputation of their boats depended upon the hospitality they extended. Captains often stood at the gangway to greet passengers, particularly if they were people of "standing" whom the company favored. Sooner or later, on every trip, the captain circulated about the decks and chatted with the passengers, as best his personality would permit. Some captains entertained favored ones among them at a meal or perhaps, if no one seemed to object, to a drink or two in the gentlemen's bar. Steamers came to be known by their masters, and captains for themselves. It was not unusual for a passenger booking passage in advance, and not knowing which boats were running or how skippers were currently assigned, to ask for a particular captain irrespective of the steamer. Captains Davis, Gourley, and Geoghegan had such a following.

Captains were hustlers within certain meanings of the word. To a considerable extent trade along the river landings depended on the captains' ability to attract shippers to place their produce, cattle, and merchandise aboard their boats or other steamers of the line. Although the Weems line enjoyed a virtual monopoly over the rivers that it served during much of its life, the growth of the regions—and indeed of the line—was linked to continued expansion of the shipping route to Baltimore (and in later years, to Norfolk). Captains were hustlers for trade, whether they liked the role or not. Some succeeded more than others.

They were hustlers also in another sense: they kept the crew in line. Until the Civil War, all deckhands, roustabouts, wood or coal passers in the fireroom, cabin stewards, and dining room waiters were slaves owned by the Weems family. After the Civil War, the same help presented a heterogeneous appearance, coming from diverse sources. Most of the deckhands and roustabouts, fireroom people, cabin help, and dining room staff were black. But lookoutsmen, quartermasters, pursers, clerks, and some of the labor force aspiring to the upper deck and promotion were white. Over the small kingdom of a steamboat, captains held nearly absolute authority, restrained only by the laws of the land. At their will, work was done, a routine maintained, and emergencies met. How well a boat functioned turned on the prodding—good-natured or ill-tempered—of its master.

A measure of what life was like aboard one of the steamers, a former Weems line boat, can be seen through the eyes of a lookoutsman turned quartermaster:

I got a job on a sidewheeler . . . as lookoutsman, $15.00 per month, but 3 meals per day. The steamer left Baltimore. . . . and landed Washington, D.C. . . . 3 trips per week. I kept job as lookoutsman 2 months and advanced to quartermaster. . . . The run to Washington . . . was very picturesque. We often carried the B & O Secretaries and the Shriners on the weekend runs.

We arrived at Wynne Wharf about 2 A.M. and discharged freight . . . at about full daylight we would be in the Coan River in Virginia. . . . Roads were not good . . . and there were no railroads. The passenger traffic was very busy on weekends. . . . On the return trip to Baltimore, especially during fall + winter the freight was very heavy. Tobacco, canned tomatoes, calves, sheep and oysters. It was a sight to pull up to a large cannery wharf . . . and see the canned goods stacked on the wharf. Sometimes we would take 2 hours loading, and the passengers mostly went ashore. . . .

In the summertime the run was delightful. Loads of pretty girls on weekends and in those days a uniform didn't have to be Army or Navy. I often wondered if a Bell Hop had them chasing after him as we did . . . . [I worked on another boat] and would have stayed longer if an irate father hadn't threatened me with a shotgun. He told me exactly what would happen to me if I did not stay away from his daughter. . . . I was at one time engaged to marry 6 different girls. One in Baltimore, one in Washington, St. Mary's City, Lodge Landing, Mundy Point, Colonial Beach. Married none of them, had some tight squeezes, tho.

Every time Capt. Bohannon caught me in a compromising position or occasion, he made me splice eyes in new manila 5 cables. One of the worst jobs because a new cable is hard tight, and the fid has to be hammered between the twist with a marlin spike, finger nails went and temper too.

Never was much of a drinking man being a Methodist minister's son, but it was to be had and cheap too. . . .

The Q.M. had to tag all calves and sheep in the ear and some of those calves were pretty husky critters. . . . I have been knocked down and dragged around all thro the mess they make in a pen many times, and had to bathe and change clothes after every episode, as many as 3 times from Bushwood to Wynne.

Lots of people went to Colonial Beach and Piney Point for the summer. Nice sandy beaches, cabins everywhere. Not many hotels.

All wharves in Yeocomico and Coan Rivers were cannery wharves. And all wharves were fertilizer stops in spring from Baltimore. It was in 167 and 200 lb bags and had to be stowed 8 + 10 bags high in the warehouses. And that was work. And we had to do it. Along with the deck hands. All was not fun and frolic on the steamboats in those days. I have been so tired after 6 hour watch that I slept like a log, and captain has relieved me many a time 1 whole hour late.

[The other day Q.M.] had to have a clean shirt every watch. I think he had a dozen shirts. I didn't have as many but I drag my washings on a heaving line off the stern at night. So did he.

[In winter] a lot of damage was done to lighthouses, buoys and steamboats. Sidewheel buckets were broken. Propellers lost and anchors too. We lost a propeller off the Calvert at 7 ft knoll and had to be towed to Balto by a tug. The buckets on the sidewheelers had to be repaired by the crews when they broke. And were they heavy. Each board was about 8 to 10 feet long, 12″ wide and 2½″ to 3″ thick. 3 boards to a bucket. Held together with Iron straps. Some of the bolts + nuts most always had to be cut off and there is many a . . . chisel + hammer on the bottom of the bay that slipped out of cold hands. During those repairing jobs we had to stand on a 12″ plank and pull the wheel down by hand, cut out the broken board and replace it. And the wind blowing, waves breaking under you and cold spray wetting us, all for $21.20 per month . . . .

The Lancaster and Middlesex had 7′ [steering] wheels and rope geared and when you put it hardover there was a rope becket to put on a spoke to hold her and when you released the becket you had better get out of the way. I knew of one Q.M. on M[iddle]sex who got a broken jaw for not moving fast enough.

One time we had Capt. Harding. . . . Capt. Bo was on vacation . . . and it was foggy. After we passed Raggity Pt above Piney Point he was in his room and came in the pilot house and asked the mate why he hadn't hauled around for Leonardtown. The mate told him rightly it wasn't time. He said he knew damn well it was and told me to haul her. I refused and he grabbed the wheel from me and rolled her hard over. Harry + I walked out of the pilothouse and she went high + dry. He had to get a tug to pull back in the channel. And had to beg us to take over again. He was about 5′5″ and knew it. But he never tried that again and it cost him $100.00 cash to the tug out of his own pocket. . . .

Jim Travis . . . quartermaster . . . rammed his head thro curved glass window to watch shell [races]. . . . Capt. Bo told me "next time you wash the windows, leave some spots on them so Jim will know they are not open." Those curved panes were difficult to get.

I bought myself a pair of [heavy] shoes with hard toes, and once at Bayside Wharf I heard a lot of yelling going on down on freight deck. So went down and as I stepped out on deck I saw the mate flat on his back with a Negro deck hand kneeling astride him. I always said, tho he denied it, that the mate said "get him

Vaughn." So I kicked him under the chin with those shoes on. I nearly killed him. The others rushed me and that's how I got blood to my clothes, and none of it mine. I stood 6′2″, weighed 195 lbs and was 20 years old, as hard as nails. . . . I have killed no one tho I have hurt a lot of bad ones.

Capt. Bohannon knew just about all the schooners of that day by their rig, and would look at a distant one thro the glass and say who she was. They all are gone now.

Signed Vaughn C. Mumford[9]

Captains were navigators. For them, navigation on the Chesapeake was more of an art than a science. For them, the instruments of navigation at sea were unknown; sextant, nautical almanac, reduction tables, Bowditch, chronometer, pelorus, were all uncomprehended and held at mystical value only. What a captain or pilot possessed was a compass to be used in low visibility or to strike a course on a very long reach of the Bay; his pocketwatch to time the run between lighthouse and channel markers or between course changes when fog or heavy weather kept him from seeing the markers or shore features for himself; and his profound knowledge of the Bay, gleaned from years of tutelage in the process of gaining a license and decades of experience as a waterman on the Chesapeake. That sort of experience was difficult to match. A skilled waterman knew the bottom of the Bay and its tributaries better than he knew the layout of his own house. He knew it by sight, by feel (even in the thickest fog), and by taste. A scoop of silt from the bottom could reveal location by its brininess or acidity or sour flatness.

By the time *Patuxent* began her systematic runs out of Baltimore in the 1830s, many of the lighthouses marking river entrances and island obstructions in the Chesapeake had been built. Twenty-one were standing by 1850. Many of the channels, particularly in the harbor approaches— most of them shoals and danger spots—were marked by spar or can buoys. Black and white spar or mast buoys—black to the north or starboard side, striped over the shoals in the channel—were numbered in sequence on the immediate approaches to Baltimore. By the Civil War, the colors and numbers had changed—red or odd numbered on the incoming starboard side, black or even numbered on the port side, black and white in midchannel—with startling consequences for navigators, since black had been shifted from right to left. By the 1880s, the buoyage system of numbering and coloring and floating buoys with bells, lights, and other designations had been established over most of the Bay.[10]

The upper Patuxent, with its narrow and twisting channels through marsh grass—channels often shifting and shoaling through the seasons—and with its eddies and strong currents coming with changes in the tide, was a continuing worry to steamboat skippers. In later years, some captains, when required to run at night above Benedict, insisted on taking aboard a certain canny black fisherman who memorized the river almost by the day. On the Rappahannock, the upper river above Carters and particularly near the Devils Woodyard—regions where the river narrowed in deep, reversing bends overshadowed by towering hills that tumbled to the water's edge—was a continuing challenge even to the most experienced.

Only a captain or pilot who knew from years of experience these constricted and tortuous waters like the back of his hand, who knew by timing and instinct every important sounding and every turn, and who was unafraid of the shadows would dare navigate a steamer at night in the upper Rappahannock. It took courage and knowledge to plunge into what appeared to be certain destruction against a black cliff, only to have the wall part and the river unfold. It took skill and certainty to skirt a steep bank so close that the wash of the steamer against the clay echoed in the darkness against the steamer's hull. Out of the blackness around the pilothouse would suddenly stab the blinding shaft of the searchlight, groping for a spar buoy or a marker on shore to certify the channel. But the searchlight was not often used because it left the captain and mate and the lookoutsman temporarily blinded from its brilliance.

Captains were shiphandlers, developing great skill in maneuvering their vessels in constricted waters and, most particularly, in coming alongside and clearing a dock. Sometimes wind and current made that operation difficult. These shiphandlers prided themselves on their prowess and were not above a bit of exhibitionism if the audiences on board or on the dock warranted it.

Oftentimes the efforts of skippers to bring their steamers alongside were embarrassing. On the upper Patuxent the current ran swift, often faster on the ebb than the flood. Steamers attempting to make a landing at midtide, when the current ran at maximum speed, often had to turn around to breast the flow; otherwise they would shoot past the dock before they could get lines out to get alongside. Some skippers tried to turn around in the narrow channel, using their engines and rudder, and were "halfway to Marlboro," as the locals put it, before they completed the turn. Other masters, including Jim Gourley, simply ran the bow in the bank and let the current sweep the steamer around. Getting alongside was an exciting undertaking with much shouting and hurling of heaving lines and hearty hauling on the manila—all to the delight of spectators who gathered to watch on the wharf.

Some docks required special skill in handling engines and lines. Particularly tricky were the landings at Coan and Bundicks—on opposite sides of the Coan River (off the Potomac) but separated by not much more than a steamer's length in the narrow river channel. The steamer ordinarily first tied up, port side to, at Coan on the north side of the river. On leaving Coan, the steamer had to perform a rather complicated maneuver in order to go alongside the wharf at Bundicks, less than a hundred yards away. The steamer could scarcely back and fill, the space in the channel leaving no room at bow and stern for such operations, particularly when the objective was to turn the boat around so that her port side was presented to Bundicks Wharf and her bow was headed downstream toward the Potomac. (At various periods, steamboats went alongside Bundicks first and then Coan.) Masters employed spring lines skillfully. To leave Coan, the steamer used a spring line aft; the propeller or paddlewheels backing would swing the bow away from the dock and toward the wharf across the river at Bundicks. With the rudder hard right, the engine nudging ahead, and the spring released, the bow would approach the wharf at Bundicks. Swift action on the part of a deckhand on the bow and the agent or his boy on the wharf would put a bow line on the piling; that line became a forward spring line to warp the steamer into place—port side to—alongside the wharf at Bundicks. The entire maneuver required precision in the use of lines and engines and the "feel" of a master for his boat.[11]

Quartermasters became second-class pilots, and second-class pilots became first-class pilots and masters by the process of licensing. Before 1852, a captain simply certified his apprentice when he thought he was ready. With enforcement by the Steamship Inspection Service, the process became somewhat more formal, with the applicant facing some sort of examination; but the recommendation of the master (and later the seconding of the American Association of Masters and Pilots of Steam Vessels of the United States) was the essential ingredient of promotion. What the aspirant had to know—and on this there was no equivocation—was the entire section of Bay (or several thousand miles of it) for which he was being licensed, every channel, every marker, every shoal, every headland, every creek and cove, in fair weather and foul. More than that, he had to demonstrate his mastery of seamanship, cargo handling, emergency procedures, and weather precautions. Not even the cub pilot cowering under the scathing demands of Horace Bixby in *Life on the Mississippi* had to answer for more.[12]

Beneath the master and mate lived some 25 to 35 members of the crew, depending on the size of the vessel and the season. The purser and clerk occupied their own world of selling staterooms, opened by huge brass keys with wooden tags large enough to float the key if dropped overboard. Their duties were to keep records of freight and passenger receipts and (in the earlier days) to run balances with straight pens and black ink in red leather ledgers in flowing Spencerian script. A purser's job could be profitable. He was given control of the bar, and some portion of the revenue (all of it in early days) went into his pocket. When beer was in short supply at country landings (through some form of prohibition or other causes), the arrival of a steamboat with open bar could net a few hundred dollars in a short time, the dirt on the saloon carpet marking the tramping of feet from field to barroom door.

In the dining room, paneled in white or ivory with gold trim and furnished with tables covered by snow-white tablecloths, gleaming silver, and swan-folded napkins, fussed the black waiters, each clad in black suit and white stiff shirt, a white napkin folded over the left arm. Before dinnertime, which was at noon, or suppertime, which began at five or six o'clock in the evening, the headwaiter paraded through the saloons, upper and lower, sounding a bell and announcing; "Supper's now being served" (at the evening meal), often holding the first syllables in a long

and musical trill.[13] The elegance of the setting and the panorama of the
Bay beyond the windows, the sweeping hospitality and courtesy of the
waiters, and the simple excellence of the food, served with style and
flourish, smacked of the Old South and days long gone.

In galleys too narrow for passage, black cooks prepared meals
equaled only by the best hotels in Baltimore. For example, a supper
aboard a later Weems line steamer might consist of the following[14]:

Tea	Iced	Coffee	Milk
	Broiled		
	Beef Steak	Lamb Chops	
	Fried		
Potatoes	Oysters	Clams	Fish	Chicken
	Stewed Oysters		
Tomatoes Sliced	Salad	Celery	Slaw
	Cold Meats		
Ham	Beef	Corned Beef	Bologna	Tongue
	Bread		
Hot Rolls	Corn Bread		Cold Bread
	Crackers and Cheese		

Assorted Cake	Graham Wafers	Jelly
	Fruits	
Peaches	Grapes	Oranges	Bananas

Offerings on earlier menus were even more lavish: codfish, mutton
shoulder, roast goose, veal cutlet, roast turkey, bear steak, venison, terrapin, salmon, with all sorts of vegetable combinations, and a range of
desserts including mince pie and almond cake. Prices ranged from 50
cents in the early days to $1.00 at the end. A full stock of liquors and
wines occupied the barroom shelves.

At Christmastime, the Weems line steamers served a special eggnog
from a Weems recipe[15]:

Twelve eggs, 1¼ pounds of sugar, 1 quart of *good* whiskey (such as Virginia Gentleman), ½ pint of rum, ½ pint of brandy (Courvoisier), 3 quarts of coffee cream.
Beat the eggs until light, then add the first pint of whiskey drop by drop. This
cooks the eggs and makes it thick. The remaining pint of whiskey should be
poured in very slowly. Add the other ingredients. Chill and serve with nutmeg
sprinkled on top.

The boat's reputation depended in large measure upon her cuisine
and upon the attentiveness of her dining room staff. For some reason, no
one thought very much about the engineers, their assistants, and the
gang manning the shovels and grates beneath the boilers. Not too many
engineers ranked among the names memorialized by the line or remem-

bered with affection by the passengers. John McGoldrick, longest in service as an engineer, became chief engineer for the entire line—a kind of engineering commodore—and supervised the shipyard construction of the engines and machinery of many of the later steamers. But he was an exception. For those passengers adventurous enough to seek out the engineroom, and even more horrendous, the fireroom, the experience was unnerving.

On the big sidewheelers, the control platform stood in front of the huge steam valves, admitting steam from the boiler to the cylinder on one stroke and releasing it from the cylinder to the condenser on the next; the long and dangerous scissorlike toes and wipers, propelled by the eccentric rods, sliced vertically at the unwary head; and behind the valves stood the massive cylinder, as much as 10 feet high, from which shot up and down the long piston rod projected by the piston in the cylinder. The vertical-thrusting piston rod drove the walking beam, a massive, 15-ton diamond swinging in the sky visible from the control platform through a slit in the roof of the two-story superstructure above the engineroom. At the other end of the walking beam swung the crank turning the paddlewheel shaft in monstrous strokes. The effect of this tremendous oscillation of power was awe inspiring—even terrifying to the uninitiated. For the more experienced, the sight of the engineer swinging the starting bar to set the machinery in motion when the boat was maneuvering or getting up to speed for automatic operation epitomized man's power over such massive machinery.

Aboard steamers with compound or triple-expansion engines, a visit to the engineroom was less inspiring. The engine itself was more like an internal combustion (automobile) engine, mounted vertically, with the connecting rods turning cranks around the propeller shaft just above the bilge. The entire machinery, including auxiliary equipment, fitted in the hull below main deck level, somewhere about midships. With a head clearance of six or seven feet, the engineroom space seemed cramped and often cluttered. Flailing piston rods and crankshafts were disconcerting. And the thought of crawling through narrow passages and down dark, metal, and often slippery ladders never encouraged passengers, even the least timid, to visit. On the metal decks of the engineroom, before the controls admitting steam from the boiler to the engine, stood the engineer and the oilers, intent in the light of a bulb or two to keep the engine running and the bells answered. In summertime, air brought from the hurricane deck by big scoop ventilators to the engineroom and fireroom scarcely cooled the men who labored there.

Most passengers, if they were that inquisitive, took one look down the vertical ladder to the fireroom and the scene below and drew back in horror. Across the steel deck plates, in front of blazing furnaces beneath the boiler (or boilers) shoveled sweating men—their rough clothes and bandanas soaked—swinging back and forth, hurling coal from the bunkers on either side to the furnace doors thrown open to the white heat of the grates inside. In Baltimore, most steamers loaded some 100 tons of coal, depending on the grade; more of a cheaper coal had to be loaded because it produced less heat. The coal was stored in bunkers, port and starboard. From side to side, the men worked to stoke the fires. Periodically, they would thrust long hoes into the inferno to rake and work the coals or to strike the clinkers to break them up. Their glistening faces reflected the fire in front of them. Then, at intervals, they would use the same hoes to rake out the ashes beneath the grates, shovel the hot ashes into bins or hoppers, hoist them to the main deck, and dump the ashes overboard. On later boats, a scuttle could be opened beneath the guards to throw out the ashes. On the very latest steamers, the ashes were ejected by steam pressure through an orifice below the guards; most of the earlier Weems boats never knew such a luxury.[16]

The men worked in shifts, coming up to the sideports on the freight deck for air; they were a smelly, sweaty, often repulsive sight. They were joined there by the deck force—stevedores or roustabouts, nearly always, as were the men in the fireroom, black. In the days before the Civil War, all of them were slaves. In the postwar years, the heritage lingered on.

When a boat came alongside a landing, the stevedores, wearing leather aprons or equivalents made from burlap sacks, trundled the gangplank ashore through the sideports and began swinging freight from forward deck to wharf, from wharf to freight deck on handtrucks, which they propelled with speed and grace, moving in rapid sequence behind each other, and dancing in a little jig or sidestep to the tune of a rhythmic chant drawn straight from their tribal heritage. Mingled in the staccato sounds, mostly incomprehensible, were brief but clearly pronounced words, often good-humored jibes directed at the quartermaster or the purser or any particularly flamboyant target visible among the passengers. Huge barrels of fish and oysters, great hogsheads of tobacco weighing 500 pounds, and crates of canned goods and produce were handled with an astonishing ease, often requiring incredible dexterity to mount them in tiers on the freight deck.

Sheep had to be manhandled and carried bodily to pens near the bow. Cattle, particularly frightened steers, required several men at the head to pull on an attached rope, a few behind to push, and one man to twist the tail. Many a steer broke loose, scattering stevedores and sightseers in frantic escape, leaping into the water or gathering momentum on the pier. A wild melee, reminiscent of a western rodeo would erupt to capture the recalcitrant animal and bring him to tether at a pole fastened across the freight deck. Spectators would of course applaud from the safety of the warehouse roof.

The story goes that one mule, about to be loaded aboard in Baltimore, stopped short, planted his feet in all directions, and refused to budge. An attempt to lash him up with ropes ended abruptly when his rear heels flew in the air, projecting a 250-pound, self-appointed mule expert to the bottom of a nearby barrel and scattering spectators over most of Light Street. The captain came down and spoke gently to the animal, slyly slipping a noose around each pair of legs and a blindfold over the mule's head. When suddenly tightened, the nooses hobbled the mule, and the blindfold slid over his eyes; the entire deck force picked him up bodily and deposited him on the freight deck.[17]

A colorful, dirty, sometimes unruly, often kindly lot, the roustabouts were a loyal part of the steamer's family. The sounds of their singing—a mixture of the rhythms of Africa and the melodies of plantation life—were haunting. To the very end of the line the Weems family cared for the blacks aboard their vessels with a sort of paternalistic pride and considerable affection.

Some of the deckhands earned particular fame. One named only as Horace sported a battered silk hat, which he wore in every season, rain or shine, indoors and out—creating awe among his peers. Another named Warren could neither read nor write but could tell by the configuration of labels, and his years of experience in seeing them, where the freight was to be unloaded; his accuracy was as unvarying as that of the literate purser or quartermaster.

Black passengers aboard steamboats in the waters of Maryland and Virginia suffered under the rigid social opprobrium of segregation. Aboard Weems line boats, an effort was made to keep their sleeping quarters clean, not always the case with other steamers; but the social lines were strictly drawn between blacks and whites.

In most vessels, second-class accommodations, to which blacks were assigned, occupied a space in the hull below the main deck, often in the stern. The area was divided—male and female, black and white—with berths, sometimes in curtained cubicles, around the edge. A few portholes gave feeble ventilation. Most steamers had a second-class lounge or saloon with chairs, a mirror or two, and some sort of adjoining washroom and toilet, all segregated by sex and color.

An incident occurred in 1884 which rocked the steamboat world's concept of segregation. On August 15 of that year, the Stewart sisters—Martha, Mary, Lucy, and Winnie—bought first-class tickets in Baltimore at $3.00 for passage to Kinsale, Virginia, aboard *Sue*, then operating under the Potomac Transportation Company before its sale to Charles R. Lewis and eventually to the Weems line. The Stewart sisters were black and traveled each year to visit relatives in Westmoreland County. Because of the tickets they held, the purser assigned the Stewart sisters to staterooms at the other end of the boat from those used by white women. The staterooms to which the Stewarts were assigned were poorly furnished, unmade, and filthy. The women demanded first-class staterooms commensurate with those assigned to the whites; they were refused. So they spent the night, sitting upright, in chairs in the segregated portion of the saloon.

Before the year was out, they filed suit against *Sue* in U.S. District Court (*Sue* was engaged in interstate commerce) charging unjust discrimination. The court held that two issues were at stake: one, whether owners could separate passengers on the basis of color; and two, whether the cabins were equal in comfort and convenience. Up until that point, Congress had shied away from passing segregation laws. The Supreme Court leaned to the view that some segregation was permissible; and the rules of common law prevailed, allowing steamboat owners to provide for the comfort of passengers generally and to offer equal accommodations for the same price. The court's ruling, however, was only slightly blurred: "The separation of the colored from the white passengers, solely on the ground of race and color, goes to the verge of the carrier's legal right, and such a regulation cannot be upheld unless bona fide and diligently the officers of the ship see to it that the separation is free from any discrimination in comfort or attention." The sisters were each awarded $100.00.[18]

When *Sue* joined the Weems line, she was greeted upon her arrival in the Rappahannock from a Norfolk run by storms of protest because the U.S. mail was being handled on board by a mulatto clerk assigned by Washington. Passengers on board were indignant because the man performed his duties in the regular clerk's office and ate his meals in the dining room at the same time as the white passengers. Captain Joseph Smith and Henry Williams promised to try to make a change when the steamer reached Baltimore.[19]

In 1890 a celebrated segregation case hit the Weems line. On July 6, 1887, Robert A. McGuinn, a black Baptist pastor of an Annapolis church, had bought a ticket from Baltimore to Millenbeck, Virginia, aboard *Mason L. Weems.* When the supperbell rang, he seated himself in the dining room at a table at which two ladies and a gentlemen were already seated; he refused to move when asked to do so by the captain; under instructions the waiters removed the food and dishes to another table, where all the passengers then seated themselves, leaving him alone. Some of the passengers threatened to push him overboard, and he left the boat at Monaskon, eight hours before his destination. McGuinn brought suit in U.S. District Court against Georgeanna Williams, Matilda Forbes, and Captain Thomas J. Cooper. In its 1890 verdict, the court ruled that although equal accommodations must be furnished by the carrier, public sentiment expressed in demands of passengers for separation must be gratified lest the carrier sacrifice his business; furthermore, the plaintiff was not obliged to leave the table, he was served, and although he suffered some humiliation, it was not enough for damages.[20]

The full weight of the Jim Crow laws descended on Virginia in 1900 (amended in 1901) followed by Maryland in 1904. The laws were remarkably similar, in fact, identical in most provisions.

It shall be the duty of any captain, purser, or other officer in command of any steamboat carrying passengers . . . to assign white and colored passengers . . . to the respective locations they are to occupy . . . and that it shall be [his] duty to separate . . . the white and colored passengers . . . in the sitting, sleeping, and eating apartments; provided, however, that no discrimination shall be made in the quality and convenience of accommodations afforded passengers in said locations. . . .

Any captain, purser, or other officer in command . . . who shall fail or refuse to carry out the provisions [above] shall be deemed guilty of a misdemeanor, and may be proceeded against according to law, and upon conviction thereof, shall be fined not less than twenty-five dollars nor more than one hundred dollars for each offense.

Any passenger or passengers traveling on any steamboat . . . who willfully refuse to occupy the location . . . assigned . . . or behave in a riotous or disorderly manner, he, she, or they shall be deemed guilty of a misdemeanor and on conviction thereof shall be fined not less than five dollars nor more than fifty dollars, or confined in jail not less than thirty days, or both, in the discretion of the court; and such person may be ejected from said boat by the officers thereof at any landing place of said boat, and, if necessary, such assistance may be invoked by the persons in charge of said boat as they may require to eject such passenger; and provided, that in case of such ejectment neither the captain nor other person in charge . . . nor the steamboat company . . . shall be liable.[21]

The ugly shadow of Jim Crow fell across the decks of the Weems line and darkened them to the very end. At times there were suspicions that some of the Weems skippers, even Daniel Moncure Davis, were sidestepping, if not flouting, the law, but no charges were leveled, no indictments issued. Aboard the boats, in spite of the rebel taint in the past war, sympathy for the blacks was keenly felt.

The palatial saloons, the dining rooms, the cabins, the barrooms, and the sweep of open decks belonged to the whites, and in their world they lived above the perceived seaminess of the lower decks.

The silk-hatted, starched-collared men and long-skirted, flowered-hatted women who sat primly about the decks and saloons of the steamboats of the late 1860s and 1870s stepped into a setting not unlike what they imagined for the leisure class. It whispered of romance, of starlit nights, and magical sunsets. It spoke of escape. They posed and frolicked, feasted and caroused—and steamboat owners vied with each other to please them.

The less privileged traveled, also. The farmer, trailed by his labor-beaten wife and children, clad in homespun and rough clothes of the field, dragged the dung of the cattle across the gangplank and into the carpet of the cabins. Other malodorous passengers from factories and rows of corn rode the boats as well. Hawkers and drummers and peddlers, charlatans and Bible-thumping missionaries flocked aboard. And the gentlemen's bar was never quite free of the spirited gambler. On the freight deck, the black hands shuffled and chanted, their songs straight from the soul of slavery. A steamboat was an earthy scene. The actors on board played out the drama of postwar Tidewater and preserved much of the nostalgic flavor of the era that preceded it.

The steamers of the 1890s and early 1900s were not dissimilar in atmosphere and clientele from the postwar boats. The costumes were somewhat different, the music moved to an altered tempo, but the sense of a step back in time was very much the same.

Although Fair Haven never drew the crowds of Tolchester, it enjoyed a steady clientele. The Patuxent-bound steamers and the special excursion boats of the Weems line crowded aboard hundreds of one-day or weeklong vacationers each trip. Bowler-hatted or straw-hatted men, vested and gold-chained, often mustached and bewhiskered—and parasoled, cartwheel-hatted, skirt-dragging, well-corseted women—sat sedately around the shaded or open decks and drank in the beauty of the Bay. On the evening return trip, they might loosen up the stays a bit to dance a waltz or a polka to Mr. Itzel's orchestra. Or someone might produce a newly fashionable mandolin, and in the darkness of the afterdeck they would sing "Come Back to Erin" and "Love's Old Sweet Song" and "In the Gloaming" and often the songs of the old country they had left behind.

The comfortable accommodations at the hotel, superb meals in the dining room and aboard the boats, lazy days on the hotel porch or in the groves (where local residents often came by carriage) or along the lapping waters of the sandy shore from which the cliffs of Calvert were clearly visible drew visitors season after season. In spite of scares from drinking water at one time considered polluted or from hordes of mosquitoes and biting flies that came with a change in the wind, Fair Haven kept its reputation for unsurpassed hospitality.

Travelers rode the steamers for many reasons. Around 1900 sportsmen began to book passage for Bristol, located at the head of navigation on the Patuxent.

At the turn of the century, Bristol, Hills Landing, and Mount Calvert were centers of a sport peculiar to the marshland of the Patuxent River. A small bird, the sora rail—long-legged, brown, white underneath, succulent—migrated south in early fall of each year and gathered there in great numbers to feed in the marsh grass. Sometime in the early 19th century, an unusual form of hunting developed. Hunters engaged a guide called a *pusher,* who poled a narrow flat-bottomed "railbird skiff" through the marsh at high tide while the hunters fired at the railbirds that rose from the grass in great clouds. Because the tidal range was less than two feet and the waters in the marshes dropped to mud at low tide, the trip in the hidden crannies of the marshes could last only an hour or an hour and a half at best, otherwise the boat would be stranded. A good pusher who knew the marshes and the habitat of the railbirds could earn up to $10.00 a day, a huge wage at the time. Gun clubs sprang up near Bristol and Hills Landing. Well-to-do sportsmen arrived by private yacht, the Chesapeake Beach Railway, and steamboat to stay at the gun clubs and indulge in the wholesale slaughter of the birds until the season changed and signaled the departure of both the prey and their hunters.[22]

Oddities punctuated the routine of steamboat life. On a trip down the Bay *Westmoreland* ran into a heavy gale, with wind whipping seas over the upper deck. After the steamer found shelter from the storm, two live fish were discovered on the deck near the wheelhouse. Captain Burroughs enjoyed one for his Sunday morning breakfast; the mate preserved the other as a souvenir. Sailors on the steamers were a superstitious lot, and the preserved fish was mounted for good luck.

On the other hand, sailors could make up a gloomy crew if the omens were wrong. On one occasion, *Richmond* sailed from Baltimore on Friday the 13th. She had damaged a paddlewheel slightly in the ice, thereby requiring painful underway repairs in the cold and danger inside the paddlebox. Three corpses were aboard for shipment, and, most horrendous and portentous, three captains were aboard at the same time. The vessel tied up a wharf where, it was announced, the wharf-owner had just died. And on leaving the wharf, the steamer's feline mascot and prime "ratter," Old Nance, was inadvertently left behind. With a crew so demoralized, *Richmond* barely made it to Fredericksburg.[23]

The steamers and the wharves on Light Street and around Baltimore Harbor were infested with rats and mice. Early in the war on the rodents, *Essex* acquired three cats—one black, one gray, one yellow—and one was placed on each deck; they never left the deck to which they were assigned; they fattened and basked in the praise of crew and passengers. Cats became "deckhands" aboard *Richmond, Westmoreland,* and *Sue. Potomac* was presented with a fine Maltese by a young lady. Other boats sought cats, and the practice of kidnapping good ratters became commonplace. Nevertheless, passengers were constantly startled by the ugly creatures scuttling along the paneling of ornate saloons or peering from a hole in a washroom at an embarrassing moment. All too frequent were the shrieks of female passengers, scurrying about in fright, skirts aloft, or unceremoniously climbing atop the nearest table.

Other animals intruded on the peace and tranquility of the Weems line. In early 1895, a red and white cow—one of a drove shipped from Tappahannock aboard *Essex* and herded off the boat and up Light Street—elected instead to explore the offices of the company. Turning suddenly, it climbed the 24 steps of Pier 2, Light Street, and started down the 140-foot hallway of the executive offices at an easy trot. Office doors opened and hastily shut. The cow arrived at the end of the hall, poked her head through a window, contemplated the harbor, and started to climb through the window for the roof of a shed below. Several men, quickly summoned, persuaded her to retrace her steps. At the head of the steps, several stevedores collared her, dragged her down, and sent her packing after the others in the drove. The occupants of the executive offices recovered their aplomb and considered what to do about the smelly evidence of the cow's recent presence in their sacrosanct quarters.[24]

Some captains of the boats recalled that strange animal events had always stirred up people on the line. For example, during one summer, someone caught an eight-foot shark at Hills Landing on the Patuxent, 40 or so miles from the Bay, and so upset excursionists and vacationers that the steamboat service suffered for a week.[25] Animal problems were at most minor annoyances compared with the major confrontations affecting the company.

The Weems line survived its confrontations and its catastrophes and met the public with composure. It took its cue from a long heritage— that of being the oldest steamboat line in continuous service in the United States.

When the announcement came in late 1904 that the Weems line was selling out to the Philadelphia syndicate, the news was met with dismay and apprehension along the shores of the Patuxent, the Potomac, and the Rappahannock. The shippers, the farmers, the merchants, and the vaca- tioners shuddered at the thought of an uncaring management, far away to the north, indifferent to their supplications and requests.

Who would replace Henry Williams and his genial overview of their welfare? Who would perform the myriad kindnesses of the pursers and mates and even captains of the Weems line—those employees who shepherded their customers' produce to the proper and most profitable commission merchants, who performed their shopping in the city for them—even down to the part for the hand cultivator, or suit of clothes off the rack, or a yard of trim for a homemade gown? What would it be like without the Weems line? They had become like part of the family— dependable and comfortable to have around.

CHAPTER 9

The End of
an Era

With the sale of the Weems line, Henry Williams retired from the steam-boat life of the Chesapeake, but he did not retire from the business world. Nor did he retire from politics. Maintaining an office in the Union Trust Building, he managed a substantial estate of investments and served as director of a number of banks. He held on to the office of city collector in spite of the political hostility of Mayor Timanus and contin-ued in the post under his successor, J. Barry Mahool, until 1908.

In 1907, while still serving in this post, Henry Williams briefly oc-cupied the limelight when he was induced to run for governor by Balti-more Democrats. The coalition supporting him disintegrated at the last minute, and opposition to Williams developed in the person of S[olomon] Davies Warfield (later to become president of the Seaboard Airline Rail-road and of the Old Bay Line and source of the name of the famous steamer *President Warfield*),[1] who was expected to finance most of the campaign. When the Baltimore *Sun* suddenly editorialized against Henry Williams, as it had done in his two mayoral compaigns, his support collapsed. On the floor of the convention, just 15 minutes before he was to be nominated, Williams was informed that his nomination would be withdrawn. Even the press itself had to report that few men in the state had been given as shabby treatment as that bestowed on Williams. Many delegates later expressed publicly their shame at the turn of events (Appendix E).[2]

During the last years of his life, Williams lived at 108 West 39th Street, near the line between Guilford and Roland Park in Baltimore. He died there in his sleep on March 20, 1916, so quietly that a valet (in attendance because the 76-year-old Williams had complained of not feeling well) did not realize that Williams had died. He was eulogized in the press, in financial journals, and in memorials read in churches and court houses all over the state and in Virginia.

His sons were not content to put aside the family's maritime legacy nor the name of Weems. Led by the eldest brother, Mason Locke Weems Williams, they decided to explore the possibilities of establishing a steamship line to run the coast between Baltimore and a southern port. If they had the thought of starting up another Weems line on the Chesapeake, the notion was fleeting; there seemed to be little room for a successor line in competition to the monopoly of the packet routes and the established runs of the Old Bay Line and the Chesapeake line to Norfolk. However, with a coastal line, similar to that of the Old Dominion Line, or that of the Merchants and Miners Transportation Company, a trade between selected cities and Baltimore could be developed—at least in the judgment of Mason L. W. Williams.

Mason searched the Atlantic coast below Norfolk. One small port caught his attention. Georgetown, South Carolina, handled considerable lumber sawed from the pine of the region and distributed merchandise to merchants and farmers brought in by small craft. But its commerce was hampered by the lack of regular steamer service, and its citizens welcomed the idea of establishing a freight link to Baltimore.

In 1906, out of the efforts of Mason L. W. Williams, emerged the Baltimore and Carolina Steamship Company (B & C), beginning with *George Weems*, a sleek ex-government vessel used by the B & C first as a freighter running to Georgetown, South Carolina, then as a family yacht. The Williams brothers (with Theodore Weems Forbes, son of Sydney and Matilda Weems Forbes), as directors, persuaded the Maryland, Delaware, and Virginia Railroad (MD & V) to permit the B & C to use the old house flag. The red ball on the blue field flew once again from the masthead of a vessel owned in the Weems lineage. The line prospered. In the period from 1906 to 1929, the expansion of the B & C under Mason Locke Weems Williams as president and, after his death, under his brother Henry Williams, Jr., was little short of spectacular. The need for increased coastal freight service and the upsurge in passenger travel to Florida during the period combined to make the line an extremely profitable undertaking. During those years, the line acquired no less than 15 large oceangoing ships and extended its services to include Miami, West Palm Beach, Philadelphia, New York, Beaumont, Corpus Christi, and Lake Charles.

All of its ships—except one, named for Henry Williams—were named for members of the Weems family. Most of the ships were bought from the U.S. Shipping Board—surplus from World War I. All were virtually rebuilt and completely refurbished (Appendix E).

Mary Weems and *Esther Weems* were among the finest passenger vessels engaged in coastal trade. Redesigned specifically for the Miami-bound, jazz-playing, mink-coated, Charleston-dancing, leisure set of Baltimore, Philadelphia, and New York, they carried the ultimate in interior furnishings: lounge rooms with sliding glass doors to garden decks; dance halls with stages for big bands and variety shows; two-level dining rooms lighted by art-glass panels and canopy; Gothic-style smoking and game rooms paneled in oak and furnished in black leather; bedrooms with private bathrooms, twin beds, sofas, mahogany dressing tables, and silk-shaded lamps. Both ships were welcomed in Miami with the keys to the city.

To the surprise of the shipping world, on July 22, 1929, Henry Williams, Jr., announced the sale of the B & C to A. H. Bull and Company, a New York organization operating the Baltimore Insular Line in a coastwise business from Baltimore to Pensacola, St. Petersburg, Tampa, and Puerto Rico. The sale marked the end of the maritime interests of the Weems dynasty.

For a brief period the A. H. Bull interests perpetuated the Weems name on the ships; but in 1931 the president, Ernest A. Bull, decreed that the Weems portion of each name would be dropped. By the end of January 1932, the surname had disappeared. *Frances Weems* became simply *Frances; Jean Weems* sailed as *Jean; Dora Weems* cleared as *Dora;* and all the steamers expunged the name of Weems from the name plates.[3] And with the gesture, the name of Weems left the maritime world, to be revived only briefly in World War II with the naming of a liberty ship *George Weems* as a memorial to her illustrious namesake.

During their quarter-century travels down the Bay from Baltimore to the open ocean and coastal voyages along the Atlantic Seaboard, the large black-hulled freighters and passenger ships of the B & C line passed the wide entrances of the Patuxent and the Potomac and the Rappahannock. If there was any recognition of the long history of Weems steamboats on these waters, the red ball flag was never dipped in acknowledgment. Yet after January 1905, the date when that flag came down from the mastheads of the overnight packets, these same steamers continued to ply the routes established by the Weems progenitors. By that 1905 transaction the MD & V acquired some of the handsomest steamboats on the Chesapeake: *St. Mary's, Westmoreland, Lancaster, Potomac, Essex, Caroline, Northumberland, Middlesex, Calvert,* and *Anne Arundel.* The new company, dominated by the Pennsylvania Railroad, gained the services of most of the distinguished shipmasters and mates and engineers who had manned the same boats under Henry Williams. Proudly, the steamers followed the routes where they were still greeted with affection.

New steamers were built to join them as trade expanded in the years before World War I. For example, *Dorchester* and *Talbot,* sister ships launched by the Maryland Steel Company at Sparrows Point in 1912 for the Baltimore, Chesapeake, and Atlantic Railway Company (BC & A), earned a particular place in the affections of Tidewater people. Large boats—192 feet long, with a beam of 59 feet over the guards and a depth of hold of 10.2 feet—they were designed to make 15 miles per hour. Each was propelled by an inclined engine and small paddlewheels with a lever system to feather the buckets for maximum vertical thrust in the water. Their normal cruising speed was about 11 miles per hour. Built at a cost of $185,000, each boat was luxuriously outfitted and carried passengers in exceptional comfort, with hurricane deck staterooms opening to vistas of the Bay. Both boats were intended for the Choptank River route to replace *Avalon* and *Joppa,* but in the 1920s they found themselves on the western rivers, particularly on the Potomac route in service between Baltimore and Washington. The residents and vacationers of Piney Point, the Coan River, and Lodge Landing accepted them with the same good grace they had given to the Weems boats. When *Dorchester* and *Talbot* were substituted for other boats, the residents along the Patuxent came to know them well.

Another steamer joining the parade was the *Three Rivers,* built for the MD & V in 1910 by the Maryland Steel Company for $125,000. Like *Dorchester* and *Talbot* that followed her and which were constructed somewhat to resemble her, she had especially fine staterooms on the topdeck, an inclined engine, and the lines of a large packet boat. She steamed on the Potomac route for many years. Her burning off Cove Point, at the mouth of the Patuxent, on July 5, 1924, resulting in the loss of 10 lives (four of them were young members of the *Evening Sun* Newsboys Band) was tragic. *Middlesex,* under Captain James Gresham, with a young quartermaster by the name of John D. Davis beside him, came alongside the blazing vessel and rescued the survivors.

Except for the years of World War I and its immediate aftermath, the period from 1905 to the 1920s marked the golden age of steamboating on the Chesapeake. Although the number of Baltimore steamboats running throughout the tributaries of the Bay dropped from a high of 51 in 1905 to 33 by 1930, the kind of steamboats running the Bay differed greatly from that of boats operating before the turn of the century. The former Weems boats, particularly those built in the first few years of the century, exemplified the style and elegance that became the hallmark of first-class travel on the Bay; *Three Rivers, Dorchester,* and *Talbot* carried on the tradition. But new packets were being built, especially for the Baltimore-Norfolk trade (and the York River run), which exceeded the dreams of earlier steamboat owners.

In 1905 the Baltimore Steam Packet Company (the Old Bay Line) had built the steamer *Virginia* and two years later, the *Florida.* Both resembled the earlier *Alabama* (built 1893)—palatial, high-speed packets (14 miles per hour, cruising speed) with staterooms extending the length of the gallery or hurricane deck from abaft the pilothouse to a point only a short distance from the stern. Not to be outdone, the rival Chesapeake Steamship Company brought out the sleek, steel-hulled sister ships, *City of Baltimore* and *City of Norfolk,* in 1911. They were all three-deckers

and stately. Three hundred feet long, propeller-driven, first-class floating hotels, they were designed to traverse the Bay from Baltimore to
Norfolk with clocklike precision, glistening in white paint from waterline to pilothouse, the upper decks lined with windows, the freight deck
with portholes. The Old Bay Line steamers and those of the Chesapeake
line looked more like oceanliners than the overnight packets from which
they sprang.

Competition between the bitter rivals had brought new construction
through the years. For the Chesapeake line had emerged *City of Annapolis* and *City of Richmond*, handsome vessels that collided on February
24, 1927, resulting in the sinking of the *City of Annapolis* by her sister
ship. The final Norfolk and York River packet of the Chesapeake line was
Yorktown, launched February 25, 1928. She was a lithe, clean-cut 275-
footer that ended her days as the target of a Nazi submarine on a fateful
Atlantic crossing in World War II.

The finest boats of the Old Bay Line appeared between 1922 and
1928. *State of Maryland* (1922), *State of Virginia* (1923), and *President
Warfield* (1928) were nearly sister ships, except that *President Warfield*
was more splendidly appointed with accommodations for the president
of the Seaboard Airline Railroad and owner of the Old Bay Line, the
aforementioned S. Davies Warfield, political nemesis of Henry Williams. The steamer was named for Warfield after his death. A certain
niece of Warfield's might have launched the boat from the yard of Pusey
and Jones in Wilmington had she not been preoccupied abroad in
gathering up her second husband, little realizing at the time that her
third marriage would shake the very foundations of the British throne.

These three vessels were the epitome of packet travel on the Chesapeake—steel-hulled and steel-sheathed even up to the passenger deck,
with ivory-paneled saloons, mahogany-pilastered smoking rooms, glass-
enclosed palm rooms on the gallery deck, and grand stairways overlooking a scene replete with chandeliers, gold trim, and oil paintings. Built
at costs from $718,000 to $960,000, these three-deckers measured 330
feet in length, 58 feet in beam, and 15.6 feet depth of hold; and with
triple-expansion engines, they could travel at 17 miles per hour. Each
had 170 first-class staterooms, 38 with private baths, and they boasted a
quality of luxury unheard of on the Bay.[4]

President Warfield ran with destiny. Requisitioned by the War Shipping Administration in July 1942, she was transferred under lend-lease
to the British and sailed off across the Atlantic in a convoy of river
steamers, including the Norfolk-Washington packets *Northland* and
Southland, and *Yorktown* of the Chesapeake line. On September 21,
1942, the convoy found itself under attack by Nazi U-boats, and *Yorktown* sank in a torpedo explosion that broke her back. *President Warfield*
made it to Devon, where she became an amphibious training ship until
she abruptly found herself in a huge convoy bound for Normandy. Off
Omaha Beach, she served as a control ship during the landing.

Brought back to the United States, she was laid up in the James River with other discards from the war, until in 1946 she was pulled out in a strange sale and mysteriously appeared in various dealings around Baltimore and the Delaware River. Abruptly, with British intelligence dogging her heels, she cleared the capes, appeared in the Mediterranean in various guises, and, outwitting Italian and French surveillance, appeared in Sette, near Marseilles. There she loaded 4,500 Jewish refugees who had fled concentration camps across Europe. Under the Haganah, which owned her, *President Warfield* cleared Sette and headed across the Mediterranean—destination, Palestine. She joined a long parade of decrepit ships carrying refugees from the Holocaust in an attempt to break through the British blockade (intended to deny further immigration into Palestine) and reach sanctuary in "Eretz Israel." She had scarcely begun her voyage when HMS *Ajax* (cruiser) and destroyers *Chequers, Chieftain,* and *Charity* fell in beside her, and it was clear that *Warfield's* passage to Palestine would be met with force. On the night of July 17, 1947, the destroyers rammed the *Warfield* and boarded her. A raging but uneven battle swept her decks. At the heat of it, her name board above the pilothouse was flipped over and a new name was exposed: *Exodus 1947.* Seized, forced into Haifa, her refugee-passengers placed aboard a British transport and returned to the camps in Europe from whence they had come, *Exodus 1947* became a symbol that evoked an international outcry and contributed directly to the emergence of the State of Israel.[5]

President Warfield's experience was unique in the annals of steamboat history on the Bay. Certainly Baltimore's boats dominated that history, if only because most of the steamers hailed from that focal point in the life of the Bay.

Out of Washington in the period from the early 1900s to the 1920s came a parade of Potomac steamers. Matching the Norfolk-bound packets out of Baltimore were the "queen" packets from Washington, operated by the Norfolk and Washington Steamboat Company. Earlier boats included *Norfolk, Washington,* and *Newport News;* later boats were *Northland* and *Southland,* handsome vessels that crossed the Atlantic with *President Warfield* in the fateful riverboat convoy of September 1942 which saw the torpedoing of *Yorktown.* Finally in succession of construction came *District of Columbia.* Purchased by the Old Bay Line in 1949, she brought to an end packet service from Norfolk to Washington in 1957.

Running the river was a fleet of large excursion boats, bearing pleasure seekers to the joys of Colonial Beach, Glymont, Fort Washington, Marshall Hall, Chapel Point, and River View. One of the more illustrious of the excursion boats on the Potomac was *River Queen* (bearer of President Lincoln to meet the Confederate peace commissioners at Hampton Roads), which bore the crowds to Marshall Hall and Mount Vernon just prior to the turn of the century, and Negro excursionists to Notley Hall afterward—a venerable boat indeed. Another was *Charles Macalester,* beloved sidewheeler of the Mount Vernon and Marshall

Hall Steamboat Company; she continued to operate for a very long life. And there was *Potomac*, a huge 315-foot sidewheeler out of the New York–Albany run in 1934, boasting a speed of 23 miles per hour, 29-foot paddlewheels, three stacks side by side athwartships, and mahogany-paneled saloons, richly carpeted, decorated with sculptures and oil paintings. She had a capacity of 3,000 passengers, who often danced to the music of Paul Whiteman and Benny Goodman while heading for picnics at Chapel Point, Colonial Beach, and Liverpool Point.[6]

Steamers of the Potomac and Chesapeake Line—*Majestic*, the venerable *Wakefield*, *Frederick de Barry*, *Gratitude*, and *Volunteer*—traveled down through the landings of Westmoreland and Northumberland Counties and St. Mary's County to Nomini and Machadoc Creeks and the Wicomico River. And by a subsidiary ran *St. John's* to Colonial Beach or for a journey of two days and a night on the Mattox Creek route, or delighted excursionists on day runs to River View and Marshall Hall. Many other steamers joined that white parade on the Potomac.[7]

In 1902, on the James River out of Norfolk, the Old Dominion Line introduced two of the finest packets in the Chesapeake region, the thousand-ton steel vessels *Berkeley* and *Brandon*, two-deckers for overnight service between Norfolk and Richmond and named for two renowned plantations overlooking the James. Until the First World War terminated the service, these vessels carried freight from the river landings to Norfolk and a lengthy and distinguished passenger list between the cities on the James. Connecting as they did with Old Dominion oceangoing ships, they afforded water travel from Richmond to New York. Although the Old Dominion was forced to abandon its North Carolina Division in 1905 because of the paucity of trade and the slowness of travel through the Albemarle and Chesapeake Canal, its Virginia Division prospered. *Hampton* (renamed *Smithfield*) and *Mobjack* ran to Gloucester and Mathews Counties. *Virginia Dare*, *Hampton Roads*, *Ocracoke*, *Smithfield*, the packets *Berkeley* and *Brandon*, and the beloved *Pocohontas* steamed out of Norfolk on busy but dwindling schedules. On April 6, 1920, the Old Dominion Line suspended its steamboat river service. For a time, its steamers operated under independent ownership around the region, but the inexorable march of time eventually left them stranded on the shoals of economics.

From 1922 to 1925, the Richmond–New York Steamship Company ran three 251-foot sister ships—*Virginia Limited*, *Virginia Empress*, and *Virginia Despatch*, all oceangoing freighters—out of Richmond. Their black, tall-sided hulls offered a jarring contrast to the white gracefulness of river steamboats on the James. And the Buxton Line, organized in 1920 to resume steamboat service on the James, suffered a tragic setback in April 1922 when five of the company's vessels (a tug, two freight boats, an auxiliary passenger boat *Martha Stevens*, and *Rosedale*, a 216-foot excursion steamer) were all lost from one form of catastrophe or another in a matter of days. *Westover*, named for the Byrd estate, *Virginia*, *Car-*

olina, and *Richmond* (former Queen Anne's ferry *Queen Caroline*) were acquired as replacements. In 1937 the company bought *Northumberland* (the old Weems boat) and called her *Norfolk.*[8]

Held in particular affection around the James and among travelers coming down by rail along the Eastern Shore from the North were the ferries running from Cape Charles across the mouth of the Bay to Norfolk. They were not the double-ended, boxlike tubs that earned the derision (and the loyalty) of steamboat connoisseurs. Instead, the vessels that breasted the often-troubled waters of the Chesapeake entrance, where the chop of the Bay met the swell of the Atlantic, were sturdy, sleek, white-sided Bay steamers, bowing to the title of *ferry* by having the capacity to load and unload automobiles or, as was the case with an earlier vessel, *Cape Charles,* built in 1885, to carry four Pullman cars resting on tracks on her forward freight deck. *Elisha Lee,* a graceful, two-stacked vessel, and *Maryland,* just as comely under way and a veteran of 42 years service on the route, operated for the Pennsylvania Railroad to connect the NYP & N with Norfolk and the South; and their daily voyages between that city, Old Point Comfort, and Cape Charles, in the quiet trips of summer and the pounding gales of winter when their mettle was sorely tested, endeared them not only to the region's inhabitants but also to those wayfarers from New York to Florida who remembered their comeliness and their comforts.[9]

The panorama of steamboating on the Chesapeake embroidered a rich and colorful tapestry on the region's history. But in the late 1920s and early 1930s, many observers, including most steamboatmen, realized that the pattern was playing out. Although steamers still plied the waters of tidewater Maryland and Virginia, there was more than a hint that steamboating was resting precariously on little more than nostalgia. Only with difficulty could observers make explicit their disquiet at the sight of macadam roads and trucking lines reaching into Tidewater country and at the statistics of a burgeoning automobile and truckbuilding industry that made steamboating a thing of the past.

For a brief period after the First World War, the steamboat lines seemed to hold their own, dropping in number on the Chesapeake and its tributaries from 60-odd in 1914 to about 10 less in 1919; but the decline thereafter was steep. By 1935, only about 20 boats remained; World War II reduced the total to less than 10. By 1963, all had disappeared except for the occasional diesel-driven tour boat (often made to look like a Mississippi riverboat with false side-by-side stacks and a fake sternwheel) that defiled the steamboat heritage of the Chesapeake. For 150 years— from the creation of little *Chesapeake* in 1813 to the departure of *Bay Belle* from Baltimore in 1963—the Chesapeake Bay had a love affair with the steamboat, and the memory of it lingered long after the sesquicentennium came to an end.

Nostalgia scarcely cast its veil over the last days of the former Weems line packets, until it was too late. For most of them, the end was ignominious. Only a few were touched by the emotions of farewell. The most poignant demise was that of *St. Mary's.* Wednesday, December 4, 1907, was one of the roughest nights on record on the Bay. A howling wind drove a number of steamers aground, and many others sought shelter or delayed sailing to escape the ferocity of the gale. *St. Mary's* was in the Patuxent River. Off Hallowing Point, some 20 miles from the river entrance, she went hard aground. One report attributed her grounding to the force of the gale. Another account tells a more interesting story. The steamer came upriver, bound for landings north. A man at Hallowing Point had the job of placing a lantern on a spar buoy off the shallow point when the MD & V boats came upriver at night; however, on this cold and blustery night he failed to do so. It was also his task to place a lantern at the end of the wharf, the light lining up as a range with a light kept burning in the window of a house above the landing. In the cold the man decided to leave the end of the pier to seek warmth elsewhere, and he deposited the lantern halfway down the 300-foot wharf. So, *St. Mary's* was unable to find the spar buoy for lack of the lantern on it, lined up the misplaced lantern light on the wharf with the light in the house, and promptly went hard aground at 11:00 P.M.

Later Captain Gourley narrated the events of the grounding. During the night he and his crew tried in vain to free the vessel, and in the morning, awaiting flood tide, they were able to attract the attention of a gasoline barge, which tried unsuccessfully throughout the day to pull the steamer off the sandbar. Exhausted from their exertions, the crew retired early, and the engineers banked the fires. Later, Captain Gourley was aroused by shouts of his crewmen that the vessel was afire. Flames were rushing out around the smokestack and up the engineroom casing. Sounding the alarm, Captain Gourley ordered the steamer abandoned, a lifeboat lowered, and the crew landed on a barge nearby. A second yawl was lowered. The only passenger on board, the wife of the assistant purser, went off in the first boat. The crew left for the barge in shifts. When Gourley, with the last group to leave the burning vessel, reached the barge, he began a muster that accounted for all of the crew except a black steward named Thomas A. Thompson, whose body was found the next morning, facedown on deck, burned to death. So intense was the fire that engulfed the steamer from bow to stern that spectators on the Hallowing Point shore could read a book by the light of it. The fire destroyed a large cargo of oysters, hogsheads of tobacco, and other freight. A prized cat, which had spent its life on board, left the boat at the last landing and refused to return, perhaps scenting the smoldering blaze. Nothing was left but a charred hull. Even the engine was a twisted mass of metal. It had been the *George Weems* engine, built by Charles Reeder and Sons in 1858. That same engine had been pulled from *George Weems* when she burned in June 10, 1871, and had been placed in *Theodore Weems,* built the following year. When *Theodore Weems* burned on September 10, 1889, and then was rebuilt as *St. Mary's,* the same engine that had propelled *George Weems* served her to the end on December 5, 1907.[10]

Caroline, the little browbeaten combatant with *Tourist,* continued her dwindling day service on the upper Rappahannock to Fredericksburg and filled in on other routes until June 1911, when the MD & V sold her to the Dover and Philadelphia Navigation Company, Inc., which changed her name to *City of Dover.* She ended her days in the scrapyard in 1917. *Essex,* showing her age, partially burned on May 2, 1911; she was rebuilt as a fishing boat by the Machine and Boiler Works of Baltimore and was sold to George D. Weaver of Baltimore and thence to the Indian Creek Fertilizer Company. Her configuration was altered. She was owned by John T. Donohue and homeported in Reedville, Virginia, who sold her in 1916 to the Northern Transportation Company for runs out of Portland, Maine. She ended her days in 1923 as a barge (Appendix A).

In mid-1922, it was clear to the Pennsylvania Railroad that the MD & V, which had earned no profit since 1911, had no option except foreclosure. At the same time, the Pennsy was unwilling to relinquish the notion that a profit could be made from packet service on the major rivers of the Bay and on steamboat linkage to its viable rail lines remaining on the Eastern Shore. A scheme was hatched and proposed to the Public Service Commission: the Pennsy itself would absorb the MD & V but would abandon certain rail lines and steamer services on the Eastern Shore. It would sell such steamboats and rail equipment as it deemed unnecessary in bankruptcy proceedings of the MD & V. It would create for reduced operations a new company of its own, to be called the Baltimore and Virginia Steamboat Company. And it would purchase from such bankruptcy proceedings the boats and other property for continued steamboat operations on the Western Shore, all of these stipulations subject to the grant of an annual subsidy by the state of Maryland. A governor's commission found that given the advantages obtained by the Pennsy, a subsidy was unnecessary. The bankruptcy proceedings, beginning in 1923 and extending into 1924, affected considerable property held by the MD & V not related to the former Weems line boats. Nevertheless, the Baltimore and Virginia Steamboat Company (B & V) as the front for the Pennsylvania Railroad held the position of picking and choosing the steamboats it wanted for its services on the Patuxent, the Potomac, and the Rappahannock.

Accordingly, during 1923 and early 1924, under the terms of receivership, the steamboats of the MD & V were transferred to William B. Shelton and the Girard Trust Company (a Philadelphia institution representing the interests of the Pennsylvania Railroad) as receivers, and then they were sold to interested parties. The boats on the block were the older sidewheelers *Westmoreland* and *Lancaster;* the *Potomac,* older but a sturdy screw vessel; and the newer *Northumberland, Calvert, Middlesex,* and *Anne Arundel.*

Westmoreland and *Lancaster* were not selected to carry on the tradition of the Weems line and the MD & V on the western rivers. They were sacrificed to pay for the declining fortunes of the MD & V and to augment the capital needed by the Pennsylvania Railroad to inaugurate the new Baltimore and Virginia Steamboat Company. *Westmoreland* was sold to the Marine Sand and Gravel Company; she met the graveyard in 1925. *Lancaster* was sold in the same proceedings to the New York, Albany, and Western Steamship Company, Inc., and operated on runs to Albany and Troy, New York, until she was sold at auction by the U.S. Marshall in 1925 to E. B. Leaf and Company of Philadelphia for $5,000. She was dismantled in 1929, her hull used as a dock at Hastings-on-Hudson (Appendix A).

The newer boats under the B & V continued to ply the waters of the Bay. They served the Rappahannock and the Potomac very much as before. But in 1924, immediately after assuming control, the B & V sharply cut its services to the Patuxent, a measure reflecting declining trade on the river. The MD & V sent only two trips per week on the route. After 1925, the B & V eliminated all passenger service on the river, with the Potomac steamers calling only at Solomons and Millstone near the river mouth. Except for excursions, the fortunes of the Patuxent route were left in limbo.

In the late 1920s, the steamers of the B & V sailed along the rivers and into the creeks in a last display of what appeared to be a kind of post-Edwardian elegance and a style of leisurely travel fast becoming anachronistic. At various times the Pennsy syndicates made modifications to increase their passenger capacity. For example, in 1910 and early 1911, *Middlesex* spent time in the Newport News Drydock yard so that 26 additional staterooms could be mounted on her hurricane deck. It was an alteration that was expected to increase her compatibility with the latest in packet trends but which altered drastically her appearance and the graceful sheer so much admired on the Bay. New paddlewheels, requiring the shaft to be raised, were expected to increase the boat's speed, but the additional weight from the staterooms and engineering only reduced it. Nevertheless, neat and trim even with her disfigurement, *Middlesex* rejoined the fleet on April 9, 1911.

In spite of their brave and immaculate appearance, the former Weems line steamers of the B & V fleet felt the economic realities of the times. Freight on which the line depended went instead by truck over highways from farm to city, leaving the wharves to the leftover goods of loyal friends. The Great Depression collapsed markets and trade and the personal livelihood on which steamboat travel and shipping depended. Costs mounted, cutting in on schedules, reducing maintenance, and making major repairs prohibitive. *Middlesex*, idled in 1925 by the costs of running her and her redundancy, became a candidate for disposal. *Northumberland* was laid up in 1928, her engine working loose from its bed. *Anne Arundel* and *Calvert,* both considered underpowered, suffered from lack of maintenance. *Potomac* carried on as indomitable as ever. Routes were varied to meet the status of the vessels and the shifting needs of the line. For a time, all of the steamers in turn except *Middlesex* served on a run to Cambridge, a railroad terminus on the Eastern Shore. In early 1930, *Middlesex* was sold first to Charles A. Jording, then from him to George P. Ellis of Somerville, Massachusetts, and then to the Nantasket Beach Steamboat Company out of Boston. Her name was changed to *Plymouth*. In 1936 she was sold again to the Marine Operating Corporation of New Jersey and her name changed to *Manhattan*. In 1937 she was operated by the Sound Steamship Line, Inc., from Pier 31, East River, New York. She burned at Tottenville, New York, in 1939. After being sold to the Maxwell Company of New Bern, North Carolina, and being converted to a barge, she was sold again in 1945 to an outfit in Peru and disappeared from American waters (Appendix A).

By 1930, the B & V had only four of the former Weems steamboats in its fleet: *Potomac* and *Anne Arundel*, running on the Rappahannock; *Calvert*, continuing on the Cambridge–Choptank River route; and *Northumberland*, serving as a spare boat. *Talbot* and *Dorchester*, sister ships that had been built in 1912 for the BC & A, plied the Potomac River. The Patuxent River no longer enjoyed steamboat service above Solomons. Until 1929, the steamers bound for the Potomac stopped there and at Millstone on the opposite shore; in 1930, *Piankatank*, another steamer of the B & V, stopped at these two wharves once a week on her way to landings on the Piankatank and Great Wicomico River. On all of its routes—Rappahannock, Choptank, Potomac, Patuxent, Piankatank, and lower Eastern Shore—the B & V reached the limits of its resources in the Great Depression aftermath of 1930 and 1931.

In January 1932, the B & V declared bankruptcy. All nine of its steamers, including the four former Weems boats, were scheduled for lay-up and sale. On March 1, 1932, the darkest day in the history of steamboating on the Chesapeake, the B & V steamers ceased operations, their fires drawn, their boilers cold, their officers and crew departed. In May 1932, the boats were transferred to the American Contract and Trust Company as trustees under the mortgage indenture and were put up for sale.

On February 28, 1932, *Anne Arundel* bade farewell to Washington and the Potomac landings she had known so well. As she left her wharf in the capital, Captain Herbert Bohannon played his sad farewell on the whistle: three longs and a short—"goodbye and good luck." As he passed Alexandria, Colonial Beach, and each of the wharves below, he sounded the signal of farewell. At Kinsale, *Anne Arundel* encountered heavy weather and went aground, just as the circulator pump broke in the engineroom. With the offending pump repaired, *Anne Arundel* backed and filled her way off the mud, pivoted about in the high wind by the aid of spring lines to the wharf, and continued on her way to Baltimore. At Light Street, the wharfman's little dog, as usual, caught the heaving line thrown from the steamer, and carried it to his master—for the last time. Bohannon carried off his suitcase and personal papers. Service by steamboat from Baltimore to Washington thus came to an end.[11]

Calvert, through Ernest E. Fuchs of the Thames River Line, New York, was sold in 1934 to the Sound Steamship Lines, New York, modified to burn oil, then dieselized, and ran the route from New York to Bridgeport. She was requisitioned in 1942 and served the U.S. Navy in Boston Harbor and met the breaker's torch in Alexandria, Virginia, in 1957 (some sources show Bordentown, New Jersey).

Northumberland fetched up as an excursion boat around New York for Excursion Steamboats, Inc., but the company went broke. She was sold at auction for $2,500 by the U.S. marshall to the Buxton Lines of Norfolk, Virginia, to work as a freighter, and her name was changed to *Norfolk*. While laid up near Clermont on the James River in 1945, she burned and was then relegated to the scrapper's yard.

Potomac and *Anne Arundel* enjoyed a somewhat more sanguine future. When the B & V made clear its intentions to cease operations on March 1, 1932, a group of Baltimore steamboat men, joined by some merchants and tradesmen, were persuaded that steamboating on the Bay was not dead. Determined to see it survive, they pooled their resources and started a new company. They were led by Captain James Gresham, who became the company's first president. Initially called the Western Shore Freight Company (it soon found, however, that carrying passengers could help the revenues), it changed its name to the Western Shore Steamboat Company, chartered a boat named *Hampton Roads*, which it soon released, bought *Potomac* and *Virginia* (the sidewheeler proved to be too slow), which it exchanged for *Anne Arundel* in agreement with the trustees of the defunct B & V.

Potomac and *Anne Arundel*, the stalwarts of the old Weems line and the pride of the MD & V and B & V, began a series of daylong excursions to various parts of the Bay—Annapolis, Solomons, Oxford (on the Tred Avon), St. Michaels (on the Miles), Chestertown, and the Bayside resort of Betterton, near the mouth of the Sassafras River. These were well patronized, but freight passage was minimal. Primary was the objective of the company to continue some sort of freight and passenger service to the Rappahannock, the Piankatank, and a few landings near the mouth of the Potomac.[12]

The overnight trips of *Anne Arundel* and *Potomac* on these routes were designed to appeal to the nostalgia of those who wanted to relive steamboat days and to those city residents who wanted a brief vacation from the heat of the streets. For the grand total of $9.00 the sun-seeking traveler could, on a Sunday evening, board one of the steamers at Pier 3, Light Street, steam overnight down the Bay, greet the dawn at Westland (tip of Lancaster County in the Northern Neck), enjoy the panorama of Rappahannock landings from Irvington in Carter's Creek and Urbanna to Tappahannock, trace the landings in return down the river, spend another night of cruising up the Bay, and arrive in Baltimore on Tuesday morning. The $9.00 included not only the trip but accommodations in a clean and comfortable stateroom and five superb meals as well. For $7.50, the vacationer could leave on Tuesday (returning Thursday) or Thursday (returning Saturday) and enjoy a slightly foreshortened Rappahannock. After Labor Day, the line ran special excursions to Fredericksburg, leaving Saturday afternoon, returning Tuesday. The four-day trip, stateroom, and eight Southern-cooked meals cost $12.00. The three-day Potomac cruise cost $7.50; all-day cruises to Cambridge, round-trip, $1.00. And the all-expense weekend cruise running to Cambridge, Solomons, Kinsale, Coan, Mundy Point, Bundicks and other landings taxed the vacationer to the tune of $8.50.[13] However, passengers (in the gloom of the Depression, when $12.00 could be a week's wage for a clerk or factory worker), failed to respond in sufficient numbers to the induce-ments of the overnight trips to the Rappahannock and the Potomac. Freight shipments dwindled to a few parcels and a barrel or two at each landing. The costs of operating a steamboat (in contrast to those of run-ning a diesel freighter) continued to mount.

A major setback occurred on August 23, 1933, when a hurricane plowed in the mouth of the Chesapeake and swept the waters of the Bay before it. Steamships in the open fought for their lives. In the morning some vessels at Light Street wharves were stranded on their own piling from high water. *Anne Arundel,* which bore the reputation of being un-der powered, won a battle with wind and sea and proved her mettle as a fine seakeeping vessel. The gale hit her full force off Sandy Point (mouth of the Severn River), 20 miles below Baltimore. So heavy were the seas that she pitched her propeller clear of the water and her bow under; slowing enough to keep the propeller engaged, she inched her way into the Severn in a wall of rain and spume, and anchored with 300 feet of chain in Annapolis Harbor. Most disastrous to the Western Shore Steamboat Company was the storm's demolition of 18 of the 30 wharves that the company could potentially use. No money could be found from any source to replace them.

Then on February 22, 1936, *Potomac,* caught in the ice near Seven Foot Knoll, was rammed on the starboard quarter by the Bull Line freighter *Jean* (formerly *Jean Weems*). Although the damage was not ex-tensive and *Potomac* could operate under her own power, repair costs were more than the company could handle. Laid up until 1938, *Potomac* was sold to the Chesapeake Corporation of West Point, Virginia, and converted into a barge for hauling pulp wood. In Newport News, Vir-ginia, she was dismantled in 1956 (Appendix A).[14]

Alone after *Potomac's* mishap on February 22, 1936, *Anne Arundel* carried on for another year. By summer, the owners of the Western Shore Steamboat Company knew that the end was near. Then on July 29, 1937, an event, like the hurricane of 1933, occurred and spelled doom. On that evening, the *City of Baltimore* of the Chesapeake line burned off Bodkin Point, with the loss of four lives. When *Anne Arundel* arrived in Baltimore from her Rappahannock run two days later, she was met by officers of the Bureau of Marine Inspection and Navigation of the Department of Commerce. The bureau announced that as a result of the burning of the *City of Baltimore,* it would enforce the safety-at-sea reg-ulations passed by Congress on June 30, 1936, and to be placed in effect on October 1, 1937. All passenger vessels with 50 or more berths were affected by the act. Until these vessels—which included the Norfolk boats of the Chesapeake line—complied with the law, requiring the installation of fireproof bulkheads and automatic sprinkler systems, the steamers could carry freight only. Spokesmen of the Chesapeake line said that the management was hastening to comply, and *City of Richmond* would be fully equipped with the safety measures and ready for passengers on October 15.

When confronted by the steamboat inspectors with a notice that *Anne Arundel* would not be permitted to carry passengers after October 1, 1937, unless a bulkhead and automatic sprinkler system were installed, the directors of the Western Shore Steamboat Company knew immediately what the tidings meant. The company lacked the means and, even by borrowing the money, the ability to realize sufficient profit to pay off the indebtedness. After an anguished but fruitless session of searching for a means to continue, they reached the painful decision to cease operations on September 30.

Captain John D. Davis, popular skipper of *Anne Arundel* and son of Captain Daniel Davis, master of *Mary Washington, Wenonah, Theodore Weems, Mason L. Weems, Essex, Westmoreland, Richmond,* and *Lancaster,* had one last request: he wanted to make one more round trip from Baltimore to Fredericksburg, to relive for one brief voyage all the days of romance and color of the old Tidewater steamboats. He proposed to fill the passenger list, if necessary, with all the friends and clients who had been his loyal supporters through the years. The directors agreed.

Little publicity attended the departure of *Anne Arundel* for Fredericksburg on September 11, 1937. Preoccupied with the headlines of Hitler in Europe, Japan's invasion of China, and other matters, the public seemed to have scant interest in the lonely steamer at Pier 3, Light Street. A few days before, a small notice had appeared in the newspaper[15]:

TRIP TO FREDERICKSBURG
Via Rappahannock River. Steamer *Anne Arundel* leaves Pier 3, Light Street, 2 P.M., Saturday, September 11. No sailing to Rappahannock River Sunday. Phone Plaza 1634.

Western Shore Steamship [*sic*] Company

At the appointed time, *Anne Arundel,* flaunting all the bunting she could muster, sounded her warning blast and backed clear of the wharf. Passengers—a full complement of mostly friends from the steamboat world and well-wishers—crowded her decks, sentimentally lamenting the last few days. She swung about astern in the basin, dug in her propeller full ahead with a shudder and pivoted about, white water foaming under her counter, her head pointed to the open channel. In the afternoon heat, she slipped by Fort McHenry and Fort Carroll, gained speed in the Patapsco entrance, pirouetted gracefully at Seven Foot Knoll, and took her departure for the long haul down the Chesapeake. In the afterglow of a late summer's evening, she watched the amber of water and sky fade to aquamarine and the line of wave and cloud merge in a darkening blue. The horizon winked with the lights of Cove Point and Point Lookout. Farther down the Bay, stretching broadly like the open sea, was the loom of the light at Windmill Point, where the Rappahannock opened to the West.

During the next two days, she ran the old route—past the winding way of Carter's Creek and Irvington, the majestic span of the river below Tappahannock, the cliffs above Carters Wharf, the gentle riverside at Leedstown, the somber, narrow, and curving river near Hop Yard and Devils Wood Yard, with densely forested hills tumbling to the water's edge, and the long reach to Fredericksburg. Then she threaded her way downriver for the last time. Many of the old wharves showed no more than piling standing stark in the flowing tide, victims of hurricane and neglect. But those that were still standing, warehouses leaning and unused, heard the old steamer sound a long, plaintive, and final bleat on its whistle. It echoed in the hills—and was heard no more.

In the night, on the run back to Baltimore, her stateroom windows glowing in the darkness, her pilothouse shadowed except for the glow of the binnacle, *Anne Arundel* passed the haunts of her youth, the great span of open water where the Potomac entered the Bay, where she used to swing about and begin her long journey around the river wharves to Washington, the curving bowl of the Patuxent entrance, where she spent so much of her life enroute to the landings and byways of the scenic river.

She sounded a long serenade on her whistle as she slid past the piling to her Light Street wharf. Her passengers, in the gray light of morning, had little to say. What they felt as they crossed the gangplank for the last time can only be imagined. The fires beneath the boilers died; the staterooms and dining room emptied; the crew departed; and Captain Davis locked the pilothouse and went ashore—his days as a steamboat captain at an end.

Anne Arundel marked the close of an era.[16] The history of the white packets in tidewater Maryland and Virginia had been long and colorful, and it ended in a lonely performance. *Anne Arundel* was sold in receivership to the American Contract and Trust Company on October 15, 1937, and in turn to the Stony Creek Improvement Company for excursions to Fairview Beach. She underwent major surgery—her staterooms ripped out, her decks opened up to accommodate hordes of day picnickers, and her name changed to *Mohawk*, complete with an Indian holding bow and arrow mounted on her smokestack. She was acquired by the Tolchester line in 1941, requisitioned by the War Shipping Administration in World War II for duties around Hampton Roads, placed on a Boston-Nantasket run for a brief period, laid up in 1948, and scrapped in 1952 at Baltimore (Appendix A).

With the passing of *Anne Arundel* from the Chesapeake, the legacy of George Weems came to an end. She had been the last Bay boat remaining among the packets to have flown the red ball flag; her lineage ran back for nearly 120 years to the beginnings with *Surprise*.

During the long years that raced by, the name of Weems became almost synonymous with steamboat history on the Chesapeake. It had seen every type of steamer on the Bay evolve and the structure and design of steamboats change; it had tried every type of engine; and it had experienced the trials and triumphs of steamboat management in all its forms.

From the schoonerlike hulls of little *Surprise* and *Eagle,* complete with clipper bows, bowsprits, masts and sails, to the flat-floored, knife-bowed, white-sided *Planter,* to the two-decked elegance of *Lancaster* and *Middlesex,* the Weems steamers had spanned the century of change from wood to steel in steamboat building and design. The Weems boats had known every type of engine. There was the unique rotary engine of *Surprise,* forerunner of the turbine; the crosshead "square" engine of *Eagle* and *Patuxent;* the vertical "walking" beam engine of *Planter, Mary Washington, George Weems, Matilda, Wenonah, Mason L. Weems, Richmond, St. Mary's, Sue, Westmoreland,* and *Lancaster;* and the compound (two-cylinder) inclined engine of *Middlesex.* All turned "stick-shaft" paddlewheels of large diameter except the sidewheels on *Middlesex,* which were small with feathering buckets. And there were the compound engines of *Potomac, Calvert,* and *Essex,* and the triple-expansion (three-cylinder) engines of *Northumberland* and *Anne Arundel,* all resembling modern vertical internal combustion engines, except steam instead of burning fuel provided the thrust, and all turned screw propellers at the end of shafts under the counter. And there were the double, triple-expansion engines of *Caroline,* driving twin screws, enabling the little vessel to "back on one, go ahead on the other" in a feat of maneuverability. As a contributing force to the development of the special breed of steamboat that inhabited the Chesapeake Bay, the Weems line held a special place in the annals of steamboat history.[17]

The significance of the Weems line in the life of the Chesapeake Bay was more far reaching, however. It can be argued that the Patuxent and Rappahannock valleys and the Northern Neck of Virginia would never have opened up and developed as they did without the vision, pioneering effort, and enterprising spirit of George Weems, Mason Locke Weems, and Henry Williams. The steamboats of the Weems line became the very lifeblood that sustained the economic growth of the regions around three of the four major rivers of the Western Shore. They brought the harvests of field and stream to Baltimore and eventually to Norfolk and then brought back the products of the city to the countryside. They provided the essential bridge—economic, social, and cultural—for the continued flourishing of the area. Without the steamboat—and with no passable roads—the vast farming country of tidewater Maryland and Virginia would have depended on sailing vessels. When a lapse of steamboat service was threatened, one editorialist in 1889 took up the cudgel, saying, "tillers of the soil do not see much profit in tedious potatoes, melons, etc., when they have to depend upon leaky old sailing craft in the calmest season of the year to get their produce to market a hundred miles away. Think of a people growing prosperous and rich in a community where . . . steamboats were not known; where a crop of vegetables can be cultivated and gathered in the time that it takes for the same to reach the market to which it has been consigned."[18]

The waterways of the Patuxent, the Rappahannock, and the Potomac were the highways of the 19th and early 20th centuries. Upon them, the Weems steamers kept open the lines of communication. On the fourth great river of the Western Shore there was frequent envy of the Rappahannock and its experience with the Weems line. When a new steamboat line was proposed for the James River, one reporter wrote, "there is no reason why this new line . . . should not be for the valley of the James what the Weems line steamers have done for the country along the Rappahannock River, which has been made to blossom like the rose."[19]

The ghostly memory of white packets rounding the bend and emerging from the wisps of time still haunts the byways of the Patuxent, the Potomac, and the Rappahannock. On these great rivers, inexorably moving with the seasons and the tides, history flows in the minds of the people. The curling of these waters by these little steamboats in a span of a mere 120 years was a fleeting thing, but the beauty of its presence has left its mark, poignant and indelible.

Epilogue

The steamboats on the rivers of the Chesapeake vanished without a trace; and with their passing, there ended an epoch as colorful as any in American history. The recording of that period when steamboats plied the Bay cannot be told alone in a cataloging of boats and a narrative of steamboat lines and their trials and triumphs. The sense of what it was like to ride the boats—the sounds, the sights, the smells, the essence of the steamboat experience—becomes an intrinsic part of the portrayal of the era. Memories, gleaned from those who rode the boats and from written recollections, take many turns. They consist of vignettes such as the following, which help to bring to life those days aboard the river packets of the Chesapeake.

Light Street in Baltimore at steamboat time is a maelstrom of clattering wagons, swearing mule drivers, scampering passengers trying to cross a narrow and dangerous street, cobblestones reeking with garbage and animal dung, cavernous warehouses, and flimsy wooden wharves hiding a row of clean white steamboats at the slips.

The wharf is like a warehouse filled with barrels and boxes and crates and farm machinery and stacked with bags of fertilizer; the gangplank extends from the rough planking of the wharf between the piling through the sideport of the steamer to the freight deck; roustabouts with burlap bags for aprons barely slow their handtrucks to allow a passenger to board; the freight thunders as it is loaded and tiered aboard the steamer.

It is departure time, when a dozen steamers bow-in to their slips, belch black smoke in readiness for their journeys on the Bay, their brass ladder rails glistening and their white upper works glowing warmly in the evening sun, the gilt and color of their paddlewheels splashing in great semicircles on their sides. Farther down the line, first one steamboat and then another sound long wails on their whistles, then back into the basin, turn in a froth of churning water, and head in sequence down the channel. A startling blast on the whistle overhead follows the call on deck and in the saloon, "all ashore that's going ashore." A gangplank rattles as it is taken through the port. Hawsers thud when they are brought aboard. A shudder travels below decks as the paddlewheels begin to back and passengers rush to the rail to watch the steamer leave and to wave last goodbyes toward the upturned faces on the pier. The vessel quivers as the engines on the turn in the basin are suddenly reversed and pile the water in foaming cir-

197

cles astern, and the images of Federal Hill and steamers yet to leave from their piers at Light Street recede.

The grand stairway, carved and darkly polished, ascends from the main deck to the ivory-paneled and green-upholstered saloon. Passengers mill about the purser's office; tickets are purchased and staterooms assigned at a barred window. A heavy brass key with wooden tag is inserted into the stateroom lock and a small, sparsely furnished stateroom presents itself: upper and lower berths covered with white candlewick spreads, a chair and a small table, and a corner washbasin with running water and a mirror on one side; a glass window and a louvered shutter that could be lowered in turn, but no screen to fend off the mosquitoes that come with evening along the distant creeks.

"Suppertime" is announced in the steamer's dining room, its soft lights against the ivory paneling blank out the dark waters beyond the windows. Attentive waiters, napkin over the left arm and white gloves on each hand, hover about. A menu boasts of duck, terrapin, crabs, fish, oysters, clams, cornbread, a wide variety of vegetables, and pie prepared according to the unreciped skills of Tidewater cooks.

The unsettling motion of the boat as it meets the chop off Point Lookout and the 30-mile sweep of Pocomoke Sound is not a deep roll or a pitch but a sidestepping movement, as though the bow were searching for a path through the oncoming seas.

The loveliness of the night, when the decks are deserted, casts its spell. The breeze whispers in the stays; the ship pulses in a languorous rhythm; and far-off lights on shore and a star-studded sky pinpoint the darkness of the mysterious Bay. The eerie call of the lookoutsman, "all's well," echoes from the bow, and the mournful bong of a bell buoy riding in the swell as the steamer passes sounds in the night. The wash of the waves beneath the guards slaps with each rise and fall. And there is magic when the moon casts a shimmering path across the waves and catches in silhouette the embrace of a young couple on the upper deck.

The smells of the steamboat vary by the deck. On the hurricane deck, the sulfurous odor of coal smoke from the stack mixes with that of steam bearing the taint of oil or grease emanating around the walking beam from the engine far below. In the saloon and staterooms, the scent of disinfectant, soap, and wood polish permeates the spaces with its pungency. Near the galley, rich foods under preparation spread their own aroma. And on the freight deck, the sweetness of crated fruit and produce vies with the stench of cattle. From the boat itself comes the tang of old wood, tar, hemp, and the brine of the Bay.

In the pilothouse, where darkness has settled quietly and gently, the silence is broken by the creak of the great wooden steering wheel in its posts and the cryptic orders of the master or mate to the quartermaster. The dim glow of the binnacle and the windows squaring off the blue-gray waters of the Bay punctuate the darkness. The lonely loom of a distant lighthouse reflects briefly against a cloud on the horizon. The running lights of a freighter glimmer miles away in the inbound channel. The master or mate in due course breaks the silence to spin a yarn told many times before in the same drawl, in the same accent, flavored with ancient words known only to Tidewater.

A stroll through the sumptuous cabin lounge encounters a talented lady passenger playing a piano surrounded by a group of young songsters, trying out the strains of "Listen to the Mocking Bird," "Sally in Our Alley," and "My Old Kentucky Home," or tunes from the *Remick Favorite Collection of "Old Home Songs."* In the second-class saloon, a Gramophone scratches raucous music from a modest collection of thick and very breakable records, with hymns dominating the repertoire. A mandolin is strummed in the shadows of the upper deck. By an open sideport, deckhands hum in the darkness to the strains of spirituals learned in plantation days.

Lying in an upper berth in a darkened stateroom, a young passenger listens to the sounds of the boat and feels its movement: the tremor within the bowels of the boat with each thrust of its walking beam engine, the rattle behind the paneling of an unshut door, the swish and slap of waves beyond the shuttered window, the lowing of cows and bleating of sheep on the freight deck. He stays awake to obey the parental admonition to keep the upper sheet folded over the blanket, which was not to be touched for unspecified reasons; he leaps up to peer through the louvered window at the dark sea and the reflection of lights from the boat on the passing waves.

The gray of dawn lifts on the oceanlike expanse of Bay, with the broad entrance to the Potomac or the Rappahannock or the Patuxent stretching away to the West; rolling shorelines and flatlands recede to a distant bend; a ballet of porpoises performs in the wake and bow wave.

Heavy dew laces the boat when she approaches Coan or another landing in the early morning hours; so heavy are the droplets that walking to the rail leaves a path of footprints on the glossy gray-painted canvas deck; the railing is too wet to touch. In the air are the scent of autumn fields and pine forests, the earthy odor of loam and rotting seaweed, and the cloying sweetness of vine-ripened grapes. Acres of leaves float like a colored tapestry on the narrow waters. Fishermen in the morning mist cast their nets and lines. Distant vistas of the river are vaguely outlined in haze. The melody of the steamer's whistle echoes around the creek, stirring the birds to flight and the ducks to skimming, awakening the still figures on a lonely wharf at the base of a hill, and bringing down the wagons through the trees along a dusty road. The agent slides open the heavy warehouse door; a Negro boy waits on the cluster to catch the heaving line led by the monkey fist thrown from the upper decks. A few wagons and horses and figures cast long and silent shadows across the dock. At the upper rail the weathered captain snaps the pulls to ring down full astern to the engineroom, and the water cascades under the paddlewheels and boils beneath the pilings. The dock suddenly comes to life, roustabouts rotating between dock and freight deck, their aprons flapping and their straw hats flopping; tired passengers board, and sleep-besotted passengers leave. Day breaks in a riot of color.

The morning carnival at Solomons (or, for that matter, any number of town landings) begins with the steamboat's arrival; crowds of villagers and countryfolk gathering on the dock, almost by ritual an hour or so ahead of time to show off their finery, exchange the most worthy gossip and gospel, flirt a bit, and speculate on the identity and prestige of passengers debarking when the boat arrives. Oxen-pulled carts are laden with tobacco hogsheads, and barrels and crates with produce. There is much awestruck gaping at the white-walled steamer as it slips beside the dock, its guards squealing against the piling, its huge paddlewheels churning the water like a millrace, the ship's officers strutting about the upper decks in their brass-buttoned splendor. The gangplank crosses from sideport to pier and the passengers, tugging their suitcases, bound to the dock to the waiting arms of relatives and friends. Mothers and aunts kiss embarrassed little boys, and lovers kiss lovers under hat brims and parasols, hoping not to be noticed. The activity surges as jigging deckhands, chanting to the sounds of another continent, race their handtrucks and barrels over the gangplank in both directions, lug sheep and crated chickens, narrowly miss passengers, and encourage recalcitrant steers aboard for a trip to the slaughterhouse. The dust rises in clouds from the road with the belated arrival of a farmer driving his team hard to catch the boat. Farewells are tearful when the whistle blows and the steamer moves slowly away from the dock, the handkerchief-waving figures on deck becoming mere dots in the distance.

The sights and smells of Solomons vie with each other for attention. The raked masts of fishing boats etch the sky in Back and Mill Creeks. Little boys splash in the water like frogs leaping from the steamboat dock. An old pot-bellied black man fastens a half-decayed chicken carcass to a hook, lowers his line in the water, and waits with net ready for the unwary crab. The odor of the fish and oyster cannery fills the air with oily, pungent saltiness. Oyster shells are heaped about organic matter decaying. Wooden dwellings scatter around the narrow lanes; and the river, broad and sun flecked, stretches to the edges of the Bay.

In the morning hours an odd assortment parades through Burhans and Urbanna: hoary-headed men, toothless old women, frizzled old maids on whose painted charms the morning's dew has left a disastrous effect, obstreperous young men, simpering belles, sleepy nurses with squalling babies. They all arrive on foot or by four-in-hand at the steamboat wharf; all are members of Christ Episcopal Church, headed on an outing at Naylors Hole, a look at the "city life" of Tappahannock, and a return by downriver steamer before sundown.

Time has no meaning on a leisurely cruise up a lazy river. The days on deck are sun filled, and hours slip away in utter idleness; bodies sink deep into carpet-backed deck chairs, with toes tucked in the diamond-shaped mesh of the railing. The clean, briny breeze of the Bay and the sweet-smelling air of the river banks brush over the warming faces of passengers. The sound of the waves curling at the bow and the rhythm of the boat, like the measured ticking of an old clock, have a lulling, sleep-inducing effect. Some ladies indulge in games of solitaire in direct violation of rules, posted in every stateroom, prohibiting card playing; children romp about the boat, investigating the freight deck, engineroom door, and pilothouse steps. Under the awning of the hurricane deck and in the shelter of the foredeck, passengers lounge about on folding chairs (the prized chairs have armrests and are grabbed off early by the more experienced travelers); ladies, on the lee side to escape the wind's devastation to hat, coiffure, and complexion, primly engage in conversation, needlework, or the vicissitudes of *Beverly of Graustark* or *Dorothy Vernon of Haddon Hall.* Black passengers in the shade of the afterdeck, often called the "back porch," sit clustered together in the narrow space—women invariably dressed in starched white or bright colored long dresses in summertime, with men following the lead of the whites; their language, often punctuated by hearty laughter, has its own vocabulary which the white man fails to understand.

On a run up the river on a rainy evening, when the lowering sky brings early darkness, the searchlight, hunting for spar buoys and stakes in the channel and groping for wharves under forboding banks and bluffs catches the raindrops in an effect like that of falling snow.

In the wintertime coziness of the cabin, when cold blasts rattle the windows and the steamer shakes from boarding seas, passengers huddle together to comfort one another with homespun yarns and a touch of cheer from the ready bar.

Ice fills the upper river in the wintertime and, when not too thick, is cut by the steel prow of the steamboat (to the jeers of ice-skaters) but stacks up in great sheets when it breaks up from the pull and tug of tide and current and shears off the wharf pilings as though they were saplings in its path.

There is an occasional burst of phosphorescence in the river, a curious luminous mass that seems to swim about in warm weather, often in such density that the water appears to blaze with greenish light, a weird effect alongside a steamer as it lies at a wharf at night.

Farewells at country landings are sad, with distance and finality measured by the length of the steamer's journey to Baltimore; relatives part, sons leave home for the great adventure, the sick go off to sanctuary in the city, the dead in coffins are trundled aboard to be carried with sober escort to a distant burial. Farewells are tearful in Baltimore too, when the trip is over and there are goodbyes to be said to new-found friends. With an upward glance at the graceful sheer and homely elegance of the white-sided steamboat, the passenger on the gangplank senses a loss—the adventure is over, and nothing else can ever quite match it.

The era of the river steamboat ended in a quiet and lonely performance. However, the memory of it lingered on, and the lapse of time and a belated nostalgia brought an acute awareness that an important and colorful epoch of history had run its course.

Memories are made up of many things. But there were those who remembered the summer spectacle at sunset and into the twilight hours at the mouth of the Patapsco—a memory poignant and compelling. Downstream from Baltimore came the parade of white packets, their departures scheduled between 4:00 and 8:00 P.M., so that they swept by in unbroken and proud procession to the Bay. One after the other, they rounded the turn at Seven Foot Knoll and, catching the faint glimmer of the western afterglow, they split off on their various routes—one for the lower Eastern Shore, another for the Choptank, this one for the Piankatank, that one for the Rappahannock or the Potomac or the Patuxent, another for the upper Bay—and two three-deckers, twinkling like Christmas trees, racing off to Norfolk. Even hardened observers felt a sentimental tug at the sight of the white fleet scattering and disappearing in the gathering darkness. Perhaps they sensed in the spectacle a transitory image of the course of life itself.

With the passing of the steamboats, a way of life left the Chesapeake and was never to be seen again.

Appendixes

APPENDIX A

Specification, Enrollment, Descriptive, and Other Data on Steamboats of the Weems Line

Explanation

The number assigned to the steamboat on its initial enrollment is shown in parentheses after the steamboat name. Early steamboats were not given numbers. Abbreviations used in this appendix are: p.stbt., paddlewheel steamboat; s.stbt., screw (propeller) steamboat; (w), wood hull; (i), iron hull; (s), steel hull. Example: p.stbt.(w) means wood hull paddlewheel steamboat.

Length, beam, and depth-of-hold data are shown in a series of numbers separated by ×. Thus, 178.6 × 36.2 × 10.4 would indicate a steamboat length of 178 feet 6 inches, beam of 36 feet 2 inches, and depth of hold of 10 feet 4 inches. The decimal point does not usually indicate the use of tenths of feet but serves only as a useful means of separating feet and inches. If the figure behind the decimal point is in two digits above .12 then the metric decimal does apply. The system of using a decimal point to separate feet and inches also applies to data on paddlewheel diameter, bucket size, boiler dimension, and extent of sheer fore and aft. Data are derived from enrollment or documentation certificates in the National Archives; from *Merchant Vessels of the United States, 1870–1962* (Washington, D.C.: Government Printing Office, published annually); from *Merchant Vessels of the United States, 1790–1868* (Lytle-Holdcamper List) (Staten Island, N.Y.: Steamship Historical Society of America, 1975); from Eads Johnson, *Steam Vessels of the Atlantic Coast* (published by the author, 1921). Data from these sources or from newspaper or journal information are often conflicting, indefinite, or inaccurate. Length, for example, is often given as *overall*, meaning the extreme measurement from stem to stern over the guards. Occa-

sionally, it is designated as such with the use of the letters *oa*. Frequently, length is measured *between the perpendiculars*, meaning a measurement between the first full perpendicular frame at the forward end of the boat and the last full perpendicular frame near the stern, thus excluding the upward contour of the hull above the rudder and the extension of the guard at the stern. More often than not the reader is left without a clue as to the type of measurement presented, leaving his data ambiguous and often conflicting. In the data presented in this appendix, the letters *oa* in parentheses will accompany data that clearly identify the length as *overall* or *bp* as *between the perpendiculars;* otherwise the numbers will be presented as they appear in the source.

Beam data are equally confusing; *oa* may or may not be used in presenting the width of the steamer from side to side, over the guards. On Bay steamers, the guards, even on screw vessels, always extended beyond the hull so that the actual hull width could be several feet less than the extreme beam. In the data the actual width of the hull rather than the overall width is often presented, without notice to the reader. Paddleboxes on paddlewheel steamers were each at least 10 feet wide; a steamboat with a hull beam of 30 feet would therefore have an extreme beam of at least 50 feet. Sources seldom identify the type of beam measurement, but reflection on the part of the reader will tend to set the record straight.

Depth of hold is not clearly defined in the sources since the measurement between the bottom of the main or freight deck to the floor of the hold would vary with the sheer of the boat and, because of design, with the characteristics of each boat (location of engine, boiler, hold, and other spaces). Depth of hold is not to be confused with draft since the latter depended on cargo, bunkers, stores, and other weights, including passengers, loaded aboard.

Tonnage is specified as *gross tonnage* (GT) or *net tonnage* (NT), the latter excluding all the spaces of the vessel not used for cargo or passengers (engine, boiler, other machinery, crew quarters, pilothouse, bunkers, storage, and similar areas would be removed from the calculation of gross tonnage). Sources often disagree on these figures. *Indicated horsepower* (IHP), used on more recent vessels, and *nominal horsepower* (NHP) or simply *horsepower* (HP) recorded for earlier vessels are confusing and again conflictual, sources often disagreeing on data and meaning. To the extent that this information is useful, it is reflected in this appendix.

Because there are variations in the data on length, beam, and depth of hold and because the practical means of verification have been lost with the disappearance of the steamboats themselves, this appendix will present alternative sets of data where pertinent.

Abbreviations for place names and other data used frequently in this appendix are: Patx., Patuxent; Potm., Potomac; Rappa., Rappahannock; Frdbg., Fredericksburg; Balto., Baltimore; Wash., Washington; Phila., Philadelphia; hp., home port; ldg., landing; MD & V, Maryland, Delaware and Virginia Railroad Company; BC & A, Baltimore, Chesapeake, and Atlantic Railway Company; Md. & Va., Maryland and Virginia Steamboat Company; B & V, Baltimore and Virginia Steamboat Company; USQMD, U.S. (Army) Quartermaster Department (Civil War).

The Steamboats

Anne Arundel (201088)

Built Balto. Shipbuilding & Drydock Co. for Weems Steamboat Co., hp. Balto., s.stbt.(s). 174.2 × 36.0 (oa) × 10.2; GT 795, NT 630 (enrollment data); 174.0 × 36.0 × 10.2; GT 795, NT 638 MVUS; 183.0 × 40.0 × 11.8. Triple-expansion engine; cylinder diameters 12½, 20½, and 36-inch with 24-inch stroke. Single-end, three-furnace, Scotch return tubular boiler 11.6 × 11.6 feet; 165 p.s.i.; propeller 8-foot diameter, 11½-inch pitch. IHP 500 (518). Engine reported to have been designed for tug; underpowered for steamboat. Below main deck: forward and aft holds fitted with compartments for 100 second-class passengers divided for male and female, white and colored; main deck completely enclosed bow to stern; freight deck extending aft almost to engine housing; abaft of engine room, a galley, pantry, purser's office, social hall extending across the vessel; and at the stern, a dining room finished in white and gold with polished hardwood deck. Passenger deck: balustraded grand stairway leading from social hall up to saloon, decorated in quartered oak paneling with vaulted ceiling in white and gold, 39 staterooms opening from saloon each with porcelain wash basin, mirror, chair, and oak-trimmed double berth (except four bridal chambers forward with double brass bedsteads and more elaborate decoration); open decks forward and aft passenger deck fitted with seats and awnings (hurricane deck ended just forward of pilothouse, unlike most Weems paddlewheel boats where hurricane deck extended to very bow). Pilothouse: finished in quartered oak with steam steering by Williamson & Brothers and Rushmore electric searchlight, captain's cabin adjoining aft, with officers' staterooms farther aft. Electric lighting throughout vessel and large bronze chandeliers in saloon; saloon and stateroom decks covered in Brussels carpet; oak chairs and sofas upholstered in green leather; suppliers Charles Spindler (furniture), John Trumbull & Co. (carpets), J. Seth Hopkins (crockery and glassware), M. V. O'Neal (navigation equipment and charts), John E. Hurst & Co. (linens). Launched 5/14/1904, first enrollment 7/5/1904, first trip Balto.–Wash. 7/7/1904. Sold 1/28/1905 to MD & V; sold 4/2/1924 Girard Trust Co. and William B. Shelton to B & V; sold 6/3/1932 to American Contract & Trust Co. of Phila., then 9/3/1932 to Western Shore Freight Lines, becoming Western Shore Steamboat Co. (mortgage $21,500). Made last run Balto.–Frdbg. 1937. Sold 10/5/1937 to American Contract & Trust Co., thence 11/4/1937 to Stony Creek Improvement Co. and name changed 5/20/1939 to *Mohawk*, modified as excursion boat: 174.0 × 36.0 × 10.2. GT 419, NT 254. Crew 44. Acquired by Tolchester line 1941; requisitioned by War Shipping Administration World War II; operated in Hampton Roads; served on Boston to Nantasket run, laid up 1948; scrapped 1952.

Calvert (127606)

Built 1901, Neafie & Levy, Phila. (hull 952) for Weems Steamboat Co., hp. Balto., s.stbt.(s). 180.0 (bp) × 40.0 (oa) × 10.3; GT 887, NT 604;

Top, Steamer *Anne Arundel*, high and dry, under repair off Key Highway, Baltimore, 1935. Photo by the author. *Middle*, Steamer *Calvert* in Baltimore Harbor. From the collection of Herman Hollerith. *Bottom*, Steamer *Eagle* from an early print. Note the crosshead engine, mast and sails, clipper-bow and bowsprit, square stern, and recessed paddlebox. Middle and bottom illustrations courtesy of the Mariners' Museum

190.0 (oa) × 38.8 × 12.0; GT 889, NT 604; IHP 1,500 (1,800; 726); inclined compound (two-cylinder) engine; cylinder diameters 20 and 40 inches, with 28-inch stroke. Single-end Scotch boiler 14.9 × 12.0 feet. Odd placement of smokestack (30 feet high, thin) considerably aft of midships position. Launched 11/23/1901. Christened by Matilda Williams, daughter of Henry Williams, pres. Initial enrollment 3/4/1902. Crew 35. First trip on Rappa.; a few days later took place of *Westmoreland* on Patx., latter laid up for repairs; operated on Potm. Sold to MD & V 2/11/1905; in bankruptcy proceedings of MD & V transferred 7/19/24 through American Contract & Trust Co. of Phila. to B & V; transferred 6/1932 in bankruptcy proceedings of B & V through American Contract & Trust Co. of Phila. to Ernest E. Fuchs, Belle Harbor, N.Y. (Thames River Line, N.Y.) 10/26/1933; sold to Sound Steamship Lines, Inc., New York 4/12/1934; modified to oil-burning screw 7/20/1939. GT 545.71, NT 370; further dieselized; 1940 on New York City–Bridgeport run for Sound SS Lines, Inc., New York; licensed to carry 1,300 passengers 1942, ran Orient Point–New London service, suspended 7/18/1942 for lack of business; requisitioned 10/7/1942, service in Boston Harbor; new CO committed suicide aboard 10/13/1942; 1947 still in war paint laid up in Boston Harbor; sold to be broken up in Alexandria, Va. 7/16/1957 (some records show Bordentown, N.J.).

Caroline (136822)
See *Emma Reis*.

Eagle (unnumbered)

Built 1813, J & F Brice, at Northern Liberties, County of Philadelphia, hp. Phila., p.stbt.(w). 111.5 × 46.0 (oa) or 19.3 × ? (Marestier, one version); 130.0 (46 forward of paddleshaft), 92 aft (oa) × 20.4 × 7.21 (Marestier, second version); 108.0 × 29.8 × 9.12 and 291–49/95 T (enrollment data); paddlewheels 17.4 diameter with 12 buckets 3.11 long, 1.8 high; steam cylinder 2 to 4-inch diameter (Marestier), 20-foot stack. Attached to crosshead a large wooden beam painted green which pivoted to operate force pumps below. Crosshead engine built by Daniel Large. Covered paddleboxes recessed into hull and overhang. Flush deck, schooner-bowed, square-sterned. Awning aft provided shade for deck passengers. Cabins below, separated for men and women, the former doubling as a dining room.

Single mast forward with sails. Enrolled Phila. 3/29/1814, owners: Moses Rogers, Daniel Large, etc. First enrollment Balto. 8/26/1817; owners: Samuel Briscoe, with Levi Hollingsworth, Elias Green, James Partridge, all of Balto.; and John Partridge, James Sewell, Alexander Scott, Joshua Richardson, and Henry Bennett (Elkton); William Howell, master. Operated on Upper Delaware River (Phila.–Bordentown, N.J.) until 1815, then on Balto.–Elkton, Md. route, 1815–18. In 1815, became second (or third) steamer to sail the Atlantic by running from Phila. to Norfolk under command of Capt. Moses Rogers (later master of *Savannah*); initiated Balto.–Norfolk route. Sold 1819 to Union Co. and 4/5/1820 sold to George Weems, James Harwood, Jeremiah Perry, et al.; operated Balto., Annapolis, Patx. River. Boiler exploded 4/17/1824 on trip Annapolis–Balto., burned below decks; flames extinguished by *Constitution* of Union line; Capt. George Weems severely burned; one passenger died from injuries. Engine removed. Abandoned 1827. What happened after the boiler explosion is not clear. Documentation seems to indicate that engine was removed, possibly for scrap, and the hull abandoned in 1827 (one source says 1829). In the account of Lafayette's visit to Baltimore and the reception given him, as he arrived aboard the steamer *United States* (Capt. Trippe) on October 7, 1824, the steamers *Eagle, Maryland, Virginia,* and *Philadelphia* are recorded as joining up in escort. Still other reports show *Eagle* in service as late as 1838.

Emma Reis/Caroline (136822)

Built 1900 Milford, Del., hp. Wilmington, twin s.stbt.(w); 114.6 × 21.0 × 6.0, GT 187 (GT 187.57), NT 102 (NT 107.97), IHP 190. Launched 5/11/1900. Initial enrollment 8/8/1900, Milford & Phila. Transportation Co.; service between Lewes, Del., and Cape May, N.J.; sold 4/1903 for $17,905 to Weems Steamboat Co., renamed *Caroline,* for service on Rappa. River ldgs. as feeder to Balto. steamers. Crew 12. Collision with *Tourist* of People line 5/15/1903 at Port Royal, Va.; slight damage to both vessels. Sold 1/28/1903 to MD & V. Sold 6/23/1911 to Dover & Phila. Navigation Co., Inc. (Del.); hp. Wilmington; name changed to *City of Dover.* Dismantled 6/23/1917.

Essex (135855)

Built 1885 at William Skinner & Sons, Balto., for Weems line, hp. Balto., s.stbt.(w). (First screw

Top, Steamer *Caroline*, the former *Emma Reis*. Photograph was probably taken in April 1903 when she arrived in the Rappahannock. Her old name has been painted out in readiness for the name *Caroline*. From the collection of T. H. Franklin. Courtesy of the Steamship Historical Society, University of Baltimore library. *Bottom*, Steamer *Essex*. Courtesy of the Mariners' Museum

Steamer *George Weems* offloads supplies at City Point on the James River about 1864–65. Photo by Mathew Brady. Courtesy of the Mariners' Museum

steamboat built for Weems.) 146.8 (oa) × 27.5 × 9.2; 141.5 (bp) × 28.0 (oa) × 12.2; 156.0 × 28.0 × 7; GT 601.21 (GT 580.80; GT 601.0); NT 512.3 (NT 484.88; NT 512). NHP 200; IHP 450. Compound engine; machinery built by James Clark & Co. Forward part of saloon completely surrounded in windows (like a day boat); accommodations for only 50 first-class passengers; designed to carry 250 tons of freight, service as shuttle between Rappa. and Norfolk. Estimated cost $40,000. Keel laid 2/14/1885; launched 8/1/1885. Initial enrollment 10/3/1885; owners: Georgeana Weems Williams ½, Matilda Sparrow Weems Forbes ½, James Gourley, master. First-class cabins 26.90 T; second-class cabin space 16.98 T; saloon 176.94 T. Crew 40. Burned 9/1/1887 at Pier 8, Light St., damage $15,000–18,000; rebuilt. Operated on Rappa. run. By 1891,

ran 6 months of year Rappa. ldgs. to Norfolk and later through service Frdbg.–Norfolk, connecting with Balto. boats on Rappa. In storm of 1905 broke off rudder and stern post in Carter's Creek. Sold 1/28/1905 to MD & V. Partially burned 5/2/1911; rebuilt as fishing boat at Marine Railway, Machine & Boiler Works, Balto. Masters listed on enrollment: James B. Sanford, J. M. H. Burroughs, W. H. VanDyke, John A. Clark, A. M. Long, H. A. Bohannon, James Gourley, M. W. Gourley, D. M. Davis, M. H. H. Perry. Sold 5/8/1912, owner: George D. Weaver (Balto. County, Md.), transferred 5/18/1912 to Indian Creek Fertilizer Co.; Benjamin F. Evans, master. Configuration changed: GT 375, NT 255, crew 30, hp. Tappahannock, Va.; sold 5/6/1916, owner: John T. Donohue (Balto. County, Md.), hp. Reedville, Va., transferred by owner to hp. New

Top, Steamer *Lancaster* under construction after launch at the Maryland Steel Company, Sparrows Point, Maryland, summer 1892. *Bottom,* Same ship on the building ways, early spring 1892, at the Maryland Steel Company, Sparrows Point, Maryland. Both illustrations courtesy of the Mariners' Museum

York, and 9/6/1916 operating in Portland, Me., by Northern Transportation Co. (John C. Anderson, Boston, Mass.); converted into tug, hp. Wilmington, Del. Foundered 6/3/1923, Beach Haven, N.J., 16 on board saved. Sunk, total loss, shown on certificate 10/23/1923, as a barge operated by Northern Barge Co. (Del.).

George Weems (10040)

Built 1858 in Balto. for Weems line to replace *Patuxent*, hp. Balto., p.stbt.(w). Round stern. 177.50 × 30.70 (30.8; 53 oa) × 8.60; T (not specified G or N) 640.71 (T 447). Vertical beam engine; cylinder diameter 40 inches × 10-foot stroke. Early enrollment certificates missing from archives. Enrollment 6/21/1865, owners: George W. Weems ½, Theodore Weems ½. Operated on Patx., excursions to Fair Haven through 1861. Civil War: entry USQMD 8/14/1862, discharged 4/12/1863 ($125/day); entry 4/1863 ($170.87 + $87.63); entry 4/22/1864, discharged 3/31/1865 ($200/day). Burned partially 6/20/1868, rebuilt; burned at wharf in Balto. 6/10/1871, property damage $45,000; engine placed in *Theodore Weems* (see Appendix D for additional details).

John E. Tygert (76075)

Built 1879, hp. Phila. (*Merchant Vessels of the United States* listed hp. as Pittsburgh in error, 1879–87), s.stbt.(i). 109.0 × 22.0 × 7.0; GT 206.87 (368.82 in 1892–93), NT 165.37 (310.27 in 1892–93). NHP 100 (109 in 1892–93). Initial enrollment 7/23/1879; owners: John E. Tygert and Vernon S. Tygert (Smyrna, Del.), copartners; hp. Wilmington; John E. Tygert, master. 7/11/1882, owners: William F. Brown 1/64, George W. Bush 1/4, Henry W. Tygert 1/64, and John E. Tygert 46/64. 7/2/1886, owner: John E. Tygert, pres. Phila. & Smyrna Transportation Co., hp. Phila. 5/18/1889, new owners: William R. Lewis ¼, John A. Ketcham, master, Franklin C. Lewis ¼, Charles R. Lewis ¼, Andrew I. Lewis ¼, of Accomac County, Va.; hp. Onancock, Va. Listed (*MVUS*) as "belonging to the country." Burned 5/18/1889, rebuilt. Change in tonnage: GT 206.87, NT 163.37. Transferred 1891 to Md. & Va. Steamboat Co., operations on Potm. Sold 2/21/1895 (enrollment data) to Weems Stbt. Co., new tonnage: GT 368.82, NT 310.27. Operations on Potm.; sold 12/31/1896 (enrollment) to Albion W. Higgins for Laflin & Rand Powder Co. (New York) $7,000. Sold 11/28/1904 to Thomas E. Hardinger, sec., Singer Mfg. Co., Elizabeth, N.J.; GT

226, NT 154, then transferred to Newark Bay Short Line, hp. Newark, N.J. Name changed 11/16/1905 to *Douglas Alexander*. 8/15/1907 data: 109.0 × 22.0 × 7.0; GT 248, NT 168. Dismantled 11/29/1920.

Lancaster (141217)

Built 1892 by Maryland Steel Co. (hull 5) cost $113,307.37 for Weems Stbt. Co., p.stbt.(s). First steel steamer of the line, 205.4 (bp) × 56.1 (oa) × 10.7; 213.0 × 57.0 × 10.7; 205.4 × 32.0 × 12.0. GT 919.62, NT 692.57, NHP 650, IHP 980 (IHP 1,332). Hull of mild ⅜-inch steel; keel of dished plate forming a waterway; stern post and rudder frames of cast steel; heavy framing spaced 32-inches apart connected by seven keelsons for rigidity; steel deck aft of engine and boiler. Main deck of 4-inch pine bow to stern. Steel enclosed engine and boiler casings and framing of paddleboxes. Vertical beam engine; wheels 30-foot diameter; cylinder diameter 48 inches, with 11.0 stroke. Two Scotch boilers 10.9 diameter, 15.6 length; 50 p.s.i. working pressure; 40 staterooms, 80 first-class passengers, 97 second-class passengers. Saloon with joiner work in bass and sycamore with carving, molding, ornamental alcoves, paneled doorways, ceiling in white and gold. Four staterooms aft equipped with brass bedsteads and painted in white, gold, and blue pastel; staterooms and saloon carpeted in body Brussels; gold mirrors mounted in saloon; furniture oak-framed upholstered in green leather. On main deck: ladies' social cabin, paneled in hardwood, ladies' washroom with hot and cold running water and marble fixtures; barroom furnished in walnut like a British pub; mailroom, galley, quarters for officers and crew; forward and aft of engine room enclosure, in the hold, cabin space for 97 second-class passengers. Two broad stairways with carved balustrades in cherry and bass between main and passenger decks. Hurricane deck from stem to stern: pilothouse in tongue-and-groove paneling, aft the captain's cabin in bass and sycamore with built-in bedstead, and quarters for first and second mates. Crew 42. Launched by Jane D. (Jennie Forbes) 4/15/1892; trial run 8/13/1892. Ran Patx., Potm., and Rappa. routes at various times but principally on last. Sold 2/1/1905 to MD & V. After 1912 used primarily as spare boat and for freight. Sold 9/10/1924 as result of MD & V bankruptcy through Girard Trust Co. to New York, Albany & Western Steamship Co., Inc. (Del.), Pier 12, East

Top, Main saloon of steamer *Lancaster.* To the *right* is an area at one time used as the dining room. From a brochure used by the Weems line and the Maryland Steel Company to celebrate her maiden voyage, 1892. *Bottom,* Steamer *Lancaster* sets out on her trial run, August 13, 1892, from the Maryland Steel Company, Sparrows Point, Maryland, where she was launched on April 15, 1892. Both illustrations courtesy of the Mariners' Museum

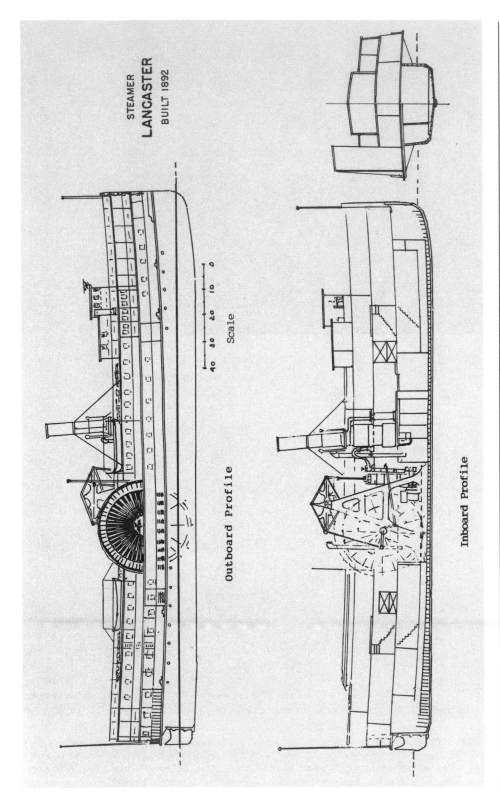

STEAMER
LANCASTER
BUILT 1892

Scale

40 30 20 10 0

Outboard Profile

Inboard Profile

Inboard and outboard profile drawings of *Lancaster*, 1892. Reconstructed from inboard profile builder's drawing in the collection of the Maryland Historical Society and photocopy of outboard drawing in the collection of H. Graham Wood. Drawings matched and reconciled with photographs of *Lancaster* on trial run

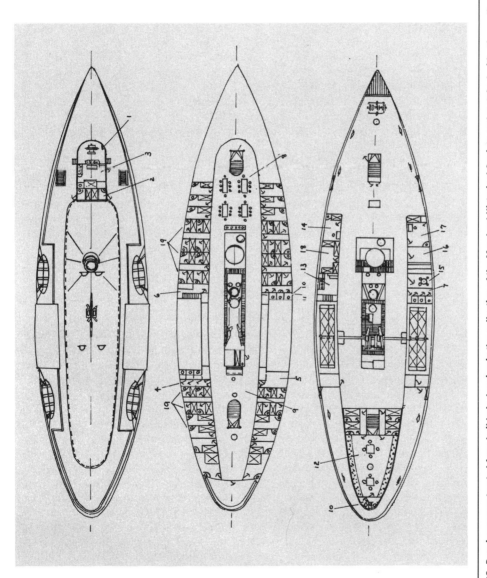

Steamer *Lancaster*, 1892. Drawing reconstructed from builder's drawing in the collection of the Maryland Historical Society and matched with other outboard and inboard profile drawings and photographs. *1*, pilothouse; *2*, officers; *3*, captain; *4*, ladies' toilet; *5*, barber shop; *6*, pantry; *7*, men's toilet; *8*, dining room; *9*, saloon; *10*, WC; *11*, washroom; *12*, main deck saloon; *13*, galley; *14*, mailroom; *15*, barroom; *16*, package room; *17*, purser; *18*, crew; *19*, staterooms

215

River, N.Y. Ran to Albany and Troy. Sold by U.S. Marshall at Stapleton, Long Island. 11/4/1925 to E. B. Leaf & Co. (Phila.) for $5,000. Laid up 1926, dismantled 1927, hull used as dock at Hastings-on-Hudson.

Mary Washington (16104)

Built Balto. 1845–46 for Balto. & Rappa. Steam Packet Co., p.stbt.(w). 165.0 × 26.0 × 10.4; 149.7 (bp) × 26.0 × 10.4. Tonnage (GT and NT not specified) 422-52/95, NT 772. Initial enrollment 6/17/1846; owner: Balto. & Rappa. Steam Packet Co., James Harwood, pres., Noah Fairbank, master. Hp. Balto. Advertised to be sold at auction by U.S. Marshall 1/5/1847 as result of suits brought by William and Hazlett McKim (copper mfgrs. of Balto.) and William and Wilson Procter (hardware merchants of Balto.) for bills unpaid by the Balto. & Rappa. Steam Packet Co. As result of complaint brought to Chancery Court, Balto., against the Balto. & Rappa. Steam Packet Co. (Fielding Lucas and John A. Robb) by Horace Abbott, Joseph Rogers, John Ferguson, John Watchman, and Henry Thompson & Sons, *Mary Washington* sold at auction 2/3/1847 for $26,000 to John Glenn, attorney for Md. & Va., chartered 2/12/1847, James Harwood, pres. Enrollment 9/28/1847; owner: Md. & Va., John S. Shriver (Balto.), pres. Sold 12/22/1854 to Mason L. Weems and Theodore Weems. Enrollment 3/5/1855; owners: Theodore Weems and Mason L. Weems, each ½. Enrollment 4/16/1855, Mason L. Weems, sole owner. Operated Balto., Frdbg., Rappa. ldgs. Civil War: entry 1/8/1862 ($148.47/day), 4/2/1862 ($38.30/day), 7/10/1862 (100.00/day), 4/21/1864 ($175.00/day as of 6/4/1863), discharged 4/1/1865. Lengthened and altered 1865: 194.0 × 26.30 × 10.35; GT 639.31, NT 566.1. Operated primarily on Rappa. 1866 on. After death of Mason L. Weems in 1874, ownership changed 6/18/1875 (certificate date) to Georgeanna Williams and Matilda S. Forbes. Enrollment 5/3/1878; owners: Georgeanna Weems Williams ½ and Matilda S. Weems Forbes ½, Henry Williams, agent; J. M. H. Burroughs, master. Dismantled and abandoned in Balto. 1888. (See Appendix D for details on specifications and construction materials and costs.)

Mason L. Weems (91372)

Built 1881 in Balto. by William Skinner & Sons for Weems line. Launched 6/13/1881, p.stbt.(w). 221.0 × 55.0 (oa) × 12.0; 221.7 × 52.9 (oa) × 12.3; 231.0 × 58.0 (oa) × 12.3; 221.0 × 32.8 × 12.0. Vertical beam engine by James Clark & Co.; cylinder diameter 56 inches, with stroke 138 inches. GT 1209.46 (GT 880.35 in 1887), NT 829.15 (NT 503.68 in 1887). Designed for speed: 7:1 hull ratio, length to beam; large paddlewheels, massive engine. Paneling handcrafted by Charles Morris; saloon gallery; stained-glass skylights; lavish staterooms. Total cost exceeded $100,000. Initial enrollment 9/23/1881; owners: Georgeanna Williams ½, Matilda S. Forbes ½; James Gourley, master. Stranded at Urbanna, off Rappa. 8/14/1882, hauled off undamaged. Collided 11/10/1882 with schooner *Brooklyn* near Sandy Point, officers of steamer exonerated. Reportedly drew too much water for creeks of Rappa. and Patx. Sold 4/26/1890; owner: Jacob H. Tremper, pres., Romer & Tremper Stbt. Co. (Kingston, N.Y.). Name changed to *William F. Romer*. This company reportedly bought by Cornell Steamboat Co. Sold 11/6/1913 to Herbert R. Odell, Newburgh, N.Y., sec., Central-Hudson Stbt. Co., New York. Reportedly on one run, made record speed New York–Stony Point, unchallenged except for *City of Kingston*. Enrollment surrendered 6/30/1920, reportedly unfit for use, broken up for junk.

Matilda (16103)

Built 1864 in Balto. intended eventually for Patx., Fdbg., and Rappa. ldgs. service of Weems line, hp. Balto., p.stbt.(w). 220.5 × 30.9 × 10.2; 200 × 28 × 9; 192 (prob. bp) × 33 × 10; GT 928.05 (GT or NT unspecified, 650 and 707). Weems line reportedly wanted to keep some service going after three boats had been seized by USQMD, but this vessel built for this purpose nevertheless was immediately requisitioned and chartered by govt. While under govt. service, boiler exploded in James River; eng. Thomas Brannon killed, and others injured. Civil War: entry 4/12/1864 ($500/day), discharged 5/11/1865. Operated 1865–66 on Patx. and Rappa. Operated 1866–74 Frdbg. and Rappa. ldgs. for Balto. & Va. Steamship Co. incorporated 2/21/1866 (Mason L. Weems and Jacob Tome, principal owners); Jacob Tome, principal owner of Balto. & Susquehanna Steam Co. Enrollment 6/4/1875, owners: Matilda S. Forbes (Balto.) ¼, Georgeanna Williams (Calvert County) ¼, estate of Theodore Weems (Balto.) ½, James Gourley, master. Sold 5/11/1883 to Wesley Ricketts, converted to barge 6/25/1883. Engine removed and placed in new steamer *Westmoreland*.

Hills Landing,

Drawing of steamer *Mary Washington* alongside dock at Hills Landing, Prince George's County, with toll bridge built by W. B. Hill in background. Date of drawing unknown but after 1854 and before the Civil War. Courtesy of Roland and Helen Sasscer Sliker

Top, Steamer *Mason L. Weems.* From a painting by J. S. Bohannon. *Middle*, Steamer *Matilda* at Light Street, Baltimore, 1871. From the collection of H. Graham Wood. Top and middle illustration courtesy of the Mariners' Museum. *Bottom*, Steamer *Middlesex* at Irvington in Carter's Creek about 1912. From the collection of H. Graham Wood. Courtesy of the Steamship Historical Society, University of Baltimore library

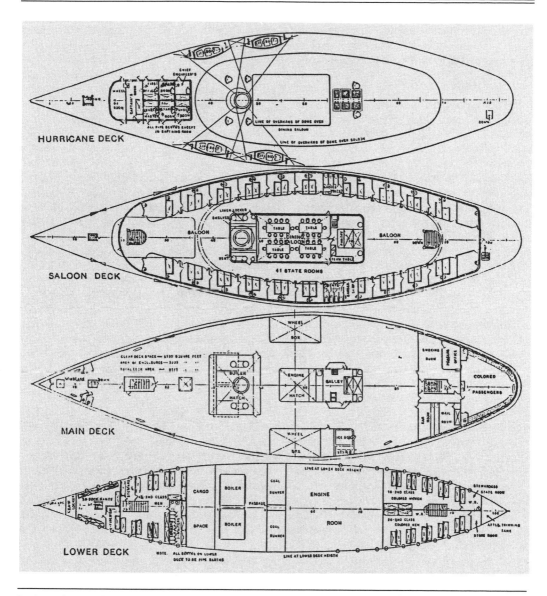

Deck drawing of *Middlesex* published by Neafie and Levy Ship and Engine Building Company on the launching of the vessel, 1902, and reproduced in *Marine Engineering* (July 1903), 364. Courtesy of *Marine Log*

Enrollment surrendered, John King (New York), owner and master, stating that barge had not been heard from since 2/16/1889, assumed lost.

Middlesex (93331)

Built 1902 by Neafie & Levy (hull 955), Phila., for Weems Steamboat Co., p.stbt.(s). Used inclined compound engine and nine curved buckets per paddlewheel with a feathering mechanism to permit bucket to remain vertical during water immersion for maximum thrust; paddlewheels small (13.2 diameter) and rapid moving; paddleboxes faired into contour of vessel's sides, hence steamer often mistaken for being propeller driven. 200 (bp) × 36 (hull width) × 12.3; 207 (oa) × 59 (oa) × 11.5, GT 1190, NT 754. Crew 42. IHP 500 (IHP 1,300, IHP 800). Compound engine (two cylinders) diameters 24 and 53 inches with 84 inch stroke; 45 rpm, stick shaft. Two single-end Scotch boilers, 12.9 diameter, 10.6 length. Because of sheer (4.6 forward and 2.0 aft) and small paddleboxes faired into each side, vessel had very pleasing lines. Below main deck, hull forward of collision bulkhead held 18-ton ballast tank and chain locker; aft, 17-foot room with 24 bunks for deckhands and stokers; farther aft, second-class cabin for men with 45 berths reached by stairway from main deck; farther aft, room for waiters and cooks; boiler and engine room occupied 70 feet of hull, separated by coal bunkers on either side (each with 60-ton capacity); aft of engine room bulkhead, three second-class cabins for women with 48 berths and room for stewardess, entered by stairway from main deck; 3,500-gallon fresh water tanks beneath this cabin, trimming tank at stern. Main deck: at stern, for second-class passengers, large social hall trimmed in oak and white-painted soft wood and fitted with toilets and washstand, passageway leading forward to freight deck flanked on port side by dark-paneled bar and mailroom and on starboard side by smoking room and purser's office; aft of crankroom (for enclosed paddlewheels), a large galley of steel with tile floor connected by lift to saloon deck; forward deck for freight, space of steam capstan, windlass, crew toilet, and boatswain's stores. Main saloon 150 feet on passenger deck: 41 outside staterooms opening directly to saloon, many communicating, fitted with two berths each, washstands, electric lights, call bells, decorated in carved cherry wood; four large rooms at aft end equipped with double brass bedsteads; saloon paneled in richly

carved oak, furnished with heavy oak furniture upholstered in green leather; dome extended fore and aft painted white and leafed in gold; aft of stack paneling was dining room, 32 feet long, 20 feet wide, raised 12 feet to a second dome extending above saloon dome, seating 42; enclosed pantry on main deck above galley served by lift; hurricane deck (extending from stem to stern): awning-covered promenade from pilothouse aft; stairs from saloon and after passenger deck; pilothouse paneled in tongue-and-groove, steam-driven steering; binnacle, engine bellpulls, bench, overhead controls for searchlight; captain's cabin and six officers' staterooms aft (*Marine Engineering*, July 1903, 363–65). Launched July 1902, christened by Jane (Jennie) D. Forbes. Delivery 8 months late. Trial run 12/16/1902 on Delaware River. Initial enrollment 12/30/1902. Operated by Weems Steamboat Co. principally on Rappa. route but on Potm. and Patx. at intervals. Sold 1/30/1905 to MD & V. Contract 11/29/1910, Newport News Drydock, for construction of 26 additional staterooms on hurricane deck; new paddlewheels; shaft raised; returned to service 4/9/1911. Sold 4/24/1924 in bankruptcy proceedings of MD & V through Girard Trust Co. and William B. Shelton to B & V. Sold 2/9/1929 and 3/10/1930 to George P. Ellis (Somerville, Mass.). Name changed to *Plymouth* in Balto. where work in progress. Transferred 8/20/1930 to Nantasket Beach Steamboat Co. (Boston). Sold 5/28/1936 to Marine Operating Corp. of New Jersey, hp. Newark, N.J. Sold 4/9/1937 to Sound Steamship Lines, Inc., and name changed to *Manhattan*. Operated 4/16/1937 by Sound Steamship Lines, Inc., from Pier 31, East River, N.Y. Burned 3/13/1939 at Tottenville, N.Y. Sold 7/20/1939 to C. G. Willis, Maxwell Co., hp. Norfolk, changed hp. Wilmington, N.C. Converted 5/23/1941 into barge by Maxwell Co., New Bern, N.C. Enrollment surrendered, sold to Peruvian flag, 6/5/1945, approved by U.S. Maritime Commission.

Northumberland (130855)

Built 1899–1900 by Neafie & Levy, Phila. (hull 930) for Weems Steamboat Co., s.stbt.(s). Cost $127,256.49 cash. Launched by Elizabeth Chew Williams March 3, 1930. First steamboat to be built for line outside of Balto. Intended for Potm. run. 190 (bp) or 200 (oa) × 39.8 or 41 (oa) × 11.0 (12.0). GT 993, NT 675, IHP 1,500. Steel hulled, propeller driven. Crew 26. Two steel Scotch boilers, gunboat type, each 9.6 (9.1 diameter,

Top, Northumberland steams out of Baltimore. From the collection of R. Loren Graham. Courtesy of the Steamship Historical Society, University of Baltimore library. *Bottom,* Steamer *Planter* in the service of the Union army at Whitehouse Landing, Pamunkey River, Virginia, during the Civil War. Photo by Mathew Brady. Courtesy of the National Archives

20.0 length). Triple-expansion engine; cylinder; diameters 18, 28, (25), 45 inches with 30-inch stroke. Saloon paneled in carved oak, 43 staterooms, berths for 72 second-class passengers; social hall for music and dancing; pub-style smoking room. Ran Balto.–Wash. route. Initial enrollment 5/7/1900, Weems Steamboat Co. Sold 1/28/1905 to MD & V. In bankruptcy proceedings of MD & V, sold 4/2/1924 through Girard Trust Co. and William P. Shelton to B & V, sold 6/3/1932 through American Contract & Trust Co. of Phila. to Excursion Steamboats Inc., Newark, N.J. Operated as excursion boat around New York. In bankruptcy proceedings of Excursion Steamboats Inc., sold at public auction 3/5/1934 by U.S. Marshall at Quinian's Coal Yard, Staten Island, N.Y. Sold 4/11/1934 to J. A. Cheatham, Norfolk, Va. for $2,500; operated to carry freight, Norfolk–Richmond. Sold 5/14/1937 to Buxton Lines, Norfolk, Va., hp. Norfolk. Name changed 8/5/1937 to *Norfolk*. While laid up at Clermont on the James River, burned 9/30/1945, hull sold, and subsequently scrapped.

Patuxent (5284)

Built 1826 in Balto. by Andrew Flanigan for new company organized by George Weems as master, hp. Balto., p.stbt.(w). 122.6 × 24.9 × 7.1. Tonnage 219-68/95. Schooner hull without bowsprit or mast. Crosshead engine built by John Watchman and John Bratt (Hughes St., Balto. plant). Cabin areas with small cubicles separating men and women (men's area used alternately as dining room). Enrollment 5/5/1827; owners: James Corner (Balto. merchant) and Hugh McElderry (Balto.); George Weems, master. Enrollment 6/23/1828; owners: Charles Nicols [*sic*], Hugh McElderry, and James Corner; George Weems, master. Enrollment 1/9/1830; owners: George Weems, John Watchman, John Bratt, James Corner, James Johnson, Charles Nichols, Duncan McCullough, and Hugh McElderry; George Weems, master. Enrollment 3/12/1831; owners: same as for 1/9/1830 but adding Walter Fernandis, Edward D. Kemp. Enrollment 8/18/1831; owners: George Weems, John Watchman, Duncan McCullough, John Bratt, James Johnson, Charles Nichols, Edward D. Kemp. Enrollment 4/23/1835; owners: George Weems, John Watchman, John Bratt, Charles Nichols, James Johnson, Edward D. Kemp; George Weems, master. As of 4/23/1835, major modification completed: 144.9 × 24.9 × 9.1; tonnage 265–12/95. Enrollment 10/12/1838;

owners: George Weems, John Watchman, John Bratt, James Johnson, Charles Nichols, Edward D. Kemp. Enrollment 12/14/1838; owners: George Weems, James Johnson, Edward D. Kemp; Mason L. Weems, master. Enrollment 3/20/1849; owners: Theodore Weems, Gustavus Weems, George W. Weems, Mason L. Weems; Theodore Weems, master. Operated on the Patx. route throughout Weems ownership. August 1828–May 1830 ran to Frdbg. and Rappa. ldgs.; July 1828 to Sassafras River; second attempt at Frdbg. route, August 1833–October 1834; 1830–41, Wicomico–Salisbury and Whitehaven; 1849–50, Patx. via Green Landing. New engine 1849 by Charles Reeder; cylinder diameter 38 inches, with stroke of 96 inches, low pressure. Collision 11/15/1854 with schooner in Chesapeake Bay. Sold 4/23/1861 to Calvin Taggart, et al., Phila. & Bridgeton Steamboat Co. and to W. Whilldin 12/7/1861. Civil War: entry USQMD 12/18/61 ($125/day, reduced to $100/day, 5/1/1863); purchased by USQMD 7/1/1864 at Phila. for $16,000; sold at public auction to S. & J. Flanagan, Balto., 10/19/1865 for $3,200. Redocumented 4/12/1866 as *Cumberland*. Abandoned 1868. [Note: as result of death of James Harwood 7/7/1847, his ⅛ share in name of Edward D. Kemp then held by wife and executrix Susan Harwood required court action and sale by auction (5/1/1848) for liquidation; buyer at $7,000 Edward G. Leach (Leitch) transferred vessel to Mason L. Weems, Theodore Weems, George W. Weems, and Gustavus Weems, in agreement with executrix.]

Planter (19543)

Built 1845, probably by Flanigan Shipyard, Balto., for Weems line, as a partial replacement for *Patuxent*, p.stbt.(w). Initial enrollment 6/18/1845: 162.25 × 25.80 × 8.65; tonnage (GT or NT not specified) 509.96. Enrollment 1851: 168.0 × 25.0 × 8.0; tonnage 473. Enrollment 3/5/1855: 161.5 × 25.8 × 8.7; tonnage 338-51/95. Enrollment 6/11/1872: 196.0 × 30.9 × 9.45; tonnage 688.04. Vertical beam engine, cylinder diameter 36 inches with stroke 120 inches. Single boiler. Main deck forward enclosed for freight; gallery aft of paddleboxes surrounded cabin and dining areas; promenade deck had cabin running two-thirds length of vessel containing staterooms and saloon; covered deck surrounded cabin aft of paddleboxes. Pilothouse square box forward of passenger cabin, with roof raised for windows fore and aft to provide all-around view. In hull, engine and

Top, Steamer *Potomac* as a Weems line boat, c. 1900. From the collection of H. Graham Wood. *Middle*, Steamer *Potomac* backs from her Light Street slip, July 18, 1933. From the Boyles Collection. Top and middle illustration courtesy of the Steamship Historical Society, University of Baltimore library. *Bottom*, Steamer *Richmond* in Baltimore Harbor. Courtesy of Alice Forbes Bowie boiler rooms, cooking facilities, berths and benches for Negro passengers and crew. Wood stacked on deck for fuel. Operated on Patx. through 1857; 1847–48 trips to Green Landing. In late 1846 and early 1847 to Frdbg. and Rappa. ldgs., excursions Frdbg. to Port Royal. Reported on Norfolk run 1/1/1848. With *Thomas Jefferson* on 1/15/1848 went to assistance of *Columbus* ashore near Magothy River. Collided 5/17/1855 with Ft. Carroll, Patapsco River, sank during night, damage $9,000; raised, repaired. In 1859 ran to York, East, and Great Wicomico Rivers. Prior to seizure by U.S. govt. operated in Potm. seized at Wash. Civil War: entry 1/1862, 2/1862, 7/1862 ($66/day and $65.88/day), 8/15/1862 ($100/ day), discharged 3/12/1863; 4/21/1864 ($175/day), discharged 6/12/1865. Resumed Patx. route, 1866. Enrollment 6/19/1868; owners: Mason L. Weems ½, estate of Theodore Weems ½. Enrollment 7/22/1879, transfer through trustees D. W. Crain to Georgeanna Williams and Matilda S. Forbes, value $23,500. Sold 2/26/1881 to junk dealers, Balto.; broken up by wreckers, 6/1881.

Potomac (150672)

Built 1894 by Neafie & Levy, Phila. (hull 870), for Md. & Va. for service on Potm., Balto.–Wash., s.stbt.(s), hp. Balto. 176.8 (180 oa) × 35.8 (41.0 oa) × 11.0; GT 763.46, NT 688.88, NHP 1000, IHP 450. Crew 30. One single-end Scotch boiler 11.9 × 11.6. Compound (two-cylinder) engine; cylinder diameters 20 and 30 inches with 26-inch stroke. 37 first-class staterooms, well-decorated saloon, dining room aft on main deck. Initial enrollment 6/28/1894; conditionally assigned to Md. & Va. 7/2/1894. Sold 1895 by Neafie & Levy (enrollment 1/10/1896) to Weems Steamboat Co. Operated on Patx., Potm., and Rappa. Sold 2/1/1905 to MD & V. Sold 4/24/1924 in bankruptcy proceedings of MD & V through Girard Trust Co. of Phila. to B & V. Reported 12/29/1928 that vessel made last run with B & V. Sold in bankruptcy proceedings of B & V through American Contract & Trust Co. 6/13/1932 to Western Shore Freight Lines, Inc., Balto., and 10/5/1932 by company name change to Western Shore Steamboat Co. Sold 3/21/1936 to Chesapeake Corp, Newport News, Va.; converted into barge. Dismantled 10/26/1956, Newport News, Va.

Richmond (110862)

Built 1890 by William Skinner & Sons, Balto., for Weems line to replace *Mason L. Weems*.

p.stbt.(w). Last wood-hulled steamer built for line. Launched 6/26/1890. 205.0 (213.0 oa) × 32.8 (56.2 oa) × 11.3; GT 865.57, NT 648.59. IHP 952. Vertical beam engine constructed by James Clark & Co.; cylinder diameter 48 inches, stroke 132 inches. Two steel Scotch boilers, 11.0 × 15.0, each furnishing power independently to drive the engine and auxiliaries, if necessary. 125 first-class passengers, 175 second-class passengers. Saloon designed by Charles Morris finished in mosaic of oak, sycamore, and cherry; ladies' cabin in cypress; staterooms forward reached through alcoves; those aft fitted as bridal suites; latest materials in plumbing; cabins heated by steam, lighted by electricity; searchlight on bow operated by lookoutsman later moved to roof of pilothouse. Placed on Rappa. route. 8/28/1890 strap on walking beam broke, damaging cylinder head and surface condenser, all requiring replacement at cost of $5,000–10,000; hurricane deck around piston rod smashed; only a ventilator saved engineer from being crushed. 11/14/1901, burned at Frdbg. wharf, destroyed. Insured for $70,000 (market value only).

St. Mary's
See *Theodore Weems*.

Sue (23471)

Built 1867 by Harlan & Hollinsworth Shipbuilding Co., Wilmington, Del. Named for Sue Harlan, daughter of one of firm's partners, who was interested in Eastern Shore Railroad. Firm idle much of 1867, and *Sue* built on speculation and hope that vessel would be sold to Eastern Shore railroad interests. p.stbt.(i). 175.1 × 27.0 × 9.9, GT 688.84, NT 569.20, NHP 122, IHP 400. Vertical beam engine, cylinder diameter 32 inches with stroke of 9 feet. Crew 27. Initial enrollment 7/17/1867; Harlan & Hollingsworth Shipbldg. Co. Enrollment 7/16/1870; owner: Samuel Harlan, Jr., for Eastern Shore Steamboat Co. (Balto.). Ran Crisfield–Norfolk. On York River line 1874. 11/8/1874 ran into Ft. Carroll, Patapsco River; minor repairs. Placed on Potm. route; then to Norfolk as opposition to Old Bay Line; withdrawn; returned to Potm. route to Wash. Sold 6/26/1875 to Express Steamboat Co., Phila., hp. Wilmington, Del., then 1/29/1890 to Balto., Chesapeake & Richmond Steamboat Co. of Balto., thence to Potm. Transportation Co. and 3/25/1891 to Charles R. Lewis, Westmoreland County, Va., hp. Tappahannock, Va.; W. C.

Top, Saloon deck, forward, of steamer *Richmond,* showing dining tables, port and starboard. *Bottom,* Saloon deck, aft, of steamer *Richmond.* Both illustrations courtesy of Alice Forbes Bowie

Steamer *Sue* about 1904, prior to her conversion to the name *Bristol*. From the collection of Thomas A. Franklin. Courtesy of the Steamship Historical Society, University of Baltimore library

Geoghegan, master. Sold 8/20/1891 ($50,000) to Md. & Va. Sold 1/30/1895 to Weems Steamboat Co. ($150,000 for three steamboats plus wharves and other property). Sold 10/24/1903 to Peter Hagen for $990 and thence 11/4/1903 to Herman Schell ¼. Sold 2/25/1905 to Henry Brown (Phila.) ½, Henry B. Massey ½; hp. Camden, N.J., for Delaware River Navigation Co., name changed to *Bristol*. Operated by Camden Shipbldg. Co., 1920; burned at Camden, N.J., 10/28/1923. Scrapped 3/31/1924.

Surprise (unnumbered)

Built 1816 Balto. by George Stiles, p.stbt.(w). First enrollment 8/14/1817, 90.0 × 16.8 × 6.7. Marestier: 28.65 meters (94.0) × 4.75 meters (15.6) × 1.22 meters (4.0). Tonnage 132. Used rotary engine patented by James Curtis (Balto.) and Royal Yeamans (Balto., Plymouth, N.Y., and Westfield, Mass.). Inner cylinder diameter 53 inches, outer cylinder diameter 59 inches; unit 19 inches long. Marestier: outside cylinder 1.8 me-

ters (4.9) diameter; annular spaces between inside and outside cylinders 0.15 meters (0.49); two end plates 0.48 meters (1.57) apart, stick shaft; paddlewheels 4.9 meters (16.0) diameter, 12 buckets 1.8 meters (5.9) long, 0.5–0.6 meters (1.6–2.0) wide; 18 rpm; steam pressure 73.5 p.s.i. Weight of engine 5 tons. Three iron boilers beneath engine, each with firebox, with flues through all three, uniting in a single flue above deck; total of 7 tons of water, total weight empty 8 tons. Cost as estimated by Stiles: boat and iron boilers 66,000 francs ($12,500), engine 44,000 francs ($8,250). Pine wood consumption 0.31 cords per hour; HP 60; ran 139 nautical miles in 16 hours (8.7 kts). Seen slowing to a dead stop off Annapolis 1821. Initial enrollment 8/14/1817; owners: George Stiles and John S. Stiles (son); George Stiles, master. Enrollment 4/1/1819; owner: George Stiles; George Weems, master. Enrollment 8/7/1820; owners: Christopher Daushon, Solomon Etting; George Weems, master. Enrollment 8/29/1825; owners: Robert

Top, Steamers *Essex* (*left*) and *St. Mary's* (*center*) at the Weems line pier, Light Street, Baltimore. *B. S. Ford* is at the *right*. From the Eldredge Collection. Courtesy of the Mariners' Museum. *Bottom*, Steamer *Wenonah*, serving as a transport, on the Pamunkey River, Virginia, during the Civil War. Courtesy of the National Archives and the Calvert Marine Museum

Taylor, agent, for Surprise Steamboat Co. (hp. Georgetown, D.C.). Last enrollment Georgetown 9/20/1826; document never surrendered; vessel apparently abandoned 1828. During operation by George Weems ran between Balto., Patx., Bay ldgs., Miles River, Chester River, and Annapolis.

Theodore Weems/St. Mary's (24908)

Built 1872 by William Skinner & Sons, Balto., to replace *George Weems* (engine from latter installed), p.stbt.(w). 196.2 (207.0 oa) × 30.0 (50.0 oa) × 9.45; 192.2 × 30.4 (30.9) × 9.4. GT 688.04; NT 535.50. NHP 1121. Resembled *George Weems* in design. Hurricane deck extended from stem to stern, thus affording shade on bow and stern and open air on upper deck for full length. Limited number of staterooms and second-class accommodations. Ran excursions Fair Haven; initiated excursions to Bay Ridge resort 1879; on Patx. route. Burned 9/10/1889 at Light St. wharf, damage $50,000. Rebuilt and renamed *St. Mary's;* ready for service 1890. Sold 2/11/1905 to MD & V. Burned 12/5/1907 off Benedict on Patx., total loss.

Wenonah (26064)

Built 1863–64 by J. S. Fardy & Bros., Balto. (designed by Charles Woodall) for Balto. & Susquehanna Steam Towing Co. to haul stones. p.stbt.(w). 194 (204 oa) × 33.0 × 10.0; 200.0 × 28.0 × 9.6; 192.0 × 35.0 × 10.0; 196.5 × 33.4 × 10.25. Tonnage 700: GT 644.43, NT 569.52, NHP 890. Civil War: entry 4/24/1864 ($375/day), discharged 4/25/1865, used as transport Balto.–Cape Hatteras. Ran from 1866 for Balto. & Susquehanna

Steamboat Co., Balto.–Frdbg. and Rappa. ldgs., owners: Jacob Tome ½, Mason L. Weems ½. Enrollment 2/5/1875; owners: Matilda S. Forbes (Balto.) ½, Georgeanna Williams (Calvert County) ½. Became passenger boat for Balto.–Frdbg. route. Laid up 1887. Spare boat 1892. Sold 12/27/1892 to John Rooney (Balto.) for $894, converted to a barge, dismantled 1892.

Westmoreland (80995)

Built 1883 by William Skinner & Sons, Balto., for Weems line, using engine from *Matilda*. p.stbt.(w). 199.3 (bp) or 210 (oa) × 32.3 (hull), or 52.0 (55.0 oa), × 12.5. *MVUS* carried length for 11 years in error as 119.0. GT 846.76, NT 673.0, IHP 875. Vertical beam engine; cylinder diameter 48 inches, stroke 132 inches. Crew 32. Ran Rappa. and Patx. Staterooms surrounding saloon on passenger deck arranged in two banks, inside and outside, connected by inside corridors; paneled saloon with dining room at forward end; gaslight from tankards connected to piping; running water in first-class staterooms. Carved eagle on paddleboxes and above pilothouse. Name on paddleboxes in Old English letters was first to use county names (Maryland or Virginia). Sold 1/26/1905 to MD & V. March–May 1909 outfitted by James Clark & Co. as excursion boat to replace *Love Point* for train connection to Rehobeth and Ocean City; operated by BC & A (PRR subsidiary). 1/4/1924 sold in bankruptcy proceedings of MD & V through Girard Trust Co. of Phila. and Charles A. Jording 8/9/1924 to Marine Sand and Gravel Co. Sold at auction 8/25/1932; dismantled 1/30/1925.

Steamer *Westmoreland* in Baltimore Harbor. Courtesy of Alice Forbes Bowie

Schedule Data for Steamboats of the Weems Line, 1819–1905

Explanation

The year-by-year schedules of the departures and arrivals of the Weems line steamboats reflect the advertising in Baltimore newspapers, primarily the Baltimore *Sun*, and occasionally other sources such as Baltimore City directories and advertising in the newspapers of other areas, for example, those of St. Mary's County, Fredericksburg, Virginia, and Easton, Maryland. Wherever possible, the data show the spring/summer and fall/winter schedules. In the early period, however, advertising was often sketchy and infrequent. Even in later periods, unexplained gaps appeared in the frequency of newspaper advertising, with the result that the data appear to be inconsistent or incomplete at certain times.

Until 1890, Weems line advertising generally identified each steamboat with its route; for example, in June 1889, on Tuesday *Westmoreland* left Baltimore for the Rappahannock River and Fredericksburg, and on Sunday she departed for landings on the Patuxent River to Bristol. On Wednesday and Saturday, *Theodore Weems* made the rounds of Patuxent landings as far as Benedict. Early in 1890, the linking of steamboat and route began to disappear, with some exceptions, from Weems notices, largely because the steamers often replaced each other on the routes. Throughout the data, as presented, the names of the steamboats operating during a particular season of a year will be shown in the heading for each date.

Where the notices permit, steamers will be identified with the route; otherwise, the assumption can be made that the steamers listed at a particular time were interchanged on the routes with some frequency even though certain steamers came to be known by the routes they served.

The abbreviations used are as follows: lv., leave; ret., return; whf., wharf; ldg., landing; R/T, round trip; whse., warehouse. Days of the week are abbreviated as follows: Su, Sunday; M, Monday; Tu, Tuesday; W, Wednesday; Th, Thursday; F, Friday; Sa, Saturday. Frequently used place names are abbreviated as follows: R., river; Patx., Patuxent; Rappa., Rappahannock; Potm., Potomac; FH, Fair Haven; PP, Plum Point; GR, Governors Run; Bndct., Benedict; Frdbg., Fredericksburg; Wash., Washington; Balto., Baltimore; Alex., Alexandria; Md., Maryland; Va., Virginia; HB, Herring Bay; Phila., Philadelphia.

The names of landings of wharves do not use an apostrophe (i.e., Pearson's or Parker's). Steamboat schedules and maps and early gazetteers and writers omitted the apostrophe, as did the large name boards attached to wharves and landings. Furthermore, omission of the apostrophe avoids the problem of dealing with an anachronism such as *Sollers's* or *Saunders's*, unacceptable in regional geography. Other place names, such as those of creeks or counties (i.e., St. Leonard's or St. Mary's) use the apostrophe. Both the appendixes and the chapters follow the above-stated practice.

Table B.1. Schedule Data for Weems Line

Year	Schedule
1819–25	*4/1/1819–6/14/1822 Surprise* Patx. ldgs.: *7/7/1819* lv. Balto. W 8 A.M. lv. Nottingham Sa 6 A.M. lv. Annapolis, Miles R. & Chester R.: lv. Balto. M & Th 6 A.M., ret. Tu & F 8 A.M. Centreville: lv. W & Sa, ret. same day. *1822–23 Eagle:* During session of legislature (exclusive of *Maryland,* W & Sa) lv. Light St. Su, Tu, Th 9 A.M.; Patx. ldgs "during residue [*sic*] of year." *1825* Patx ldgs. & Annapolis.
1827–30	*1827 Patuxent* Patx. ldgs.: *3/1828* Annapolis, Easton & Choptank R. ldgs. (during lay-up of *Maryland)* lv. Balto. Sa 7 A.M., Annapolis 11 A.M. for Castlehaven, Easton, ret. lv. Easton Su 7 A.M. *7/1828* Sassafras R. ldgs., Patx., Rappa. ldgs., *8/1/1828* Rappa. R.: lv. Balto. Tu 8 A.M.; arr. HB 1 P.M., Town Creek 5 P.M. lv. 6 P.M. for Rappa., Frdbg.; ret. arr. Town Creek Sa 6 A.M., HB 11 A.M.; thence Balto. *Summers 1828–29* excursions Frdbg. to Port Royal & Port Tobago. *10/1828–5/15/1830:* lv. Balto. W 8 A.M., ret. lv. Frdbg. Sa 8 A.M. via Port Royal, Tappahannock, Carter's Creek, Urbanna.
1830–42	*1830–41 Patuxent* to Salisbury & Whitehaven on Wicomico R.: lv. lower end Dugans Whf. M 5 P.M. *(1833–34* Tu 6 P.M.; *1838* F 4 P.M.), ret. W A.M. In *1830,* connections with Phila. boats of Union Line in Patapsco R. Patx. ldgs.: lv. Th 7 A.M. *(1833–34* F 6 A.M.) to Bndct. via Town Creek, HB, other ldgs., ret. Su (James Harwood, agent, 7 Light St.); *7/1838:* lv. Md. Whf. Tu 6 A.M. for Bndct. F 4 P.M., Su 7:30 A.M. FH only *8/7/1833–10/1834* Rappa. R.: lv. Balto. W 6 A.M., lv. Frdbg. Sa 6 A.M. *(3/1/1834:* lv. Balto. Th, Frdbg. Su.)
1845–49	*7/1845 Planter* Patx. ldgs.: lv. Balto. W & Sa 7 A.M. for Green Ldg.; *Patuxent* lv. Balto. for FH. *1–12/1847 Planter* Rappa. R. ldgs. (Balto–Frdbg.); *8/6–20/1847* excursions F P.M. Frdbg.–Port Royal; *1847–49 Planter* Patx. ldgs.: lv. Md. Whf. W 7 A.M. to Green Ldg.; *Patuxent* Sa 7 A.M. same route. *1/1/1848 Planter* lv. Balto. W midnight for Norfolk.
1853–54	*Planter* Patx. ldgs.: lv. Dugans Whf. W 6 A.M., ret. lv. Bndct. Sa A.M.; *Patuxent:* lv. Sa via FH, ret. Bndct. W.
1855–56	*Patuxent* Patx. ldgs.: lv. Dugans Whf. Sa 6 A.M. via FH to Hills Ldg., ret. lv. Tu 6 A.M. via Bndct., lv. W 6 A.M. for Balto. *Planter* Patx. ldgs.: same route lv. W 6 A.M. Hills Ldg. F 6 A.M. *Mary Washington* Rappa. R. (although sold *12/12/1854* to Mason L. & Theodore Weems, advertising under Md. & Va. Steam Packet Co. continued *1855):* lv. Hughes Quay F P.M. Frdbg.). *Summer 1855: Patuxent* to FH only M & Sa, *Mary Washington* Patx. ldgs.: lv. Balto. W 6 A.M. to Hills Ldg.
1857–61	*Patuxent* Patx. ldgs.: lv. Dugans Whf. Sa 6 A.M. for FH, ret. same day; lv. Tu 6 A.M. to Lyons Creek ldg.; lv. W to Bndct., ret. Th via FH; *Planter* lv. Sa 6 A.M. via PP to Hills Ldg., ret. lv. Tu 6 A.M. to Bndct., lv. W 6 A.M. via PP for Balto.; *Mary Washington* lv. W 6 A.M. via PP to Hills Ldg., ret. lv. F 6 A.M. to Bndct., lv. Sa 6 A.M. via PP to Balto. *Planter* on charter part of year to Nor-

(Continued)

231

Table B.1. (Continued)

Year	Schedule
	folk; 7/1859: on charter, York, East, Great Wicomico R.; 1861: Potm. R. to Wash.; 7/1860: *Planter & George Weems* lv. Sa & W 6 A.M. for FH. 1861 *Patuxent, Planter & Mary Washington* seized by USQMD (see Appendix A).
1863	7/29/1863 Patx. ldgs.: *George Weems* lv. W 6 A.M. to Hills Ldg. 8/1/1863: *Planter* lv. Sa 6 A.M. to Hills Ldg. (short-lived; both boats, discharged by USQMD, were seized again).

Year	Schedule	
	Patuxent Route	Rappahannock Route
1865–66	*George Weems* lv. Balto. W 6 A.M. via FH, PP to Hills Ldg.; *Planter* lv. Sa same route; *Matilda* lv. F same route.	*Wenonah* (owned by M. L. Weems & Jacob Tome) lv. foot South St. Su 4 P.M. to Frdbg.; ret. lv. Tu 4 A.M., arr. Balto. W A.M..
1867–68	*George Weems* lv. 1 Tobacco Whse. F 6 A.M. via FH, PP to Hills Ldg., ret. M A.M. to Bndct.; lv. Tu 8 A.M. to Balto. *Planter* W & Sa 6 A.M. to Bndct.; Summer 1868: *George Weems*, 33 excursions to Chester R. & Tred Avon R.	*Wenonah* lv. Su 5 P.M., ret. lv. Frdbg. M 8 P.M. on arr. Richmond train.
1868–69	*Mary Washington* lv. 1 Tobacco Whse. Th 11 P.M. to Hills Ldg., ret. lv. M A.M. for Nottingham; lv. Tu 5 A.M.; calling at ldgs. below Bndct., passengers only. *Planter* lv. M, W & Sa 6:30 A.M. to Bndct., FH, PP, both ways.	*Wenonah* lv. foot Spears Whf. Tu 4 P.M.; ret. lv. Frdbg. Th 8 P.M. on arr. Richmond train. *Matilda* lv. F, ret. M, same route. (Note: *George Weems*, excursions to FH, Bruff's Island, charters to Susquehanna, Chester, Little Choptank, Tred Avon. *Mary Washington & Matilda* on excursions.)
1870	*Planter* lv. 1 Tobacco Whse. W & Sa 6:30 A.M. via FH, PP to Bndct., ret. lv. Th & M 6 A.M. *Mary Washington* Th 11 P.M. to Hills Ldg; ret. lv. M to Nottingham, lv. Tu 5 A.M. Balto.	*Matilda* lv. foot Spears Whf. Tu 4 P.M., ret. lv. Frdbg. Th at high water. *Wenonah* lv. F 4 P.M., ret. lv. Frdbg. M P.M. at high water.
1871	*George Weems* lv. Pier 8 Light St., W & Sa 7 A.M. via FH, PP, ldgs. to Bndct., ret. lv. Th & M 6 A.M. *Mary Washington* lv. Th 10 P.M. to Hills Ldg.; ret. lv. M to Nottingham, lv. Tu 5 A.M. Balto. *Matilda* excursions FH.	*Matilda* lv. foot Spears Whf. F 4 P.M., ret. lv. Frdbg. M 8 P.M. *Wenonah* lv. Tu 4 P.M., ret. lv. Frdbg. Th 8 P.M.

1872–74	Planter lv. Pier 8 Light St. W & Sa 6:30 A.M. via FH, PP, GR to Bndct., ret. lv. Th & M 6 A.M. Mary Washington lv. Th 10 P.M. to Hills Ldg., ret. to Nottingham M, lv. Tu 5 A.M. 9/18/1872: Theodore Weems replaced Mary Washington same route.	*Matilda, Wenonah, same schedule as 1871.*
1875	Planter & Mary Washington same as 1874, except lv. Nottingham below Bndct. for passengers only. 6/21/1875: Wenonah, Theodore Weems, Matilda, excursions to FH, lv. Pier 8 Light St., Wenonah, M 8:30 A.M.; Theodore Weems, M 2 P.M., Tu 8:30 A.M., W 8:30 A.M., Th 2 P.M., F 8:30 A.M., Sa 2 P.M.: Matilda Th 8:30 A.M., ret. 8 & 10:30 P.M. R/T $1; children & servants 50¢.	*Matilda, Wenonah had sketchy schedules, generally same as 1871–74. (Note: Wenonah, Theodore Weems, & Matilda available for charter only up to 6/20/1875; Planter, Mary Washington during June & July).*
1876	Wenonah lv. Balto. Su 9 P.M. for Hills Ldg.; lv. W. Planter lv. W & Sa to Bdnct. 6/19/1876: excursions FH as in summer 1875. Added in ads: boats that lv. 8:30 A.M. remain at FH 4 h.; those that lv. at 2 P.M. remain 1 or 2 h. Prof. Itzel's Band at FH & on board.	*Matilda lv. Pie– 9 Light St. Tu 4:30 P.M., ret. lv. Frdbg. Th 8 P.M., Wenonah lv. F 4:30 P.M., ret. lv. Frdbg. M 8 P.M.*
1878	Mary Washington lv. Pier 8 F 6:30 A.M. via FH, PP, GR, ldgs. (except Parkers, Planters) for Hills Ldg.; ret. lv. M for Trent Hall, lv. Tu 8 A.M. to Balto. 5/23/1878: Planter lv. Sa & W 6:30 A.M. via FH, PP, GR, to Bndct.; lv. M & Th 6 A.M. Wenonah lv. Su 9 P.M. direct to Hills Ldg., ret. lv. Bristol M noon (last entry for Hills Ldg.).	*Matilda lv. Pie– 9 F 4 P.M., ret. lv. Frdbg. M 5 P.M. for Leedstown, lv. Tu A.M. to Balto. 5/23/1878 Wenonah lv. Tu 4:30 P.M., ret. lv. Frdbg. M 5 P.M., Matilda lv. F, ret. M.*
1880	1/9/1880: Mary Washington lv. Pier 8 & Sa 6:30 A.M. via FH, PP, GR, ldgs. to Bristol (except Planters, Abells, Parkers, Williams); ret. lv. M 9 A.M., Trent Hall Tu 7 A.M. 6/3/1880: Planter lv. Pier 8 Sa & W 6 A.M. via FH, PP, GR, ldgs. to Bndct.; ret. lv. M & Th 6 A.M., Millstone Ldg. 10 A.M., PP 12:30 P.M., FH 2 P.M. Wenonah lv. Su 9 P.M. direct to Bristol, ret. lv. M noon. 7/1880: Planter lv. Tu, Th & Sa 7 A.M. for ldgs. to St. Leonards. Mary Washington lv. Su & W 10 P.M. to Bristol.	*1/9/1880: Theodore Weems lv. Pier 9 Sa 4:30 P.M., ret. lv. Frdbg. M 4 P.M., Saunders Whf. Tu 5 A.M.* *6/3/1880: Theodore Weems & Wenonah lv. F & Tu 4:30 P.M., ret. lv. Frdbg. M & Th P.M. (Note: with opening of Bay Ridge resort, at the mouth of the Severn R., Theodore Weems made excursions 9 A.M. & 4 P.M. daily from Pier 8, fare 5¢. M & F stop at Md. Sttt. Whf., Annapolis, music on board).*

(Continued)

Table B.1. (Continued)

Year	Patuxent Route	Schedule	Rappahannock Route
1881	*1/21/1881: Mary Washington* lv. Pier 8 F 6:30 A.M. via FH, PP, GR, ldgs. (except Abells, Planters); ret. lv. M A.M., lv. Trent Hall Tu 6 A.M. *6/4/1881: Wenonah* lv. W & Sa 6:30 À.M. via FH, PP, GR, ldgs. to Bndct.; ret. lv. M & Th 6 A.M. *Theodore Weems* lv. Su 9 P.M. for Bristol direct, lv. M noon for ldgs. below for passenger only.		*1/21/1881: Theodore Weems* lv. Pier 9 F 4:30 P.M., ret. lv. Frdbg. M 4 P.M., Leedstown Tu 5 A.M. *6/4/1881: Theodore Weems & Matilda* lv. Tu & F 4:30 P.M., ret. lv. Frdbg. M & Th P.M. (Note: *Theodore Weems* to Bay Ridge, 1880 schedule.)
1882	*3/4/1882: Wenonah* lv. Pier 8 W & Sa 6:30 A.M. via FH, PP, GR, ldgs. to Bndct.; lv. M & Th 6 A.M. *Theodore Weems* lv. Su 9 P.M. direct to Bristol; ret. lv. M noon, ldgs. below for passengers only. (*Theodore Weems* summer excursions to FH & Bay Ridge daily.)		*3/4/1882: Mason L. Weems* lv. Pier 9 W 4:30 P.M. via Mill Creek, River View, Urbanna, Monaskon, Sharps, Bowlers, Water View, Wares, to Tappahannock; lv. Th 10 A.M. via above ldgs. & Millenbeck, Merry Point, Carter's Creek. *Theodore Weems, Mason L. Weems*, lv. T & F 4:30 P.M. to Frdbg.; ret. lv. M & Th P.M.
1883	*1/6/1883: Mary Washington* lv. Pier 8 F 6:30 A.M. via FH, PP, GR to Bristol; ret. lv. M A.M. to Jones Whf., lv. Tu 7 A.M. *3/2/1883:* same as 3/4/1882. *7/1883: Wenonah* lv. T, Th & Sa 6:30 A.M. ldgs. to St. Leonards. *Mary Washington* lv. 11 P.M. to Bristol. (*Theodore Weems*; summer excursions to FH & Bay Ridge daily. See 1880 schedule.)		*1/6/1883: Theodore Weems* lv. Pier 9 F 4:30 P.M., ret. lv. Frdbg. M P.M. high water to Leedstown, lv. T 6 A.M. *3/2/1883:* same as 3/4/1882. *9/20/1883: Mason L. Weems & Westmoreland* lv. T & F for Frdbg. *10/16/1883: Mary Washington* lv. Frdbg. T & F 8 A.M. (after arrival morning trains), Port Royal 12:30 P.M., Tappahannock 4:30 P.M., Urbanna 7 P.M., other ldgs., arr. Norfolk W & Sa A.M., ret. lv. Old Dominion SS Co. Whf. Su & W 8 P.M., Urbanna 7 A.M., Tappahannock 11 A.M., Port Royal 3 P.M., arr. Frdbg. for evening trains N & S (Norfolk connections with Old Dominion SS Co. for NY, passage 1st cl $1.50, 2nd cl $1.00).
1884	*1/4/1884: Theodore Weems* lv. Pier 8 Sa 6:30 A.M. via FH, PP & GR, ldgs. to St. Leonards, ret. lv. M Tu 7:30 A.M. Lv. Tu 6:30 A.M. via FH, PP, GR, ldgs. to Bristol; lv. W noon, Bndct.		*1/4/1884: Westmoreland* lv. Pier 9 F 4:30 P.M., ret. lv. Frdbg. M 4 P.M., Leedstown Tu 5 A.M. Lv. W 4:30 P.M., ret. lv. Tappahannock Th 10 A.M. *6/8/1884: Mason L. Weems* lv. W

Th 5:30 A.M. 6/8/1884: lv. W & Sa to Bndct.; lv. Bndct. M & Th 5:30 A.M. (Summer excursions to FH, Bay Ridge; see earlier entries.) *Westmoreland* lv. Su 4 P.M. direct to Bristol, ret. lv. M noon; ldgs. below for passengers only.

4:30 P.M., lv. Tappahannock Th 10 A.M. *Westmoreland* lv. Tu 4:30 P.M., lv. Frdbg. Th P.M.

1885

1/2/1885: *Theodore Weems* lv. F 6:30 A.M. (ice permitting) via FH, PP, GR, ldgs. to Bristol; ret. lv. M 10 A.M., Bndct. T 5:30 A.M. (Summer excursions to FH & Bay Ridge; see earlier entries.) 6/27/1885: lv. W & Su 6:30 A.M. via PP, GR, ldgs. to Bndct.; ret. M & Th 5:30 A.M. *Westmoreland* (same as 6/8/1884.)

1/2/1885: *Westm-oreland,* same as 1/4/1884. 3/6/1885: add *Mason L. Weems* for Tu & F schedule as above. *Mary Washington,* same as 3/6/1883. 6/27/1885: same as 10/16/1383. 10/6/1885: *Essex* lv. Frdbg. Tu & F 9 A.M. ldgs. to Norfolk, arr. W & Sa A.M.; ret. lv. Balto Stm. Packet Co. Whf. W & Su 7 P.M., arr. Frdbg. M & Th connecting with evening trains N & S (Norfolk connections with Old Dominion SS Co. for NY) (Excursions to Norfolk R/T $1.50, statrm $1.)

1886

1/4/1886: *Theodore Weems,* same as 1/2/1885. 6/26/1886: same as 6/27/1885. *Westmoreland,* same as 6/8/1884 & 6/27/1885.

1/4/1886: *Westmoreland,* same as 1/4/1884. 6/26/1886: *Mason L. Weems,* same as 6/8/1884. *Westmoreland & Mason L. Weems* lv. Tu 4:30 P.M., lv. Frdbg. M & Th P.M. *Essex,* same as 10/6/1885.

1887

6/4/1887: *Wenonah* lv. Tu, Th & Sa 7 A.M. via FH, PP, GR, ldgs. to Bndct.; ret. lv. M, W, F 6:30 A.M. (*Theodore Weems,* summer excursions FH & Bay Ridge; see earlier entries.) *Westmoreland,* same as 1/8/1884 except lv. 9 P.M.

Same schedule as 1886.

1888

Same schedule as 1887, except *Wenonah* is replaced by *Theodore Weems.*

Same schedule as 1887.

1889

1/14/1889: *Theodore Weems* lv. Pier 8 F 7 A.M. via FH, PP, GR, ldgs.; ret. Tu (Summer excursions FH & Bay Ridge; see earlier entries.) 6/8/1889: lv. W & Sa 6:30 A.M. via FH, PP, GR, ldgs. to Bndct.; ret. lv. M & Th 5:30 A.M. *Westmoreland* lv. Su 9 P.M. direct to Bristol, ret. lv. M noon; ldgs. below for passengers only.

1/14/1889: *Westmoreland* lv. F 4:30 P.M., lv. Frdbg. W A.M. to Naylors, lv. W 4:30 P.M. 6/8/1889: *Mason L. Weems* lv. W 4:30 P.M. ldgs. to Naylors, ret. lv. Tappahannock Th 10 A.M. *Westmoreland & Mason L. Weems* lv. Tu & F 4:30 P.M., ret. lv. Frdbg. M & Th P.M. 10/20/1889: *Essex* lv. Balto. Stm. Packet Co. Whf. Norfolk Su & W 7 P.M. via ldgs. to Frdbg.; lv. Urbanna 5 A.M., Port Royal 12 noon; lv. Frdbg. Tu & F 7 A.M., Port Royal 9:3C A.M., Tappahannock 2 P.M.; arr. Norfolk Sa & W A.M.

(Continued)

Table B.1. (Continued)

Year	Schedule	
	Patuxent Route	Rappahannock Route
1890	*St. Mary's* & *Westmoreland* *2/8/1890:* lv. Pier 8 W & Sa 7 A.M. via FH, PP, GR, ldgs. to Bndct.; Bndct. to Bristol M; lv. Trent Hall Tu & Th 6 A.M. *6/7/1890:* lv. Sa 7 A.M. via FH, PP, GR, ldgs. Lv. Su & W 11 P.M. ldgs. direct.	*St. Mary's* & *Westmoreland* *2/8/1890:* lv. F 4:30 P.M. to Frdbg. Lv. W 4:30 P.M. to Naylors. *6/7/1890:* lv. Tu & F 4:30 P.M. to Frdbg. Lv. Su 4:30 P.M. to Naylor's except Weems, Carter's Creek, Jones. Lv. W 4:30 P.M. to Naylors, ldgs. except Bay Port, Millenbeck, Merry Point. *9/5/1890: Richmond* & *Westmoreland* lv. Tu & F 4:30 P.M. to Frdbg., ret. lv. M & Th 4 P.M. tide permitting, Leedstown Tu & F 5 A.M. Lv. W 4:30 P.M. to Naylors, ldgs. except Bay Port, ret. lv. Naylors Th 9:30 A.M. *Essex,* same as 10/20/1889.
1891	*St. Mary's, Westmoreland* & *Richmond* *2/20/1890:* same as 2/8/1890, except lv. Bristol Tu & Th 5:30 A.M. *5/30/1891:* lv. Pier 8 W & Sa 6:30 A.M. via FH, PP, GR, ldgs. to Bndct. Lv. Pier 8 Su 9 P.M. direct to Bristol.	*St. Mary's, Westmoreland* & *Richmond* *2/20/1890:* same as 2/8/1890. Pier 2 used, Rappa. route. *6/7/1891:* lv. Pier 2 Tu & F 4:30 P.M. to Frdbg.; ret. lv. M & Th 4 P.M. tide permitting, Leedstown Tu & F 4:30 A.M. Lv. W 4:30 P.M. to Naylors, ldgs. except Bay Port; ret. lv. Th 9:30 A.M. *Essex,* same as 10/20/1889.
1892	Same as 1891. (*Wenonah* as spare used for summer harvest.)	Same as 1891.
1893	*1/14/1893: St. Mary's* & *Westmoreland* lv. Pier 8 W & Sa 7 A.M. via FH, PP, GR, ldgs. to Bndct.; to Bristol & ret. M, lv. Bndct. Tu & Th 5:30 A.M. Lv. Su 9 P.M. direct to Bristol.	*1/14/1893: Lancaster* & *Richmond* lv. Pier 2 W & F 4:30 P.M., W to Tappahannock, F to Frdbg. *2/28/1893:* same except ret. lv. Frdbg. M & Th 4 P.M., Leedstown T & F 4:30 A.M., W trip to Naylors, ldgs. except Bay Port, ret. lv. Th 9:30 A.M. *3/2/1893: Essex* lv. Balto. Stm. Packet Co. Whf. Norfolk Tu & F 7 P.M., Urbanna W & Sa 4:30 A.M., Tappahannock 8:30 A.M., Port Royal noon; ret. lv. Frdbg. M & Th 7 A.M., Port Royal 10 A.M., Tappahannock 2 P.M., Urbanna 7 P.M.; arr. Norfolk Tu & F A.M. *4/2/1893:* special trips Tappahannock/Balto. M & W 10 A.M., ldgs. except Millenbeck, Merry Point; ret. lv. Balto. Sa & T 4:30 P.M.

Year	Schedule		
	Patuxent Route	Potomac Route	Rapphannock Route
1894	1/20/1894: *St. Mary's & Westmoreland* lv. Pier 8 W & Sa 6:30 A.M. via FH, PP, GR, ldgs. to Bndct.; W trip going on to Bristol; ret. Tu & Th 7 P.M. 6/9/1894: same as 1/20/1894.		1/20/1894: *Lancaster & Richmond* lv. F 4:30 P.M. to Frdbg., lv. Su, Tu, W, & Th 4:30 P.M. to Tappahannock. 6/9/1894: same except Su trip to Naylors.
1895	1/12/1895: *St. Mary's & Westmoreland*, same as 1/20/1894 except Sa trip extended to Bristol. 3/8/1895: lv. W & Sa 6:30 A.M. via FH, PP, GR, ldgs. to Bndct.; lv. Su 9 P.M. direct to Bristol.	2/22/1895: *Potomac* lv. Pier 8 this day 5:30 A.M. to Leonardtown. 3/8/1895: *Potomac, Sue & John E. Tygert* lv. F via ldgs. to Wash., lv. 6 P.M. to Stones. Ret. lv. Wash. Su 4 P.M. 6/8/1895: lv. Pier 9 Su & W 6 P.M. via ldgs. to Wash., ret. lv. 7th St. Wash. W, M & Tu 6 P.M. (Su 4 P.M.). Lv. Pier 9 Tu 5 P.M. ldgs. to Stones. 12/27/1895: *Potomac* lv. Pier 9 Tu & F 5 P.M. via lower ldgs.[a] F only via upper ldgs.[b] Ret. lv. Wash. Su 1 P.M. all ldgs., lv. Leonardtown M & Th 6 A.M., Kinsale noon, Bacons 5:30 P.M., arr. Balto T & F A.M.	1/10/1895: *Essex* lv. Pier 2 Tu & Th 2:30 P.M. to Tappahannock, ret. lv. M & W 9:30 A.M., ldgs. except Millenbeck, Merry Point, Bay Port; ret. lv. Tappahannock M & W 9:30 A.M. Lv. Tappahannock F noon ldgs., arr. Norfolk Sa 5 A.M., ret. lv. Balto. Stm. Packet Co. Whf. 9 A.M., ldgs. below Tappahannock. 1/4/1895: *Richmond* lv. Pier 2 F 4:30 P.M. to Frdbg., ret. lv. M 4 P.M., Leedstown Tu 4:30 A.M. Lv. Pier 2 W 4:30 P.M. to Tappahannock, ldgs. except Bay Port; ret. lv. Th 5:30 A.M. 1/12/1895: *Lancaster* replaced *Richmond* above. 3/8/1895: lv. Tu & F 4:30 P.M. to Frdbg.; lv. W 4:30 P.M. to Naylors. 12/24/1895: same as 1/4/1895 except to Naylors, ret. lv. Th 9 A.M. *Essex*; same as 1/10/1895.
1896–97	*St. Mary's, Westmoreland, Potomac, Sue, John E. Tygert, Lancaster, Richmond, Essex*		
	1/14/1896: lv. Pier 8 W & Sa 6:30 A.M. via FH, PP, Dares, GR, ldgs. to Bndct.; ret. Tu, Th & Sa direct to Bristol. 6/13/1896: same except Su & W lv. 6 P.M. direct to Bristol.	1/14/1896: lv. Pier 9 F 5 P.M. to Wash. Lv. Tu 5 P.M. to Stone's. 6/13/1896: lv. W & F 5 P.M. to Wash., Tu to Stones. Ret. lv. Su & M 4 P.M. Lv. Wash. F 4 P.M., ldgs. to Mil-	1/14/1896: lv. Pier 2 F 4:30 P.M. to Frdbg.; Lv. Tu & Th 2:30 P.M. to Tappahannock; lv. W 4:30 P.M. to Naylors. 6/13/1896: lv. T & F 4:30 P.M. to Frdbg.; lv. Su 2:30 P.M., W 4:30 P.M. to Naylor's. 12/25/1896: *Richmond* lv. F 4:30 P.M. to Frdbg., ret. lv. M 3 P.M. (tide permitting) to Leedstown, lv. Tu 4:30 A.M. Lv. 4:30 P.M. to Naylors, ldgs. except Bay Port;

(Continued)

Table B.1. (Continued)

Year	Schedule		
	Patuxent Route	Potomac Route	Rappahannock Route
		lers, ret. lv. Su 4 A.M., arr. Wash. Su P.M.	ret. lv. Th 9 A.M. *Essex* lv. Tu 2:30 P.M., F 4:30 P.M., to Tappahannock; ret. lv. M & W 9:30 A.M., ldgs. except Millenbeck, Merry Point, Bay Port.
1898	*St. Mary's & Westmoreland* 1/8/1898: lv. Pier 8 W & Sa 6:30 A.M. via FH, PP, Dares, GR, ldgs. to Bndct., trip extended M to Bristol. 6/4/1898: same, except lv. Su & W 6 P.M. direct to Bristol.	*Potomac & Sue* 1/8/1898: lv. Pier 9 Tu 5 P.M., ldgs. to Wash. Lv. Sa 5 P.M., ldgs. to Stones. 6/4/1898: lv. Tu & F 5 P.M., ldgs. to Wash. Lv. Sa 5 P.M. ldgs. to Stones.	*Lancaster & Richmond* 1/8/1898: lv. Pier 2 daily except Sa & Su 4:30 P.M. to Tappahannock; lv. Su 2:30 P.M. to Tappahannock. 6/4/1898: lv. Tu & F 4:30 P.M. to Frdbg. Lv. W & Th 4:30 P.M. to Tappahannock. 6/27/1898: *Essex* lv. Tappahannock Tu noon to Norfolk; ret. lv. W 4 P.M., ldgs. to Frdbg.
1899	*St. Mary's & Westmoreland* 1/14/1899: lv. Pier 8 W & Sa 6:30 A.M. via FH, PP, Dares, GR, ldgs. to Bndct. Sa trip extended M to Bristol. 6/10/1899: lv. Pier 8 W & Sa via FH, Chesapeake Beach, PP, Dares, GR, ldgs. to Bndct; lv. Su 7 P.M. direct to Bristol.	*Potomac & Sue* 1/14/1899: lv. Pier 9 Tu 5 P.M. to Wash. Lv. Sa 5 P.M. to Stones. Tu only for Lancaster, Burhans, Riverside, Liverpool Point, Glymont, Alex., Wash. Ret. lv. 7th St. Whf. 7 P.M., arr. Balto. Tu & Sa A.M. 3/10/1899: same as 1/14/1899. 6/10/1899: same as 1/14/1899.	*Lancaster, Richmond & Essex* 1/3/1899: lv. Pier 2 M–F 4:30 P.M., Su 2:30 P.M. to Tappahannock, ldgs. except Weems, Irvington, Millenbeck, Merry Point, Bay Port (stop only Sa & Tu A.M.); ret. lv. T & Sa 8 A.M., M, W, Th & F 9 A.M., ldgs. except Millenbeck, Merry Point (stops made only Tu, Th & Sa; Bay Port, Tu & Sa). Trip F extended to Frdbg.; ret. lv. M & F 2:30 P.M. to Leedstown; lv. Tu & Sa 4:30 A.M. *Essex* lv. Tappahannock Tu noon to Norfolk; ret. lv. W 4 P.M. to Frdbg.; lv. Tappahannock Th 8 A.M. 3/10/1899: lv. Tu & F 4 P.M. to Frdbg., ret. lv. M & Th 2:30 P.M. to Leedstown, lv. Tu & F 4 A.M. Lv. Balto. W 4:30 P.M. to Naylors, ldgs. except Bay Port; ret. lv. Th 8 A.M. Lv. Balto. Th 4 P.M. to Tappahannock; ret. lv. M A.M. *Essex*, same as 1/3/1899 except lv. F noon, ret. lv. Norfolk Sa 6 P.M. 6/10/1899: same as 3/10/1899. 12/31/1899: lv. Pier 2 daily except Sa & Sun 4:30 P.M., Sun 2:30 P.M. to Tappahannock, extending F trip to Frdbg. Lv. Tu & Sa to Bay Port, call Tu & Sa upriver at Millenbeck, Merry Point; Tu, Th & Sa downriver at Weems, Irvington call Sa & Tu. Lv. Tap-

1900

St. Mary's & Westmoreland
1/6/1900: lv. Pier 8 W & Sa 6:30 A.M. via FH, Chesapeake Beach, PP, Dares, GR, ldgs. to Bndct.; Sa trip extended to Bristol. 6/2/1900: same as above except lv. Su 7 P.M. direct to Bristol.

Potomac, Sue & Northumberland
1/6/1900: lv. Pier 9 Tu 5 P.M. to Wash.; lv. Sa 5 P.M. ldgs. to Stones. 6/2/1900: same as above. 7/4/1900: *Potomac & Northumberland* lv. Pier 9 Tu, Th & Sa 5 P.M. ldgs. to Wash.; ret. lv. Th, Su & Tu 4 P.M. to Leonardtown; lv. M, W & F 7 A.M.

pahannock Tu & Sa 8 A.M., M, W, Th & F 9 A.M. Lv. Tappahannock to Norfolk Tu & F noon; ret. lv. W & Sa 4 P.M. to Frdbg. Lv. Frdbg. M & F 2:30 P.M. to Leedstown; lv. Tu & Sa 4:30 A.M. to Balto.

Lancaster, Richmond & Essex
3/9/1900: *Express* lv. Tappahannock F noon to Norfolk, ret. lv. Sa 6 P.M. *Essex* (resumes route). *Lancaster & Richmond* lv. Pier 2 Tu & F 4:30 P.M. to Frdbg., ret. lv. M & Th 2:30 P.M. (tide permitting), Leedstown Tu & F 4:30 A.M. Lv. Balto. W 4:30 P.M. to Naylors, ret. lv. Th 8:30 A.M. Lv. Balto. Th 4:30 P.M. to Tappahannock, ldgs. except Bay Port, Millenbeck, Merry Point, ret. lv. M 8 A.M. 6/2/1900: lv. Tu & F 4:30 P.M. to Frdbg. Lv. W & Th 4:30 P.M. to Tappahannock. 7/4/1900: lv. Balto. Tu & F 4:30 P.M. to Frdbg.; ret. lv. M & Th 2:30 P.M. (tide permitting), Leedstown 4:30 A.M. Lv. Balto. W 4:30 P.M. to Naylors, ldgs. except Bay Port; ret. lv. Th 8:30 A.M. Lv. Balto. Th 4:30 P.M. Su 2:30 P.M. to Tappahannock; ret. lv. M 9 A.M. *Essex* lv. Norfolk Su 4 P.M. to Frdbg., arr. M 5 P.M., ret. lv. Tappahannock F noon (Frdbg. pass. & frt. transferred from Balto. boat F P.M. to *Essex*).

1901

1/12/1901: same as 11/6/1900 except no calls at Chesapeake Beach. 6/1/1901: lv. Pier 8 W & Sa 6:30 A.M. via FH, PP, Dares, GR, ldgs. to Bndct. Lv. Su 8 P.M. to Bristol.

1/12/1901: same as 1/6/1900. 3/26/1901: lv. Tu, Th, Sa 5 P.M. ldgs. to Wash., ret. lv. Th, Su & Tu 4 P.M. to Leonardtown, lv. 6 A.M. 6/1/1901: same as 3/26/1901. 12/24/1901: lv. Pier 9 Tu & Sa 5 P.M. via ldgs. lower river; Tu via ldgs. to Leonardtown to Wash. Ret. lv. Wash. Th 4 P.M., Leonardtown M & F 6 A.M.

1/12/1901: lv. Pier 2 daily except Sa 4:30 P.M., Su 2:30 P.M. to Tappahannock. 3/20/1901: lv. Tu & F 4:30 P.M. to Frdbg.; ret. lv. M & Th 2:30 P.M. (tide permitting). Leedstown Tu & F 4:30 P.M. Lv. Balto. W & Th 4:30 P.M. to Tappahannock, ldgs. except Bay Port; ret. lv. M & Th 8 A.M. *Essex* lv. Tappahannock F 1 P.M. to Norfolk; ret. lv. Sa 6 P.M. 6/30/1901: lv. Tu & F 4:30 P.M. to Tappahannock, ldgs. except Irvington, Weems, Morans, Merry Point, Millenbeck, Bay Port. Lv. Th 4:30 P.M., Su 2:30 P.M. to Tappahannock, ldgs. except Bay Port, Millenbeck, Merry Point, Morans. Lv. Tappahannock to Balto. M, Tu, W & F 8 A.M., Th 9 A.M., direct W 4 P.M.; for Frdbg. M 8 A.M., W noon, Sa 1 P.M.; for Norfolk F 1 P.M., ret. lv. Norfolk Su 3 P.M. to Frdbg.; lv. Frdbg. to Balto. ldgs. M & Th 2 P.M.; lv. Tap-

(Continued)

Table B.1. (Continued)

Year	Patuxent Route	Potomac Route	Schedule Rappahannock Route
			pahannock W 7 A.M. 12/29/1901: lv. daily (except Sa) 4:30 P.M., Su 2:30 P.M., ldgs. to Tappahannock, extending F to Frdbg.; Tu & Sa lv. Bay Port to Balto. (inbound call at Millenbeck, Merry Point Tu & Sa; outbound M, Tu & Sa; call at Weems, Irvington Sa & M). Lv. Tappahannock, ldgs. to Balto. Tu & Sa 8 A.M., M, W, Th & F 9 A.M. Lv. Tappahannock to Norfolk Tu 2 P.M., ret. lv. W 4 P.M. to Frdbg.; lv. Tappahannock Th 9 A.M. Lv. Frdbg. M & F 2 P.M. to Leedstown; lv. Tu & Sa 4:30 A.M.
1902	*St. Mary's & Westmoreland* 1/4/1902: same as 1/12/1901. 12/16/1902: lv. Pier 8 W & Sa 6:30 A.M. via FH, PP, Dares, GR, ldgs. to Bndct. Lv. Su & Th 8 P.M. direct to Bristol.	*Potomac & Sue* 1/4/1902: lv. Pier 9 Tu 5 P.M., ldgs. to Wash. Lv. Sa 5 P.M. ldgs. to Stones. 6/3/1902: lv. Pier 9 Tu, Th & Sa 5 P.M., ldgs. to Wash.; ret. lv. 7th St. Whf. Th, Su, Tu 4 P.M. to Leonardtown; lv. 6 A.M. to Balto., arr. following A.M. 12/16/1902: same as 1/4/1902. 12/23/1903: same as above.	*Lancaster, Essex & Calvert* (Note: *Calvert* began operations 3/1902, temporarily replacing *Westmoreland* on Patx. route, then *Richmond* on Rappa. route, and then settled into routine service on Potm. route.) 1/4/1902: lv. Pier 2 daily except Sa & Su 4:30 P.M., ldgs. to Frdbg. Lv. Su 2:30 P.M. to Tappahannock. 3/18/1902: lv. Tu & F 4:30 P.M. ldgs. to Frdbg.; ret. lv. M & Th 2:30 P.M., Leedstown T & F 4:30 A.M. Lv. Balto. W & Th 4:30 P.M. to Tappahannock, ldgs. except Bay Port; ret. lv. M 8 A.M., W & Th 9 A.M. (outbound W will not call in Corotoman R.) Lv. Tappahannock to Norfolk F, ret. lv. Sa 6 P.M. 7/20/1902: lv. Pier 2 Tu & F 4:30 P.M., ldgs. to Frdbg. Lv. W 4:30 P.M., ldgs. to Tappahannock except Irvington, Weems, Morans, Merry Point, Ottomans, Millenbeck, Bay Port. Lv. 4:30 P.M. Su 2:30 P.M., ldgs. to Tappahannock except Bay Port, Millenbeck, Merry Point, Ottomans, Morans. Lv. Tappahannock to Balto. M, Tu & F 8 A.M., Th 9 A.M., except Bay Port (Tu & F only). Lv. Tappahannock to Balto. direct W 4 P.M. (Urbanna only); for Frdbg. M A.M., lv. Port Royal 12:30 P.M.; for Frdbg. W noon, Port Royal 4 P.M. Lv. Frdbg. ldgs. to Balto. M & Th 2 P.M. via Tappahannock, Urbanna W 5 A.M.

	St. Mary's & Westmoreland	Potomac, Sue, Calvert & Northumberland	Middlesex, Lancaster, Essex & Caroline
1903	6/3/1903: same as 6/1/1901 & 6/1/1902. 11/3/1903: same as 12/16/1902.	6/3/1903: same as 6/1/1901 & 6/1/1902. 11/3/1903: same as 12/16/1902.	3/17/1903. lv. Pier 2 Tu & F 4:30 P.M. ldgs. to Frdbg.; ret. lv. M & Th 2 P.M., Leedstown Tu & F 4:30 A.M. Lv. Balto. W & Th 4:30 P.M., ldgs. to Tappahannock except Bay Port; ret. lv. M 8 A.M., W & Th 9 A.M. (no stops inbound at Tappahannock; Th at Bowlers, Wares, Wellfords). Lv. Tappahannock F 2 P.M. ldgs. to Norfolk; ret. lv. Sa 6 P.M. 4/1/1903: *Caroline* (in response to competition from *Tourist* of People's Steamboat line; see advertising[c]) lv. Frdbg. M, W & F 11 A.M., ldgs. to Urbanna; ret. lv. Tu, Th & Sa 6 A.M., Tappahannock 10 A.M. 6/3/1903: same as 6/1/1901 & 6/1/1902. 11/3/1903: same as 12/25/1901.
	St. Mary's & Westmoreland	Potomac, Calvert & Northumberland	Middlesex, Lancaster, Essex, Caroline & Anne Arundel
1904	1/1/1904: same as 1/12/1901. 7/7/1904: same as 12/16/1902.	1/1/1904: lv. Pier 9 Tu, Th & Sa 5 P.M., ldgs. to Wash. 7/7/1904: same as above.	1/1/1904: lv. Pier 2 Tu & F 4:30 P.M., Su noon, ldgs. to Frdbg. Lv. W & Th 4:30 P.M., ldgs. to Tappahannock. 3/15/1904: essentially same as 3/17/1903 & 4/1/1903. 7/7/1904: same as 1/1/1904. 9/6/1904: essentially same as 1903.
1905	As above.	As above.	1/3/1905: lv. Pier 2 daily (except Sa) 4:30 P.M., Su noon, to Tappahannock, extending F to Frdbg.; ret. lv. M & F 2 P.M., Leedstown Tu & Sa 4:30 A.M. Lv. Tappahannock daily except Su, Tu & Sa 8 A.M., M, W, Th & F 9 A.M. to Balto. Lv. Tappahannock to Norfolk Tu 2 P.M., ret. lv. W 4 P.M. from NYP & NRR ldg.

[a] Lower river landings include Millers, Bromes, Bacons, Grasons, Lewisetta, Bundicks, Cowarts, Coan, Kinsale, Mundy Point, Lodge, Sandy Point, Adams, Piney Point, Abells, Leonardtown, Cobrums, Howards, and Stones.

[b] Upper river landings include Lancaster, Bushwood, Riverside, Liverpool Point, Glymont, Alexandria, and Washington.

[c] Advertising of *Caroline* in local newspapers: "New and attractive steamer *Caroline* carrying the U.S. Mail" will leave Fredericksburg Monday, Wednesday, Friday A.M. for Urbanna; returning leave Urbanna 6 A.M. Tuesday, Thursday, Saturday, leave Tappahannock 10 A.M., arrive Fredericksburg 5 P.M. "Passenger accommodations first class. Fare—Fredericksburg to Port Royal 10 cents. From Fredericksburg and points between Port Royal and Tappahannock, 15 cents. From Fredericksburg to all points below Tappahannock, 25 cents. Freight on oysters, flour cakes, crackers, sugar and all drug barrels 10 cents; on molasses, coal oil, and wet barrels 20 cents a barrel. Bacon, 5 cents per 100 lbs. All other freight carried at proportionate low rates." The appearance of *Caroline* was in response to the following: "The People's Steamboat Line. The handsome and swift steamer *Tourist* will leave Fredericksburg for Urbanna and intervening wharves every Monday, Wednesday, and Friday at 11 A.M. Returning, will leave Urbanna every Tuesday, Thursday, and Saturday at 6 A.M., arriving at Fredericksburg in time for supper the same day. Excellent accommodations for both passengers and freight. W. D. Carter, President, Business Men's Association."

Financial Summaries

Summary of Account Sheets/Account Books of Steamboats *Patuxent*
(1835 and 1860), *Planter* (1855–60 and 1868–69), *George Weems* (1868–69),
Mary Washington (1868–69), and *Matilda*(1868–69); Summary of Cash
Expenditures for Wharf Property and Repairs, 1866; and Summary of Invoices
from Charles Reeder, Jr., Engine Builder, for repairs on *George Weems* during the
period of service with USQMD of the Union Army*

Statement of the Steamboat *Patuxent*, 1835

The steamer in this account is treated as a person. Accounts receivable are termed *due to Patuxent;* accounts payable are included in the statement as *Patuxent indebted to the sum of.* Identification in parentheses of merchants and individuals was not stated on the original account sheets; these notes came from the Baltimore City directory for 1835. *Patuxent* was built in 1826; disbursements made from this account sheet undoubtedly represent payments toward the discharge of remaining debts from construction and from accumulated operating costs. George Weems apparently contributed substantially toward the building; James Harwood, not a stockholder, loaned substantial sums for operating costs.

May 11, 1835. Due to *Patuxent* 219.57; received on account in 1835 71.45. Balance   148.12

May 1, 1835.
   Patuxent indebted to the sum of $9,880.79 to the following: George Weems 2,886.80, Watchman & Bratt (eng. bldg.) 1,669.89; G. Goodwin & Co. (ship carpenter) 1,591.11; Mathew Drake (hardward mrcht.) 113.82; Jacob McLane (blacksmith) 31.04; F. Erickson 395.44; Job Smith (lumber mrcht.) 131.74; Albert Koster (china, glass) 47.79; Walter Crook (upholsterer) 35.63; W.F. Bartlett 261.43; John McKim & Son (copper) 581.59; Josiah Share (brass) 46.92; Benjamin Buck & Son (sailmaker) 81.38; William Wallace (copper plate) 58.62; James Harwood 1,935.70.

Received May 1, 1835 to Jan. 1, 1836 for freight and passages 14,268.22; debts due in 1834 and paid 71.45
                                                   14,339.6

Appropriations made as follows: paid to George Weems on a/c 2,433.21; Watchman & Bratt on a/c 1,000.00; G. Goodwin & Co., 1,591.11; Mathew Drake 113.82; J. McLane 31.04; F. Erickson 384.44; Job Smith 131.74; Albert Koster 47.79. Total 5,734.15.

Account of the Steamboat *Planter* for the Period 1855–60, with Reference to the Steamboat *Patuxent*

Tables C.1 and C.2 are summaries of the account book of the steamer *Planter*, 1855–60. The original handwritten account book treats the steamboat as a person, with entries shown as *amounts due Steamer Planter* or *amounts Steamer Planter owes.* The following table uses the terminology *receipts* for accounts received and *expenditures* for bills paid.

The original account book, 302 pages in length, consists of very long lists of planters and merchants with the amounts of their bills for consignments shipped aboard *Planter*, the entries in the ledger made at the time of payment. Many of the consignees were clearly tardy in paying their bills, often as much as a year or two. Therefore, the amount of money earned by the steamboat on any particular trip is not reflected in the account book; instead, the receipts from current and past due accounts are shown by the date of payment.

---

*Derived from original documents in the Forbes Collection.

Nevertheless, over an extended period, the earnings of the boat can be ascertained.

In the case of the *accounts paid or owed* by *Planter,* the steamboat was tardy as often in paying bills due as shippers were in paying *Planter.* Some payments were obviously made on time, particularly those relating to wages. Some terminology used in the account book is difficult to define. For example, *marketing and wages* probably includes wages for deckhands, stokers, stewards, and other crew not officers and for provisions for dining room and crew fare, although this deduction is based on the fact that no other entries for such disbursements are made. On the listing of disbursements, in parentheses after the name of each payee is shown the individual's trade or profession; this information came from the Baltimore City directories for the years indicated.

Bookkeepers for *Planter* were not consistent in their methods, and irregularities appear. Also, their adding up of long columns, their subtraction, and their methods of carrying figures for-

Table C.1. Summary of the Account Book of the Steamboat *Planter* for the Period 1855–60, with Reference to the Steamboat *Patuxent*[a]

	Planter				*Planter Patuxent*
	1855	1856	1857	1858	1859
Number of regular trips	32	30	39	25	
Number of excursion/ charters	1	2	1		*Planter* bal.
Total receipts	$13,645.69	$20,600.74	$24,020.90	$17,118.73	$10,244.25
Passages (fares)	4,183.89	5,874.28	7,321.85	4,468.99	
Freight	5,392.74	7,085.15	10,461.41	7,197.25	
Charter	300.00	2,029.16	1,025.71	Norfolk	
Other, incl. bill pd.	769.06	5,212.15	5,211.93	1,677.00	237.97
Sale of boiler		400.00			99.95
Patuxent freight				3,775.00	
Average receipts per trip					
Passages	149.42[b]	195.81	187.74	178.76	
Freight	262.27	253.04[c]	268.24	287.89	
Charters (per day)	50.00	53.00	52.00		
High/low receipts					
High					
Passages	391.50	496.00	267.50	383.75	
Freight	429.94	462.48	443.35	504.12	
Low					
Passages	56.50	97.00	89.75	59.00	
Freight	21.37	71.51	131.67	137.91	
Total expenditures	19,355.89	20,132.21	15,734.90	6,941.71	6,226.49
Net profit/loss	(−)5,710.20	468.53	8,286.00	10,177.02	4,355.68
Acct. book balance	(−)5,710.20	1,255.53	7,358.22	10,244.25	4,355.68

[a]Principal disbursements, see Table C.2.
[b]28 trips; no passengers carried on trips 12, 14, 16, and 17.
[c]28 trips; no freight carried on trips 28 and 30.

ward were inaccurate, often leading to errors. Nevertheless, the portrayal of the business transactions of *Planter* in the pre-Civil War period is remarkably revealing.

At the end, the net profits of *Patuxent* were added to the receipts of *Planter* in the original account book, and the two steamers were joined in a final accounting.

Table C.2. Principal Disbursements of the Steamboat *Planter* for the Period 1855–60, with References to the Steamboat *Patuxent (in dollars)*

					Planter *Patuxent*
		Planter			
Disbursements	1855	1856	1857	1858	1859
J. P. Pindle (wood)	2,077.80				
Marketing & wages	2,051.64	3,467.34	4,488.49	2,612.50	
John Turnbull (carpet)	1,288.00				
W. A. Padgett (comm. mrcht.)	51.84				
John Henderson (chandler)	125.82	95.91	30.82		
Hugh Bolton (glass, oil paint, porcelain)	420.78	254.88	306.18	151.59	
Capt. C. L. Wise, salary	1,624.43				
Wharfage	37.50	80.00	80.00	70.50	
C. Kelly (coppersmith)	42.00	43.00			
W. B. Hill (atty. fee & conveyance, Hills Ldg.)	125.00				
W. B. Hill, rent Hills Ldg.		238.55	250.00		375.00
W. B. Hill, planking & wood		35.49			
Taxes, Magruder Ferry	1.12				
Driving piles	0.50				
Wharfage, Magruder Ferry	31.96				
Mill Stone Ldg.	125.00				
Advertising	5.00				
Advertising (*American Patriot*)			21.25	37.50	
Taxes on *Planter*	79.96				
Taxes on *Planter* & *Patuxent*		120.84	126.00	144.57	403.14
Gustavus Weems, wages @ 65/ mo.		709.00	780.00	455.00	
Theodore Weems, wages @ 75/ mo.	900.00	900.00	900.00	525.00	
George W. Weems, wages	744.00				
James Gourley	6.06				
Theodore Weems, dividend	588.00				
Gustavus Weems, dividend	588.00				
George W. Weems, dividend	588.00				
Charles Reeder (eng. bldr.)		4,678.13	169.10		
Custom house		39.20	39.60		
Insurance		79.00	200.72	200.72	302.20
Geo. Crooke (coal: *Planter* converted from wood 5/1856)		75.00			

Table C.2. (Continued)

Disbursements	Planter				Planter Patuxent
	1855	1856	1857	1858	1859
Stephen Lee (coal)		765.00	2,232.44	516.50	78.00
Dobbins & Warfield (comm. mrcht.)		1,055.13	175.00		
E. L. Tarr (cabinet work)		130.00			
James Stewart (glass, paint)		80.00	159.25	67.83	
E. T. Norris		310.00			
Latta & Clarke		365.00		100.00	
J. T. Turner (washrooms)		265.85			
George & Jenkins (comm. mrcht.)			91.99	36.70	
A. Flanigan (shipbldg.)			125.00		
Wm. McKinnon			1,380.26		
Hollingsworth (glass, supplies)			936.67		
Walter Crooke (upholstery)			113.25		
Wharf repairs			412.00		
Lyons Creek Wharf				75.00	
Bristol Wharf				.68	145.58
Thomas B. Billingslea				23.05	
B. H. Hooper				100.71	
J. K. Booth				325.65	
County Court				5.07	
J. Forrest					105.39
Capt. L. Thomas					187.50
C. H. Young					342.36
State of Maryland					500.00
W. R. Thomas					262.50
Handtruck					9.00
W. Bowman					270.00
Mt. Calvert rent					145.83
Repairing scow					16.85
Water rent					65.24
John E. Turlton					112.50
James Harrison					45.00
State wharfage					583.32
Wages					20.12
Prince George County taxes					2.75
Lower Marlboro warehouse					114.11
Rent on wharves					28.00
Duke					
James Hanson					25.00
Mrs. Thomas					62.50
St. Leonards					135.97
Holland Cliffs					425.65
Lower Marlboro					400.00

Summary of Account Sheets of Steamers *Planter, George Weems, Mary Washington,* and *Matilda,* 1868 and 1869

The original handwritten account sheets for tables C.3 and C.4 simply tally each trip by *passages and fares, freight receipts,* and *expenses.* What is included in *expenses* is not indicated. The figure could presumably include wages, fuel, and food. Whether repairs, wharfage, taxes, renovation, resupply, and other long-term costs are included is not clear although the fluctuations in the amounts would indicate that at least some are added in the figure, and the large year-end expenditures would suggest that the term *expenses*

represents bills coming due and paid. Distribution to Mason L. Weems of $666.67 as salary is indicated. Occasional errors in addition or subtraction occur in the original.

George Weems was under charter at various times in 1868, as shown by accounts received. In 1869, the charter/excursions are listed by each sponsoring organization.

Matilda operated on the Rappahannock during both years and carried the mail. Furthermore, in 1868, she carried "money packages" for various purposes, including purchases in Baltimore for river residents and bank deposits. Fees for these services and postage are reflected in the entries.

Table C.3. Summary of Account Sheets of Steamers *Planter* and *George Weems,* 1868 and 1869

	Planter		George Weems	
	1868	1869	1868	1869
Number of regular trips	69	86	28	10
Number of excursion/ charters			13	33
Total receipts	$32,911.33	$43,798.36	$22,707.36	$17,584.99
Passages (fares)	16,182.92	19,168.30	5,968.25	1,400.35
Freight	16,728.41	24,630.06	14,461.46	7,781.19
Charter			2,250.75	7,595.00
Other receipts			26.90	808.45
Average receipts per trip				
Passages	234.54	222.89	213.15	140.04
Freight	242.44	286.40	516.48	778.12
Charter (per day)			173.13	230.15[a]
High/low receipts				
High				
Passages	492.35	634.35	332.25	226.30
Freight	574.51	537.33	970.64	1,084.48
Low				
Passages	69.00	47.00	76.75	93.75
Freight	100.30	141.25	173.25	170.57
Total expenditures	21,406.17	26,366.66	13,706.25	14,640.80[b]
Net profit	11,505.16	17,431.70	9,001.11	2,944.19
Account sheet balance	12,172.69	16,862.85	6,483.01[c]	2,589.02

[a]High/low 1868: $25–300; for 1869, $39–600. See Table C.4 for excursion charters.
[b]Includes added expenditure of $10,659.11.
[c]Account sheet closes with addition of *Planter* account ($7,417.11) for total of $13,900.12.

Table C.4. Summary of Account Sheets of Steamers *Mary Washington* and *Matilda*, 1868 and 1869

	Mary Washington		Matilda	
	1868	1869	1868	1869
Number of regular trips	30	41	43	43
Number of excursion/ charters	1	1		
Total receipts	$26,101.36	$35,041.52	$44,684.33	$46,394.33
Passages (fares)	5,708.41	7,279.95	18,000.70	16,637.45
Freight	20,021.63	27,553.57	26,530.91	28,407.24
Charter	371.32	205.00		1,029.50
Other receipts		3.00	152.72[d]	320.64[e]
Average receipts per trip				
Passages	190.28	177.56	418.62	386.92
Freight	667.39	672.04	617.00	660.63
Charter (per day)	371.32	205.00		343.16
High/low receipts				
High				
Passages	324.00	317.60	602.75	538.25
Freight	1,032.17	1,162.20	1,407.56	1,247.60
Low				
Passage	112.25	64.25	258.50	163.25
Freight	210.95	349.32	230.43	310.35
Total expenditures	14,275.40	23,388.22	36,343.34	35,614.60
Net profit	11,825.96	11,753.30	8,340.99	10,780.23
Account sheet balance	8,536.80[f]	11,380.14	8,324.35	9,860.52

[d]Includes $141.70 for 17 money packets and $11.02 for postage receipts.
[e]Includes four postage receipts for $56.64; receipts from Tappahannock Wharf $156.68; freight received from Baltimore Steam Packet Company $100.00.
[f]Adjustment of $3,289.16.

Excursion/Charters of Steamboat *George Weems* Included in Account Sheets for 1869

Druid Hill Association 200.00; Monument Street Church 150.00; Jefferson Street Sunday School 150.00; Chestertown Cold [reference to Washington College?] 300.00; Hanover Street Sunday School 150.00; Franklin Street Ch. Ch. [Church Choir?] 185.00; Excelsior Assembly 200.00; Can Makers 200.00; Woodbury Schl. 200.00; Knights Pythias 200.00; Stone Masons 200.00; American Protes. P. [?] 200.00; Bennett Club 150.00; Patuxent River 304.00; Iron Moulders [sic] 200.00; Med. Turners [?] 200.00; Immaculate Con. [Conception?] 195.00; Ebenezer Cold. [College?] 300.00; Chestertown Cold. 300.00; Union Lodge 200.00; Eureka Lodge 200.00; Port Deposit [Susquehanna run?] 300.00; Chestertown Cold. 225.00; Waiters Assoc. 250.00; Atlantic Lodge 200.00; Pocahontas Tribe 200.00; North East 350.00; Tobacco Stick [Little Choptank River run?] 300.00; Fair Haven 100.00; Catholics 150.00; Chest. & Balto. 500.00; Schomer M. Alice 39.00; Chester to Tred [Avon Rivers?] 600.00.

Summary of Invoices from Charles Reeder, Jr., Engine Builder, for Repairs on Steamboat *George Weems* during the Period of Service with USQMD of the Union Army

There were three lengthy periods of overhaul: (1) June 21 to November 29, 1861 (cost $103.14); (2) March 21 to July 4, 1862 (cost $119.50 less $5.00 discount) recorded with March 13 to December 25, 1863 (cost $255.56); (3) June 10 to August 19, 1864 (cost $646.82 less 5 percent discount). In the listing below, the numbers in parentheses after each item refer to the periods of overhaul, as numbered above. The numbers after the parentheses indicate the quantity.

Parts and Materials: Tube & wrought socket @.50 (1)1; 1⅛" bolts for followers @.16 (1) 6; lugs for furnace bolts @.40 (1) 4; iron & bearing @1.50 (1) 4; boiler iron or iron forging @.06/in. or @.10/lb. (1) 71¾, (2) 740½, (3) 32; ⅝" bolts @.12 (1) 18, (2) 88, (3) 29; cast iron bonnet for steam chest @.42 (1) 1; farriages @.03 (1) 14, (2) 19; ½" bolts @.10 (1) 3; steel packing springs @.50 (1) 2; copper air valve @1.35 (1) 1; ½" copper rivets @.02½ (1) 8; ⅝" rivets @.06 (1) 2, (2) 27; 2" em-

ery @.28 (1) 1; ¾ " bolts @.28 (1) 3, (2) 157; 6 30" furnace bars @1.58 (1) 12; 5" cylinder head bolts @.54 (1) 1; packing hook @.28 (1) 1; cement @.06/lb. (2) 48, (3) 4; grate bars @1.65 (2) 6; ⅛" bolts @1.38 (3) 2; eccentric key bolt @.66 (2) 1; copper steam air valve @.44 (2) 1; slice bar @2.34 (2) 1; deck pump bolts @.02 (2) 10; red/white lead @.15 lb. (3) 6; hooks for chimney bolts @1.00 (2) 47; mercury @1.00/lb. (2) 5; (3) 2½; files @.90 (2) 3, (3) 3; brass liners @.50 (2) 5; ½" steel plugs for shaft @.15 (2) 3; washers @.02 (2) 235, (3) 56; follower bolts @.43 (2) 2; mixed gum @.90/lb. (2) 1¼; cast iron bonnet for stop valve @1.05 (2) 1; pine boards @.04/ft. (3) 6; iron wrenches for packing bolts @.14 (3) 47; copper bolts & keys @.80 (3) 6; candles @.35 (3) 7½; iron scrapers, hook bolts for anchor davits, chain hooks @.18 (3) 24; charcoal @.30/ bushel (3) 2½; oak boards for sidewheels @.08/ft. (3) 38; piecing hook @.54 (1) 1.

Labor: Forging @.50/hr. (1) 24, (2) 114½, (3) 56; boiler maker @2.00/day (1) 5½, (2) 28¾, (3) 475; finish work on board @1.75/day (1) 7½, (2) 31½, (3) 32½; carpenter @1.00/day (1) ½; lathe work @3.00/day (1) ½, (2) ½, (3) 1; valve grinding @10.00/day (1) ½; hauling @1.00/day (1) ½, (2) 1; pattern making @1.50/day (2) 1¼, (3) ½; milling @4.00/day (3) 9; helper @2.50/day (3) 34½; crane hoist @8.00/day (3) 2.

Construction Costs
and Agreements

Extract of the Account Book of the Steamboat *George Weems*, August–September
1858; Bills Due for the Construction and Outfitting of the Steamboat
Mary Washington in 1845–46; and Agreements for Construction Work
on *Mary Washington* Made in 1844

Extracts from the Account Book of the Steamboat *George Weems*, August–September 1858

The steamboat *George Weems* was built in 1858.
Bills paid in 1858 as entered in the account book
for the steamer reflect the total cost for her construction and outfitting. The occupation or trade
shown in parentheses was added from information derived from the Baltimore City directory for
1858. The extracts are from documents in the
Forbes Collection.

8/27. Abraham & Ashcraft (ship carpenters) 11,333.65;
8/20 C. Reeder, Jr. (eng. bldr.) 14,920.80; 8/20 George W.
Morris (carpenter) 5,094.40; 9/30 R. C. Waite (chandler)
1,130.57; 8/26 Hugh Bolton (glass, porcelain, paint)
262.21; 9/3 James Stewart (paint) 953.28; 10/9 Walter
Crook, Jr. (upholstery) 907.12; 9/10 William Knabe
(piano) 247.00; 8/18 H. Bass (plumber) 169.79; 8/18
Regester & Webb (brass bell mfr.) 44.60; 8/3 E. L. Tarr
(cabinet maker) 130.00; 8/18 James Stewart (paint and
glass) 100.37; 5/7 Hollingsworth & Co. (glass, porcelain,
interiors, paint) 1,352.92; 8/18 John Turnbull (carpet, oil
cloth, floor-clothing) 507.97; 11/19 Hollingsworth & Co.
601.74; 5/25 insurance and a number of unidentified
merchants 30.00
Total $41,384.55

Bills Due for the Construction and Outfitting of the Steamboat *Mary Washington* in 1845 and 1846

The bills included here are those presented for
payment in the case of Abbot et al. vs. The Baltimore and Rappahannock Steam Packet Company
in the Court of Chancery, Baltimore, October
1846, and in the case of William and Hazlett
McKim vs. The Baltimore and Rappahannock

Steam Packet Company in the U.S. District
Court for Maryland, August 1846.

William and Hazlett McKim

Bill August 19, 1846 for $1,958.49. 45 boiler plates
1,151.87; 97 copper rods 374.29; 35 sheets copper
plates or pattern copper 169.04; 44 lb. copper nails
13.20; 22 sheets brazier copper sheets 225.40; 13
sheets sheathing copper 24.69.

James Russell

Bill 1846 for $46.19. Windlass casting, 400 lbs. 16.26;
turning iron necks 2.50; composition boxes 3.60; Pr
iron hawse pipes fitted 8.00; brass fittings, nuts for
wheel, bushing 9.80; turning, iron shaft 1.00; spikes
2.12; iron sheaves for blocks 2.12; 2 sheaves for
chocks 1.00.

John A. Robb & Co.

Bill May 9, 1846 for $859.56, submitted by John Bratt,
Chairman, Building Committee:

Materials: 3,139 ft. pine lumber @.03½/ft.; 1,016 iron
bolts @.07; 22 lb. iron spikes @.05/lb; 2,657 ft. YP
or WP plank @.04/ft.; 38 sheets tarred paper @.02/
sheet; 1 sheet paper tacks @.09/sheet; 6 bbls. pitch
and tar @2.30/bbl.; 781 ft. oak timber @.04/ft.;
7,600 deck plugs @.04/hundred; 1,375 lb. oakum
@.02½/lb.

Labor: 1 day joiner work @2.00/day; 3½ days hauling
(men and horses) @3.00/day; 15½ days carpenter
@2.00/day; 7½ days caulking @1.75/day; 1,862 ft.
sawing @.02½/ft.

Bill June 15, 1846 for $1,122.54 submitted by Noah
Fairbank:

Materials: 5.612 ft. pine lumber @.03½/ft.; 2,392 ft.
WP plank @.04/ft; 160 sheets tarred paper @.02/

sheet; 2 sheets paper tacks @.09/sheet; 2 bbl. pitch @2.30/bbl.; 120 ft. oak timber @.04/ft.; 36 lb. oakum @.02½ lb.; 6 lb. nails @.16/lb.; 100 lb. B oakum @.08½/lb.; 1¾ reams paper @3.00/ream; 297 spikes @.10; 675 lb. iron @.08/lb; 3 shores @.25; 60 rings ¾ @.06; 4 mops @.25; 4 dressers @.25; 1,152 ft. cedar @.06/ft.

Labor: 6½ days O-Boy @.75/day; 1½ days hauling (men and horses) @3.00/day; 140½ days carpenter @2.00/day; 42 days caulking @1.75/day; 546 ft. sawing @.02½/ft.; 58 days F. stages @1.50/day; 10 days P. kettle @.25/day.

Hergeshimer & Sherwood

Bill March 4 for $162.23¾. Bill consists of costs of labor and materials for the installation of the windlass, rudder, steering wheel, and steering assembly. Materials include a variety of bolts, nails, rings, hoops, plates, collars, straps, brass fittings, eyes, swivels, brackets, spindles, sheaves, blocks, and thimbles. Labor includes welding, machining, and installing.

Thomas C. Morris & Sons

Bill $266.56.

Materials: 2,164 ft. board various sizes @ avg. .03½/ft. $60.94; 180 lbs. cut & wrought nails @avg. .06/lb. 11.60; 125 ft. timber @.05/ft. plus .50 hauling 6.75; 16 ft. coaming @.03/ft. .48; 291 ft. scantling @.01½ ft. 6.71; 240 ft. oak for steering chock 9.50; 500 sprigs .18; 10½ doz. screws 1.11; 9 ft. mahogany @.20/ft. 1.80; 128 ft. Yellow P @.03/ft. 3.84; 54 ft. ash @avg. .03/ft. 1.67; 8 Brop screws .20; 750 ft. cullings @.00½/ft. 11.25; 30 ft. board stanchions .75; 3 turned stanchions .75.

Labor: 158.75 days work, avg. $1.75/h. 277.84; work on waist 50.00; work around engine upper deck 20.00.

Total: 470.16, less 203.60 by hardware received of William Proctor & Son. Balance 266.56.

William Proctor & Son

Bill $54.44. Miscellaneous hardware consisting of nails, wire, screws, sharps, hooks, hinges, bolts, chain, paper, staples, lamp hooks, door hooks, flat files, saws, smooth files, tacks, hammers, and a few gravy spoons, mustard spoons, and tea spoons.

John Watchman

Bill $12,611.13. Bill consists of costs of labor and materials for the installation of the engine and other mechanical parts.

Materials: bolts, washers, cock valves, kelsam bolts, castings, copper strainers, cast iron rings, guard braces, bevel plates, rivets, charcoal, brackets, augurs & chisels & other tools, caulk, patterns, grate bars, rudder rivets, iron rolling bars, keel bolts, cast iron air pump (117.00), air pump piston & rods, gas-

kets, pedestals, rod for starting bar, cast iron plates for condenser and discharge, iron braces for slides, wrought iron rings for force pump, force pump rods, gaskets, iron spindle for cut-off, boiler iron, bilge water pump valve, eye bolts, steam gauge. 2,165.98

Labor: @avg. 1.50 to 1.75/day. 945.15

Steam Engine Contract: 9,500.00

Total: 12,611.13

[Note. There are a few pencil marks opposite some items, and the following note appears at the bottom of the last sheet: "Mr. Bratt says the Items X in pencil are all included in the contract for the Engine. The residue of the bill is submitted. So says Mr. Bratt."]

Wells & Miller

Bill $414.55½. Making piston patterns and stuff $40.00; making patterns and stuff for packing 5.85; cast iron piston 31.99; 2 rings for packing 15.05; boring for pump 100.00; hand (labor) planing slides 12.00; hand (labor) at lathe on piston 6.00; do at lathe on piston rod 5.00; 2 keys for air pump rod .08½; hand (labor) drilling chipping key hold 4.50; turning piston rod or air pump 9.00; 8 springs 3.92; round steel for springs 9.85; 2 ring and 2 set bolts 1.25; turning piston, grinding packing, making & fitting steel springs for same, fitting piston rod, and putting into cylinder 151.00; 28 bolts & washers .08½; making grate bar pattern & stuff 1.25; 9 feet oak .27; augur handle .12½; 29 grate bar 14.00; small wrench .50; drayage .25.

W. Christopher Rabas, Jr.

Bill December 23, 1846 for $159.11½ submitted by Noah Fairbank. 48 lb. shot lead 4.87; 4 scuppers @.12½ ea. .37; 2 scuppers .37; 1 lg square tin steamer 1.88; bottom (.75 & .50) 1.25; 8 pieces tin ware 9.00; bottom to bucket, cover, steakpan .50; 39 bbl. coal plus drayage 31.02; 2 pieces copper 5.92; 1 lg. coffee canister .75; 10 sheets japanned tin 3.12½; tinning lg. square Camboose ladle 2.25; 2 of next size 2.50; tinning 2 stew pans 2.00; 1 less size .63; 1 lg. double tin coffee boiler, 18.00; 2 lg. double tin O'Barath pans 2.50; 11 deep bath pans 2.50; 11 shallow bath pans 1.25; small bath pans .35; 1 lg. oval steak pan with cover 1.87; 6 tin plates & 6 riveted tin cups 1.25; 1 tin cover for pan & 1 wash basin .69; 2 hanging lamps, 1 with 2 panes with 1 spout .62; 1 coffee boiler & ladle .88; 1 gal. saucepan 1.25; 1 lg. tumbler drainer 2.50; 1 square sugar canister, 1 collander, & 1 hand lamp .94; 5 dust pans 1.87; 5 lamp shades 1.00; 3 petticoat lamps .60; lantern .20; 3 lb. mill'd lead 5.30; 2 glass lanterns 3.00; 2 sugar canisters 2.38; 1 qt. machine oil .44; 3 doz. japanned spittoons 12.00; 1 light glass to lanterns .20; 1 lg. square lid to Camboose copper .75; 2 smaller 1.00; 2 water coolers 5.00; 6 lb. copper tacks 3.90; glass lanterns 1.50; bottom of lamp .50; 1 water ladle .25; small glass lanterns 1.00; 2 stand lamps .50; 2 water buckets 1.13; 1 water ladle .25; oil feeder .25; 2 coach lights .50; 2 black tin tea pots

4.00; 2 petticoat lamps .40; 4 lights glass to lanterns .75.

Henry T. Baker

Bill $17.50 for pane glass.

Wesley & S. Earnest Cowles

Bill $140.59. 3 doz. egg cut plates 4.00; 2 sets caster 5 holes 2.75; 4 doz. fluted tumblers 5.00; 6 pc. blue bakers 5.25; 5 doz. blue plates 5.65; 4 doz. blue plates (small) 4.40; 4 doz. raised fig. coffee, bowls & saucers 7. 00; ½ doz. creams 1.25; ½ doz. sugars 2.50; 3 prs. glass salts 1.50; ½ doz. lg. blue pitchers 4.50; 5 doz. fluted tumblers 6.25.

Bill $403.19. 89 sq. yd. oil cloth 111.25; 65 yd. Brussels carpeting 113.75; 42¾ yd. in-grain carpeting 42.75; 165 yd. binding 6.75; 15 yd. in-grain 15.75; 1 binding .75; 85¾ yd. in-grain carpeting 85.75; 2 mats 5.00; 25 yd. ¼ matting 6.25; 12¾ yd. damask 9.50; 1 yd. 4/4 matting .75; 2 yd. oil cloth 2.50; 1 table cover 5.00.

John Welsh

Bill $71.82 for paint, white lead, varnish, oil.

Walter Cook

Bill $415.89. Curtain materials, beds, mattresses, upholstery for cabin 184.10; sofa 2.00; plus bed lace, satin, Turkey red, curtains for staterooms, cushions.

David C. Harris

Bill $28.00. Basket of champagne wine 12.00; gal. brandy 2.00; basket of champagne (pts.) 14.00.

Julia A. Fairbanks, Eliz. Berlin, Ann Clinton, and Others

Bill $156.74. Making & fitting 14 feather beds 3.00; making & fitting 2 lg. feather beds 2.00; 2 doz. pillows 18.00; 2¹¹⁄₁₂ doz. tablecloths 3.87½; 8 doz. towels 6.00; ⁶⁄₁₂ doz. rollers .75; 11 doz. pillow cases 22.00; 25⁵⁄₁₂ doz. curtain 42.62; binding 48 yd. carpet 3.00; placing drapery in gentlemen's cabin & 16 berths 16.00; pulling up 16 berths 3.00.

Thomas C. Morris & Sons

Bill $369.49.

Materials: 1,733 ft. boards $48.81; 19 lb. wrought & cut nails 4.14; 16 ft. coaming .48; 2 clamps 3.50; 72 lb. nails 4.11; 175 ft. timber for bell post 1.15; 10½ doz. screws 1.08; 500 sprigs .88; 9 ft. mahogany 1.80; 5 ft. YP coaming 1.50; 60 ft. steering chocks 2.10; 54 ft. ash 1.67; 30 ft. oak 1.20; 141 ft. scantling 2.11; 320 ft. cuttings 4.80; 430 ft. cullings 6.45.

Labor: 2 days mfr. pine for boiler 3.31; work on after part paddlewheel over waist 50.00; work, companionway, 7.00; 9 days work, water closets 15.75; joiner work around engine, upper saloon, 20.00; 4 days work on refrigerator 7.00; hauling .50; work on bell post 3.50; general labor 99.5 days 174.12.

These agreements include certain specifications for the construction of the steamer.

Agreements for Certain Construction Work on *Mary Washington*

Agreement between on the One Hand James Harwood and Members of the Building Committee of the Baltimore and Rappahannock Steam Packet Company and on the Other Hand John A. Robb, November 5, 1844

This Agreement entered into this 5th day of November 1844, Between the President and Director of the Baltimore & Rappahannock Steam Packet Company, on the one part, and John A. Robb of the City of Baltimore on the other Part, Witnesseth, that for and in consideration of the price hereafter named, the said John A. Robb & Co. doth agree to build for said Steam Packet Company, a Steam Boat of the following dimensions and specifications: to wit, Length on Deck 160 feet, Breadth of Beam from outside to outside 26 feet, Depth of Hold 10 feet. The Keel to be of White Oak 16 inches in the center and 12 inches at the stem and Stern Post, the Apron, Knightshead and main transom to be of Live Oak or Locust, the frame to be of White Oak and Cedar, the top timbers entire of Cedar and as many cedar frames forward and aft as it may be possible to work. To have one center kelson, 4 Side Kelsons, and 2 bilge kelsons fore and aft with 2 boiler kelsons 40 feet long the whole to be 12 by 14 inches of yellow Pine free from sap and bolted with copper bolts. The Bottom Plank to be of White Pine 3½ inches thick, the bends and clamps of yellow pine 4 inches thick free from sap. The deck Beams of yellow pine free from sap and kneed outside and in wherever it may be requisite. The deck plank 3¼ inches thick and plugged. The counter timbers and guard stanchions to be of Cedar. The hull to be copper fastened and tree nailed to the bends. The deck clamps to be secured with ¾ inch Screw Bolts, one in each frame. The floors to be 6 by 14 inches and 22 inches from center to center. To be ceiled from the clamps to the bilge Kelson with white pine 2½ inches thick. The said John A. Robb & Co. to do all the carpenters work to the hull (except such as appertain to the engine and machinery). To do also the outboard joiner work and find the customary materials and fastening for the same, also the carved work for the head and Stern. The boat to be launched on or before the first of November 1845.

The said Steam Packet Company doth agree to pay unto the Said John A. Robb & Co. Twenty Six Dollars per ton Carpenters measurement in the following payments, to wit

$2500 on signing this Contract

2500 on January 1, 1845

2500 on January 1, 1846

and the Balance on or before the 1st October 1846.

Witness: James Harwood, President
J. M. Shoemaker   Samuel Elliott, Jr.
                           M. N. Falls
                              Building Committee
                           John A. Robb

Agreement between George W. Morris and C. T.
Morris on the One Part and James Harwood,
President of the Baltimore and Rappahannock
Steam Packet Company on the Other

It is understood and agreed that the said Morris shall do
the Joiner work of the new Steamer now building at the
shipyard of the Messrs. John A. Robb & Co. It is understood and agreed that all the planks (except the Passmill
oak used for this work) shall not exceed Four (4) Inches
in width and be entirely free from Knots splits sap +
wind shakes. It is understood that Messrs. Morris shall
herewith use such material or planks in the Cabin floor
Bulkheads and Bench Linings as they may see fit—It is
understood and agreed that there shall be a Ladies
Cabin below the main Deck Aft with (22) Twenty Two
berths finished and put up Complete. Also a forward
cabin with six lengths of Berths. Bar Room complete.
On the main Deck aft a Ladies and Gentlemens Dining
Saloon with closets, water closets, and wash room
finished complete in the style of the main saloon of the
steamer *Planter,* said Dining Saloon to be 40 feet in
length and to have doors leading into the Ladies cabin.
Forward of the saloon there is to be [paddle] wheel
Houses. Six rooms on each side six feet square, Kitchen
to be furnished with necessary shelves. The other
Rooms to be fitted up as mens Room and Pantry. The
whole Engine on the main + Promenade decks to be
cased in. Companion way sky lighted. Decks stanchioned, awning stanchioned on the promenade deck.

To have a cabin forward + aft with six state Rooms on
each side aft with Two Berths in Each and Tier of three
Berths each forward with Steering House, and rail
around the forward part and on the after part to have a
Rail with seats. A dunnage floor to be put in. And it is
distinctly understood and agreed that the said Geo. W.
and C. T. Morris shall will and truly finish all the joiner
work of said steamer in a complete and workmanlike
manner and that there shall be no bill of Extra Charges
or any other change unless hereafter agreed upon. That
the sum hereinafter mentioned as the price of said work
and that there shall be no exceptions to this but those
hereinafter mentioned in this contract.—And that it is
understood + agreed that these exceptions shall be as
follows. That the said S & B & Co. shall furnish the
Botto Locks and rings for the rooms, the copper nails for
the wheel House. The Blacksmith work to secure the
Rail around the Promenade Deck and also such Blacksmith work as may be necessary to secure the cabins
and wheel or steerage house to the rest of the vessel.
And it is distinctly understood and agreed that the foregoing contract shall be in good faith to the full accom-
plishment of the Joiner work to be done to the said
steamer for the sum of Five Thousand Three Hundred
dollars to be paid as follows:
   $500 on the signing of this contract.
   500 on November 10, 1845.
   500 on December 10, 1845.
Note for $1000 from 1st October, 3 months to be re-
newed for 3 months longer when due (to be renewed by
Messrs. Morris)—Note for $1000 at 4 months from 1st
March 1846 to be renewed for 4 months longer when
due (to be renewed by Messrs. Morris). Note for $1000
at 12 months from the 1st March 1846 interest to be
added to all of the foregoing notes after 4 months.
   Signed: T. E. Clifton (true copy of the original)

The Weems Family

Long-standing tradition held that the Weems family name began with John MacDuff, who was created earl by Malcolm III of Scotland in 1056 and assumed the title of earl of Wemyss (or Weems, from the Gaelic name for coves that indented the east coast of Scotland). His descendant was David, earl of Wemyss, created lord high admiral of Scotland by Queen Anne. Because of its participation in the Stuart uprising of 1715, the family forfeited its right to the title, not to be restored until 1786. According to family legend, William, third son of David, the fourth earl of Wemyss (1678–1720) died in battle, Sunday, November 12, 1715, at Preston. Verification is difficult; Burke's *Peerage* contains no reference to any son by the name of William in the titled line. However, it is noted that the fourth earl's successors included "one sorrowing son." There is no evidence to deny the validity of linkage to the lord high admiral of Scotland.

The widow, Elizabeth Loch Wemyss (Weems), after the death of William, decided to travel to the New World with her three children, David, James, and Williamina, to live under the roof of her brother, Dr. William Loch, who had settled in Anne Arundel County, Maryland, in about 1706 and who owned the estate of Loch Eden, located between Herring Bay and the West River. Whether she came alone with the children or if Dr. Loch traveled to Scotland to accompany her was never settled in the family history. A likely version of the story held that Dr. Loch brought over James, the older son, as his heir in 1715, and Lady Elizabeth, David, and Williamina in 1720 (Douglas Andes Weems, *History of the Weems Family* [Annapolis: Weems System of Navigation, 1945]).

Notwithstanding the order of arrival, the children of Elizabeth Weems grew up comfortably in the four-storied mansion of Loch Eden overlooking the Bay. In time James practiced medicine in Calvert County and produced a line prominent in southern Maryland. Williamina's progeny married into leading families in Pennsylvania. The tendency of the landowning gentry of Maryland to intermarry is exemplified in the genealogy of the Weems family (E. C. Papenfuse et al., *A Biographical Dictionary of the Maryland Legislature, 1635–1789* [Baltimore: The Johns Hopkins University Press, 1985], 893–96; Weems family narrative handwritten at Loch Eden, 1854, in the Forbes Collection; data on Weems genealogy, courtesy of Jane McWilliams, Maryland Archives).

Dr. William Loch, after living as a widower through the years, married a lady upward of 50 years of age, who, contrary to expectations, delivered a son in her 51st year. The estate of Loch Eden (or Lochedon, as it was spelled in legal documents) was divided between that son, who became Dr. William Loch, Jr., and David and James Weems, his cousins. David bequeathed his share to Loch Weems, Jr. (Anne Arundel County Land Records for 1757–63, BB 2, p. 330). The divided estate passed for the most part to the heirs of James Weems.

David (1706–79), the younger son of Elizabeth, became a planter. Because of the prosperity of the tobacco trade and the need to expand land holdings to meet the ravages of tobacco on the light soil of Anne Arundel County, he purchased ever-increasing acreage, using at first as collateral to purchase additional land whatever moiety was available to him in his uncle's settlement and then the profits from his plantation. In February 1733, he purchased from William Vernon for 220 pounds a tract of land called Marches Seat (later titled Marshes Seat) on Herring Creek, which ran into Herring Bay. The tract consisted of 150 acres; bordering it was another tract of 100 acres called Barnetts Plantation; Weems signed a mortgage to the seller for 60 pounds sterling (Land Records of Anne Arundel County, 1733–37, RD 2, p. 42, Maryland Archives). This was the first of numerous land purchases. The largest occurred on June 14, 1740, when he bought from Skipworth Cole of Baltimore County for 165 pounds 13 shillings 4 pence in cash a tract of 2,000 acres part of the Mannour [*sic*] of Portland, and lying on a branch of Lyon's Creek (Land Records of Anne Arundel County, 1740–44, RD 1, p. 21, Maryland Archives). David Weems settled on his estate at Marshes Seat, built a manor house 100 feet in length, and basked in the pleasures of the Bay.

David married twice. His first wife, Elizabeth, and his second wife, Ester (died in 1776), had in sequence a total of 19 children. Among the children by his second wife was a series of newborn infants named David. Three by that name died shortly after birth, and the fourth David was the father of George Weems. The last child was Mason Loch Weems (1759–1825), the first and perhaps most controversial biographer of George Washington.

Mason Loch Weems, the itinerant clergyman who brought down the wrath of his own Episcopal clergy for his passion in defense of slaves, Tom Paine, and other "firebrands," for his earthy style of living and flamboyant sermons, yet won their respect for gaining ordination in the wake of the Revolution by the bishop of Chester and admission to the priesthood by the archbishop of Canterbury, served congregations in All Hallows and St. Margaret's parishes in Anne Arundel County and preached at Pohick Church near Mount Vernon. At Pohick, he became an intimate friend of the Washington family. The famous biography by Parson Weems, portraying the first president as a paragon of virtue, wisdom, and courage, contains the famous story of the little hatchet and the cherry tree, denounced by critics as apocryphal, defended by others as simply a transcription of a story about Washington which had circulated for 20 years before the writing. Parson Weems, even more than his biography, became a part of the American heritage. The vision of this cheerful, crusading, eccentric, Bible-thumping man, riding in his rickety wagon, pounding the back roads at the turn of the century, was embroidered in the fabric of American history (*Dictionary of American Biography*, xix, p. 604; Emily E. F. Skeel, ed., *Mason Locke Weems, Works and Ways* [New York: Plimpton Press, 1929]; Lawrence Wroth, *Parson Weems: A Biographical and Critical Study* [Baltimore: Eschelbarger Book Company, 1911]; Harold Kellock, *Parson Weems of the Cherry Tree* [New York: np, 1928]; Alexander M. Saunders, ed., "An Unpublished Letter of 'Parson' Weems," *Maryland Historical Magazine* 46 (1951); "Parson Weems, Reformer, as his Church Knew Him" and "The Reverend Mason Locke Weems" in the Elizabeth Chew Williams Papers, MS 909, Mary-

land Historical Society; Emily Lantz, "Washington's First Biographer," series of articles in the Henry Williams Papers, MS 907, Maryland Historical Society; "There is Proof of the Cherry Tree," Baltimore *Sun*, March 17, 1912).

Of the 19 children of David Weems, seven died before the age of one year. One more ended up in suicide; another drowned at sea (Weems family Bible, Maryland Room, Enoch Pratt Free Library). All of them were nurtured in the stately pace of life at Marshes Seat. Some of the progeny crossed the Appalachians and started a branch of the family in the Midwest. Most of the members of the Weems family trace their origin in America to the first David. When David died on May 3, 1779, at age 73, the division of his extensive property specified that Marshes Seat was to pass to his namesake, David Weems. [Note: the Herring Creek adjoining Marshes Seat became known as Rockhold Creek in the 19th century; its mouth lies less than a mile southeast of Deale in Anne Arundel County. Marshes Seat was located between this creek, emptying into the most northern part of Herring Bay (an indentation of the western shore of the Chesapeake Bay), and Tracy's Landing, a community lying a few miles to the west. The 2,000-acre tract bought from Skipworth Cole adjoined Marshes Seat (*Gazetteer of Maryland*, 1941, pp. 96, 179).

David Weems, the younger, born August 8, 1751, followed the sea in his youth and, with three other seafarers, outfitted two privateers for action against British shipping in the Revolutionary War. He married Margaret Harrison on April 15, 1777. Their children were David (born March 2, 1778), who became a British subject after being impressed by the British at sea in the War of 1812; Gustavus (born April 2, 1779); Rachel (born August 16, 1780); Sidney (born October 3, 1782); George (born May 23, 1784); Theodore (born March 9, 1786); and Mason L. (born January 20, 1789).

In an indenture signed January 7, 1819, David Weems bequeathed the 400-acre estate of Marshes Seat and part of the adjoining Pascals Purchase to two of his sons, Gustavus and George. Gustavus bought up large tracts of land around Huntingtown, just north of Prince Frederick, Calvert County (some 2,000 acres known variously as Trent, Tillington, Devils Wood Yard, Evans Purchase, Sheridans Point, Rock Hall, Reserve, Penmenmore, Rawlings Mill Swamp) and operated a general store and warehouse employing nine

Left, David Weems (1751–1820), mariner, shipbuilder, privateer in the Revolutionary War, and father of George Weems, progenitor of the Weems line. Courtesy of Orlando Ridout IV and Richard Forbes. *Middle,* Mason L. Weems (1814–74), son of George Weems and master of steamers on the Patuxent and Rappahannock for many years. Courtesy of Richard Forbes. *Right,* Henry Williams, general manager and president of the Weems line, 1875–1905. Courtesy of Alice Forbes Bowie

clerks handling shipments at nearby Plum Point landing (Land Records, Anne Arundel County, 1818–20, WSG-6, pp. 302–3; 1815–16, WSG 2, p. 452; 1823–25, WSG 10, p. 255; Abstract Index of Deeds, Calvert County, SR 511, deeds 6/17/1815, 8/12/1812, 1/19/1813, 4/14/1809, 1/6/1808, 9/29/1807, 8/27/1816; Lantz, "X- The Good Ship Surprise"). David Weems died on January 20, 1820.

George Weems married Sarah Sutton of Baltimore in 1808, bought a house at 47 Philpott Street, Fells Point, and had five children: Ann Margaret (born 1809); Thomas Sutton (October 25, 1812–August 22, 1837); Mason Locke (April 12, 1814–October 13, 1874); Gustavus (September 30, 1816–July 6, 1859); Theodore (March 22, 1818–September 7, 1871); and George W. (December 2, 1819–July 26, 1865). Margaret later ran off and married "a common fellow Jones," as the family journal recorded it, had a child, and returned to Marshes Seat. Thomas Sutton, George's young son, blown through *Eagle's* skylight, at an early age commanded an icebreaker in Baltimore harbor, contracted consumption, and died on August 22, 1837, at the age of 24 (Forbes collection). George Weems lost his house on Philpott Street from debts on *Surprise* and rented a house at Charles and Barre Streets until the explosion occurred on *Eagle.* Then, after recuperating at Marshes Seat, he moved into a dwelling on Conway Street east of Howard, only a block or two from the Light Street wharves.

George Weems came to depend on his sons in 1843: Mason L. to manage his affairs and serve as master of *Patuxent,* Gustavus as engineer, Theodore as mate, and George W. as occasional mate and, at home, assistant to his father. They were a close-knit family.

As early as 1829, George Weems had weighed transferring *Patuxent* to his sons. In that year, he executed a document in his own handwriting agreeing to sell the steamer (or seven-eighths portion of it) to them for $21,000 (retaining one-eighth for himself). The terms were apparently never carried out (Weems papers, MS 909, Maryland Historical Society). At age 60, George Weems was acutely conscious of his mortality and celebrated his birthday by executing a bond with his four sons. By the agreement, they collectively posted $50,000; the terms stipulated that "whereas the above named George Weems has by much care industry and economy accumulated considerable real and personal property and feeling desirous to apportion the same among his four sons . . . and whereas he has already had certain real estate decreed in fee to two of his sons . . . to . . . the farm which he bought of Thomas Croxall to Mason L. Weems and the farm in Calvert County which he purchased of the two M. W. Longs to George W. Weems . . . [he] conveyed all . . . right and title . . . to the Steam Boat *Patuxent* and all the [N]egro slaves which are now employed in manning said boat . . . as regular hands and all her tackle, fixtures, boats, wharfs, furniture belonging to said boat . . . [but] the said George Weems [hold] title to said property during his life [and that he not] be disturbed in any manner . . . by his said sons or any other persons . . . but to use, occupy, possess, and enjoy the same as he had heretofore done" (Forbes Collection).

On April 5, 1847, George Weems transferred one-half interest in *Planter* to Mason L., who owned the other half, and sold Fair Haven to him for $10,000. Theodore held substantial real estate in Baltimore; George W. Weems operated a business as commission merchant in Baltimore in 1847. George Weems (senior) lived at Fair Haven and also bought a house in 1835 for $6,000 at 125 South Exeter Street (at Duke Street) in Baltimore (Forbes Collection). After a lingering illness, George Weems died at Fair Haven on March 6, 1853, and was buried in Herring Creek Churchyard, St. James Parish. Mason L. Weems took control of *Patuxent* and *Planter* (built 1845). He lived at 35 North Eutaw Street (at Pratt Street) in 1859 (Baltimore City directory). The new steamer *George Weems*, launched in 1859, was a memorial to the patriarch. Gustavus Weems, engineer and close associate of Mason L., died on July 6, 1859.

Mason Locke Weems lived at 6 North Carey Street, Baltimore, from 1858. In 1844, he had married Matilda Sparrow. They had six children, all but two of whom died in childhood: Mary (December 9, 1846–July 21, 1847); Mason Locke (June 16, 1850–April 3, 1854); John Sparrow (June 16, 1852–January 25, 1859); Thomas Henry (October 21, 1853–April 26, 1855); Georgeanna (May 27, 1845–August 24, 1924); Matilda (June 8, 1848–October 23, 1910). Matilda, his wife, died on September 26, 1861. The steamer *Matilda*, launched April 1864, was named for her.

George W. Weems, the youngest of the brothers, died on July 26, 1865. He had lived at 506 West Fayette Street. Theodore Weems, in failing health, in the terms of his will dated July 26, 1871, bequeathed one-half share of his steamboat property to his nieces, Gustavia and Rachel, daughters of George W., who had nursed him during his illness. (The terms of the will were retired by Henry Williams in 1879.) Theodore died on September 13, 1871. A new boat was named for him (the engine was removed from the wreckage of *George Weems*).

Georgeanna Weems married Henry Williams on June 11, 1868. They lived in Prince Frederick

where he practiced law with James T. Briscoe. Born October 9, 1840, at the parsonage of All Saints Church in Calvert County, where his father was the rector, Henry Williams came of old Maryland stock. Educated by private tutors and at Toppings School in Baltimore, Henry Williams read law under the guidance of Charles J. M. Gwins, later attorney general of Maryland. During the Civil War, Henry Williams won election to the house of delegates and then in 1871 to the state senate.

Georgeanna and Henry Williams had seven children: Mason Locke (born March 13, 1869); Henry (born March 15, 1871); Elizabeth Chew (born December 5, 1872); George Weems (born June 25, 1874); John Hamilton Chew (born June 11, 1875); Ferdinand (born in Scotland September 19, 1876; died July 4, 1877); and Matilda Weems (born January 3, 1878).

Matilda Sparrow Weems married Sydney Hume Forbes on April 15, 1873. Their children were Theodore (born July 18, 1874); Jane (Jennie) Dawson (born 1876); James D. and Matilda (died as infants).

Mason Locke Weems, after a period of exhaustive work, died (most likely of a stroke) on October 15, 1874. Sydney and Matilda lived at 6 North Carey Street after the death of Mason Locke. Sydney Hume Forbes died in 1902.

When they first came to Baltimore in 1875, after the death of Mason Locke Weems, Henry Williams and Georgeanna lived at 6 Waverley Terrace. Within a year, however, they moved to 407 West Lanvale Street, at McCullough, where they lived for many years. Henry Williams was principally responsible for the buildup of the Weems fleet of steamboats, 1875–1905, particularly during the period of steamboat prosperity around the turn of the century. He sold the line to the Maryland, Delaware, and Virginia Railroad Company (subsidiary of the Pennsylvania Railroad) in early 1905.

In addition to his management of the Weems steamboat line and to his extensive business interests, Henry Williams played an intermittent game with politics. Many years before, during and immediately after the Civil War, he was twice elected delegate to the state legislature from Calvert County and received every vote cast in the county in both elections. In 1871, he was elected for a four-year term in the Maryland Senate. While in the House of Delegates, he had used his influence in the enactment of legislation to reenfranchise southern sympathizers and to complete the building of the railroad to Pope's Creek. A staunch Democrat, he carried his affiliation to the political contest in Baltimore in 1895. His bid for mayor on the Democratic ticket in 1895 was ill timed. For 20 years, Maryland politics had been controlled by a Democratic machine dominated by Arthur Pue Gorman of Howard County and in Baltimore City by Isaac Freeman Rasin. Underneath their hold on power, the seeds of reform were taking root, attacking the spoils system of the machine. The politics were clouded further by racial tension and by press hysteria over conditions in the slums. The result of the election was catastrophe for the Democratic slate. For the first time since the Civil War, the Republicans held the balance of power in the state and in the city. The Democrats awaited the reforms promised by the Republicans. When they were not specifically forthcoming, the Democratic machine tried again. Henry Williams's second bid for mayor in 1897 went down to defeat along with the Gorman-Rasin machine.

Henry Williams was a wealthy man. Not only had the Weems Steamboat Company consistently earned for him a substantial profit but also his investments, most in regional enterprise, had prospered. His portfolio included stock holdings in railroads, real estate, and banks. In the commercial life of the city, he held a prominent place.

His bid for a return to political power met with initial success. The election of 1901, remarkably quiet after the bloody ones of the 1890s, resulted in the triumph of Thomas G. Hayes as mayor and Henry Williams as president of the second branch of the city council; in this office, he took the mayor's place in his absence. He was a member, ex officio, of the board of estimates and of the harbor board. The mayoral elections of 1903 brought Robert McLane to office. But Henry Williams, largely because of the heavy turnout of Negroes in his district and their fear of disenfranchisement at the hands of the Democratic machine, failed to hold his seat. Mayor McLane immediately appointed Williams as tax collector for the city. The death of McLane in 1904 not only foreshortened the most promising career on the Democratic horizon but also brought to office E. Clay Timanus, a likable but stalwart Republican who would have cleared out from City Hall all of McLane's appointees had not the charter prevented him from firing the heads of department named by his predecessor. Henry Williams stayed on and was sub-

jected to mounting harassment from Timanus. A particular form of needling was an abrupt order that Williams physically occupy his office in City Hall from 9:30 A.M. to 3:00 P.M. each day, a departure from the discretionary office hours observed by tax collectors for many years. Stubbornly, Henry Williams held on, obeying the onerous injunctions. He served his full four-year term, largely to protect Democratic appointees beneath him from the hatchet of Mayor Timanus.

In 1907, while still serving as city tax collector, Henry Williams briefly occupied the limelight when he was induced to run for governor by Baltimore Democrats. For some months, he held the balance of support, at least 100 of the 121 convention votes, with the Talbott-Gorman faction working in his behalf. But the coalition supporting him disintegrated at the last minute, and opposition to Williams developed in the person of S.[olomon] Davies Warfield (later to become president of the Seaboard Airline Railroad and the Old Bay line, and source of the name of the famous steamer *President Warfield*), who was expected to finance most of the campaign—and the Baltimore *Sun*. On the floor of the convention—just 15 minutes before he was to be nominated—Henry Williams learned that his nomination would be withdrawn. Even the press condemned the shabby treatment given Henry Williams.

During the last years of his life, Henry Williams lived at 108 West 39th Street, near the line between Guilford and Roland Park in Baltimore. He died there on March 20, 1916. He was eulogized in the press, in financial journals, and in memorials read in churches and courthouses all over the state and in Virginia.

His sons (and the son of Matilda Forbes) were not content to put aside the family's maritime legacy or the name of Weems. Not seeing any future in steamboat operations on the Chesapeake, they decided to explore the possibilities of establishing a steamship line to run the coast between Baltimore and southern ports (similar to the Old Dominion Line or the Merchants and Miners Transportation Co.). Beginning with service to Georgetown, South Carolina, and a small but handsome former government vessel renamed *George Weems* (so comely that they ceased to use her as a freighter and made her into a yacht), they rapidly expanded their coastal trade, eventually to include Wilmington, North Carolina; Charleston, South Carolina; Miami; West Palm Beach; Philadelphia; New York; Beaumont;

Corpus Christi; and Lake Charles—and developed a fleet of 15 oceangoing ships, mostly bought from World War I surplus through the U.S. Shipping Board and rebuilt into profitable freighters and handsome passenger liners, rivaling the best ships running the coast. All 15 of the ships bore the name of Weems (one was *Henry Williams*). *Mary Weems* and *Esther Weems*, designed specifically for the fashionable Miami passenger trade, boasted luxuries unheard of at the time. At the very start of the Baltimore–Carolina Steamship Company, as they called the enterprise at the start with the acquisition of *George Weems*, the brothers (and Theodore Weems Forbes) persuaded the MD & V to permit the use of the old house flag. The red ball on the blue field flew once again from the masthead of a Weems vessel. In the period from 1908 to 1929, the expansion of the B & C under Mason Locke Weems Williams, and, after his death, under his brother Henry Williams, Jr., was little short of spectacular. Nev-

ertheless, on July 22, 1929, Henry Williams, Jr., to the surprise of the shipping world, announced the sale of the Baltimore & Carolina Steamship Company to A. & H. Bull and Company, a New York organization operating the Baltimore Insular line in a coastwise business. The sale marked the end of the maritime interests of the Weems dynasty. For a brief period the new owners perpetuated the Weems name on the ships, but in 1931 the president, Ernest A. Bull, decreed that the Weems portion of each name would be dropped. With the gesture, the name of Weems disappeared from the coastal trade. During World War II, a liberty ship was christened *George Weems*. When she was renamed at the end of the war, the name of Weems left the maritime world forever (data in vertical files, Maryland Room, Enoch Pratt Free Library; *Baltimore Municipal Journal,* August 2, 1929; Williams papers, MS 907; and Weems Scrapbook, MS 888, Maryland Historical Society).

Notes on Landings and Other Features of the Patuxent, Potomac, and Rappahannock Routes of the Weems Line around the Turn of the Century

These notes reflect the scheduled routes of the Weems Steamboat Company in the period 1900–4. Many wharves visited by the Weems line boats in earlier years are not mentioned. The listings included in these notes are arranged in the sequence in which they would be encountered by a steamer entering the river from the Bay and proceeding toward the head of navigation. Following each entry in parentheses is a letter (L) or (R) indicating the left or right side of the river on which the particular feature was located.

The apostrophe or possessive form is not used in the spelling of landings or wharves (i.e., Pearson's or Ware's). Steamboat schedulers and mapmakers, early gazetteers and writers, and painters of the large name boards displayed on wharves omitted the apostrophe. Omission of the apostrophe avoids such anachronistic spelling as *Saunders's* or *Solomons's,* unacceptable in regional geography. Other place names, such as those of creeks or counties, carry the apostrophe. The text follows the above-stated practice.

Patuxent River Route

During 80 years on the river, the Weems line touched more than 30 landings on the Patuxent; some were dropped and others added because of changes in trade and because of siltation of the river channel. Five counties flanked the river. Except for Prince George's their names reflected the baronial origins of Maryland: St. Mary's, for the Virgin worshipped when the colonists led by

the Calverts landed in 1634; Charles, for Charles Calvert, son of Cecil, second Lord Baltimore; Anne Arundel, wife of Cecil; Calvert (originally Patuxent), for the family name of the Lords Baltimore; Prince George's, carved out in 1695, for the Danish husband of Queen Anne. Many of the landings carried names reflecting the tumultuous colonial history and the families who engaged in it. The Patuxent lay in the shape of an old fashioned pistol lying on its left side—its long thin barrel pointed far to the north. The head of steamboat navigation had been Hills Landing (Green Landing) in early days, 48 miles from the river's mouth. Between Hills Landing and Bristol (two miles downstream on the opposite shore), the river's width was about 200 to 300 feet, winding through wetlands; from Bristol to Hollands Wharf, about seven miles above Benedict, the river widened to about 1,500 feet; between the town of Benedict to its mouth it opened to about two miles and narrowed at its mouth at Drum Point to about one mile. At the mouth, the river was about 20 to 30 feet deep, but inside the great curve it deepened to more than 100 feet.

Landings

Pearsons (L) The wharf was named for the family owner.

Millstone (L) Located at the southern hook of the river near the entrance, it was used in the Civil War as a transit point for the underground movement of supplies and spies across St. Mary's County to the Potomac and south.

General map of the Chesapeake Bay

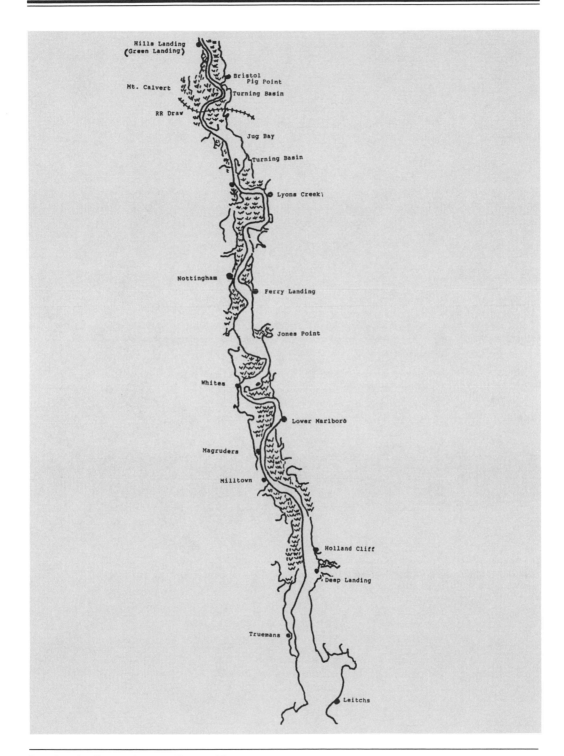

Steamboat landings on the upper Patuxent River

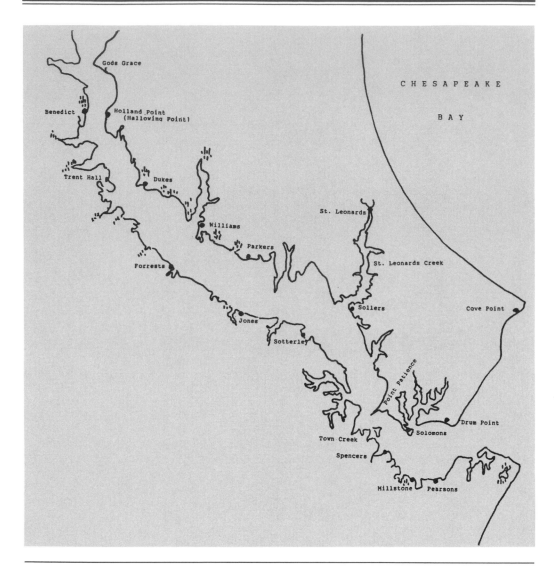

Steamboat landings on the lower Patuxent River

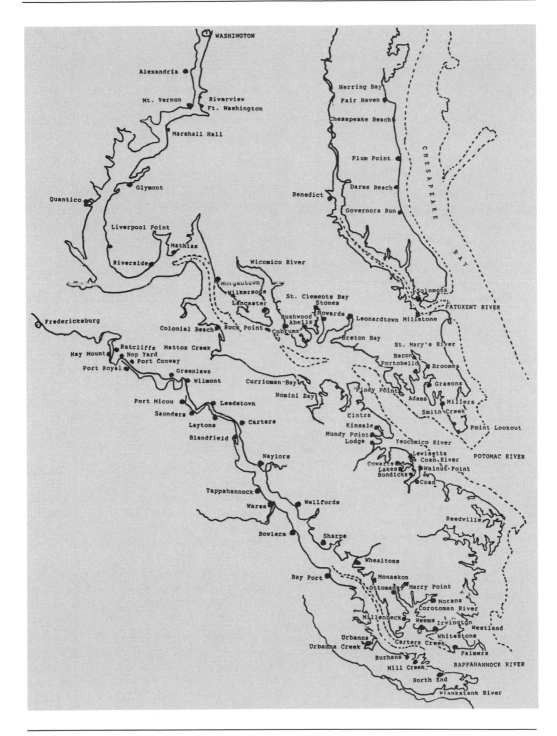

Steamboat landings on the Potomac and Rappahannock Rivers

Solomons (R)   Originally Bourse Island, part of the 5,000-acre Eltonhead Manor (Edward Eltonhead, member of the British bar, arrived in 1649 with his brother and later was executed by the Puritans after the Battle of the Severn), Bourse Island became Solomons Island (Captain Isaac Solomon, Philadelphia, established first large oyster packing house in Calvert County, 1879). The wharf property was arranged with Isaac Solomon by Mason L. Weems, 1869 (Document, Forbes Collection). The site consisted of a warehouse, cannery, and a small town.

Spencers (L)   This landing was named for its family owner.

Sollers (R)   Inside St. Leonard's Creek on the right side, it was named for John Sollers who first settled in Anne Arundel County in 1670 before moving to Calvert County. It included a general store, warehouse, and a cattlepen. A bell on the end of the wharf was used to summon the shopkeeper who lived at Old Spout Farm on the hill.

St. Leonards (R)   Near the head of St. Leonard's Creek, this landing was named for the patron saint of captives and for Leonard Calvert. It was abandoned after the Civil War by the Weems steamers because of shoaling. The town itself moved twice in colonial days (last move, 1735) to be closer to deeper water. On the shores of St. Leonard's Creek originated the story of Thomas Johnson who, in Yarmouth, England, fell in love with a young girl whom, as a ward of the court, he could not legally marry. They wed secretly, fled to America, and settled on St. Leonard's Creek. He was denounced as a Royalist, sailed for England to plead his case, was captured by the Spanish, escaped, reached Canada, walked to Maryland, and found his wife dead, his house destroyed, and a son to raise. (The son fathered his own son, Thomas Johnson, first elected governor of Maryland, who nominated George Washington as commander-in-chief of the Continental army.) Here Joshua Barney fought the so-called Battle of the Barges in August 1814, when he met the barges of the marauding British with barges of his own.

Mackalls (R)   Located across St. Leonard's Creek from Sollers, the wharf was sometimes called St. Leonards. It was not used by the Weems line but may have become an intermittent stop for former Weems boats under the MD & V.

Sotterley (L)   The plantation and mansion were named for Soterlega, seat of the Plate family in Suffolk, England. The grandson of George Plater, early governor of Maryland, also named George, married Ann Rousby and gained large plantation holdings. The long plantation house was imposing, with handsomely carved woodwork. It overlooked the river, and a brick passageway from the cellar to the foot of the hill gave rise to speculation about its use, ulterior and romantic. Duels were fought on the grounds, and pirates were rumored to have raided the estate. It became a hiding place for Confederate spies. The estate was finally lost on a throw of the dice by the Platers to Colonel Summerville of Mulberry Fields on the Potomac.

Jones (L)   The landing bore the name of the plantation family owner.

Parkers (R)   Attributed to Dr. John Claire Parker, landowning physician and president of the state senate, the landing adjoined a small village.

Forrests (L)   It was named for the plantation family owner.

Williams (R)   Named for the plantation family owner, it became a "flag-stop" for Weems steamers. Passengers wishing to board waved a white flag by day and a lantern at night.

Dukes (R)   The wharf was often called Sheridans. It was named for James Duke, who arrived in 1634, served on the council, and returned to England, leaving behind children and a tavern that bore his name; the wharf was tucked in a cove. Below Dukes lay Battle Creek (two-mile indentation in the river bank). On a hill above it stood a brick mansion, the ancestral home of Roger Brook Taney, chief justice of the United States. Above Godsgrace (a point named for John Godsgrace, early settler), the river narrowed, and marsh grass encroached on the channel.

Trent Hall (L)   The wharf adjoined the site of the home of Major Thomas Truman, who violated a treaty with the Indians in 1675, massacred their peace delegation, and laid siege to their fort; he was dismissed from the council.

Holland (Hallowing) Point (R)   The name originated with a rude ferry existing as early as Indian and first-settlement times and with the need to summon the boat from the opposite shore by hollering (hallowing). The name changed to Holland

Top, Loading tobacco aboard the steamer at Millstone Landing on the Patuxent. *Middle*, Steamer *Anne Arundel* alongside the wharf at Benedict on the Patuxent River. *Bottom*, The upper Patuxent River not very far from the head of steamboat navigation. From the collection of H. Graham Wood. Above illustrations courtesy of the Mariners' Museum

Point as used on the steamboat schedules. Above, on a bluff was the site of the estate of the same name surveyed by John Ashcombe in 1653. The original house was burned by the British in 1815; the rebuilt house descended to the Gourleys (Weems steamboat family) and by sale to their descendants, the Brooks family.

Benedict (L)   The town became an overnight steamboat layover point, the terminus for shorter runs out of Baltimore. It marked the dividing line between the upper and lower river. Benedict was recognized as a town in 1653. Named for Benedict Leonard Calvert, fourth Lord Baltimore (1675–1715), it gained an early reputation for whiskey and gambling. There were three stores, a tobacco inspection station, a hotel, several boarding-houses, tobacco warehouses, a seafood cannery, numerous houses, several bars, and a wharf. In August 1814, the British under General Ross landed enroute to Washington, marched along the river, trailed by British men-of-war in the river; the marchers unaccountably remained unmolested by the inhabitants. In October 1863, Camp Stanton was established by Union forces for the recruitment and training of the 7th, 9th, and 30th U.S. Colored Infantry.

Leitches (R)   This was named for the plantation family owners. Members of the Weems family lived here.

Truemans Point (L)   This wharf served a Negro community, with a sandy beach and a sheltered harbor just inside dangerous shoals.

Deep Landing and Holland Cliffs (R)   These two landings were separated only by a narrow creek; the wharves were at the foot of high clay banks. Above this point, marshes filled most of the river, backed by woods and rolling uplands.

Milltown (L)   This landing was named for a flour mill that once stood there; it had since been abandoned.

Magruders Ferry (L)   Named for man who, in colonial days, rowed a ferry across the river to Lower Marlboro, this was a busy wharf in summertime. It served a small rural community.

Lower Marlboro (R)   Originally called Coxtown in 1683, then Marlborough, "lower" was added to distinguish it from Upper Marlborough. It was a colonial port of entry at which royal customs were

collected and naval jurisdiction exercised. It boasted a number of handsome 18th-century houses, stores, inns, warehouses, and a sawmill. It had a physician who went by skiff to treat patients at landings along the river (for hospital care, a sick person at the turn of the century had no option except to travel by boat to Baltimore).

Whites (L)   This landing was already in decline at the turn of the century.

Ferry Landing (R)   The terminus of the ferry from Nottingham, it was in decline at the turn of the century.

Nottingham (L)   From this wharf departed the ferry to Ferry Landing, the ferry being an old scow with hinged gangways fore and aft and rails along the side and rowed by several stout black men. It was an 18th-century port for shipping tobacco to England. The town of 1,500 people before the Revolution became a ghost town, a hamlet with a tavern, inn, seven stores, and a sprinkling of old houses. In August 1814, Joshua Barney viewed the British advance and considered a march overland to Bladensburg. Above, the channel became constricted by marshes and narrowed to 300 feet.

Lyons Creek (R)   This was a wharf serving a small community.

Chesapeake Beach Railway Bridge   A span had to be opened to allow steamers to pass.

Bristol (R)   Located at Pig Point—named for a nearby source of pig iron in colonial days— Bristol in earlier steamboat days had been a substantial community of mills, inns, warehouses, stores, and dwellings. It was a center of trade for the region but was in decline at the turn of the century. The river grew heavily silted. Above here on August 12, 1814, Joshua Barney's flotilla of barges, unable to proceed further up the river, went up in flames to prevent their capture by British naval units under Cockburn, and Barney began his march overland for his stand at Bladensburg.

Hills (Green Landing) (L)   The silt and marsh grass led to its extinction. Earlier it had been the site of a thriving community of mills, warehouses, and dwellings, with Mt. Calvert nearby. (For an illustration of Hills Landing, see Appendix A, *Mary Washington*.)

Top, Steamer *Potomac* in the upper Patuxent in 1908 alongside landing at Lower Marlboro. From the collection of H. Graham Wood. *Bottom,* Steamer *Northumberland* leaving the wharf at Cintra, Virginia, on her Potomac run. Above illustrations courtesy of the Mariners' Museum

*Advertising for Boarding Houses on the
Patuxent Route*

Ms. C. B. Belt's on St. Leonard's Creek: "Saltwater bathing, fishing, and crabbing, oysters, fresh vegetables, and milk." John H. Marburger's at Point Patience: "One of the Garden Spots of Maryland," furnishing "an excellent table, with Spring Chicken, Crabs, Oysters and Fish daily" and "dancing every night" at $1 per day, $5 per week. The Maples at Solomons: "No Mosquitoes." Holland Point of Mrs. Thomas B. Gourley: "A pleasantly situated Farm House, directly on the River Bank, overlooking Four Counties, and 300 yards from Steamboat Landing, Good Bathing and Crabbing at $5 per week."

Sources

Material for coverage of the Patuxent included the following. Charles Francis Stein, *A History of Calvert County, Maryland,* rev. ed. (published by the author in cooperation with the Calvert County Historical Society, 1976). R. Lee Van Horn, *Out of the Past* (Riverdale, Md.: Prince George's County Historical Trust, 1976). *Inventory of Historic Sites in Calvert County, Charles County, and St. Mary's County* (Annapolis: Maryland Historic Trust, 1980). Alan Virta, *Prince George's County* (Norfolk: Donning Company, 1984). Margaret Brown Klapthor and Paul Dennis Brown, *History of Charles County, Maryland* (La Plata, Md.: Charles County Tercentenary, 1958). Frederick Gutheim, *The Potomac* (Baltimore: The Johns Hopkins University Press, 1986). Regina Combs Hammett, *History of St. Mary's County, Maryland* (published by the author, 1977). Donald Marquand Dozer, *Portrait of the Free State* (Cambridge, Md.: Tidewater, 1976). Hamill Thomas Kenney, *The Place Names of Maryland: Their Origin and Meaning* (Baltimore: The Maryland Historical Society, 1984). Katherine Scarborough, *Homes of the Cavaliers* (Cambridge, Md.: Tidewater, 1969). Donald G. Shomette, *Flotilla: Battle for the Patuxent* (Solomons, Md.: Calvert Marine Museum Press, 1981). Series of letters written by George Alfred Townsend (GATH) under the pen name of Jinkie Jinkins, "Life and Legends of the Patuxent River," "A Tale of Old Nottingham on the Patuxent," and others untitled for the Hagerstown *Herald,* July 1899. Theodore Ford Murray, "Bay Boat Adventures of Long Ago," Baltimore *Sun,* June

12, 1960; W. E. Northam, "Steamboat Days," *Calvert Independent,* January 5, 1950; Weems Line Brochure, 1896. Interview with Perry Bowen, Sr., December 22, 1988, and Clyde Watson, November 8, 1988.

Potomac River Route

From its mouth (more than four miles wide) the Potomac River ran in a broad water corridor for 95 miles to the head of navigation at Washington, D.C. Even at Alexandria, just a few miles below the capital, the river was nearly two miles wide. Numerous lesser estuaries emptied into the Potomac, the whole creating a system of waterways serving the lower reaches of the Northern Neck on the Virginia side as well as the counties of southern Maryland. Its shores reeked with the history of the Revolution and the Civil War. Around St. Mary's, the colony of Maryland was born, its inception with the arrival in 1628 in Virginia of George Calvert, Baron Baltimore, from his estate of Avalon in Newfoundland and his encounter, when he reached Virginia, with a reception no less frigid than the icy island he had left behind. He sought a grant from King Charles for land south of the Chesapeake to be called Carolana (after Charles) but settled for land on the Potomac. He died before the seal was affixed in 1632, leaving the settlement to be undertaken by his son, Cecil, in the face of the continued hostility of Virginians, particularly in the person of William Claiborne. Leonard and George, brothers of Cecil, led a company of 127 in the *Ark* and the *Dove*—Catholics all but forced by the commonwealth to take the oath of allegiance—to Blakiston's Island at the juncture of the Potomac and St. Mary's River. Their arrival on March 25, 1634 marked the actual birth of Maryland.

Landings

Millers (R) On Smith's Creek, near the Potomac River entrance, this was originally Tennysons Wharf consisting of a pier, a warehouse, a fish-packing plant, a general store, a hotel, and a dozen or so cottages. It was the site of Wynne, named for John Wynne, its 17th-century owner. The creek was named for John Smith; early settlers called it Trinity Creek until the connotation became unpalatable in the colony's history. The 20th-century storekeeper and postmaster was Charles R. Lewis, followed by his son.

Top, Steamer *Anne Arundel* at St. Mary's, Maryland. From the collection of Richard Edgerton. Courtesy of the Steamship Historical Society, University of Baltimore library. *Bottom,* Steamer *Anne Arundel* at Grasons Wharf on the Potomac about 1930. From the collection of Richard Edgerton. Courtesy of the Mariners' Museum

Bromes (R)   On St. Mary's River, where the first settlers landed. This was the site of St. Mary's City, the first capital of the colony under the Calverts. In 1900, only archaeological findings remained of the capital left behind in 1694 when Governor Nicholson convened the assembly in Annapolis, where he felt less Catholic influence prevailed. By 1708, only the village remained. In 1900, two churches, a seminary, and a monument stood on the site.

Bacons (R)   This landing was on St. Mary's River, opposite Bromes.

Portabello (R)   Located on St. Mary's River, below Bacons. The landing was named by William Hobb (or Edward Cooke) for his experiences in the Royal Navy during the campaign of Admiral Vernon (for whom the Washingtons named Mount Vernon) against the Spanish and the engagements at Cartegena and Portabello. On the site was a low, rambling manor house.

Grasons (R)   On St. Mary's River where St. Inigoe's Creek shallowed, Grasons was known also as Jones Wharf for a former owner. It was surmounted by Cross Manor, home of the state senator Charles S. Grason. Several plantation houses were located in area, including one built in 1656 by Governor Cornwalleys.

Coan (L)   At the head of steamboat navigation of Coan River, where the river was not much wider than a steamer's length lay Coan with Bundicks on the opposite shore. It was the official port of entry in Northumberland County for the collection of crown revenues and for vessels from Britain and the West Indies. In 1900 it was the major wharf for the shipment of oysters, tobacco, produce, and livestock. During the Civil War when the Potomac became the dividing line between the North and the South and legitimate trade on the river virtually ceased, the seclusion of Coan, far up its own tributary, served the purposes of smugglers, spies, and others bent on escaping scrutiny: the Tennessee regiment in June 1861 awaiting the arrival of *St. Nicholas* and Colonel Richard Thomas Zarvona, the "French lady" spy, the crews of the prize sailing vessels seized by *St. Nicholas*, Zarvona's men in the pungy bent on new depredations on Baltimore steamboats. It was a small community in 1900 consisting of a hotel, a boarding house on the hill, and a packing plant near the water.

Bundicks (L)   Bundicks lay opposite Coan. To go alongside after leaving Coan, a steamer had to undergo a complicated maneuver with spring lines to turn around in the narrow channel. Named for a resident prominent as a local warehouse owner and storeowner of the late 1800s, this was a small community of a few dwellings, an agent's house, a store, wharf, shed, and cattlepen.

Cowarts (L)   At mouth of the Glebe, a finger of the Coan River, Cowarts was named for the family owning the seafood- and tomato-packing plants.

Lewisetta (L)   On north side of the mouth of Coan River as it entered the Potomac lay this complex of seafood-packing and tomato-canning factories, a grove of summer cottages, a general store, and warehouse. It was the legacy of Charles R. Lewis, dominant in 1900 and was named in 1753 for Etta Lewis, the daughter of a local landowner. The wharf was kept busy in loading products from the local canneries.

Walnut Point (L)   On opposite side of Coan River entrance from Lewisetta was Walnut Point, home of packing houses. The Weems steamer no longer called there at the turn of the century.

Kinsale (L)   On the West Yeocomico River off the Potomac stood this pleasant, hilly town of orderly streets, a hotel, dwellings, small factories, a lumber mill, a packing plant, and a basin for sailing craft. Reputed to be the oldest river town on the Potomac in Virginia, it was founded in the first decade of the 18th century. Streets were planned from its beginning. Export of tobacco, trade with the West Indies, lumbering, and shipbuilding made it thrive. Early sailing convoys were formed even before the Revolution. On August 4–5, 1814, the force of Rear Admiral George Cockburn, RN, drove off the defenders of Kinsale, burned down the warehouses, seized five schooners, destroyed all available tobacco and flour, and scorched the countryside. Nothing was spared except the hovel of a poor black woman; Cockburn was labeled "The Scourge of the Potomac." In the early days of the Civil War, the town was the link with Leonardtown for smuggling operations across the Potomac (see Chapter 4).

Mundy Point (L)   Across the West Yeocomico River from Kinsale was this site of one of the Potomac's largest seafood-packing plants, with a tomato cannery and a community surrounding a

Top, The wharf at Coan, Virginia, about 1925. The cable ferry at *right* was used to cross the Coan River to Bundicks, a short distance on the opposite bank. From the collection of J. S. Bohannon. *Middle,* Steamer leaving Walnut Point, Virginia. Cowarts Landing can be seen in the background to the *left,* Lewisetta Landing to the *right.* From the collection of H. Graham Wood. *Bottom,* Steamer *Dorchester* at Kinsale, Virginia, on a Potomac run, August 1931. Photo by A. Aubrey Bodine. Above illustrations courtesy of the Mariners' Museum store and post office. Named for Henry Mundy, a British seafarer who lived there at end of 17th century, the town shared the fate of Kinsale in the depredations of Admiral Cockburn in 1814.

Lodge Landing (L)   On the South Yeocomico River off the Potomac, this landing was named for Exeter Lodge, whose nearby plantation was patented in 1651. For decades its sawmill produced cordwood for shipment; freight shipments were heavy in the harvest season.

Adams (R)   On the creek at the entrance to St. George's River on the Maryland side of the Potomac lay Adams. Nearby was Hobbs Wharf, a former steamboat landing and a resort with hotels for summer visitors.

Piney Point (R)   A long narrow neck of land appeared as a line of pines outlined against a crescent of white sand. Its 30-foot lighthouse, built in 1836, was the first lighthouse on the Potomac River. Piney Point Hotel and rows of quaint summer cottages graced the fashionable resort for politically and socially prominent residents of Washington. In the past, presidents James Monroe, Franklin Pierce, and Theodore Roosevelt, as well as John C. Calhoun, Henry Clay, and Daniel Webster were vacationers there. Washington newspapers listed notables vacationing at Piney Point. For entertainment, there were bands and orchestras all summer long, as well as bathing, blackberrying, rowing, fishing for perch, straw rides, group singing in gazebos after dark, and dancing through the night. The choir of St. James Episcopal Church came to stay each summer and there developed its repertoire. The Capital Bicycle Club, bringing their vehicles by steamer, explored nearby roads and countryside. "Old Tom Kosten," the lighthouse keeper, played host to visitors. The wharf was a two-story structure complete with a bar and smoking room; it replaced the earlier one destroyed in the fire of 1881.

Leonardtown (R)   This town lay seven miles inside Breton Bay off the Potomac (on the Maryland shore), where the stream narrowed and became a marsh. Streets and lanes criss-crossed on the hillside. Originally called Seymour Town in 1704 for John Seymour, it was later named for Benedict Leonard Calvert, fourth Lord Baltimore. From the 17th century on, more tobacco was shipped from Blakiston Wharf than from any other Potomac port; this wharf, near Foxwell Point, then became a steamboat wharf. Leonardtown became the center of commercial life of St. Mary's County. A warehouse, stores, granaries, oyster-shucking houses, tomato canneries, banks, an ice plant, a hotel, a herring fish factory, and houses lined the wandering streets. The town was featured in a few skirmishes between the British and local militia in the Revolutionary War. On July 19, 1814, Rear Admiral George Cockburn, RN, and his men plundered every house in town, wrecked the courthouse, seized all the tobacco, rummaged through the graveyard for valuables, and used upset tombstones as field ovens for their evening meal. During the Civil War, the town was linked with Kinsale for smuggling operations across the Potomac (see Chapter 4).

Howards and Stones (later known as Bayside) (R)   On St. Clement's Bay (on the Maryland shore), named for St. Clement's Day of November 23, 1633, when a plot was discovered in Yarmouth, England, to prevent the sailing of *Ark* and *Dove,* both wharves were named for local residents. Both became fishing centers for herring and shad.

Cobrums (R)   Sometimes incorrectly spelled *Coburn,* this landing lay on the western side of St. Clement's Bay.

Abells (R)   On a sandy point near the entrance to St. Clement's Bay, this landing was named for a large family inhabiting the area. Steamers usually called on their return trip.

Bushwood (R)   On the western shore of the Wicomico River (Maryland shore) near the entrance, one of several Chesapeake tributaries of the same name, it was named for Bushwood Lodge, homestead of the Key family, ancestors of the writer of "The Star-spangled Banner." The landing dated from 1683; the lord proprietor decided the site should be used for minting coins for the new colony, an idea squelched by the Crown. Rented by Union forces in 1862 as a supply depot, it grew to a commercial center, with a tomato cannery, large flour mill, several oyster-packing houses, three general stores, an ice cream parlor, and boardinghouses. Nearby was the summer resort at Bullock's Island, complete with a ballroom for cotillion dances.

Lancaster (R)   This was a landing on the shore of the Wicomico River opposite Bushwood.

Bushwood Wharf, Maryland, on the Potomac run, July 1907. Courtesy of the Mariners' Museum

Riverside (R)   This was a country landing with a store on the Maryland shore.

Liverpool (R)   On the Maryland shore, this landing was named for Liverpool, England. The wharf was active in the shipment of canned fish from the local factory.

Glymont (R)   This was a landing on the Maryland shore and served the naval depot at Indian Head and a dwindling summer resort for some Washingtonians.

Alexandria (L)   This Virginia city below Washington was renowned in history.

Washington (R)   Weems steamers tied up here at the 7th Street Wharf. The trip from Light Street Wharf, Baltimore, took 37 hours to complete; by train, the trip could be made in less than two hours.

Advertising for Boarding Houses on the Potomac Route

Calvert's Rest at Ridge near Millers: "With good water, bathing, fishing, crabbing, and boating, $6 per week, $1 per day." Garrett's at Piney Point: "Offering special inducements to Young People and Families, and sailing, dancing, saltwater bathing, and carriages to meet guests at the landing." Moore's Hotel at Leonardtown: "With croquet and 'livery in connection' at $9 per week, $1.50 per day." Kinsale Hotel: "Fine table with Delicacies of River and Surrounding Country, Artesia Drinking Water, Livery, No Mosquitoes." J. D. Statesman's Piney Point: "Comfortable Rooms and Good Table, Will Accommodate a few Colored Boarders for Summer Months. Terms Reasonable."

Sources

Material for coverage of the Potomac route came from the following. Edwin A. Beitzell, *Life on the Potomac* (Abell, Md.: published by the author, 1968, 1979), and especially from Appendix F: Frederick Tilp, "Derivation of Potomac River Place Names." Frederick Tilp, *This Was Potomac River*, 3rd ed. (Alexandria, Va.: published by the author, 1987). Regina Combs Hammett, *History of St. Mary's County, Maryland* (published by the author, 1977). Frederick Gutheim, *The Potomac* (Baltimore: The Johns Hopkins University Press, 1986). Margaret Brown Klapthor and Paul Dennis Brown, *History of Charles County, Maryland* (La Plata, Md.: Charles County Ter-

centenary, 1958). Donald Marquand Dozer, *Portrait of the Free State* (Cambridge, Md.: Tidewater, 1976). Robert de Gast, *The Lighthouses of the Chesapeake Bay* (Baltimore: The Johns Hopkins University Press, 1973). *Summer Homes and Historical Points Along the Routes of the Weems Steamboat Company* (brochure published by the Weems Steamboat Company, 1896). Robert H. Burgess, "Gone Are the Days," Baltimore *Sun*, July 3, 1949. Edwin A. Beitzell, "Steamboating on the Potomac River," *Chronicles of St. Mary's* 16 (February 1969). Ames W. Williams, "The Baltimore Boats," *Virginia Cavalcade* 15 (1965–66). George Alfred Townsend (GATH), series of articles written 1897–99 including "A Journey by Water . . . from Baltimore to Washington" in Weems Scrapbook, MS 888, Maryland Historical Society. Betty M. Snyder, "Floating Lazily to Washington," Baltimore *Sun*, October 21, 1928. Robert H. Burgess, "Vanished White Fleet," Baltimore *Sun*, March 30, 1947. Robert H. Burgess, "Steamboat Reveries" in *This Was Chesapeake Bay* (Cambridge, Md.: Tidewater, 1963). BC & A and MD & V brochure, published by the companies jointly in the 1920s.

Rappahannock River Route

Wharves had come and gone. During the 75-year span of Weems line contact on the river, perhaps as many wharves as years had been sighted by its boats. Some disappeared, victims of neglect, abandonment, ice, high water, and storm. Others were bypassed as trade diminished; new wharves appeared as demand increased or shifted. At the turn of the century, Weems steamboats called at some 32 landings on the Rappahannock.

The river ran for 93 miles from its mouth to Fredericksburg at the head of navigation. By various criteria, the river tended to be divided into "upper" and "lower." At Bowlers, for example, oyster beds tended to disappear. Instead of oystermen tonging or dredging, there appeared the long nets fishermen placed between stakes to harvest herring and shad. For many practical reasons, Tappahannock in Essex County, a major town approximately midway between the river's mouth and Fredericksburg, was considered the dividing point. The interests of residents surrounding that community differed markedly from those of their counterparts in Fredericksburg. By another standard, Leedstown, some 17 miles upriver from Tappahannock, was considered the

Top, The Rappahannock River from the pilothouse of *Potomac*, July 5, 1935. Photo by the author. *Middle*, Steamboat time at a Rappahannock River wharf about 1912, as *Middlesex* arrives. Photo by A. Spencer Marsellis. *Bottom*, Steamer *Calvert* pulls away from the landing at Irvington, Carter's Creek, on a Rappahannock run. From the collection of David E. Willing. Middle and bottom illustrations courtesy of the Mariners' Museum point of division. There, the Weems steamboats on certain schedules lay overnight, thereby bisecting the long trip between Fredericksburg and Baltimore. And at Leedstown, the scenery of the river changed markedly. Below Leedstown, the river sprawled like a widening bay toward its mouth, until at the place where its water emptied into the Chesapeake Bay it measured almost four miles from shore to shore. Above Leedstown, the river began to narrow, and the rolling hills of the lower Piedmont plunged straight-sided and wildly forested in many places to the very water's edge. In the upper reaches, the river bent back and forth in spectacular vistas of high hills shadowing one another over a narrow stream.

Landings

Northend and Mill Creek (L)   These landings on the south shore were exposed to the open Chesapeake.

Riverview (R)   This landing served the north shore near the mouth of the river.

Weems (R)   This was a landing at the mouth of Carter's Creek, which emptied into the river. Its name was derived from the fact that the Weems line built and owned it. It had a long wharf extending from shallow water, a warehouse, a shed, a store, an agent's house, and docking for sailing vessels. It became a center for fishermen and oystermen and a shipping point for products of two nearby factories at which fish were boiled and pressed to extract oil used as a lubricant, and the refuse ("chum") was mixed with mortar and used for fertilizer; it had an unbearable odor. Near Weems Wharf was the wharf (between Corotoman Creek, the mouth of the Corotoman River, and the mouth of Carter's Creek) built by "King" Carter in the heyday of his empire. Robert Carter, son of John (offspring of a London vintner) who emigrated to Virginia, carried the myth of Virginia aristocratic dynasties to its ultimate dimension (most of the founders of the Virginia plantation system were ruthless, hard-fisted men who advantaged themselves from the acquisition of land and merchant enterprise; few were gentry in the British meaning). His house at Corotoman, occupied in the 1650s, commanded a view of the river, an overview of his plantation of more than 18,000 acres, and a place from which to dominate the 18th-century politics and society of Virginia. In his 60s, he owned more than 300,000 acres on 44 tobacco-producing plantations in 24 counties;

1,000 slaves; 2,000 cattle; herds of sheep, hogs, and horses; and his mansion (burned in 1729 and completely destroyed by the British in the Revolutionary War). Robert Carter became the agent of Lord Fairfax in extending the domain of the Proprietary, from 1,470,000 to 5,282,000 acres, to the Shenandoah Valley and parts of what became West Virginia. He served as rector of William and Mary College, speaker of the House of Burgesses, treasurer, and acting governor; he built the courthouse of Lancaster County; an industrial complex of gristmill, cloth factory, carpenter, joiner, and wheelwright shops and countinghouse near his wharf; and Christ Church, a handsome cross-shaped chapel (built without architects) in the community of Irvington. He died in 1732, after a long bout with excessive flatulence, gout, and a large stock of fine wine in his cellar.

Irvington (R)   This town at the head of Carter's Creek, on a confined channel, was the site of old tree-shaded residences and of Christ Church.

Millenbeck (R)   This landing was at the mouth of the Corotoman River where it emptied into the Rappahannock. Named for the estate of its original owner, it was the seat of the Ball family; Mary Ball was the mother of George Washington.

Merry Point (R)   This landing was noted for its soft-shell crabs, for the mansion for which it was named, and for an old, blind preacher named James Waddel who, in 1762, delivered thunderbolt sermons attracting crowds from all over the valley.

Burhans (L)   This landing on the south shore was named for a family.

Urbanna (L)   This town stood at the head of shallow and winding Urbanna Creek. Its entrance was difficult to navigate because of a sharp bend and a spit of land with a shoal extending into the channel. The town was laid out in the early 1700s as an urban center and port of entry for Middlesex County. In 1729, Robert, son of "King" Carter, attempted to convenience himself by having the office of the Crown revenue collector removed to Corotoman, but he was outshouted by protesters and displaced by his brother. The steamboat wharf rested in a jumble of makeshift shacks and fishing boats. A warehouse, packing plant, commercial buildings and dwellings comprised the town. A heavy volume of freight moved through Urbanna in the harvest and oyster seasons.

Top, Saunders Wharf on the Rappahannock River as it appeared in 1990. *Middle*, Saunders Wharf as it appeared in 1990, showing the cattlepen. *Bottom*, Saunders Wharf as it appeared in 1990, showing the passenger waiting room. Above photos by the author. Courtesy of Fielding Dickinson, Jr.

Monaskon (R)   Noted in 1900 for its 2,000-acre garden seed farms laid out by David Landreth (Philadelphia), with its attendant barns, drying and packaging houses, cottages for workers, and boardinghouses, the community in later years became a resort.

Waterview (L)   This landing fronted the river. A colony of Russian Jewish refugees arrived in 1883 and tried unsuccessfully to farm. They scattered, some to Baltimore (similar to the experience of the colony in Charles County, Maryland). Here about 1850, John J. Hurkamp began growing sumach (used as a dye in the tanning industry; it had formerly been grown in Sicily) and shipping it to Fredericksburg for grinding and transshipment by rail.

Whealtons (R)   This landing was named for a family.

Bayport (L)   The landing was in decline by 1900.

Sharps (R)   A long wharf here extended from the north shore. Named for a family, the landing was busy at harvest time.

Bowlers (L)   This landing on the south bank served a small community. The wharf was adjacent to the Bowlers Rock lighthouse, a small tower built in 1868 to replace the lightship that had functioned for 33 years; it was the only lighthouse ever constructed on the Rappahannock.

Wares (L)   This was a wharf on the south bank. Nearby, old Confederate earthworks were thrown up to shield guns firing at Union gunboats on their way to Fredericksburg.

Wellfords (R)   Serving the plantation of one of the oldest families of Virginia, this wharf was damaged many times by weather. Ice destroyed it in the 1890s, and an alternate wharf in conjunction with the Weems line was constructed in front of the house occupied by Captain Pratt. Wellfords was rebuilt and busy in 1900.

Tappahannock (L)   This country town became a busy metropolis at steamboat time. A long steamboat wharf and other landings for sailing vessels occupied the town center. Warehouses, fish factories, crabhouses, banks, commercial buildings, hotels, boardinghouses, and dwellings lined the streets; large plantations lay nearby. Passengers used the landing as a transfer point at which steamers for Norfolk met steamers from Fredericksburg and Baltimore.

Naylors (R)   This was a resort community on the sandy shore of an old plantation and a wharf serving a local packing plant. In the stream, long fishing nets were cast to catch runs of herring and shad.

Blandfield (L)   This wharf lay at the end of a long flat point covered with marsh grass. Its road was made of planks chopped from logs. Blandfield was named for the plantation of the Beverleys, a 2,500-acre tract acquired in 1680 by Robert Beverley, friend of Sir William Berkeley, despotic governor challenged by Nathaniel Bacon. The estate remained in the family. The Beverley who joined William D. Carter in belaboring Henry Williams and the Weems line lived here. The plantation was occupied by Union forces in the Civil War. Above Blandfield, the river began to narrow, and on hills high above the north shore were the heavily forested habitats of bald eagles, osprey, turkey buzzards, blue heron, mallard, teal, and red-headed ducks.

Carters (R)   This small wharf nestled beneath a 70-foot cliff on the north shore. It was generally inactive. A wooden chute from the slope was used to expedite the loading of timber and lumber to schooners and occasionally to steamboats.

Laytons (L)   This was a small community with an active lumber mill (pulpwood) and nearby plantations.

Leedstown (R)   In colonial days the community was overly ambitious when its inhabitants mapped it out as a town and projected it as a major port. It declined, and in 1900 it was only a short wharf leading to an unplanned scattering of homes on a flat plain, with a mansion in the offing, a store, and a warehouse.

Brook's Bank (L)   Not a landing, this was rather a brick mansion built in 1731 on land given to Sarah Tolliver for her husband's service to George II. The house was shelled by Union gunboats in the Civil War (shots went through without exploding) and sold for debts incurred during the war. Later it was refurbished as a showplace of Georgian stateliness.

Saunders (L)   This wharf was surmounted by a one-story building containing a freight room, cattlepen, passenger waitingroom (heated by a potbellied stove) and serving also as an agent's office. The wharf served Wheatlands, the ancestral plantation of the Saunders family. The handsome,

Top, Steamer *Potomac,* headed down the Rappahannock, lies alongside the landing at Port Royal. From the collection of Richard Edgerton. *Bottom,* The steamer approaches the landing at Hop Yard in the upper reaches of the Rappahannock. From the collection of Captain J. D. Davis. Above illustrations courtesy of the Mariners' Museum white-framed mansion was built in 1791 and was fired on by the British in the War of 1812. In the Civil War, the captain of a Union gunboat sent word ashore to John Saunders to evacuate the house before the shelling began, but Saunders collected all the women and children on the plantation and placed them on the back veranda in full view of the river, whereupon the gunboat captain changed his target to a granary between the wharf and the house. The mansion, constructed from a builder's sketch, followed the pattern of many plantation houses; servants, cooking in an out-building, brought food to the English (above-ground) basement for family dining; the basement also served as a schoolroom for household and neighboring pupils taught by a governess in residence, and as a dispensary where the sick on the plantation were nursed to health. The wharf was a busy place at steamboat time, serving merchants from Loretto and other communities; farmers driving wagons and livestock, even across the mansion's lawns, to the cattlepen for shipment; and passengers in carriages and on horseback. A garden on the grounds had a fence around it to keep out cattle, grazing mules, and people. A bell in the yard rang at mealtimes. Mules pulling plows or wagons stopped in their tracks by habit and headed for the house for hay and water; farmhands would eat a huge midday meal, sleep in the shade, and then return to the fields to work until sundown. In the mansion were a drawing and dining room, a wide hallway and stairway, all perfectly proportioned. There were two entrances, a carriage on the landward side, and veranda on the river side.

Port Micou (L)   This seldom used landing was once the site of a community of French Huguenots. The river narrowed with hills, 70 feet high, on either side.

Wilmont (R)   This wharf lay at the base of a cliff on the north bank. Nearby were the remains of the Bristol Iron Works, founded 1721 by John Bristol to ship iron ore to England.

Greenlaws (R)   Greenlaws was a small landing on the north bank. Upstream, the river formed a deep bend called Horsehead Turn. Another bend in the twisting stream was known as Devil's Elbow. On the opposite bank was the plantation of the Baylors, its front extending for more than 15 miles on the river.

Portabago Bay (L)   This wide and shallow bay on the river was once used by excursion steamers out of Fredericksburg. It was not used in 1900. On the north shore stretched one of the 44 tobacco plantations of "King" Carter.

Port Royal (L)   On the south shore, the old port was consolidated as a town in 1744 and was one of the major ports of entry during the colonial period. Substantial dwellings marked the orderly streets. It was considered in 1790 by the U.S. Congress as a possible site for the nation's capital (along with New York, Philadelphia, Havre de Grace, Boston, Yorktown, Kingston, Newport, Washington (juncture of the Potomac and Anacostia Rivers), Trenton, Reading, Lancaster, Annapolis, and Williamsburg). The implication for the Civil War, if selected, was imponderable. Here, John Wilkes Booth crossed the river on his way to early capture.

Port Conway (R)   This wharf beneath a hill was surmounted by Belle Grove, the birthplace of James Madison. Between the wharves of Port Conway and Port Royal—three-eighths of a mile apart—*Tourist* of People's line and *Caroline* of Weems line played a game of tag in 1903. Above Port Conway were the narrow fastness of the river, heavily timbered hills 80 feet high, and on either side of stream, only several hundred yards wide, the channel often was within feet of the banks. One narrow and picturesque stretch was known as Devils Woodyard.

Hop Yard (R)   This narrow wharf beneath a steep hill served a small community named for the hops grown among the vegetables of an adjoining farm. Beer was brewed on the farm, and old beer bottles appeared on the shore long after the brewery disappeared.

Hay Mount (L)   This wharf served the rich farmland to the south; it was abandoned prior to 1900.

Ratcliffs (R)   This wharf serving a small community was named for the family owning an adjoining farm. In 1900 it became a "flag stop."

Fredericksburg (L)   A steamer would turn here in a narrow channel and tie up, starboard side to (headed downstream), alongside a wharf consisting of timber bulkheading of the bank surmounted by a two-story frame house serving as agent's quarters, warehouse, and open shed. A half-mile upstream, a bridge crossed the river to

Top, Scenery on the Rappahannock River above Ratcliffs, 1990. Photo by the author. *Middle*, Steaming up the placid Rappahannock aboard *Middlesex* about 1922. Note how close the steamer shaves the shore in the upper river. *Bottom*, Steamer *Middlesex* alongside the landing at Fredericksburg, Virginia. Middle and bottom illustrations from the collection of H. Graham Wood. Courtesy of the Mariners' Museum

Falmouth; rocky falls blocked navigation. This historic city was viewed by John Smith in his appraisal of the new colony, and it became the 10th most important port of entry in the British colonies. Nearby, George Washington spent his boyhood, walked the same lane to the waterfront used for the steamboat landing, threw the legendary coin across the river, and later in life visited his mother at the house he provided for her on Charles Street. The city was known well by Thomas Jefferson and James Monroe, who practiced law near the center of town. It suffered through four major battles of the Civil War (17,000 dead, more than 80,000 wounded) with many scars left on the town's buildings. Fredericksburg was also known to Robert E. Lee, who lived at nearby Stratford, one of the splendid plantations of the Northern Neck. A steamer would return to Baltimore from Fredericksburg; a few passengers would make the roundtrip. As one stated, "where on earth besides this route can a man get a week's first-class entertainment, besides traveling nearly a thousand miles, for the sum of $12?"

Advertisements for Boarding Houses on the Rappahannock Route

Ross House of W. C. Fitzhugh at Urbanna: "Surrounded by magnificent shade trees, bathhouses, livery, steamers daily, $5 per week." Loretto of A. T. Brooke: "An old Virginia Country Home, situated about one mile from Saunders Wharf, convenient to Churches with conveyance free, $20 per month." At Port Royal, Mrs. C. Askins: "Good board, location healthy, $1 per day, $5 per week, $18 per month." At Naylors, Mrs. W. B. Mitchell: "One or two summer boarders, situated on prominent hill commanding charming view." At Weems, Mrs. R. C. Cross: "A few summer boarders at a country home, meals three times a day, $4 per week." At Bay Port, F. C. Sadler: "One of the old country homes of Essex County, rooms large and comfortable, lawn cool, $10 per month." Farmville of Miss Shead at Monaskon: "An old country residence, no children desired." Virginia Hotel of George R. Scott: "Fine Summer Hotel, Drummers' Headquarters." Hotel Nelson of D. M. Nelson: "Urbanna Wharf, beautiful view of water, Fine Spacious Porches and Bath Houses, Telephone, delicacies of the River, from $5 to $8 per week." Irvington Beach of R. W. Long: "Fishing, Bathing, Boating, Driving, No Mosquitoes, No Malaria, $5 per week, $10 per month."

Sources

Material for coverage of the Rappahannock route included the following. DeGast, *Lighthouses of the Chesapeake Bay.* Numerous articles in the Weems scrapbook, MS 888, Maryland Historical Society. *Summer Houses and Historical Points Along the Routes of the Weems Steamboat Company,* brochure published by the Weems Steamboat Company, 1896. Wilstach, *Tidewater Virginia.* Conway, *Barons of the Potomac and Rappahannock.* Dowdey, *The Virginia Dynasties.* Wertenbacher, *The Planters of Colonial Virginia.* Women's Club of Essex County, *Old Homes of Essex County.* "In Virginia Waters: A Delightful Trip on the Rappahannock," Baltimore *Sunday News,* August 14, 1890; Frye, "Baltimore Is Not in Virginia?", Baltimore *Sun,* July 16, 1967; George Alfred Townsend (GATH), "A Journey by Water," series of articles to Chicago *Tribune,* 1897. Burgess, "Baltimore Steamboats to the Northern Neck," *Northern Neck Historical Magazine* (December 1897). Historical information furnished by William Billingsley, professor at Mary Washington College; by Fielding Dickinson, Jr., master of reconstructed Saunders Wharf and Wheatlands; by A. Thomas Embrey, Jr.; by the commentary of the master of *Captain Thomas* enroute to Fredericksburg; and by William J. Bray, Jr., from his extensive research on the steamboat history of the Rappahannock.

Extracts from "The Minutes and Proceedings of the Meetings of the Stockholders of the Weems Steamboat Company of Baltimore City," 1891–1905

December 17, 1891 (stockholders meeting at Pier 2, Light Street). Elected Henry Williams, president, and Henry S. Beal, secretary; recorded the incorporation of the company and subscription of 2907 shares each by Georgeanna Williams and Matilda S. Forbes; listed the company's property: steamers *Richmond, Essex, Westmoreland, Wenonah,* three-fourths interest in *St. Mary's* and a new steamer #5 being built by Maryland Steel Company, plus Pier 2, Light Street, other wharves, total evaluation of property $551,400.00; reported mortgage for $60,000.00; report adopted; by-laws passed.

December 28, 1891 (directors meeting, including Henry Williams, Sydney Hume Forbes, Mason L. W. Williams, John H. C. Williams, Henry S. Beal). Decided that new company on January 1, 1892, would take possession of the property of the Weems line steamers in the name of the Weems Steamboat Company.

January 10, 1893 (directors meeting). Reported receipts for 1892: gross $221,543.12 for line to Baltimore, $10,204.37 for line to Norfolk, total $231,747.49, net $66,289.35; steamer *Wenonah* advertised for private sale received no offer, sold at public sale realizing $894.87 after costs and expenses; cost of *Lancaster* $113,307.37, with $20,000.00 paid out of 1891 receipts, $38,000 borrowed from Bank of Commerce at 5 percent, remainder ($55,207.37) paid out of receipts for 1892; dividend of 2½ percent declared on capital stock; forecast "enough money on hand to pay off indebtedness on the wharf in Baltimore and to the Bank of Commerce and enough to enable the company to build or buy new steamers as may be required"; established a "duplication account" to include earnings of company above 2½ percent dividend and from sale of *Wenonah* to be used for new steamers.

January 10, 1894 (directors meeting). Reported receipts for 1893: net $62,076.57, some $39,047.51 spent in paying off balance of indebtedness for steamer *Lancaster* (fully paid off); declared 2½ percent dividend, remainder of earnings placed in "duplication account."

January 14, 1895 (directors meeting). Reported receipts of 1894: gross $232,736.61, net $60,054.37, "showing a considerable falling in gross and net receipts . . . chiefly caused by the almost total failure of the fruit crop and the low prices obtained from many articles usually shipped . . . prevented large shipments," together with fact that mortgage debt due the Johns Hopkins Hospital on Pier 2, Light Street, $20,000.00 borrowed at 5 percent, became due and paid; declared dividend of 2½ percent.

December 9, 1895 (directors meeting followed by stockholders meeting). Recommended payment for wharf property at Pier 2, Light Street; reported that on February 6, 1895 the steamers *Potomac, Sue,* and *John E. Tygert,* together with the goodwill of the Maryland and Virginia Steamboat Company, had been purchased for the sum, including broker commission, of $155,000.00, thus making the total indebtedness of the company $175,000.00, of which $53,000.00 had been paid, leaving a balance of

From the Hagley Museum and Library.

$122,000.00 borrowed from several banks and individuals at 5 percent interest; reported receipts for 1895: gross $292,989.89, net $69,724.79, some $60,784.36 of this earned on the Patuxent and Rappahannock routes ($729.99 more than previous year), $8,940.43 on the Potomac route, an amount "much smaller than it should have been because [of] boat runs in opposition, and persons connected with the Maryland and Virginia Steamboat Company, whose goodwill we had bought," and repairs on steamer *Sue;* declared 2½ percent dividend.

November 19, 1896 (directors meeting). Reported sale of steamer *John E. Tygert* to the Laflin and Rand Powder Company for $7,000.00.

January 14, 1897 (directors meeting). Reported receipts for 1896: gross $299,742.02, net $69,857.39; debt reduced from $122,000.00 to $64,600.00; declared 2½ percent dividend.

January 14, 1898 (directors meeting). Reported receipts for 1897: gross $324,288.44, net $91,875.26; entire debt paid off and surplus in treasury; declared 2½ percent dividend and establishment of fund to build another steamboat.

January 13, 1899 (directors meeting). Reported receipts for 1898: gross $324,803.37, net $82,197.55 (decline from previous year) due to $8,452.92 (in contrast to $2,194.77 for 1897) paid for wharf repair, and $820.95 more than 1897 for repairing boats, plus $1,309.16 paid for stamps on bills of lading, a new addition; declared 2½ percent dividend plus an extra dividend of 5 percent for the year; set aside $30,000 in securities for building of a new boat.

January 11, 1900 (directors meeting). Reported receipts for 1899: gross $340,659.14, net $76,291.06 (an increase of gross earnings nearly $16,000.00 more than preceding year but a decrease of nearly $6,000 in net earnings, due to "large increase in expenses [from] building and repairing wharves, the increased amount paid in repairing steamers, which as they become older require more repairs, the accident to the engine of *Westmoreland* and large sums of money spent on her"); reported that a contract had been placed with Neafie and Levy Shipbuilding Company of Philadelphia to build a new boat to be ready by the first of May, funded by a payment of $30,000.00, plus a $30,000.00 deposit at 3 percent in the National Bank of Commerce and a similar amount in the Baltimore Trust and Guarantee Company; declared a 5 percent dividend.

January 14, 1901 (directors meeting). Reported receipts for 1900: gross $380,601.93 (increase of $39,942.79 over previous year), net $77,564.66 (increase of $1,372.60 over previous year), but net would have been larger except for increase of the percentage of expenses from repairs, cost of coal, increased number of steamboat runs to accommodate the trade; reported that steamer *Northumberland* built by Neafie and Levy Shipbuilding Company cost $127,256.49, the sum entirely paid off; declared 5 percent dividend.

January 10, 1902 (directors meeting). Reported receipts for 1901: gross $403,263.31 (increase of $23,661.38 over preceding year), net $70,063.96 (decrease of $7,500.70 from preceding year), decrease attributed to increase in running expenses, cost of coal and all supplies, increase in number of trips and consumption of coal; reported the loss of *Richmond* by fire as a serious one, the boat's insurance at $70,000 (her full market value) not being enough to replace her at $140,000 for a new boat; stated that contracts for a replacement boat were being prepared; reported that steamer *Calvert* had been contracted for during year and was expected to begin service in February, $60,000 having been paid toward her cost; declared 5 percent dividend on capital stock.

January 5, 1903 (directors meeting). Declared 5 percent dividend.

December 14, 1903 (directors meeting followed by stockholders meeting). Following stockholders present, either in person or by proxy: Georgeanna Williams (her proxy Henry Williams, Jr.), 2,907 shares; Matilda S. Forbes (her proxy Theodore W. Forbes), 2,907 shares; Henry Williams, trustee, 180 shares; Henry Williams, 1 share; Henry Williams, Jr., 1 share; Mason L. W. Williams, 1 share; Henry S. Beal, 1 share; Theodore W. Forbes, 1 share, total shares 5,999. Reported receipts for 1902: gross $455,047.75, net $69,572.54; to the gross should be added the gross receipts for *Caroline* $4,563.82, making total gross receipts $459,611.57; falling off in net earnings "caused by the expense of running the boat on the Rappahannock River at nominal charges for freight and passage to put down an opposition that started there," the loss on this steamer being $7,721.77, together with the cost of a lawsuit as to the title of the wharves on the Rappahannock River at a cost of $1,146.25; price paid for *Caroline* $17,905.80; reported paid on account of the building of *Middlesex* delivered the first of the year $23,486.07; reported sale of *Sue* for $990.00 net; reported charging against net profit $15,000.00 for the rebuilding of *St. Mary's;* reported indebtedness to the National Bank of Baltimore $27,500.00 and in dispute some $12,000.00 due Neafie and Levy for last payment on *Middlesex,* this amount declined for payment because the boat was eight months behind in delivery, thereby causing considerable loss; stated that the operating expense of the steamers was much larger "in consequence of increased charges of mechanics in making repairs, increased charges of engineers for wages, increased cost of coal"; forecast that "as the opposition boats have been withdrawn, and we can get back to our former prices, we hope the present year will be a more prosperous one"; declared 3 percent dividend.

October 10, 1904 (directors meeting). Announced that stockholders were about to sell their stock in the company; proposed that "the loyal and faithful service of employees of the company should be recognized in a substantive manner" by setting aside "an amount of $25,000 . . . for employees of the company that Henry Williams may deem deserving"; reported an agreement in which Georeanna Williams, Theodore W. Forbes, Jane D. Forbes (committee of Matilda Forbes), in exchange for the property of Pier 2, Light Street (carrying on the functions of the company there by lease at $6,750 payable quarterly) would assume responsibility for the disbursements of the company and support for the last trips of the steamers leaving after midnight October 11, 1904, and receive all claims and assets of the company; Henry Williams offered his resignation as president and director of the company to take effect at noon on October 12, 1904 (his resignation was accepted); Willard Thompson elected to fill vacancy caused by the Williams resignation to take office on Wednesday, October 12, 1904, at noon.

October 10, 1904 at 3:45 P.M. (stockholders meeting held in offices of Marbury and Gosnell, Maryland Telephone Building, Baltimore). Present the following stockholders: Henry Williams, trustee, 180 shares; Henry Williams, 1 share; Henry Williams, Jr., proxy for

Georgeanna Weems Williams, 2,907 shares; Henry Williams, Jr., 1 share; Mason L. W. Williams, 1 share; Henry S. Beal, 1 share; Theodore W. Forbes, proxy for Matilda S. Forbes, 2,908 shares; Theodore W. Forbes, 1 share, these being all of the stockholders of the company; approved all of the minutes of the board of directors meeting.

October 15, 1904 (special meeting of directors in company office). Henry Williams, Jr., and Theodore W. Forbes, resigned as treasurer and secretary, respectively, and William L. Rothstein was elected to fill vacancies of both; authorized the treasurer to deposit all funds of the company in the National Bank of Commerce, Baltimore.

December 12, 1904 (stockholders meeting). Confirmed election of officers of the company: Willard Thompson as president, W. L. Rothstein as secretary and treasurer; following officers appointed by the president: T. Murdock, general freight and passenger agent; T. A. Joynes, superintendent of steamers; Thomas Benson, chief engineer, floating equipment.

January 28, 1905 (directors meeting consisting of Willard Thompson, Edward P. Hill, Ralph Robertson, William L. Rothstein). Reported the following: "I am authorized by the Maryland, Delaware, and Virginia Railroad Company of which I am president to purchase all the property of every kind and description belonging to the Weems Steamboat Company at and for the sum of $1,030,966.13, this sum to be paid in certificates of indebtedness of my company bearing 5 percent interest until paid. I therefore on behalf of my company make you a proposition to purchase the said property on the above terms. Yours truly, John S. Gibbs, President, Maryland, Delaware, and Virginia Railroad Company." Whereupon Ralph Robinson offered the following resolution: "Resolved that the offer of the Maryland, Delaware, and Virginia Railroad Company be accepted and that the president and other corporate officers be and they are hereby authorized to make the necessary deed or deeds or other instruments of writing to carry said offer into effect and to convey the title of the property of this company to the Maryland, Delaware, and Virginia Railroad Company," which resolution was duly seconded by Mr. E. P. Hill, and unanimously adopted. W. L. Rothstein, Secretary.

January 28, 1905 (stockholders meeting). Present: Scott and Company, 6,000 shares (all of the stockholders). Minutes of previous directors meeting read and approved. Resolution proposed by Henry Scott of the firm of Scott and Company: "Resolved that the action of the Board of Directors of this company on the offer of the Maryland, Delaware, and Virginia Railroad Company, as set forth in the resolution of the board, now submitted to this meeting, be and the same is hereby ratified, approved, and confirmed, and that the terms of said resolution be carried into effect by the officers of this company," which resolution was duly seconded by Mr. Harlan G. Scott of the firm of Scott and Company, and unanimously adopted. W. L. Rothstein, Secretary.

Notes

Prologue

1. The few excursion and midnight runs of *S.S. Potomac* in August 1967 could not be considered a part of the steamboat era.

2. Although the Chesapeake line called at a few landings on the York River until 1941, and *Eastern Shore,* dieselized and disfigured, went to Crisfield and a few remaining stops on the lower Eastern Shore until 1940, the last trip of *Anne Arundel* up the Rappahannock to Fredericksburg effectively marked the end of overnight steamboat service to the many landings of Tidewater and the major rivers of the Bay.

Chapter 1. The Quest for Steamboats: Trial and Error

1. U.S. census, 1790, 1810, 1820; Baltimore City directory, 1827.

2. Baltimore City directory, 1817.

3. Scott S. Sheads, *The Rockets Red Glare: The Maritime Defense of Baltimore in 1814* (Centreville, Md.: Tidewater Publishers, 1986), passim.

4. Emily E. Lantz, "X—The Good Ship Surprise," Baltimore *Sunday Sun,* March 15, 1908.

5. *Niles Weekly Register,* October 16, 1814.

6. Baltimore *Sun,* September 11, 1849.

7. Baltimore City directory, 1814–15.

8. From the partial index of reconstructed patent records, National Archives. The U.S. Patent Office and all records burned in 1856; about 25 percent or some 8,000 records could not be reconstructed. A detailed index reference exists for the Curtis-Yeamans engine.

9. John W. McGrain, "Englehart Cruse and Baltimore's First Steam Mill," *Maryland Historical Magazine,* 71 (1976).

10. *Niles Weekly Register,* October 16, 1819.

11. McGrain, "Englehart Cruse and Baltimore's First Steam Mill."

12. *Niles Weekly Register,* October 16, 1819.

13. Charles Reeder papers, vertical file, Maryland Historical Society; George N. Howard, *The Monumental City: Its Past History and Present Resources* (Baltimore: M. Curlander, 1989), 537–40.

14. Emily E. Lantz, "I—The Union Steamboat Line, Organized in 1813, and Captain Edward Trippe," Baltimore *Sunday Sun,* January 12, 1908.

15. James Thomas Flexner, *Steamboats Come True: American Inventors in Action* (Boston: Little, Brown, 1944, 1978), passim.

16. Louis C. Hunter, *Steamboats on the Western Rivers: An Economic and Technological History* (New York: Octagon Books, 1969), chap. 1.

17. John H. K. Shannahan, "Steamboats on the Chesapeake: Advent of Automobile Sounded Knell of a Flourishing Bay Traffic," Baltimore *Sun,* March 9, 1930.

18. Charles Reeder papers, vertical file, Maryland Historical Society.

19. Sheads, *The Rockets Red Glare,* 93.

20. Shannahan, "Steamboats on the Chesapeake"; Robert H. Burgess and H. Graham Wood, *Steamboats Out of Baltimore* (Cambridge, Md.: Tidewater Publishers, 1968), xvii–xx; Alexander Crosby Brown, *The Old Bay Line, 1840–1940* (New York: Bonanza Books, 1940), 11–12.

21. Eldredge Collection, Mariners' Museum.

22. *Niles Weekly Register,* October 16, 1819.

23. First enrollment, September 1816, certified by William Parsons, master carpenter.

24. Lantz, "X—The Good Ship Surprise."

25. *Easton Album,* 1820; Buse, *150 Years of Banking on the Eastern Shore,* extracts in vertical file, Enoch Pratt Free Library.

26. *Niles Weekly Register,* September 13, 1817.

27. Baltimore *Federal Gazette* and Baltimore *Daily Advertiser,* July 3, 1817.

28. Lantz, "X—The Good Ship Surprise."

29. Baltimore *Federal Gazette,* September 18, 1817.

30. Baltimore City directory, 1818; Weems family Bible, Maryland Room, Enoch Pratt Free Library; Weems family narrative, document handwritten at Loch Eden, 1854, addressed to Dr. David G. Weems, Forbes collection.

31. A silver flagon for cider or ale which

David Weems brought from England became an heirloom; also Emily E. Lantz, "III—The Weems Line," Baltimore *Sunday Sun,* January 26, 1908; and Weems family narrative. In the possession of the Calvert Marine Museum is a brass telescope encased in a mahogany sleeve; it bears the name of David Weems. In a letter addressed to George W. Weems, grandson of David, one Edward Reynolds wrote: "Dear Cousin George—This glass I have always greatly valued, but am now glad to give to one who has the same ancestors, and who I feel sure will appreciate its great value . . . . This was the property of David Weems . . . who used it on his many trips across the Atlantic, before the American Revolution" (Forbes Collection).

32. Military record of David Weems (Forbes Collection) cites *Military Records,* 16:454 and 21:175, Maryland Archives; DAR patriot index; oath of fidelity, Anne Arundel County, March 1778, calendar of Maryland papers, no. 4, part 2, and the Red Books, item 1544:244; DAR National Paper no. 362693; George F. Emmons, *Statistical History of the Navy of the United States, 1775 to 1853* (Washington, D.C.: Gideon Press, 1853).

33. Weems family Bible, Enoch Pratt Free Library.

34. Land records, Anne Arundel County, 1818–20, WSG 6:302–3, Maryland Archives.

35. Land records, Anne Arundel County, 1815–16, WSG 2:452; 1823–25, WSG 10:255; Abstract Index of Deeds, Calvert County, SR 511, deeds as follows: estate called Tillington near Huntingtown June 17, 1815; Devils Wood Yard August 12, 1812; Rock Hall January 19, 1813; Sheridans Point April 14, 1809; Reserve and Penmenmore January 6, 1808; Devils Woodyard and Rawlings Mill Swamp September 29, 1807; and deed June 27, 1816; Maryland Archives; Lantz, "X—The Good Ship Surprise."

36. Lantz, "X—The Good Ship Surprise."

37. Lantz, "X—The Good Ship Surprise." Quoted by permission of the Baltimore *Sun.*

38. Gustavus and George had worked hand in hand through the years. During the War of 1812, they operated a schooner, the *Nancy and Jane,* out of Plum Point. Gustavus had a narrow escape when, on a return trip from the Choptank River, he met two British vessels at the mouth of the river in full chase of a Choptank schooner. The latter, north of Poplar Island, came about with an agility that confounded the British and then fled up the river, thereby leaving *Nancy and Jane* to the attention of the two enemy ships.

When it became apparent that the Chesapeake schooner was outdistancing them on a reach across the Bay, the British opened fire. Their cannonballs fell short. The British tacked, hoping to cut off the American vessel in beating to windward. When it became clear that they were outmaneuvered by the handy little vessel, the British squared off for the upper Bay. Gustavus put into Londontown on the South River and jogged home by horse. He was left with a topic of conversation with which to regale his friends for years (Lantz, "X—The Good Ship Surprise").

39. Forbes Collection.

40. Baltimore *Patriot,* July 3, 1819.

41. Jean Baptiste Marestier, *Mémoire sur les Bateaux à Vapeur des Ètats-Unis d'Amérique* (Paris: Institute of France, Royal Academy of Sciences, 1824) (*Memoir on Steamboats of the United States of America,* trans. Sydney Worthington [Mystic, Conn.: Marine Historical Association, 1957] 29).

42. The difficulties of the rotary engine in *Surprise* can be attributed to a number of causes. The interior rotor had two swinging flaps or baffles. In between them, in the open position, steam was admitted and exerted its pressure for rotation. When the revolution reached the position of the exhaust pipe, the steam, having lost its power, vented to the condenser, whereupon the flap, touching an obstacle in the chamber, folded to a closed position to admit the next intake of steam. These flaps or baffles could not operate any length of time without lubrication, but they were inside the assembly and could not be lubricated without tearing down the entire engine. Furthermore, at that period of industrial history lubricants were made either of vegetable or animal fats and withstood very little heat, friction, or pressure. Trouble with the movement of these flaps or baffles was almost assured. Also, the delivery of steam to the rotor in just two big bursts or puffs per revolution kept the rotor moving in unequal surges, hard on the bearing surfaces. Modern turbines, of which the rotary engine was a primitive precursor, have a great number of blades and a complete circumference for the entry on one side and discharge on the other of steam, thereby ensuring smooth performance and a uniform pressure and temperature gradient, neither of which was provided for in the simplistic design of the rotary engine on *Surprise.*

43. Enrollment August 7, 1820, National Archives.

44. Land records, Anne Arundel County, 1820, WSG 7:465, Maryland Archives.

45. Land records, Anne Arundel County, 1822–23, WSG 9:436, Maryland Archives.

46. Lantz, "X—The Good Ship Surprise." Quoted by permission of the Baltimore *Sun*.

47. Enrollment June 4, 1822: Robert Taylor, Georgetown; Account sheet of the Union Bank of Maryland, Forbes Collection.

48. Lucretia Ramsey Bishko, "Lafayette and the Maryland Agricultural Society, 1824–32," *Maryland Historical Magazine*, 70 (1975).

49. Enrollment March 28, 1814, National Archives; Marestier, *Memoir on Steamboats of the United States*, passim; Lantz, "I—The Union Steamboat Line."

50. Edwin W. Beitzell, "Steamboating on the Potomac River," *Chronicles of St. Mary's*, monthly bulletin of the St. Mary's County Historical Society, 16 (February 1968); William L. Tazewell, *Norfolk's Waters: An Illustrated Maritime History of Hampton Roads* (Woodland Hills, Calif.: Windsor Publications, 1982), 61.

51. Brown, *The Old Bay Line*, 11.

52. Enrollment August 16, 1817, National Archives.

53. Baltimore City directories, 1817–47; correspondence of George Weems, Forbes Collection; Land records, Anne Arundel County, 1843–45, WSG 27:143, Maryland Archives.

54. Enrollment April 5, 1820, National Archives.

55. *Easton Album* and Easton *Gazette*, 7 June, 1819.

56. Baltimore City directories, 1820–22.

57. Beitzel, *Life on the Potomac River*, chap. 7.

58. U.S. census data for period; Tazewell, *Norfolk's Waters*, passim.

59. Baltimore City directories, 1825–28.

60. Enrollment May 5, 1827, National Archives.

61. Emily E. Lantz, "III—The Weems Line," Baltimore *Sunday Sun*, January 26, 1908.

Chapter 2. Probing for Trade: Risk and Frustration

1. Robert J. Brugger, *Maryland: A Middle Temperament, 1634–1980* (Baltimore: The Johns Hopkins University Press, 1988), 198.

2. Robert H. Burgess, *Chesapeake Sailing Craft* (Cambridge, Md.: Tidewater Publishers, 1975), vol. 1.

3. *Easton Album* and *Easton Gazette*, June 7, 1819.

4. U.S. census data for period; William L. Tazewell, *Norfolk's Waters: An Illustrated Maritime History of Hampton Roads* (Woodland Hills, Calif.: Windsor Publications, 1982).

5. John C. Emmerson, Jr., *The Steamboat Comes to Norfolk Harbor and Log of the First Ten Years, 1815–25*. Reported [collected and published] by the Norfolk *Gazette* and *Public Ledger*, *American Beacon*, and Norfolk and Portsmouth *Herald*, Portsmouth, Va., 1947, 1949, passim; U.S. census data for the period; Tazewell, *Norfolk's Waters*, passim.

6. U.S. census data for period.

7. Charles Francis Stein, *History of Calvert County, Maryland*, rev. ed. (published by the author in cooperation with the Calvert County Historical Society, 1976), passim.

8. Arthur Pierce Middleton, *Tobacco Coast: A Maritime History of Chesapeake Bay in the Colonial Era* (Baltimore: The Johns Hopkins University Press, 1984), passim.

9. Files of the Historical Division, Maryland-National Capital Park Planning Commission for Prince George's County.

10. Baltimore City directories for period.

11. R. Lee Van Horn, *Out of the Past* (Riverdale, Md.: Prince George's County Historical Society, 1976), 25.

12. Edwin W. Beitzell, *Life on the Potomac River* (Abell, Md.: published by the author, 1976), 112.

13. U.S. census data as follows:

County	1790	1820	1830
Lancaster	5,630 (3,236)[a]	5,517	4,800
Caroline	17,489 (10,903)	18,008	17,774
Westmoreland	7,722 (4,425)	6,901	8,411
Middlesex	4,140 (2,558)	4,057	4,122
Essex	9,122 (5,440)	9,909	10,531
Spotsylvania	11,252 (5,933)	14,254	14,697 (3,307)[b]

[a]Number of slaves included.
[b]In corporate limits of Fredericksburg.

In 1820, the population of Virginia was more than twice that of Maryland: Virginia, 1,065,366 (425,053 slaves); Maryland, 407,350 (107,398 slaves). Two-thirds of the Virginia population lived in the eastern district near the Bay. The slave population of Virginia exceeded the total population of Maryland by nearly 20,000. The largest city in the Tidewater area was Baltimore, 62,738; Richmond had 12,067; Norfolk, 8,478; and Fredericksburg, 3,307 (U.S. census data 1790, 1820, and 1830).

14.   John H. K. Shannahan, "Steamboats on the Chesapeake: Advent of the Automobile Sounded Knell of a Flourishing Bay Traffic," Baltimore *Sun*, March 9, 1930.

15.   Fredericksburg *Political Arena and Literary Museum*, August 1, 1828.

16.   Fredericksburg *Virginia Herald*, August 2, 1828. A rate schedule showed the following:

Passage: To or from Baltimore $5; Port Royal $1; Tappahannock $2; Urbanna or below $3.

Freight: Hogsheads, brown sugar, per cwt. 12½¢; loaf sugar 25¢; crates, earthern ware $1.30; barrels, whiskey 30¢; flour, tar, rosin, and fish 25¢; casks, nails 25¢, or per cwt. 10¢; bundles, shovels, spades, and scythes per doz. 20¢; casks, cheese 20¢; stoneware, per doz. 25¢; iron per ton $2.50; castings $3; coffee, pimento, allspice, and pepper per bag 25¢; boxes soap and candles per box 12½¢; hogsheads, molasses, rum $1.50; bundles, boxes, and packages of merchandise per foot 7¢. N.B. Gunpowder prohibited.

17.   Baltimore *Sun*, September 28, 1828.

18.   Fredericksburg *Political Arena and Literary Museum*, January 13, 1829.

19.   "An Act to Incorporate the Baltimore and Rappahannock Steam Packet Company," *Laws Made and Passed by the General Assembly of the State of Maryland* (Annapolis, Md., 1830), chap. 42, passed February 2, 1830.

20.   Enrollment January 9, 1830, National Archives.

21.   William J. Bray, Jr., "Captain Noah Fairbank, 'The Storm King'," *Fredericksburg Times*, November, 1987.

22.   The account written by B. B. Minor in the Fredericksburg *Star* of August 2, 1890, concerning an alleged rescue of passengers from an ill-fated steamer *Philadelphia* sunk by a snag in the Rappahannock by the fortunate arrival of *Patuxent* under Captain Weems is of questionable accuracy since neither vessel was operating in the

river at the time alleged. Nevertheless, his recollections of Noah Fairbank and the Weems father and son coincide with other opinions of them expressed at the time.

23.   Fredericksburg *Virginia Herald*, April 18, 1829; June 13, 1829; July 4, 1829; September 5, 1829; December 2, 1829; March 24, 1830.

24.   Fredericksburg *Virginia Herald*, April 24, 1830.

25.   Advertising 1830–31 in Baltimore newspapers.

26.   Enrollment March 12, 1831, National Archives.

27.   Statement of steamboat *Patuxent* (Appendix C).

28.   Fredericksburg *Virginia Herald*, August 9, 1833.

29.   Ibid.

30.   Fredericksburg *Virginia Herald*, September 24, 1834.

Chapter 3. Expansion: Acceptance of the Steamboat on the Bay

1.   Statement of steamboat *Patuxent*, Appendix C.

2.   Bills of sale, Forbes Collection.

3.   He bought a house for $6,000 at 125 South Exeter Street (at Duke Street) in Baltimore in 1835 (Forbes Collection).

4.   Baltimore City directories, 1847; obituary, Baltimore *Sun*, 7 July, 1847.

5.   Document, Forbes Collection.

6.   Rental agreement provided rent at $150 per year, workmen's bond deducted, wages @ $1.50 per week for Negroes, $2.50 per week for whites (document, Forbes Collection).

7.   This letter and subsequent letters written by James Harwood which are referenced in this chapter are included in the Forbes Collection.

8.   Drawing, Forbes Collection.

9.   Baltimore *Sun*, June 21–22, 1839.

10.   Drawing, Forbes Collection.

11.   Letters, Forbes Collection.

12.   Document, Forbes Collection.

13.   Arbitration agreement dated February 26, 1842, and arbitration award dated March 31, 1842, both in the Forbes Collection.

14.   Baltimore City directory.

15.   To the sketch he made of the hotel plan at Fair Haven, George Weems added some notes for the future, "It is a matter of Great Importance

that any improvements you make hereafter should be made to be uniform with what you have already. With that I am decidedly in favor of the above plan. You will find it far less expensive than any other that will be equally useful. If you have the ground story or Ware House part of the building of Brick, a wall of 9 inches thick and 8 feet high will take 15,000 Brick @ 11¢ per thousand $165. The wood work can be made very cheap. The flooring for the Ball Room you can get plained [*sic*] and grooved ready to be laid down for $3.50 to $4.50 per hundred. It will take 1,100 feet, say $50." On the wharf, he sketched in a warehouse and a row of cubicles to serve as bath houses. For property leases and transfers related to Fair Haven, see land records of Anne Arundel County, 1843–45, WSG 27:45, 143, 146–47.

16.   Note the letter dated in Baltimore, February 16, 1843, concerning *Patuxent* and sarcastically referring to John Watchman: "My dear Father—Your favour of the 14th was today received and it affords me pleasure to learn that you and George are well, also that you have succeeded in filling your Ice House. I am sure that you will [be] pleased to hear that 'your old friend' Mr. Watchman on last Monday Night signed the temperance Pledge. We have had such a continuation of bad weather that we have not been able to do much painting . . . .Gusty [Gustavus] & Tho [Theodore] join me in love to you and George. I remain your dutiful son, M. L. Weems. My love to Unkle [*sic*] Gusty and friends— MLW" (Forbes Colletion).

17.   Forbes Collection.

18.   Baltimore City and County Court of Chancery records, 1848, AWB 9:528.

19.   Enrollment data, National Archives.

20.   Baltimore City directory.

21.   *The Biographical Cyclopedia of Representative Men of Maryland and District of Columbia* (Baltimore: National Biographical Publishing Company, 1879), 607–8.

22.   For a detailed description of the vertical (walking) beam engine and its operation, see David C. Holly, *Steamboat on the Chesapeake: Emma Giles and the Tolchester Line* (Centreville, Md.: Tidewater Publishers, 1987), chap. 12.

23.   Baltimore *Sun* advertising through July 1845.

24.   Baltimore *Sun*, July 1845.

25.   In the midst of their confusion, the directors voted to contribute $1,000 to a prospective

canal to be built above the rapids at Fredericksburg and $400 as an annual salary to James Harwood, but "not paid until the new boat is paid off."

26.   The prospectus of *Mary Washington*, together with the work performed and materials used in her construction, is detailed and accurate.

27.   Information on the Baltimore and Rappahannock Steam Packet Company and the *Mary Washington* was derived from two court cases: (1) Baltimore County Court of Chancery, file 6000 MdHr, Horace Abbott, Joseph Rogers, John Ferguson, John Watchman, Henry Thompson and Sons vs. Baltimore and Rappahannock Steam Packet Company, October 21, 1846; and (2) U.S. District Court for the Maryland District, in Admiralty, William and Hazlett McKim vs. Baltimore and Rappahannock Steam Packet Company, September 3, 1846. Also, Baltimore *Sun*, fall 1846, advertising; "An Act to Incorporate the Baltimore and Rappahannock Steam Packet Company," *Laws Made and Passed by the General Assembly of the State of Maryland* (Annapolis, Md., 1830) chap. 42, passed February 2, 1830.

28.   "An Act to Incorporate the Maryland and Virginia Steam Packet Company," *Laws Made and Passed by the General Assembly of the State of Maryland* (Annapolis, Md., 1847), chap. 112, passed February 12, 1847.

29.   Baltimore *Sun*, March 3–14, 1847; Enrollment data, National Archives.

30.   Fredericksburg *News*, January, October, and November, 1847.

31.   Documents, Forbes Collection; *National Intelligencer*, January 1, 1846.

32.   Document, Forbes Collection.

33.   Baltimore *Sun*, May 8, 1855.

34.   Baltimore County record of deeds, 1854–55, liber 402:405, Maryland Archives.

35.   Documents, Forbes Collection; enrollment data, National Archives.

36.   Prince George's County survey sheet PG 82 B-1 and summary sheet on "Green Landing," file of the History Division of the Maryland-National Capital Park Planning Commission; John L. Shepherd, "Pig Point," *Maryland Gazette, Supplement* (1927); Bradstreet's directory, 1867. William B. Hill died in 1890, leaving Green Landing to his daughter, who sold it to the Patuxent Gun Club in 1908. It became the Marlboro Hunt Club in 1950.

37.   In 1990, four-lane Maryland Route 4

crossed the Patuxent at the site of this bridge.

38. Steam whistles gained acceptance on the Bay in the 1830s. Before that time, only bells were used for warning. The whistles, adapted from those on steam locomotives, were scorned at first by steamboatmen. By 1852, with regulations governing steamboat navigation, the number and duration of whistle blasts had gained significance.

39. U.S. census data.

40. Yearly wharf fees (rental or lease) were as follows: Bristol, $145; Mount Calvert (Green Landing), $145.83; State Warehouse, Baltimore, $583.32; W. B. Hill, $125; Dukes, $28; Magruders Ferry, $31.96; St. Leonards, $335.97; Holland Cliffs, $428.65; Mill Stone, $125; Lower Marlboro, $400 (Forbes Collection).

41. See Appendix C for a replication of the accounts of *Planter* during the years 1855–58.

42. Baltimore City directories; U.S. census data.

43. The following resolution was adopted on her trial run, August 10, 1858: "At a meeting of the Invited Guests, held on board of the Superior new Steamer 'George Weems' on her trial trip this day . . . Francis Hales Esq was called to the chair and Richard Sands Esq was appointed Secretary, when on motion it was Resolved: that a tender to the Messrs Weems, our Thanks for the Kind invitation extended to us, for their kind and courteous attention, and the very sumptuous and beautiful repasts which we enjoyed, for which they are proverbial; . . . that we consider the 'George Weems' in every respect a Superior Steamer, and that in her construction, the carpenter, engineer, painter and other mechanical and Artistic agencies employed have displayed good judgement and skill, such as we deem necessary to notice; . . . that the 'George Weems' is in our judgement in every respect fitted for the accommodation of Passengers, and in Speeds and Capacity one of the finest steamers out of our port; . . . that under the guidance of her estimable Theodore Weems, and expert and worthy engineer Tone Hembring, she will accomplish all for which she was and is designed in the carriage of passengers and freight to the mutual satisfaction of all parties and commend her to the public generally" (Forbes Collection).

Chapter 4. Civil War: Disruption and Rebuilding

1. William J. Kelley, "Baltimore Steamboats in the Civil War," *Maryland Historical Magazine*, 37 (1942).

2. U.S. Congress, *Vessels, Bought, Sold, and Chartered by the United States . . . Since 1861*, 40th Cong. 2d sess., July 16, 1868.

3. J. Thomas Scharf, *History of the Confederate States Navy* (New York: Prager & Sherwood, 1887), chap. 6; *Official Records of the Union and Confederate Navies in the War of the Rebellion* (Washington: GPO [published under direction of the secretary of the navy by Prof. Edward K. Rawson] 1897), series 1, vol. 4; Harold R. Manakee, *Maryland in the Civil War* (Baltimore: Maryland Historical Society, 1961), 63–65; Daniel Carroll Toomey, *The Civil War in Maryland* (Baltimore: Toomey Press, 1983), 17–36; Kenneth Brooks, Jr., "Coinjocks Roberts Wasn't Really His Name," *Chesapeake Bay Magazine* (May 1985); Kelley, "Baltimore Steamboats in the Civil War."

4. *Official Records of the Union and Confederate Navies*, series 1, 4:569–70, 795.

5. He was kept in Fort McHenry without being charged for several months when reports of his poor health circulated; the Confederate government made efforts to gain his release or, at least, better treatment as a prisoner of war; he was transferred to Fort Lafayette, where he tried to escape. Eventually, he was released under promise to leave the country and not return until hostilities ended. He lived in Paris until the war was over. He died in March 1875 and was buried at Deep Falls, the ancestral home at Chaptico, St. Mary's County, Md.

6. Brooks, "Coinjock Roberts Wasn't Really His Name"; "Nestor of the Bay Dead: Capt. James Gourley Was Known to Every Chesapeake Master," Baltimore *Sun*, April 18, 1912; official death certificate of James Gourley, Baltimore County records; *Official Records of the Union and Confederate Navies*, series 1, 4:557.

7. *Official Records of the Union and Confederate Navies*, series 1, 4:560.

8. Documents, Forbes Collection.

9. *St. Mary's Beacon*, July 18, 1861, quoted in Regina Combs Hammett, *History of St. Mary's County, Maryland* (published by the author, 1977), 221.

10. Document, Forbes Collection.

11. The relative costs were not high, but the yard time was certainly excessive.

12. Notes handwritten on a document by

Mason Locke Weems, Forbes Collection.

13. Document, Forbes Collection.

14. David C. Holly, *Steamboat on the Chesapeake: Emma Giles and the Tolchester Line* (Centreville, Md.: Tidewater Publishers, 1987) 219–21.

15. *Pilot Boy* and *Alice C. Price* were closely related to the history of the Tolchester line. The engine of *Alice C. Price* became the engine of *Emma Giles.* See Holly, *Steamboat on the Chesapeake,* chap. 12.

16. *Official Records of the Union and Confederate Navies,* series 1, 6:584–88; 7:709; Holly *Steamboat on the Chesapeake,* chap. 12.

17. *Official Records of the Union and Confederate Navies,* series 1, 8:578.

18. Note on photograph of *Planter* by Mathew Brady, National Archives; Eldredge Collection data, Mariners' Museum.

19. She was rebuilt, chartered to USQMD, modified, and lengthened at the end of the war, and operated by the Potomac Transportation Company from Baltimore to Washington. On the night of October 22, 1878, she sank in a gale off the Little Choptank River in one of the worst disasters of steamboat history; only 8 of 31 passengers aboard survived. (Robert H. Burgess and H. Graham Wood, *Steamboats Out of Baltimore* [Cambridge, Md.: Tidewater Publishers, 1969], 408; Eldredge Collection data; enrollment certificate, National Archives).

20. Baltimore *Sun,* November 15, 1864.

21. Baltimore *Sun,* January 1 and March 13, 1865.

22. Baltimore *Sun,* May 13, 1865.

23. She was propeller driven; length, 115.6; beam, 19.3; depth, 7.1; 149 tons, Captain Albert H. League. Owners: League, Ambrose L. Higgins, Isaac and Thomas DeFord, and James A. Hooper; homeport Baltimore (enrollment data, National Archives).

24. Baltimore *Sun,* March 3 and October 28, 1865.

25. This link across southern Maryland operated so successfully in the smuggling of contraband and intelligence that it continued to function, almost reflexively, for some months after the surrender at Appomattox.

26. Kelley, "Baltimore Steamboats in the Civil War"; Toomey, *The Civil War in Maryland,* 1148–49; *Official Records of the Union and Confederate Navies,* series 1, 5:540–44.

27. This was the last Weems boat to bear a likeness on the paddle boxes.

28. Other children included Mary (1846–47), Mason Locke (1850–54), John Sparrow (1852–59), and Thomas Henry (1853–55).

29. Enrollment data, National Archives; Kelley, "Baltimore Steamboats in the Civil War"; family records, Forbes Collection.

30. Family records, Forbes Collection.

31. Key information is tabulated as shown in table (see p. 294).

32. *Maryland: Its Resources, Industries and Institutions,* prepared for the Board of World's Fair Managers of Maryland by Members of the Johns Hopkins University and Others (1893), passim; Hamilton Owen, *Baltimore on the Chesapeake* (Garden City, N.Y.: Doubleday, Doran & Company, 1941), passim.

33. Letter of George Alfred Townsend (GATH) to Chicago *Herald,* May 28, 1869.

34. Richard Walsh and William Lloyd Fox, *Maryland: A History* (Annapolis, Md.: Hall of Records, Department of General Services, 1983), passim; Paul Wilstach, *Tidewater Maryland* (Indianapolis: Bobbs-Merrill, 1931), passim.

35. *Albemarle,* vertical beam sidewheel steamer, built 1865, 170 × 35.3 × 19.3; *Creole,* vertical compound, built 1862, 194 × 38 × 18.5; *Hatteras,* sister of *Albemarle,* built 1865; *Niagara,* built 1865; *Saratoga,* built 1865, 225 × 32 × 15, 1,025 tons, sister of *Niagara; Yazoo,* built 1865, 255 × 38 × 26, 1,353 tons.

36. John L. Lochhead, "Steamships and Steamboats of the Old Dominion Line," *Steamboat Bill* (March, June, September 1949); Richard E. Prince, *Norfolk, Southern Railroad, Old Dominion Line, and Connections* (Millard, Nebr.: R. E. Prince, 1972); Robert H. Burgess and H. Graham Wood, *Steamboats Out of Baltimore* (Cambridge, Md.: Tidewater Publishers, 1968), passim; Frederick Tilp, *This Was Potomac River,* 3d ed. (Alexandria, Va.: published by the author, 1987), 57–59; Hammett, *History of St. Mary's County, Maryland,* 216–17; Eldredge Collection, Mariners' Museum.

37. 40th Congress, *Vessels Bought, Sold, and Chartered by the United States.*

38. "An Act to Incorporate the Baltimore and Susquehanna Steam Company," *Laws Made and Passed by the General Assembly of the State of Maryland* (Annapolis, Md., 1850), chap. 159, passed February 27, 1850.

U.S. Census Data, 1860, 1870   (table cited in note 31)

Maryland County	1860	1870		
Calvert	10,447	9,865		
Prince George's	23,327	21,138		
St. Mary's	15,213	14,944		
Charles	16,517	15,738		
Anne Arundel	23,900	24,457		
Total	89,404	86,142	(−) 3,262	3% decline
Baltimore City and County	238,655	330,741	(+)92,086	38% increase
Baltimore City (alone)	212,418	267,354	(+)54,936	25% increase
Virginia County	1860	1870		
Caroline	18,464	15,128		
Essex	10,469	9,927		
King and Queen	10,318	9,709		
Northumberland	6,856	6,503		
Spotsylvania	15,576	11,728		
Westmoreland	8,282	7,682		
Lancaster	5,151	5,355		
Middlesex	4,364	4,981		
Total	79,480	71,013	(−)8, 467 10% decline	
Norfolk		19,229	(took 20 years to double)	

39. *Biographical Cyclopedia of Representative Men of Maryland and District of Columbia* (Baltimore: National Biographical Publishing Company, 1979), listed by name; Baltimore *Sun*, 9 July, 1883.

40. "An Act to Incorporate the Baltimore and Virginia Steamship Company," *Acts of the General Assembly of the State of Virginia* (Richmond, Va., 1866), chap. 279, passed February 21, 1866.

41. Personal note, Forbes Collection.

42. This addition is not explicit in the records.

43. Register of Wills, Baltimore City, 1871, liber SHB 37:404, Maryland Archives. It is to be noted that both Gustavus and George W. (Gustavus had never married) had transferred their interests in the steamboats by sale to Mason Locke Weems long before their deaths (enrollment certificate dated April 5, 1847, National Archives).

44. William Skinner and Sons, shipyard and marine railway situated at the foot of Cross Street in Baltimore, was founded by William Skinner in 1845. His sons, William H. and George W., were admitted to partnership. Subsequently, Henry G. Skinner, son of William H., became sole proprietor but preserved the name of his grandfather (George W. Englehart, *Baltimore, Maryland, Book of Its Board of Trade* [Baltimore: n.p., 1895], 24–75).

45. The configurations of the predecessor and successor differed because of the alterations.

46. Family records, Forbes Collection.

47. Obituary, Baltimore *Sun*, October 6, 1874.

Chapter 5. Red Ball on the Three Rivers

1. The four children were Mason Locke (1869), Henry (1871), Elizabeth Chew (1872), and George Weems (1874).

2. Another surviving child, Jane D., was born in 1876; two other children died in infancy.

3. They moved their residence a year later to the northeast corner of Lanvale and McCulloch Streets in Baltimore (Baltimore City directory).

4. Eldredge Collection, Mariners' Museum.

5. See David C. Holly, *Steamboat on the Chesapeake: Emma Giles and the Tolchester Line* (Centreville, Md.: Tidewater Publishers, 1987) chap. 4.

6. Baltimore *Sun* advertising, June and July, 1875–81.

7. Jane W. McWilliams and Carol C. Patterson, *Bay Ridge on the Chesapeake: An Illustrated History* (Annapolis, Md.: Brighton Editions, 1986), 40, 45, 48, 71, 80, 87.

8. Enrollment certificate, July 22, 1879, National Archives; Eldredge Collection, Mariners' Museum.

9. Mark S. Watson, "Motor Horns Sound the Bay-boats' Death Knell," Baltimore *Sun*, March 6, 1932; enrollment certificate May 11, 1863; and other enrollment data on *Matilda*, National Archives; Eldredge Collection, Mariners' Museum.

10. Enrollment data, National Archives; Eldredge Collection, Mariners' Museum.

11. Baltimore *Sun*, June 14, 1881, and August 16 and 22, 1882; Eldredge Collection, Mariners' Museum.

12. Weems scrapbook, MS 888, Maryland Historical Society.

13. Survey of Fredericksburg newspapers of the period; consultation with William J. Bray, Jr., from his exhaustive research in newspaper and other sources for the period.

14. Enrollment data, October 2–19, 1883, National Archives.

15. For a time, *Mary Washington* in spite of her age became a workhorse of the fleet.

16. Weems scrapbook, MS 888, Maryland Historical Society (collection of clippings from Fredericksburg newspapers).

17. Eldredge Collection, Mariners' Museum; Baltimore *Sun*, September 11–12, 1889, and May 10, 1890.

18. Charter records, 1878–95, Baltimore City Superior Court, JB liber 29:439, 517, December 14, 1891, and July 26, 1892; MdHR 20474-2, CR 39189-2; enrollment data, *Richmond* January 4, 1892; *Westmoreland* September 27, 1892; *Essex* April 7, 1892, National Archives.

19. Other guests on *Westmoreland* included

Sydney Forbes, Enoch Pratt, R. Anzon Hoffman (vice-president of the Seaboard Air Line Railroad), many officials of the Maryland Steel Company, Captain W. C. Almy of the Old Bay Line, Colonel William P. Craighill (corps of army engineers and designer of the Craighill Channel entering Baltimore Harbor), Dr. Samuel C. Chew, William C. Eliason (president of the Tolchester company), George Warfield, Theodore Weems Forbes, and many others prominent in the shipping and social circles of Baltimore.

20. Eldredge Collection, Mariners' Museum; Baltimore *Sun* and Baltimore *American* articles, April 16–17, August 10 and 17, 1892.

21. Robert H. Burgess and H. Graham Wood, *Steamboats Out of Baltimore* (Cambridge, Md.: Tidewater Publishers, 1968), passim; Holly, *Steamboat on the Chesapeake, passim.*

22. Eldredge Collection, Mariners' Museum; John L. Lochhead, "Steamships and Steamboats of the Old Dominion Line," *Steamboat Bill* (March, June, September, 1949); Richard E. Prince, *Norfolk, Southern Railroad, Old Dominion Line, and Connections* (Millard, Nebr.: R. E. Prince, 1972).

23. Robert H. Burgess, "Palace Steamer Pocohontas," *This Was Chesapeake Bay*, (Cambridge, Md.: Tidewater Publishers, 1963), 94–96.

24. Edwin W. Beitzell, *Life on the Potomac River* (Abell, Md.: published by the author, 1968, 1979), 111–23; Frederick Tilp, *This Was Potomac River*, 3d ed. (Alexandria, Va.: published by the author, 1987), 55–59; Regina Combs Hammett, *History of St. Mary's County, Maryland* (published by the author, 1977), 216–19.

25. Enrollment data, National Archives.

26. Beitzell, *Life on the Potomac River*, 182.

27. *Marine Journal* (November 1890); Charter records, 1876–95, Baltimore City Superior Court, JB liber 29:27 and 84, March 19, 1891, and April 17, 1891; MdHR 20474-2, CR 39189-2. During the rebuilding of *John E. Tygert*, Charles R. Lewis leased *W. W. Coit*, which ran the Baltimore to Washington route temporarily before returning to the excursion trade. By this move, Lewis clearly intended to pursue his ambitions on the Potomac. In the March 19, 1891 incorporation of the Maryland and Virginia Steamboat Company, its stock was declared at $100,000 in 1,000 shares of $100 each (paid in full by April 17, 1891); its directors included Charles R. Lewis, M. H. Bayly-Browne, Alvin P. Kennedy, John G. Johnson, William C. Geoghegan, and James Woodall; and

its management rested upon Charles R. Lewis and Thomas B. Flood, president. Prime ownership remained with Charles R. Lewis. The exclusion of his father and brothers implied that Charles R. Lewis bought them out. With William R. Lewis, the father, Charles R. Lewis had engaged in expansive commercial activities, acquiring land and starting up various enterprises; as the Lewisetta Cannery and Transportation Company, they bought the wharf property at Bundicks in 1884. Andrew Lewis made a similar stake in a cannery at Walnut Point and other ventures around the Coan River. There were some who hypothesized that the Lewises had in mind the projection of a new city so strategically located near the mouth of the Potomac.

28.   *Nautical Gazette*, August 27, 1892; in May 1892, he bought *Excelsior* (an unusual twin-walking beam vessel) at auction for $15,000 but sold her three months later to the Philadelphia, Chester, Wilmington, and Lewis Steamboat Company. The reason for the purchase and her mission were not defined.

29.   Series of articles dated 1893 in Weems scrapbook, MS 888, Maryland Historical Society.

30.   Article reporting the burning of *Lady of the Lake* and narrating her history in *Alexandria Gazette*, February 15, 1895.

31.   Article "A New Steamboat," October 1893, in Weems scrapbook, MS 888, Maryland Historical Society.

32.   Ibid.

33.   *Rappahannock Times*, October 13, 1893.

34.   Baltimore *American*, October 15, 1893.

35.   *Rappahannock Times*, October 25, 1893.

36.   *Alexandria Gazette*, February 15, 1895.

37.   Enrollment data, National Archives.

38.   The numerous shipbuilding yards on the Delaware gave the region the name of the American Clyde. Among the ones best known on the Chesapeake were Harlan and Hollingsworth and Pusey and Jones at Wilmington and Neafie and Levy at Philadelphia. The latter came into existence in 1844 as Reaney, Neafie and Co., a partnership between Thomas Reaney and Jacob G. Neafie, both machinists of long experience, and Captain John P. Levy, financial partner and practical shipwright. Their firm gained wide respect for building until 1860 more propeller engines than any other firm in the United States (they held the patent for the "curved propeller"), for turning out more than 300 iron or steel hulled

vessels until the turn of the century, for leading the way in the design and construction of boilers and various kinds of engines (including firefighting equipment), and for designing boats of superior quality. Known as the Penn works and standing at Beach and Palmer Streets in Philadelphia, the firm changed its name to Neafie and Levy in 1860. In the 1890s, it ranked near the top of shipbuilders along the Delaware (Daniel B. Tyler, *The American Clyde* [Newark, Del.: University of Delaware Press, 1958], 56–57, 89–101; Edwin T. Freedley, *Philadelphia and Its Manufactures* [Philadelphia: Edward Young, 1857], 317–18; Francis Burke Brandt, *The Majestic Delaware: The Nation's Foremost River* [Philadelphia: Brandt & Gummere, n.d.], 167).

39.   Enrollment data, National Archives.

40.   *St. Mary's Beacon*, May 4, 1893.

41.   Document of Neafie and Levy, Weems file, MS 909, Maryland Historical Society.

42.   *Northern Neck News*, December 28, 1894.

43.   *St. Mary's Beacon*, January 10, 1895.

44.   Letter of understanding dated January 29, 1895, signed by Jacob G. Neafie, president, and bill of sale of *Potomac* dated January 30, 1895, document in Weems papers file, MS 909, Maryland Historical Society; enrollment data, National Archives; advertising in Baltimore *Sun*, June 1894–February 1895; series of articles in Weems scrapbook, MS 888, Maryland Historical Society.

45.   Charles R. Lewis turned his full attention to his lagging canning business at Lewisetta. In the past he had prospered there. He canned tomatoes in season. He packed oysters for shipment to Baltimore, and he rivaled his brother Andrew who packed shad roe (brand name "Potomac View") across the Coan River. A short distance from his store and post office and factory stood the home of Charles R. Lewis, a gracious two-storied, plantation-style house with porches on both levels on all four sides, a place where he had raised his children as his interest in the steamboat business developed. In the past his canning business had prospered, and gossip had it that at one time he had trucked his money in an open wheelbarrow to his house for safekeeping. But in the 1880s, the canning business on the Coan River had become intensely competitive. His factory at Lewisetta, engaged primarily in the canning of tomatoes, depended on a continuing and adequate supply of tomatoes from local growers. In view of the fact that several factories in the area competed

in the purchase of the available harvests—one operated by L. W. Courtney at Mundy Point on the nearby Yeocomico River and another run by Thomas Fallin (and later by his son, Eugene) at Coan, just across the stream from Bundicks—Lewis found himself hard pressed to find enough tomatoes to make a decent profit. On the night of July 26, 1896, the factory of Thomas Fallin at Coan burned to the ground. The Courtney cannery at Mundy Point also burned. Shortly afterward, rumors began to spread that Charles was responsible for the burnings. Thomas Fallin, well-to-do and influential landowner, brought charges against Charles, and he was arrested on December 12, 1899. The trial lasted through February 1900. Much of the evidence was circumstantial, but the most damaging testimony came from a resident of Accomac County, who recounted how Charles had boasted about the ease of setting fire at Fallin's with burlaps soaked in gasoline and lacquer. His own brother, Andrew, testified against him, voicing a suspicion that Charles was stealing his oysters (barreled for shipment) off his wharf. Two charges were leveled against Charles in connection with the burning of the two factories; two indictments were added; one had to do with burning a barn for insurance money, the other concerned the alleged poisoning of the horse used to transport one A. Wiles, agent for the receiver of the Lewisetta property, when he came to inspect the premises under the conditions of bankruptcy which had now descended around Charles. He was found guilty and sentenced to serve for 15 years. On his release, knowing full well the feeling against him in Northumberland and Lancaster Counties, he chose to settle across the Potomac at Wynne on Smith's Creek in St. Mary's County. There, he opened a store, where he sold general merchandise, strawberries at 2 cents a quart, penny candy, diamond-back terrapins that he raised in a dirt-filled room, and the first ice cream sold in St. Mary's, brought down packed in ice by steamboat from Baltimore. He died at the age of 81, extolled in the local press as "having given Southern Maryland and Virginia the first real freight and passenger service by way of water that opened business between here and the large cities . . . the largest oyster packer in the eastern part of the United States . . . a man of quick and broad interests and great gentleness . . . intelligence, integrity and talent." He was known as a great marksman, able, as the rumors went, to hit,

with "Long Tom" his rifle, the halyards of a schooner passing Lewisetta and bring the mainsail clattering to the deck before the startled crew. He enjoyed a taste for spirits, passing his brand around in tomato cans in the days of prohibition and hiding it for ready use in castor oil bottles on the shelf. He was deeply loved by his immediate family and regarded with affection by his neighbors, in spite of his eccentric behavior that aroused the fear, respect, and curiosity of the residents of the Northern Neck. He was a legend (Northumberland County, Va., *Common Law Book, 1897–1902*, 391, December 18, 1899, indictment; 422–23, February 23, 1900 guilty verdict on Fallin charge, eight years recommended; 424, February 24, 1900, eight-year sentence; 433–34, March 12, 1900, indictment for arson of James T. Luttrell barn, L. W. Courtney factory, and poisoning of horse; 442–44, March 13, 1900, sentences confirmed by court, total 15 years; newspaper accounts in Warsaw, Va., *Northern Neck News*, February 12–23, 1900 and Lancaster County, Va., *Citizen*, February 16, 1900; articles by Glenda W. Lowery, "Lewisetta, An Island in Northumberland County" and idem., "Charlie Lewis: The Pirate of Lewisetta," *Pleasant Living* (Spring 1990); interviews: Alice Taylor and Edward Thomas; court data courtesy of Steven Thomas).

46. Baltimore *Sun*, February 4, 1895.

Chapter 6. Coping with the Nineties: Catastrophe, Confrontation, and Adjustment

1. Richard Walsh and William Lloyd Fox, *Maryland: A History* (Annapolis, Md.: Hall of Records, Department of General Services, 1983), 410–71.

2. Walsh and Fox, *Maryland*, 439, 619; Jacques Kelly, *Bygone Baltimore: A Historical Portrait* (Norfolk; Donning Company, 1982), passim.

3. Mame Warren and Marion E. Warren, *Maryland Time Exposure, 1840–1940* (Baltimore: The Johns Hopkins University Press, 1984), 128.

4. Francis F. Beirne, *The Amiable Baltimoreans* (Baltimore: The Johns Hopkins University Press, 1984), 108–9.

5. Beirne, *The Amiable Baltimoreans*, 178–85, 198–99; Kelly, *Bygone Baltimore*, 14–20, 109–27.

6. U.S. census data.

U.S. Census Data, 1890, 1900　(table cited in note 7)

Maryland County	1890	1900	
(Baltimore County)	(72,090)	(90,775)	17,866 − 24% increase
Anne Arundel	34,094	39,620	
Charles	15,191	17,662	
Prince George's	26,050	29,898	
St. Mary's	15,819	17,132	
Calvert	9,860	10,223	
Total			
(with Baltimore County)	(173,923)	(205,360)	
excl. Baltimore County	101,014	114,585	13,571 − 13% increase

Virginia County	1890	1900	
Caroline	16,681	16,709	
Essex	10,047	9,701	
King and Queen	9,669	9,265	
Lancaster	7,191	8,949	
Middlesex	7,458	8,220	
Northumberland	7,885	9,846	
Richmond	7,146	7,086	
Spotsylvania	14,238	9,289	4,949 − 34% decline
Westmoreland	8,399	9,243	
Total	88,714	88,308	406 − 0.1% decline

7. Data as shown in table (see above).

8. U.S. Congress, 1st sess. Patuxent River, Md. Justification for the project, costing $79,440, rested in some statistics on Patuxent River trade in 1887 furnished by Henry Williams.

Total value of shipments	$907,500
Total value of receipts	462,500
Number of mills, factories, business houses, etc.	
Grist mills	30
Canning factories	4
Stores for general merchandise	50
Vessels engaged in trade during 1887 (departures)	
Steam vessels, greatest draught 9 feet	160
Sailing vessels, greatest draught 8 feet	2,000
Westmoreland, making weekly trips to Bristol	
Draught unloaded	7 feet
Draught loaded	8½ feet

9. David C. Holly, *Steamboat on the Chesapeake: Emma Giles and the Tolchester Line* (Centreville, Md.: Tidewater Publishers, 1987), passim.

10. Baltimore *Sun*, April 15, 1899.

11. Weems scrapbook, MS 888, Maryland Historical Society.

12. Baltimore *Sun*, February 29, 1895.

13. Baltimore *Sun*, February 15, 1895.

14. Baltimore *Sun*, February 19, 1895.

15. Series of articles in Weems scrapbook, MS 888, Maryland Historical Society.

16. Baltimore *Sun*, September 18, 1897.

17. Articles in Weems scrapbook, MS 888, Maryland Historical Society.

18. Ibid.

19. Ibid.

20. Ibid.

21. Ibid.

22. The officers and directors of the Weems Steamboat Company met year after year during the mid-1890s to reelect themselves to office (see Appendix G).

23. Baltimore *Sun,* March 25, 1895.

24. Forbes Collection.

25. *Northern Neck News,* June 12, 1895.

26. *Northern Neck News,* February 24, 1896.

27. Series of articles dated 1895, Weems scrapbook, MS 888, Maryland Historical Society.

28. Weems scrapbook, MS 888, Maryland Historical Society.

29. Forbes Collection; Articles in Weems scrapbook, MS 888, Maryland Historical Society.

30. Baltimore *Sun,* March 29–31, 1898; advertising in Baltimore *Sun* 1899 and 1900; Ames W. Williams, *Otto Mears Goes East: The Chesapeake Beach Railway* (Prince Frederick, Md.: Calvert County Historical Society, 1981), 2–3, 8, 30–32, 55–59, 67–69; Holly, *Steamboat on the Chesapeake,* 22–23, 97, 278.

31. Fredericksburg *Necessity,* February 5 and 6, 1891.

32. Bray, "The Grocer's Boat," *Fredericksburg Times,* 15 (June 1989).

33. Richmond *Dispatch,* February 18, 1893.

34. Walsh and Fox, *Maryland,* 590–606; Frank Richardson Kent, *The Story of Maryland Politics* (Hatboro, Penn.: Tradition Press, 1968), 195–209.

35. Weems file, MS 909, Maryland Historical Society.

36. Invitations and other social documents in Weems file, MS 907, Maryland Historical Society.

Chapter 7. The Gilded Age: Palace Packets, River Conflict, and the Railroad's Grasp

1. Robert H. Burgess and H. Graham Wood, *Steamboats Out of Baltimore* (Cambridge, Md.: Tidewater Publishers, 1968), 64.

2. Ibid.

3. John L. Lochhead, "Steamships and Steamboats of the Old Dominion Line," *Steamboat Bill* (March, June, September 1949); Robert H. Burgess, "Steamboats on Mobjack Bay," *Chesapeake Circle* (Cambridge, Md.: Cornell Maritime Press, 1965); Richard E. Prince, *Norfolk, Southern Railroad, Old Dominion Line, and Connections* (Millard, Nebr.: R. E. Prince, 1972).

4. Enrollment data, National Archives; Baltimore *Sun,* March 4, 1900; Series of articles in Weems scrapbook, MS 888, Maryland Historical Society.

5. Baltimore *Sun,* November 15, 1901.

6. *Northern Neck News,* November 29, 1901.

7. Baltimore *Sun,* November 25, 1901.

8. Enrollment data, National Archives.

9. Articles in Weems scrapbook, MS 888, Maryland Historical Society.

10. The design did not prevent a disaster common among paddlewheel steamers on the Chesapeake. *Middlesex,* nosing into Pier 2 one early morning, coasted along with engine stopped, her bow aimed for her slot at the wharf. Passengers on the bow awaited to debark, stevedores on the pier stood ready to catch the heaving lines attached to the hawsers. The captain in the pilothouse rang the engine room bell for full astern. To everyone's astonishment, *Middlesex* continued on her path at the same speed—straight into the pier, demolishing wharf, piling, shed, and housing. When she stopped, her bow rested on the cobblestones of Light Street. Her engine had stuck on dead center, and nothing the engineer could do was quick enough to prevent catastrophe (Article, "The Last Link: Pratt Street and Old Steamboat Days," May 1952, in vertical file, Maryland Room, Enoch Pratt Free Library).

11. "New Steamboat *Middlesex* for the Rappahannock River," *Marine Engineering* (July 1901), 363–65; Enrollment data, National Archives; Eldredge Collection, Mariners' Museum.

12. Enrollment data, National Archives.

13. Frank Richardson Kent, *The Story of Maryland Politics* (Hatboro, Penn.: Tradition Press, 1968), xxxiv, chap. 10–20; Richard Walsh and William Lloyd Fox, *Maryland: A History* (Annapolis, Md.: Hall of Records, Department of General Services, 1983), 609–15.

14. In 1990, the location was occupied by the Baltimore Civic Center.

15. Henry L. Mencken, 24-year-old city editor, was the last to leave the Baltimore *Herald* building.

16. Baltimore *Sun,* July 4 and 9, 1904; Harold A. Williams, *Baltimore Afire* (Baltimore: Schneiderath & Sons, 1954, 1979); Walsh and Fox, *Maryland: A History,* 621–22.

17. Ibid.

18. Baltimore *Sun,* June 16, 1904.

19. Weems scrapbook, MS 888, Maryland Historical Society.

20. Extensive number of articles from Fredericksburg and Rappahannock Valley newspapers are contained in the Weems scrapbook, MS 888, Maryland Historical Society; excellent coverage and analysis are in Bray, "Rate War on the Rappahannock," *Steamboat Bill* (Spring 1990).

21. The Circuit Court, Eastern District of Virginia, Judge Waddill presiding, on October 17, 1905, found that "wharves belong to a class of property in which the public is involved" and, after a lengthy dissertation on what constituted private and public ownership, decided in favor of the People's Steamboat Company and denied the injunction requested by the Weems Steamboat Company (141 *Federal Reporter* 154 in Circuit Court, Eastern District of Virginia, October 17, 1905); Weems appealed, but the appellate court upheld the Waddill decision (152 *Federal Reporter* 1022, May 7, 1907). Refusing to accept the verdict, George Weems Williams pursued the appellate process to the U.S. Supreme Court, which granted certiorari. The case was argued on April 26, 1909, and decided June 1, 1909—overturning both the original circuit court ruling and the appellate court—that "a wharf on a navigable stream is private property and subject to the absolute control of the owner as other property is" (Charles Henry Butler, *United States Reports*, vol. 214, *Cases Adjudged in the Supreme Court at October Term, 1909* (New York: Bank Law Publishing Company, 1909). Henry Williams had—at length—won. In 1909! Ironically the People's Steamboat Company died in 1903, and the Weems Steamboat Company ceased to exist in 1905. Henry Williams was a tenacious man indeed.

22. Daniel B. Tyler, *The American Clyde* (Newark, Del.: University of Delaware Press, 1956), 99.

23. Miss Williams had arrived by carriage; the majority of the official party came on the tug *Solicitor* from Pier 2, Light Street. On her arrival, Miss Williams received a huge bouquet of American Beauty roses from John Quitman Lovell, president of the Baltimore Shipbuilding and Drydock Company. Others in the official party included George M. Shriver (assistant to the president of the B & O Railroad); J. William Middendorf; Charles F. Macklin; Douglas Huntley Gordon (president of the International Trust Company); Rufus K. Wood (Maryland Steel Company); Henry Williams, Jr.; Clarence Shriver (Ericsson Line); James Briscoe; Matilda Williams; Theodore Weems Forbes (son of Sydney Hume and Matilda S. Forbes); Captain T. A. Joynces (BC & A Railway); George Weems Williams (counsel for the Weems line and son of Henry Williams); and a host of other dignitaries from Baltimore steamboat and financial circles.

24. On board were the officials of the Baltimore Shipbuilding and Drydock Company, Mason Locke Weems Williams (vice president of the Weems Steamboat Company, son of Henry Williams); Theodore Weems Forbes (secretary of the Weems line, nephew of Henry Williams); Captain James Gourley (senior captain of the Weems line); John McGoldrick (chief engineer of the Weems line); Thomas W. Lawrence (superintending engineer of the Chesapeake Steamboat Company); George Weems Williams (counsel of the Weems line); and many members of the Williams family and their guests, together with representatives of shipping interests around Baltimore.

25. Many years later, when *Anne Arundel* became *Mohawk*, owned and operated by the Rock Creek Line as an excursion boat, one of her engineers discovered that a drain valve on one of her cylinders had never been drilled through, a defect she had endured all her life. Completing the drilling did nothing to increase her speed or performance (courtesy of Charles Efford, the engineer).

26. U.S. Department of Commerce, *Historical Statistics of the United States*, series Q, 2:148–62, "Motor-Vehicle Factory Sales and Registration 1900–70," and 2:50–53, "Mileage of Rural Roads and Municipal Streets, 1904–70."

27. John C. Hayman, *Rails Along the Chesapeake: A History of Railroading on the Delmarva Peninsula* (Marvadel Publishers, 1979), 72–89.

28. Baltimore *Sun*, January 5 and 30 and February 5, 1905; enrollment data, National Archives; Weems file, MS 907, vol. 3, Maryland Historical Society; "A Short History of the Weems Line," *Bugeye Times* 7 (Winter 1983).

29. Fair Haven continued as a resort, although diminishing in popularity, until 1923; the Pennsylvania Railroad paid rent for the use of the wharf until then. From 1923 to 1928, the Fair Haven property was used as a working farm by the Williams and Forbes families, who raised tobacco and sheep. In 1928, Fair Haven was sold to Irwin Owings for $102,000. The Williams and Forbes families retained title to Pier 2, Light Street, until 1951 when the City of Baltimore took the premises for the development of the memorial park to General Sam Smith, commander of Baltimore's defending forces in 1814, and subsequently as the site of Harbor Place (documents, Forbes Collection).

Chapter 8. Steamboat Life Through the Years

1. Mason L. Weems was not known for his sense of humor or even disposition. Judge James A. C. Bond, southern Maryland jurist of the 1800s, recalled a trip from the Patuxent to Baltimore on a vessel captained by Mason L. Weems. Dressed in his velvet suit and white collar as befitted a young gentleman of eight, Bond mounted the upper deck to watch the potentate of the wheelhouse bellow his orders for maneuvering the steamer away from the pier. Noticing mud being churned up by the paddlewheels, he shouted at the brass-buttoned skipper: "Hey! Don't you see you're running her into the bank?" Weems looked hastily astern to see that all was well, then glared down at the imp that had dared question his wisdom. "Why you little . . . ," he began, took a fresh breath, and launched into his diatribe. As the judge, narrated it 70 years later, "before he had finished, I was debating whether I should kill him right there on his own ship. But I decided not to. Instead, I retired to the cabin, leaving the entire responsibility for that ship's guidance in the hands of that inexperienced captain" (Mark S. Watson, "Motor Horns Sound the Bay-boats' Death Knell," Baltimore *Sun*, March 6, 1932).

2. Obituary and news reports in Baltimore *Sun*, April 18, 1892; enrollment data, National Archives; obituary and news reports, Baltimore *Sun*, April 18, 1912. After the sale of the Weems line in 1905, Gourley continued as master of *Anne Arundel*. He had nine children, 16 grandchildren, and attended the wedding of his grandson, James Gourley, Jr., cashier at Pier 2, Light Street, in January 1912. James Russell Gourley died on April 17, 1912. Stricken by a heart attack on board his boat the day before, he had insisted on taking a trolley car to his new suburban home at Halethorpe, fully expecting to return and take *Anne Arundel* down the Bay on her usual schedule. A second attack the following morning brought his career to an end.

3. Baltimore *Sun*, April 18, 1892.

4. To Henry Williams as president, Thomas Gourley addressed a letter dated October 24, 1904, in which he expressed his gratitude: "I do thank you most heartily and earnestly and wish to extend my thanks to Mrs. Williams and Mrs. Forbes. I wish they could know how much I appreciate their noble gift. It is not alone for the money—which will be more than you can imagine—but also that my poor efforts should be remembered . . . your kindness will always be a pleasure to remember . . . in the passing of the line I lose in you my best friend" (MS 907, Maryland Historical Society).

5. Robert H. Burgess, "Half a Century on the Chesapeake," Baltimore *Sun*, May 23, 1954.

6. Robert H. Burgess and H. Graham Wood, *Steamboats Out of Baltimore* (Cambridge, Md.: Tidewater Publishers, 1968), 130.

7. Watson, "Motor Horns Sound the Bay-boats' Death Knell," Baltimore *Sun*, March 6, 1932.

8. Baltimore *Sun*, January 26, 1907.

9. Handwritten letter of Vaughn C. Mumford (courtesy of Chesapeake Bay Marine Museum, St. Michael's, Md.).

10. David C. Holly, "Navigation on the Bay," in *Steamboat on the Chesapeake: Emma Giles and the Tolchester Line* (Centreville, Md.: Tidewater Publishers, 1967), chap. 10.

11. Interview with Captain Harry E. Slye, who was master of several steamers plying the Potomac.

12. Holly, *Steamboat on the Chesapeake*, chap. 10.

13. The Weems boats never adopted the form used aboard the Old Bay Line Steamers bound for Norfolk—the "din-n-n-e-r-r's now being served" with a trill at the end, expected by the more urbanized of its clientele.

14. Weems line menu posted at Saunders Wharf (courtesy of Fielding Dickinson, Jr.).

15. Kenneth Brooks, Jr., "Grandmother's Bay Kitchen," *Chesapeake Bay Magazine* (April 1988).

16. Holly, "Steamboat Engines," in *Steamboat on the Chesapeake*, chap. 12.

17. Baltimore *Sun*, January 7, 1890.

18. *Federal Record* 22:843; Jeffrey R. Brackett, "Notes on the Progress of the Colored People of Maryland Since the War," *The Johns Hopkins University Studies in Historical and Political Science* (July–September 1890); 70–71; Dan Rodricks, "1884 Act for Dignity Merits Historic Note," Baltimore *Evening Sun*, 15 August, 1984.

19. Article in Weem scrapbook, MS 888, Maryland Historical Society.

20. Brackett, "Notes on the Progress of Colored People of Maryland Since the War," 71.

21. "An Act to Provide for the Separate Accommodations of White and Colored Passengers

[on] Steamboats," *Acts and Joint Resolutions Passed by the General Assembly of the State of Virginia*, sess. 1899-1900, and extra sess. 1901, Richmond, 1900 and 1901, chap. 312, February 9, 1900 and chap. 169, February 15, 1901; *Maryland Code: Public General Laws* (Baltimore, 1860 on), art. 27:353–55, 1904, chap. 109, sec.1.

22. Exhibit at the Equestrian Center, Maryland-National Capital Park Planning Commission, Patuxent Park.

23. Article in Weems scrapbook, MS 888, Maryland Historical Society.

24. Weems papers, MS 907, Maryland Historical Society.

25. Baltimore *Sun*, August 31, 1894.

Chapter 9. The End of an Era

1. David C. Holly, *Exodus 1947* (Boston: Little, Brown, 1969).

2. Frank Richardson Kent, *The Story of Maryland Politics* (Hatboro, Penn.: Tradition Press, 1968), 364–69.

3. Data in vertical files, Maryland Room, Enoch Pratt Free Library; *Baltimore Municipal Journal*, August 2, 1929; Williams Papers, MS 907, Maryland Historical Society; Weems scrapbook, MS 888, Maryland Historical Society.

4. Robert H. Burgess and H. Graham Wood, *Steamboats Out of Baltimore* (Cambridge, Md.: Tidewater Publishers, 1968); Alexander Crosby Brown, *Steam Packets on the Chesapeake: A History of the Old Bay Line Since 1840* (Cambridge, Md.: Cornell Maritime Press, 1961); John Antonio Hain, *Side Wheel Steamers of the Chesapeake Bay, 1840–1947* (Glen Burnie, Md.: Glendale Press, 1947).

5. Holly, *Exodus 1947*.

6. Frederick Tilp, *This Was Potomac River*, 3d ed. (Alexandria, Va.: published by the author, 1987), 62–63.

7. Brochure: *The Steamers of the Potomac and Chesapeake Line: Potomac River Routes, Spring, Summer, and Fall Schedules*, April 1, 1916; Ames W. Williams, "The Baltimore Boats," *Virginia Cavalcade* 15 (summer 1965), 32–39; Robert H. Burgess, "Baltimore Steamboats to the

Northern Neck," *Northern Neck of Virginia Historical Magazine* (December 1987); Regina Combs Hammett, "The Final Steamboat Days" in *History of St. Mary's County, Maryland* (published by the author, 1977); Edwin W. Beitzell, *Life on the Potomac River* (Abell, Md.: published by the author, 1968, 1979), chap. 7.

8. John L. Lochhead, "Steamships and Steamboats of the Old Dominion Line," *Steamboat Bill* (March 1949); Richard E. Prince, *Norfolk, Southern Railroad, Old Dominion Line, and Connections* (Millard, Nebr.: R. E. Prince, 1972).

9. Robert H. Burgess, *Chesapeake Circle* (Cambridge, Md.: Cornell Maritime Press, 1965), 73–78.

10. Baltimore *Sun*, December 7 and 9, 1907; Kenneth Brooks, Jr., "Deep in December . . . It's Nice to Remember," *Chesapeake Bay Magazine* 3 (September 1973).

11. Baltimore *Post*, March 2, 1932.

12. Enrollment data, National Archives; Weems scrapbook, MS 888, Maryland Historical Society; Burgess and Wood, *Steamboats Out of Baltimore*, passim.

13. Western Shore Steamboat Company brochure, "Vacations and Outings in the Chesapeake Bay Country," 1935.

14. Burgess and Wood, *Steamboats Out of Baltimore*, 139; enrollment date, National Archives.

15. Baltimore *Sun*, September 9–30, 1937; Burgess, *Chesapeake Circle*, 155–58.

16. A dieselized *Eastern Shore* served a few landings in the Pocomoke Sound area, and there were a few runs to the York River by the Chesapeake line subsequent to September 1937, but steamboat packet service effectively ended with *Anne Arundel*'s last trip up the Rappahannock.

17. David C. Holly, *Steamboat on the Chesapeake: Emma Giles and the Tolchester Line* (Centreville, Md.: Tidewater Publishers, 1987). Chapters 11 and 12 contain a detailed discussion of steamboat construction and design and the workings of steamboat engines.

18. Vertical file, Maryland Room, Enoch Pratt Free Library.

19. Richmond *Times*, April 3, 1891.

Select Bibliography

Primary sources cited in the notes, generally not repeated in this bibliography, include manuscript collections; federal, state, and local documents and records; memoirs; extensive coverage of newspaper files, including the Alexandria, Virginia, *Gazette* (1895); Baltimore newspapers including the *Daily American* (1817), *Federal Gazette* (1817), *Municipal Journal* (1929), *Niles Register and Niles Weekly Register* (1814–22), *Patriot* (1818–19), *Post* (1832), *Sun* (1817–1937); the Chicago *Tribune* (1869, 1897–1901); Fredericksburg, Virginia, newspapers including the *Daily Star, Free Lance, Necessity, News, Political Arena and Literary Museum, Rappahannock Times, Virginia Herald, Virginia Star* for intermittent periods when files existed or when events involving the Weems line were covered, the Richmond *Dispatch* and *Times* (1891, 1893); the St. Mary's County, Maryland, *St. Mary's Beacon* (1893–95); the Warsaw, Virginia, *Northern Neck News* (1894–1901); the Washington *Evening Star* (1897) and *National Intelligencer* (1846); contemporary articles in various journals; various brochures and pamphlets published by steamboat lines; and a number of contemporary treatises providing specific information or background on the steamboat era. Additional sources are cited in the appendixes.

Manuscript Collections

Elwin Eldredge Collection: Manuscripts of data on steamships and steamboats. Mariners' Museum, Newport News, Va. Forbes Collection (privately held by descendants of Matilda S. Weems Forbes) consisting of handwritten Weems manuscripts. Of primary value are the following: military records of David Weems in the Revolutionary War; deeds, wills, indentures, and other papers of David Weems in the 1700s; correspondence of George Weems in the early 1800s; mortgages and instruments of money borrowing for *Surprise, Eagle,* and *Patuxent;* correspondence of James Harwood in the 1840s; deeds and other documents pertaining to the acquisition of Fair Haven property; drawing of Fair Haven hotel, 1839; deeds, arbitration agreements, indentures, property exchanges, and wills of George Weems; family narrative in notebook from original prepared by John C. Weems and copied by Rachel Weems Reynolds at Loch Eden, 1854; handwritten notes of Mason Locke Weems; notes on trial runs of various steamboats; Weems family genealogy; account books of steamers *Patuxent, Planter, George Weems, Mary Washington,* and *Matilda,* immediately before and after the Civil War; engine repair invoices for various steamboats during and after the Civil War; transfers of ownership of steamboats from George Weems to his sons and from the sons to the eldest, Mason Locke Weems, at various times; letters of the provost marshall to Mason Locke Weems regarding suspicious activities of Weems steamboats in the Civil War; account sheets of steamers *George Weems, Mary Washington,* and *Planter* during the Civil War; personal letters of Mason Locke Weems on takeover of Fredericksburg line, 1869; statements of cash outlays for wharf property and repairs, 1866; original bill of sale of steamer *Potomac* to Weems Steamboat Company; memorial documents to Henry Williams, 1916; disposition of Fair Haven property, Pier 2 Light Street, and Marshes Seat estate.

Weems Steamboat Company Papers and Scrapbooks (MS 888). Henry Williams Collection (MS 907). Elizabeth Chew Williams Papers (MS 909). Maryland Historical Society.

"The Minutes and Proceedings of the Meetings of the Stockholders of the Weems Steamboat Company of Baltimore City." Handwritten ledger of the minutes of meetings of directors and stockholders, 1892–1905. Hagley Museum and Library, Wilmington, Del.

Vertical file collections of the Calvert Marine Museum, Solomons, Md.; the Maryland Room, Enoch Pratt Free Library, Baltimore, Maryland;

the Mariners' Museum, Newport News, Va.; the Maryland Historical Society; and the Virginia Historical Society.

Selections for Further Reading

Books

Beitzell, Edwin M. *Life on the Potomac River.* Abell, Md.: published by the author, 1968, 1979.

Brown, Alexander Crosby. *Steam Packets on the Chesapeake: A History of the Old Bay Line Since 1840.* Cambridge, Md.: Cornell Maritime Press, 1961.

Brugger, Robert J. *Maryland: A Middle Temperament, 1634–1980.* Baltimore: The Johns Hopkins University Press, 1988.

Burgess, Robert H. *This Was Chesapeake Bay.* Cambridge, Md.: Tidewater Publishers, 1963.

———. *Chesapeake Circle.* Cambridge, Md.: Cornell Maritime Press, 1965.

———. *Chesapeake Sailing Craft.* Vol. 1. Cambridge, Md.: Tidewater Publishers, 1975.

Burgess, Robert H., and H. Graham Wood. *Steamboats Out of Baltimore.* Cambridge, Md.: Tidewater Publishers, 1968.

Conway, Moncure. *Barons of the Potomac and Rappahannock.* New York: Grolier Club, 1892.

Dayton, Fred Erving. *Steamboat Days.* Illustrated by John Wolcott Adams. New York: Frederick A. Stokes, 1925.

Dowdey, Clifford. *The Virginia Dynasties: The Emergence of "King Carter" and the Golden Age.* Boston: Little, Brown, 1969.

Emmerson, John C., Jr. *The Steamboat Comes to Norfolk Harbor and Log of the First Ten Years, 1815–25.* Reported [collected and published] by the Norfolk Gazette and Public Ledger, American Beacon, and Norfolk and Portsmouth Herald, Portsmouth, Va., 1947, 1949.

Flexner, James Thomas. *Steamboats Come True: American Inventors in Action.* Boston: Little, Brown, 1944.

Footner, Hulbert. *Maryland Main and the Eastern Shore.* New York: Appleton-Century, 1942.

———. *Rivers of the Eastern Shore: Seventeen Maryland Rivers.* New York: Farrar and Rinehart, 1944.

Gutheim, Frederick. *The Potomac.* Baltimore: The Johns Hopkins University Press, 1986.

Hain, John Antonio. *Side Wheel Steamers of the Chesapeake Bay, 1880–1947.* Glen Burnie, Md.: Glendale Press, 1947.

Hammett, Regina Combs. *History of St. Mary's County, Maryland.* Published by the author, 1977.

Hays, Anne M., and Harriet R. Hazleton. *Chesapeake Kaleidoscope.* Cambridge, Md.: Tidewater Publishers, 1975.

Holly, David C. *Exodus 1947.* Boston: Little, Brown, 1969.

———. *Steamboat on the Chesapeake: Emma Giles and the Tolchester Line.* Centreville, Md.: Tidewater Publishers, 1987.

Hunter, Louis C. *Steamboats on the Western Rivers: An Economic and Technological History.* New York: Octagon Books, 1969.

Klapthor, Margaret Brown, and Paul Dennis Brown. *The History of Charles County, Maryland.* La Plata, Md.: Charles County Tercentenary, 1958.

Lane, Carl D. *American Paddle Steamboats.* New York: Coward-McCann, 1943.

Middleton, Arthur Pierce. *Tobacco Coast: A Maritime History of Chesapeake Bay in the Colonial Era.* Baltimore: The Johns Hopkins University Press, 1984.

Morrison, John W. *History of American Steam Navigation.* New York: W. F. Sametz, 1908.

Prince, Richard E. *Norfolk, Southern Railroad, Old Dominion Line, and Connections.* Millard, Nebr.: R. E. Prince, 1972.

Scharf, J. Thomas. *History of the Confederate States Navy.* New York: Prager & Sherwood, 1887.

Shomette, Donald G. *Flotilla: Battle for the Patuxent.* Solomons, Md.: Calvert Marine Museum Press, 1981.

Stanton, Samuel Ward. *American Steam Vessels.* New York: Smith & Stanton, 1895.

Stein, Charles Francis. *A History of Calvert County, Maryland.* Published by the author in cooperation with the Calvert County Historical Society, 1976.

Tilp, Frederick. *This Was Potomac River.* 3d ed. Published by the author, Alexandria, Va., 1987.

Toomey, Daniel Carroll. *The Civil War in Maryland.* Baltimore: Toomey Press, 1983.

Wertenbaker, Thomas J. *The Planters of Colonial Virginia.* Princeton: Princeton University Press, 1918.

Whittier, Thomas J. *Paddle Wheel Steamers and Their Giant Engines.* Duxbury, Mass.: Seamaster Books, 1983.

Williams, Ames W. *Otto Mears Goes East: The Chesapeake Beach Railway*. Prince Frederick, Md.: Calvert County Historical Society, 1981.

Wilstach, Paul. *Tidewater Virginia*. Indianapolis: Bobbs-Merrill, 1929.

———. *Tidewater Maryland*. Indianapolis: Bobbs-Merrill, 1931.

Newspaper and Journal Articles

Bray, William J., Jr. "Captain Noah Fairbank, 'The Storm King'." *Fredericksburg Times*, November 1987, 34–42.

———. "The Grocer's Boat." *Fredericksburg Times*, June 1989, 26–35.

———. "Rate War on the Rappahannock." *Steamboat Bill*, Spring 1990, 4–12.

Brooks, Kenneth, Jr. "Deep in December . . . It's Nice to Remember." *Chesapeake Bay Magazine*, September 1973.

———. "Coinjock Roberts Wasn't Really His Name." *Chesapeake Bay Magazine*, May 1985.

Burgess, Robert H. "Steamboat Lore." *Tiller*, August 1946.

———. "Vanished White Fleet of Tidewater." Baltimore *Sun*, March 30, 1947.

———. "Gone Are the Days—When the Spotless Little Steamboats Bound Down the Chesapeake Sailed Out of Baltimore on a Summer Afternoon." Baltimore *Sunday Sun*, July 3, 1949.

———. "Half a Century on the Chesapeake: Capt. John D. Davis Keeps Alive the Name of the Bay's Oldest Steamboating Family." Baltimore *Sunday Sun*, May 23, 1954.

———. "I Remember . . . Weekend Steamer Voyages." Baltimore *Sun Magazine*, June 20, 1971.

———. "I Remember . . . the Day that 'Real Steamboating' Ended on the Bay." Baltimore *Sun Magazine*, February 27, 1972.

———. "I Remember . . . the Steamboating Era: 10-Cent Watermelons and Melodious Whistles." Baltimore *Sun Magazine*, January 8, 1978.

———. "Baltimore Steamboats to the Northern Neck." *Northern Neck Magazine*, December 1984.

Gilfillan, S. C. "Early Steamboats of the Chesapeake." Baltimore *Sun*, May 31, 1931.

Kelley, William J. "Baltimore Steamboats in the Civil War." *Maryland Historical Magazine*, 37 (1942).

Lantz, Emily E. "History of the Steamboat on Chesapeake Bay." Series of articles in Baltimore *Sunday Sun*. "Steam Navigation on the Chesapeake," January 5, 1908. "I—The Union Steamboat Line, Organized in 1813, and Captain Edward Trippe," January 12, 1908. "II—The Union Steamboat Line, Continued," January 19, 1908. "III—The Weems Line, Founded in 1817," January 26, 1908. "IV—The Weems Line Before and After the War," February 2, 1908. "V—The Weems Line in Recent Years," February 9, 1908. "X—The Good Ship Surprise," March 15, 1908.

Lochhead, John L. "Steamships and Steamboats of the Old Dominion Line," *Steamboat Bill*, March, June, September 1949.

Shannahan, John H. K. "Steamboating on the Chesapeake: Advent of the Automobile," Baltimore *Sun*, March 9, 1930.

Steuart, William C. "The Weems Line of the Chesapeake," *Steamboat Bill*, April 1944.

"Weems Genealogy," *Maryland Historical Magazine*, 28 (1933).

Wood, H. Graham. "Fredericksburg to Baltimore: Ninety Miles by Air: Two Days and Two Nights on Different Steamers," *Steamboat Bill*, Winter 1988.

Index

Numbers in italics denote illustrations; those in boldface denote maps.